Business Leasing For Dummies®

M000290718

The Fundamentals

Here are some basic definitions to orient you to leasing. A *lease* is a business arrangement in which a lessor allows a lessee to use and possess property for a period of time in exchange for rent and other payments. Rent provides a part of a lessor's return on its investment. In a true tax lease, a lessee should pay lower rents that reflect at least some of lessor's tax benefits from owning the property. See Chapter 13. A true lease finances 100 percent of the purchase price of the property. A loan or a non-tax-oriented lease may require the lessee to pledge other property as collateral or make a down payment on the "leased" property. See Chapter 1.

The *lessee* uses and possesses leased property and pays rent for it. The *lessor* owns and/or controls the property and transfers the property to the lessee under a lease.

A lessee can lease almost any personal or real property. A lessee can lease office towers, shopping centers, apartments, and much more, on the real estate side. A lessee can also lease computers, trucks and trailers, amusement park equipment, office equipment, furniture and fixtures, construction equipment, boats, and aircraft, to name a few items, on personal property side. See Chapter 1.

A *single-investor lease* is a two-party transaction between a lessor and a lessee. A *leveraged lease* consists of a transaction with three or more parties including a lessor, a lender (who loans money to the lessor), and a lessee. See Chapters 1 and 5.

Critical Tests of a True Tax Lease

Chapter 13 takes you through the criteria for a true lease. A *true tax lease* refers to a lease of property in which the lessor enjoys the benefits and accepts the burdens of ownership of the property for Federal income tax purposes. A lease should, for starters, pass these three tests to get true lease treatment:

- ✔ **Twenty percent investment at risk.** The lessor should make a 20 percent unconditional investment of its own funds in the cost of the leased property and maintain that investment "at risk" throughout the lease term.

- ✔ **Twenty percent residual value.** Estimating at the start of the lease, the leased property

should have a fair market value at the end of the lease term equal to at least 20 percent of the original lessor's cost. This percentage is a sure bet, but the courts have gone lower. For example, a $100,000 printing press should have an expected value of $20,000 at the end of the lease.

- ✔ **Twenty percent remaining useful life.** Estimating at the start of the lease, the leased property should have remaining useful life at the end of the lease term equal to at least 20 percent of the original useful life. A truck with ten years of useful life should have at least two years of life left in it at the end of the lease term.

Business Leasing For Dummies®

Cheat Sheet

Off-Balance Sheet Leases for Lessees

To keep a lease off of a lessee's balance sheet, the lease should meet the following criteria (see Chapter 15 for details):

- ✔ **No ownership transfer.** A lease must not transfer ownership of the leased property to the lessee at the end of the lease term.

- ✔ **No bargain purchase options.** A lease must not contain an option to purchase the leased property at a bargain price.

- ✔ **Limit on the length of the lease term.** The lease term of your lease cannot equal or exceed 75 percent of the estimated economic life of the leased property.

- ✔ **Limit on the present value of payments.** The present value of the rentals or other minimum lease payments must be less than 90 percent of the fair value of the leased property.

Finding Lessors

How do you find the people with the money, the lessors?

- ✔ **Network with your friendly professionals.** Ask your lawyers, accountants, and financial advisors, as well as your bankers, for names of lessors that can lease personal property to you. See Chapter 4.

- ✔ **Contact associations.** Try various leasing associations for leads, such as the site of the Equipment Leasing Association at www.elaonline.com. Look at the "Member Directory" or "Funding Source."

- ✔ **Use the Web.** E-leasing has not caught on too much yet, but some Web sites can provide access to real money and real deals. See Chapter 21.

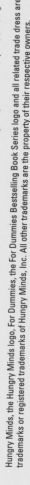

Hungry Minds™

For Dummies: Bestselling Book Series for Beginners

Business Leasing FOR DUMMIES®

by David G. Mayer

Foreword by Joseph C. Lane, President, IBM Credit Corporation

Hungry Minds™

Best-Selling Books • Digital Downloads • e-Books • Answer Networks • e-Newsletters • Branded Web Sites • e-Learning

New York, NY ◆ Cleveland, OH ◆ Indianapolis, IN

Business Leasing For Dummies®

Published by:
Hungry Minds, Inc.
909 Third Avenue
New York, NY 10022
www.hungryminds.com
www.dummies.com

Library of Congress Control Number: 2001089352

ISBN: 0-7645-5370-4

Printed in the United States of America

10 9 8 7 6 5 4 3 2 1

1O/RU/QZ/QR/IN

Distributed in the United States by Hungry Minds, Inc.

Distributed by CDG Books Canada Inc. for Canada; by Transworld Publishers Limited in the United Kingdom; by IDG Norge Books for Norway; by IDG Sweden Books for Sweden; by IDG Books Australia Publishing Corporation Pty. Ltd. for Australia and New Zealand; by TransQuest Publishers Pte Ltd. for Singapore, Malaysia, Thailand, Indonesia, and Hong Kong; by Gotop Information Inc. for Taiwan; by ICG Muse, Inc. for Japan; by Intersoft for South Africa; by Eyrolles for France; by International Thomson Publishing for Germany, Austria and Switzerland; by Distribuidora Cuspide for Argentina; by LR International for Brazil; by Galileo Libros for Chile; by Ediciones ZETA S.C.R. Ltda. for Peru; by WS Computer Publishing Corporation, Inc., for the Philippines; by Contemporanea de Ediciones for Venezuela; by Express Computer Distributors for the Caribbean and West Indies; by Micronesia Media Distributor, Inc. for Micronesia; by Chips Computadoras S.A. de C.V. for Mexico; by Editorial Norma de Panama S.A. for Panama; by American Bookshops for Finland.

For general information on Hungry Minds' products and services please contact our Customer Care department; within the U.S. at 800-762-2974, outside the U.S. at 317-572-3993 or fax 317-572-4002.

For sales inquiries and resellers information, including discounts, premium and bulk quantity sales and foreign language translations please contact our Customer Care department at 800-434-3422, fax 317-572-4002 or write to Hungry Minds, Inc., Attn: Customer Care department, 10475 Crosspoint Boulevard, Indianapolis, IN 46256.

For information on licensing foreign or domestic rights, please contact our Sub-Rights Customer Care department at 212-884-5000.

For information on using Hungry Minds' products and services in the classroom or for ordering examination copies, please contact our Educational Sales department at 800-434-2086 or fax 317-572-4005.

Please contact our Public Relations department at 212-884-5163 for press review copies or 212-884-5000 for author interviews and other publicity information or fax 212-884-5400.

For authorization to photocopy items for corporate, personal, or educational use, please contact Copyright Clearance Center, 222 Rosewood Drive, Danvers, MA 01923, or fax 978-750-4470.

Hungry Minds™ is a trademark of Hungry Minds, Inc.

About the Author

David G. Mayer has a diverse background in domestic and international business transactions. He is admitted to practice law in New York, California, and Texas and has been a practicing lawyer since 1977. David began his career in private practice in New York City and subsequently served as counsel at GATX Capital Corporation for more than 12 years. Insisting that he understand "the leasing business," David's talented colleagues at GATX gave him the opportunity to learn a wide array of leasing "industry" skills, including financial analysis, insurance, tax, marketing, equipment management, and lease documentation.

David is now a Partner at Patton Boggs LLP, an international law firm with almost 400 lawyers located in Washington, D.C., Anchorage, Boulder, Dallas, Denver, and Northern Virginia. At Patton Boggs, David structures, negotiates, drafts, and closes leases, secured loans, asset purchases and sales, syndications, and many other financing transactions primarily for lessors and lenders of all types and sizes. He devotes a substantial part of his practice to leasing and financing commercial and business aircraft, technology equipment and software, facilities, and other personal property. He is actively involved in business workouts, restructuring deals, and related bankruptcy proceedings affecting real and personal property.

David has also been active in international and domestic power, infrastructure, and real estate development projects. He has advised companies on power plant acquisitions and development projects in the United States, China, Central America, Mexico, India, and the Philippines. He often focuses on power project development in the United States and related matters.

David won a prestigious first place merit award for a unique article on copyright law from the American Society of Authors, Composers, and Publishers. He has also been published in the Fordham Law Review, a publication of the Business Law Section of the State Bar of California, and the Harvard Journal on Legislation.

David graduated in three years, summa cum laude, from Ohio University in 1974, with a Bachelor of Arts degree. He then attended Case Western Reserve Law School, where he served as a member of the Case Western Reserve Law Review. He was awarded a Juris Doctor degree in 1977.

David frequently lectures on a wide range of topics relating to domestic and international financial transactions and leasing. He can be reached at his Dallas, Texas, office at dmayer@pattonboggs.com.

Dedication

To my wife, Anne, an inspiring professional author and journalist, who had the vision to see the possibilities for this book. She helped me land this book and then encouraged me, advised me, and sacrificed for me so that I could complete it.

To my children, Ashley and Lindsay, who supported me with the kind of smiles, pride, and understanding that would make any father want to make a sustained effort to write this book.

Author's Acknowledgments

To say that many people helped make this book become a reality is a great understatement. Before I share with you the names of the many technical experts who helped infuse this book with more than 475 years of leasing, insurance, and financial services experience, let me first thank my Acquisitions Editor, Mark Butler. Mark not only saw the potential and value of this subject, but also demonstrated the kind of integrity, good judgment, and negotiating skill that I really respect and enjoy.

Thanks to Kelly Ewing, my delightful Project Editor, who used her considerable writing and editing skills acquired from working on more than 75 *For Dummies* books to clean up my act and make this book right for you.

Roy S. Powell, my friend and gym buddy from GATX Capital Corporation, graciously took on the task of commenting on the entire book. I am grateful to Roy for bringing his wide range of domestic and international leasing experience to this project — as a lawyer and a business guy. He kept a sharp mind, though I kid him sometimes, and an even sharper pencil for accuracy, clarity, and just good common sense in the text.

I am honored that my friend and mentor, Joseph C. Lane, President of IBM Credit Corporation, took time from his frenetic schedule to write the Foreword for this book.

Thanks to my Partners at Patton Boggs LLP, Clifton Jessup, for sharing his wisdom and experience in bankruptcy matters for Chapter 18, and to Timothy Mills, my maven and a teacher of Federal leasing, and contributor of deep experience to Chapter 19. Thanks also to my Associates, Terry Traveland, for her input on technology stuff in Chapters 10 and 21 and other editing suggestions, and to Andy Mittler for help on real estate issues.

I offer a special thanks to my Administrative Assistant at Patton Boggs LLP, Adrian Nicole McCoy, who skillfully and enthusiastically helped this project in countless ways, including creating the artwork, editing my materials, and copying a ton of stuff.

Thanks to the Equipment Leasing Association represented by Michael J. Fleming (President), Leslie Sterling (Vice President, Professional Development and Training), and Dennis Brown, CAE (Vice President, State Governmental

Relations). The ELA provided me with helpful research, insights on the leasing markets, and contacts in the leasing business that added to the depth and quality of this book.

To my other outside technical experts, I give my heartfelt thanks for your invaluable contributions. Your unparalleled skill, knowledge, and real-life experiences have significantly enhanced this book in many ways. The group of leasing experts (in alphabetical order) are

J. Eric (Rick) Atherholt, Senior Vice President and General Counsel for DeLage Landen Financial Services, Inc., an indirect subsidiary of Rabobank Nederland, for his comments and direction in Chapter 21 on vendor lease financing programs.

William J. Bosco, Vice President in charge of Product Development at CitiCapital (Citigroup), and Chairman of the Equipment Leasing Association Financial Accounting Committee for his in-depth review, consultation, and improvements of Chapter 15, on accounting for leases.

Joseph M. Buono, CPCU, Senior Vice President of Willis Group Limited, one of the three insurance intermediaries operating on a worldwide basis, and Adjunct Professor at The College of Insurance, for his detailed review and comments on Chapter 9 regarding insurance in leasing.

John C. Chobot, a lawyer in private practice in New Jersey and Adjunct Professor of Law at Seton Hall University Law School in commercial law (UCC Articles 2 and 9), for his knowledgeable, detailed, and professorial comments on Chapter 17 regarding UCC Revised Article 9.

Toby Cozart, a tax wiz by any standard, now a Director at KPMG, and author of a BNA tax management portfolio on leasing identified as *545 T.M., Equipment Lease Characterization*, for his analytical and knowledgeable comments on Chapter 13 on federal taxes in leasing.

Leianne S. Crittenden, Chief Counsel for Oracle Financing Division, the vendor financing division for Oracle Corporation, the largest provider of database software in the world, for her insights and comments in Chapter 10 regarding leasing high-technology assets.

Richard H. (Dick) Crofton, Senior Vice President of the Business Aircraft Finance Division of The CIT Group, for his knowledgeable input on general transactional, economic, and business aircraft issues.

Charles S. Donovan, Partner, Schnader Harrison Segal & Lewis LLP, San Francisco, California, a widely published author and expert on maritime law, for his review in Chapter 12 of leasing/chartering of vessels.

Byron Edwards, Vice President of GFSC Aircraft Acquisition Financing Corporation, a provider of lease financing for Gulfstream corporate jets, for sharing his vast business aviation experience in Chapter 11 on business aircraft leasing and finance.

Valerie L. Guerrieri, Tax Director for the CIT Technologies Corporation and Chair of the Equipment Leasing Association's State Government Relations Committee, for applying her deep technical and practical tax expertise to Chapter 14 on state sales, use, and property taxes.

Paul Haerle, Senior Vice President and Chief Operating Officer of Koch Financial Corporation, and Chairman of the Board of Directors for the Association of Governmental Leasing & Finance, the industry association for tax-exempt leasing, for his review and guidance in Chapter 19 on leasing to state and local governmental entities.

Bill Kirsch, Managing Director and cofounder of Costella Kirsch (CKI), a Menlo Park, California-based venture leasing firm, that has delivered more than $150,000,000 of capital to early stage companies, for contributing his deep industry expertise and comments in Chapter 21 on venture leasing.

Donald Paynter, Chief Financial Officer and Managing Director at Commodore Capital Corporation, an indirect subsidiary of the Nichimen Corporation, New York City, an international investment banking firm, for his thoughtful comments and direction in Chapter 20 on international and cross-border leasing.

Frank L. Polk, a partner at McAfee & Taft, a Professional Corporation, lecturer on domestic and international law affecting aircraft, and President of Global Aviation Title Insurance Agency, Oklahoma City, a premier aircraft title insurance provider, for his thorough legal review and enhancement of Chapter 11 on aircraft leasing and finance.

Michael J. Rizzo, President and CEO of U.S. Bancorp Business Equipment Finance Group, for his knowledgeable and detailed comments on Chapter 8 regarding lease terms and negotiations. Mike spent many years heading all legal affairs at U.S. Bancorp Leasing & Financial where he also serves as an Executive Vice President.

Leo Sheer, the long-time Senior Vice President and General Counsel of CIT Aerospace, a division of The CIT Group, and commercial aircraft leasing expert, for his suggestions in Chapter 11 focusing on commercial aircraft leasing.

Ann Shook, Vice President of Koch Financial Corporation, an expert at structuring and closing a wide array of tax-exempt leases, for her review and comment in Chapter 19 on leasing to state and local governmental entities.

Stephen T. Whelan, a partner at the New York law firm of Thatcher Proffitt & Wood, and Chairman of the American Bar Association subcommittees on leasing and secured transactions, for his knowledgeable and helpful observations on Chapter 16 (Article 2A of the UCC) and Chapter 17 (Revised Article 9 of the UCC).

Sharon Wilson, a financial analyst and tax expert at GATX Capital Corporation for her pricing and analytical work that greatly improved the entire discussion of economics in Chapters 6 (for lessees) and Chapter 7 (for lessors). Sharon willingly ran for more numbers than you'll see, for which I am grateful.

Before I end, thanks to you, the reader, for whom I have the greatest respect for your interest in this subject and appreciation for your wisdom to buy this book!

Publisher's Acknowledgments

We're proud of this book; please send us your comments through our Online Registration Form located at www.hungryminds.com

Some of the people who helped bring this book to market include the following:

Acquisitions, Editorial, and Media Development

Project Editor: Kelly Ewing

Senior Acquisitions Editor: Mark Butler

General Reviewer: Roy S. Powell

Editorial Manager: Jennifer Ehrlich

Editorial Coordinator: Michelle Hacker

Cover Photos: © Henry Sims/The Image Bank

Production

Project Coordinator: Maridee Ennis

Layout and Graphics: LeAndra Johnson, Jackie Nicholas, Betty Schulte, Jeremey Unger

Proofreaders: Laura Albert, Linda Quigley

Indexer: TECHBOOKS Inc.

General and Administrative

Hungry Minds, Inc.: John Kilcullen, CEO; Bill Barry, President and COO; John Ball, Executive VP, Operations & Administration; John Harris, CFO

Hungry Minds Consumer Reference Group

Business: Kathleen Nebenhaus, Vice President and Publisher; Kevin Thornton, Acquisitions Manager

Cooking/Gardening: Jennifer Feldman, Associate Vice President and Publisher; Anne Ficklen, Executive Editor; Kristi Hart, Managing Editor

Education/Reference: Diane Graves Steele, Vice President and Publisher

Lifestyles: Kathleen Nebenhaus, Vice President and Publisher; Tracy Boggier, Managing Editor

Pets: Kathleen Nebenhaus, Vice President and Publisher; Tracy Boggier, Managing Editor

Travel: Michael Spring, Vice President and Publisher; Brice Gosnell, Publishing Director; Suzanne Jannetta, Editorial Director

Hungry Minds Consumer Editorial Services: Kathleen Nebenhaus, Vice President and Publisher; Kristin A. Cocks, Editorial Director; Cindy Kitchel, Editorial Director

Hungry Minds Consumer Production: Debbie Stailey, Production Director

◆

The publisher would like to give special thanks to Patrick J. McGovern, without whom this book would not have been possible.

◆

Contents at a Glance

Cartoons at a Glance

By Rich Tennant

page 5

page 45

page 99

page 267

page 177

page 305

Cartoon Information:
Fax: 978-546-7747
E-Mail: richtennant@the5thwave.com
World Wide Web: www.the5thwave.com

Table of Contents

Foreword

Having been in the leasing and financing business for nearly 25 years, I have had an opportunity to see tax laws come and go, market conditions change and change again, and people move from one company to another while plying the same basic skills and trade. Leasing is one of those unique financial tools that many people encounter, few understand, but a select few know inside-out and use to their own advantage. David Mayer has undertaken the difficult task of explaining leasing — an undervalued, often misunderstood, sometimes archaic, and frequently leading-edge financing structure. Leasing is an under-appreciated force in the capital formation of American business; understanding its powerful potential can differentiate the reader from the uninformed majority.

David and I have teamed up on leasing transactions totaling several hundred million dollars, and I can say without reservation that he is one of the most creative, clever, and intellectually challenging characters I have had the pleasure of working with. His ability to take a complex situation and break it down into its most understandable components is exemplary. His dedicated effort on the subject of leasing is highly valuable. Meanwhile, his never-ending pursuit of clarity and understanding positions him at odds with an industry that thrives on complexity and nonconformity. David is one of the most clear-thinking, clever-reasoning people I have ever encountered. His ability to take complicated concepts and make them understandable has been proven in numerous deal negotiations we have enjoyed together. In this book, he takes some complex concepts and makes them understandable to those who do not live in the daily world of intrigue and mystery we know as leasing.

Joseph C. Lane

President, IBM Credit Corporation

Introduction

*W*elcome to *Business Leasing For Dummies,* a first of its kind, readable, informative, and personable book about leasing personal property (and some real estate). For years, I have read and tried to fully absorb some complex treatises and economic analysis on leasing. I have been privileged to work with some of the best in the business. But despite all I know and have learned, most of the books out there are just too difficult to use. You really have to work hard at it, and not everyone can, or wants to, devote that kind of effort to learn and use this stuff. In this book, you'll find that the hundreds of years of experience at work (mine plus lots of my incredible technical advisors) can help you do deals and grasp the key aspects of leasing like no other text or article or seminar ever has before.

Why You Need This Book

As I have continued to practice law in the leasing and business transactions areas in recent years, I have often noticed that many capable people do not fully know the concepts, processes, and pitfalls of leasing, even though they lease property themselves or advise others who do. I see them make avoidable mistakes that cost them (or their clients) money and aggravation.

When I planned this book, I aimed to help everyone who may participate in leasing transactions from the points of view of both lessees and lessors as well as lenders. For example, this book can help you, as a lessee, in whatever business position you hold, such as a treasury officer of a large corporation, the chief executive officer of your own small company, an analyst in a treasury department, a purchasing manager of equipment, a contracts administrator, a lawyer, an appraiser, or an accountant.

This book also helps leasing professionals, whether beginners or the advanced types, including marketing professionals, accountants, syndicators, lawyers, contract specialists, senior executives, and financial analysts. After reading this book, you may finally be able to relax a bit about the stuff that you know you need to know but probably haven't taken the time to learn.

For those of you who are beginners, this book is for you, too — perhaps as a student in business school, a lessor or lender new to the business, a journalist, a vendor, a professor, or just someone curious about financial transactions around the globe. This book describes in plain English the substance of leasing and how such a diverse financial tool can work for you however you may choose to use it.

What This Book Assumes About You

I expect that you approach this book from every part of the business or academic world including your own small business. More than 80 percent of the businesses in the United States alone lease some or all of their equipment. Perhaps you have never leased property before and want to figure out how leasing works. You may not have tried leasing before because it just seems harder than traditional loans or somewhat mysterious.

I assume that many leasing and financial professionals want to catch up, keep up, or just build a better foundation in leasing, so they can weather the winds of change, a constant in the leasing business.

My common assumption about you is that you are smart and curious, with a desire to learn about leasing as a financial tool for business, and that you want to be treated with respect when you read this book. Let me assure you that I try to demonstrate my respect and appreciation for you and your efforts throughout this book.

How to Use This Book

You can read this book cover to cover, and you are welcome to do so. However, you can also use this book as a reference, jumping into any part that interests you. It is not a tutorial, although you can use it as a road map to leasing. You can and should use the Index and Table of Contents to help you find the specifics that you need.

Because leasing usually involves negotiation, regardless of whether you are a lessee or lessor, use the opportunity when I talk about one point of view or the other to read about the issues important to the other guy (that is, lessees should read the lessor's stuff and vice versa). You may gain valuable insights that can help improve the terms of your deal, negotiate more effectively, and avoid unnecessary arguments based on your awareness of the issues of the person across the table (or telephone wires) from you.

How This Book Is Organized

This book creates a foundation for you in leasing and then builds on top of that foundation. Each part stands alone. You can use the Index to find leasing terms or concepts that you may need to supplement your knowledge from any particular chapter or section. The following sections summarize each part.

Part I: Building a Foundation

This part introduces you to the ground level definitions in leasing. To get you oriented in leasing, you may need to evaluate the benefits and risks of leasing from both the lessee's and the lessor's points of view. You also start to appreciate that some leases simply constitute disguised security agreements or loans, which can impact virtually every aspect of your lease transaction and economics.

Part II: How Leasing Works

Getting into real deals takes you into the heart of leasing. In this part, you can review the whole process of negotiating a proposal to lease and closing your lease transaction. You also find out how to work the numbers and underlying concepts for pricing the economics of a lease from the separate points of view of lessees and lessors. You also get two pictures of how to structure a deal as a single-investor lease or leveraged lease.

Part III: Taking on Documentation and Insurance

Lessees often find themselves at a disadvantage to lessors when it comes to documentation, legal, and insurance issues. Lessors often have internal experts or well-established outside specialist in these areas. In this part, I provide explanations of typical lease provisions (based on the lease form in the Appendix to this book) and negotiating hints, mostly for lessees, to level the playing field. I also take on insurance issues and make them palatable even to the uninitiated. I cover certain specialized types of property and describe to you their unique documentation and insurance features, which, if forgotten or mishandled, can lead to costly mistakes and, if handled properly, can improve your deal.

Part IV: Going by the Book: Tax, Legal, and Accounting Rules

Everyone can use some background in the legal, tax, and accounting principles that govern leasing. These principles help structure the leasing business done every day all over the planet. For those of you who don't possess a legal or accounting training, fear not! I have presented the concepts with all the definitions and basics that anyone needs to grasp and use these rules. By knowing this stuff, you can structure your transactions to get the most bang out of your leasing buck.

Part V: Products and Programs Worldwide

Leasing is a worldwide business. You can do deals inside and across the borders of the United States and many other countries. In this part, you find out how to do international deals or cross-border leases, as well as how to do business with federal, state and local government entities in the United States. You also find an introduction to leasing for vendors of goods, leasing to venture-capital backed companies, and leasing on the Internet.

Part VI: The Part of Tens

Like every book in the _For Dummies_ series, this book contains a Part of Tens. In this part, I step back from the trees and help you take a look, separately as a lessor and as a lessee, at the forest — the big issues that you should address to make a success out of your leasing efforts.

Icons Used in This Book

Throughout this book, you see a number of icons in the margins. These icons generally focus you on key points based on real experience.

This icon offers a point that you should remember because it affects the whole subject of leasing.

Used frequently throughout the book, the tip icon brings years of experience into focus to provide you with real-deal guidance and/or money-saving ideas, not just theory.

Despite all the efforts to keep information in English, some stuff just can't resist the technical spin. Use the information here as much as you can, especially if you have any technical bent, but you can pass over it if you choose and still understand the topic.

Many players in the leasing game get into trouble. Use the information next to this icon so that you won't be one of them.

Part I
Building a Foundation

The 5th Wave   By Rich Tennant

"What do you mean our Ground Lease is up?"

In this part . . .

To get you going, this part provides basic definitions, lists property that you can lease, and describes the most common types of leases and segments of the leasing market. You can evaluate the benefits and risks of leasing and determine whether leasing works for you.

Chapter 1

Getting Focused on Leasing

*O*ver the years, I have really enjoyed the leasing business. You find talented, creative people in leasing who can solve problems and figure out how to lease stuff that even surprises me sometimes. They can really work the numbers and put together documents to make deals happen.

As a result of their efforts and some significant changes in tax laws, leasing has evolved into a sophisticated financial tool that you can use to meet a variety of your needs and business objectives, whether you are a lessor or a lessee or even a lender. Over 80 percent of the businesses in the United States alone lease some or all of their equipment or other personal property, and businesses everywhere lease real estate.

Leasing has not only become a growing domestic business, but also an increasingly useful tool for international transactions in which financial institutions around the world invest hundreds of billions of dollars per year in buying, selling, and financing virtually every kind personal and real property. This property ranges from computers to aircraft, vending machines to power plants, automobiles to ships, and commercial office buildings to manufacturing facilities.

This chapter helps you build or, if you already have leasing experience, strengthen, your foundation in basic leasing concepts.

Defining a Lease

A *lease* commonly refers to an arrangement where one party, who owns or controls property, called the *lessor*, transfers possession and use of that property for a period of time to another party, called the *lessee*, in exchange for the lessee paying *rent* (cash or other valuable consideration).

A lease contract describes this arrangement (in writing, generally) and establishes the obligations of these parties to each other. Many different definitions of a lease exist, including one covered in Article 2A of the Uniform Commercial Code, which I discuss in Chapter 16.

The Uniform Commercial Code (*UCC*) is a collection of laws that provides uniform and consistent rules for the commercial transactions. The UCC, in theory (but not always in practice), represents the best approach to the business transactions that it covers.

In effect, if you are a lessee, a lease is an arrangement where you can possess property that a lessor owns or controls in exchange for paying rent to use that property. If you are a lessor, a lease allows you to transfer property that you own or control to a lessee who pays you rent to use it. That's it. Everything else that follows builds on this premise.

Parts I, II, III, and IV of this book describe the benefits, risks, and documentation involved in leasing transactions (including the impact of the UCC).

A lease is not a loan, or is it?

As leasing has grown into a huge financial services industry, I have heard occasionally that the participants in these deals or their advisors say that leases are just like loans. This confusion is understandable because you may see interchangeable terms used to describe leases such as *disguised leases, dirty leases, money over money leases, conditional sales, conditional sale leases, non-tax-oriented leases,* and *installment sales leases.* These arrangements usually constitute loans or other types of financing (even if called leases).

The idea that a lease is just like a loan is misleading and can result in some very costly mistakes for you in completing lease transactions. If you hear those words used interchangeably, you can show your knowledge gained from reading this chapter by suggesting to the speaker that the differences can significantly affect the economics of the transaction, tax benefits, and legal rights. Because of the variety of leases, a court can even characterize your lease as a secured loan or security interest when you least expect it. In other words, just because you are told that a transaction is a lease or you negotiate a transaction document called a *lease,* you should always try to distinguish a lease from a loan.

Some basic differences between a lease and a loan

You can distinguish a lease from a loan or other kinds of transactions. The following list illustrates some differences:

- ✔ **Cash sales differ from leases.** A *cash sale* occurs when a seller transfers all of his right, title, and interest in property to a buyer for cash. For example, if you buy a tractor with a purchase price of $50,000 at a dealer and pay $50,000 in cash, you have completed a sale. You receive the bill of sale or invoice to prove it. Article 2A of the Uniform Commercial Code and various other laws and rules govern leases as discussed later in Part IV.

- ✔ **Conditional sales differ from leases.** A *conditional sale* refers to a sale in which the buyer, sometimes called the *lessee,* takes possession of the property, but the seller, sometimes called the *lessor,* retains legal title to the property for security purposes until the lessee/buyer pays the full sales price to the seller. This transaction may be called a *conditional sale lease.* If a lessee enters into a conditional sale lease, the lessee buys the property by paying a series of *rents* (installment payments) over a period of time.

  After making the last payment, the lessee/buyer receives the title from the lessor/seller. Although the word "lease" appears in the name of this arrangement, it is not a lease. It constitutes a loan for the purchase of the property. In the same example, if the lessee leases the tractor from the dealer in a conditional sale, the dealer holds the title until the lessee pays the last rent payment. Those rents not only pay the $50,000, but also an interest component to compensate the dealer for financing the conditional sale.

- ✔ **Secured loans differ from leases.** A *secured loan*, in the context of equipment purchase/financing, is when a person or entity, called the *lender,* advances a sum of money, say $50,000, to a person or entity, called the *borrower*, who pledges the equipment to help repay the loan. The borrower may use the money to purchase property, say a tractor, or use the money in his business operations as working capital (daily business costs). The borrower then promises the lender that he'll repay the money with interest over a period of time. The purchased property (the tractor) serves as collateral. In other words, the borrower grants a *security interest* to the lender in the tractor to secure the payment or performance of an obligation, like the payment of the loan. The borrower agrees to compensate the lender for taking that risk by paying interest on the loan. If the borrower fails to repay the loan when it's due, the lender may take the equipment or other property (by way of a foreclosure or other remedies) and sell it to recover the outstanding loan and other amounts that the borrower owes. If, after selling the equipment or other property (the tractor), any cash remains, in a real secured loan, the lender turns over those proceeds to the borrower. If any shortfall exists, the lender requires that the borrower pay the shortfall.

In true leases, lessors generally keep the excess funds from the sale as the owner of the equipment or other property. Chapter 17 also reviews secured loans and other rules relating to leasing affected by Revised Article 9 in the Uniform Commercial Code. By reading Chapters 16 and 17 together, you can distinguish most leases from secured transactions and avoid some critical mistakes that may undo what you want to accomplish in your deals.

As you engage in a leasing transaction, consider the differences between a lease and a loan. Decide on your objectives and decide which type of deal makes sense for you. As you read this book, keep this concept in mind because virtually every analysis hinges on this distinction, whether economic (see Chapters 6 and 7) or legal, tax, or accounting (see Parts III and IV), depending on which type of transaction you select. By identifying the difference between these deals, you can gain important benefits and avoid significant problems. You should obtain legal advice here if it is important to you to make sure that you're actually entering into a lease and not a loan, or vice versa.

Roles of Lessees and Lessors

A lessor and lessee establish a creditor/debtor relationship. And in some deals, they establish a seller/buyer relationship. But generally, the lessor purchases the property, and the lessee must pay to use and possess it.

Who holds title?

The lessor usually holds the title to the property and makes the property available to a lessee. A lessor can be a leasing company, a bank or bank-affiliated leasing company, a *captive leasing company* (a leasing company formed by a manufacturer to lease its manufactured products in order to increase sales), or other financial institution as discussed in Chapter 4. A lessor can use a purchase order, purchase and sale agreement, or other similar arrangement to get the title from a third party. The seller may be the lessee(in a sale-leaseback), an intermediary, a vendor (of any description), or a manufacturer. In most cases, the lessee picks the property to lease. For example, if you are the lessor in a computer leasing transaction, you purchase the computer from ABC Computer Co., the vendor that your lessee selects, and, as the owner/lessor, you lease the computer to the lessee as the end user.

Who has possession and use of the property?

The lessee takes possession of the property and pays rent to use it for a period of time, often called the *lease term*. As the lessee of equipment and/or other personal property, you generally acquire possession directly from the seller or manufacturer when your lease begins. For example, you enter into a purchase order to purchase the computers with ABC Computer Co. As the prospective lessee, you can ask your lessor to take over your right to purchase the computers and the obligation to pay for them. You thereafter take possession and use the computers under a lease with your lessor.

Alternatively, you may purchase the computers and take possession of them even before you identify a lessor. Thereafter, you can sell the computers to a lessor, who takes the title from you instead of ABC Computer Co., and then you lease the computers from the lessor. This is called a *sale-leaseback* transaction. If you lease real property, such as an office suite, you take possession, as the tenant or lessee, after you negotiate a lease. Under the lease, your landlord hands over possession and use of the office suite to you for a period of time. You can also do sale-leaseback transactions with real estate.

Property You Can Lease

Would you believe, anything and everything can be and has been leased since the beginning of time? If you answered yes, you are close to the truth.

When people ask me today what kinds of property I lease, I sometimes say anything that rolls, floats, flies, or makes stuff and technology equipment. But in reality, the list is far longer because you can lease personal and real property of all types that you put to use in every conceivable business, such as chains, tools, and cables used on a tug boat or chairs installed on an aircraft.

Often the distinction between *personal* and *real property* blurs. *Personal property* refers to physical property other than real property. You can pick out personal property (from real property) because you do not permanently attach it to or intend to make it a permanent part of real property. You can see, weigh, measure, or touch this property, but it excludes real property. *Real property* refers to all the rights and benefits that you gain from the ownership of physical real estate (such as land, trees, bushes, and, for some people, weeds!). Lease transactions often involve real and personal property or a mixture of both types of property.

Real estate

You can lease a wide variety of real estate, ranging from office space to manufacturing sites and mini-storage facilities to retail stores. I could write a whole book about real estate leasing alone. This book, however, focuses on personal property. For now, you should simply appreciate that real estate leasing presents many opportunities and issues of its own and plays an indirect, though important, role in many aspects of leasing transactions discussed in this book.

Personal property

Here is a list of illustrative types of personal property that you can lease:

- **Agricultural/winery equipment:** Tractors, harvesters, harvesting bins, milking parlor machinery, winery oak barrels, wire and trellises, and even grape stakes

- **Amusement park equipment:** Park rides, arcade games, and jukeboxes

- **Banking equipment:** ATM machines, sorters and counting devices

- **Construction equipment:** Back loaders, bulldozers, tractors, cement trucks, cranes, jackhammers, and earth-moving equipment

- **Electrical equipment:** Electronic-testing devices, electron microscopes, drills, and transformers

- **Energy assets:** Power plant equipment (electric turbines, generators, cooling towers, control equipment, computers, environmental equipment), land-based oil rigs, oil and gas testing equipment, gas compressors, and drilling rigs

- **Entertainment equipment:** Speakers, cabling, lighting cans, sound control boards, theater seating, video screens, and cameras

- **Facilities:** Solid waste disposal plants, water-processing plants, piping, steel plants, coal processing and chemical-processing plants

- **Health-care devices:** CT scanners, X-ray machines, optical measuring devices, laboratory testing equipment, and monitors

- **Information technology equipment:** Computers, file servers, mainframes, personal computers, accessories, plotters, printers, radios, towers, and other hardware

- **Manufacturing and production equipment:** Sewing, cutting, and other textile machines, soft drink bottling equipment, pharmaceutical production equipment, and lathes

- **Material-handling equipment:** Pallets jacks, forklifts, conveyors, lifting equipment, street sweepers, and plows

- ✔ **Office equipment:** Desks, chairs, conference tables, postage machines, cabinets, file drawers, bookcases, and workstations
- ✔ **Printing/publishing:** Printing presses, paper cutters, control panels, assemblers, and photocopiers
- ✔ **Restaurant equipment:** Food-processing equipment, refrigeration, stoves, and ovens
- ✔ **Telecommunications:** Telephones, switches, fiber-optic cable, microwave towers, satellites, and radios
- ✔ **Transportation:** Trains (hopper cars, tank cars, passenger rail cars, flat cars, and locomotives), aircraft (corporate jets, helicopters, and commercial aircraft), automobiles (and other over the road vehicles like tractors, trailers, buses, and trucks), intermodal containers and vessels (tugs boats, supply boats, ships, and barges)
- ✔ **Vending machines:** Candy and soda machines and toy dispensers

Common Types of Leases

There are all kinds of leases. This section describes the four types or categories of leases: the finance lease, the true lease, the operating lease, and the service lease. Most other specialized leases tend to fall into one of these categories.

These names rarely appear on the face of your documents. Rather, they represent the substance of the leases.

The finance lease

A *finance lease* is generally the most common type of lease worldwide. It extends for a term that covers up to 85 percent (and sometimes more) of the useful life of the leased property (how long you can use property economically before it wears out). The lessor determines rent based on tax savings, residual value assumptions, cost of funds, and the time value of money, and other factors, that I discuss in Chapters 6 and 7.

In these leases, lessors must receive payments of rent for a period of time and in an amount sufficient to receive an anticipated return or yield on the lessor's investment. Lessees may nonetheless be entitled to terminate the lease before the end of its term. Property could become subject to a casualty. The lessee may default. If any of these situations occur, the lessee will be required to make a substantial payment to the lessor to compensate for a lease term that is shorter than anticipated. This payment is usually called the *stipulated loss value* or *casualty value*. For an early termination of a lease, the value may be called the *termination value*. In finance leases (and other leases where lessors use these values), these values will usually decline over the initial term of the lease. These values, when paid, make the lessor whole (return the lessor's investment and earnings and maybe a bit more) as of the date that the lessor is paid (assuming that all other amounts due under the lease have also been paid).

A finance lessor fundamentally invests her capital with the intent to receive an economic return for doing so. The lessor expects to have few real obligations other than to purchase the property, lease it to a lessee, and leave a lessee alone to use, possess, and quietly enjoy the property. Consequently, this lease imposes on a lessee comprehensive obligations to maintain, insure, and pay taxes on the property throughout the term of the lease. Because of these obligations, a finance lease may often be called a *net lease*, or a *triple net lease* (where a lessee assumes the obligation for insurance, maintenance, and taxes for the benefit of, and at no cost to, the lessor).

In this book, I use the term finance lease or a tax lease with the understanding that the lease agreement contains the net lease language. See Chapter 8 and Section 5 of the Master Lease Agreement in the Appendix.

Because of the investment nature of the finance lease, lessors carefully scrutinize the creditworthiness of the lessee. Lessors want to know that the lessee can pay the rent and other sums payable under the lease. Then, to assure that the lessee pays without fail, lessors include *hell-or-high-water provisions* in the lease agreement. See Chapter 8.

A finance lease, and other leases, often contains hell-or-high-water provisions. (In fact, you may hear a finance lease referred to as a hell-or-high-water lease.) This concept makes larger, multiparty leases, called *leveraged leases*, "financeable" with lenders' and lessor's money because they can depend on the lessee to make all payments and take responsibility for the leased property. Chapter 5 discusses leveraged leases.

The hell-or-high-water provision essentially states that the lessee's commitment to pay rent is unconditional and not subject to any setoff, counterclaim, or *abatement* (stoppage), during the term. The lessee must pay no matter what occurs. You may be thinking that this cannot be right! It is right, and it is common.

Article 2A of the UCC defines and uses the term "finance lease," but that term is not the same as the general use or categorization of a finance lease described in this section. (Stay tuned for a discussion of Article 2A of the UCC in Chapter 16.) Although some similar concepts exist in Article 2A, that type of "finance lease" carries special legal ramifications discussed there.

In short, a finance lease creates an investment vehicle where, if you are a lessor, you can and should expect to be paid by the lessee in full for all amounts you charge under your lease for the entire lease term. If you are a lessee, you should expect to enter into a very strong agreement that imposes on you the burden of remaining in control of the leased property, taking care of it, and paying all costs for it, including the rent.

The true lease

A *true lease* refers to a lease of property in which the lessor demonstrates that he has assumed the benefits and burdens of ownership of the property in a manner that entitles the lessor alone to claim all applicable benefits of a tax owner of property under federal tax law. You can determine whether a true lease exists based on all of the facts and circumstances of a transaction, legal precedent from applicable case law, and rulings issued by the Internal Revenue Service (IRS). A true lease is not a conditional sale or security agreement.

As I discuss in Chapter 13, to determine whether your lease is a true lease, you can apply criteria, sometimes called the *Guidelines*, established in 1975 by the IRS. The Guidelines primarily cover leveraged leases, but you can use the Guidelines for all leases in which a lessor wants tax benefits derived from owner property. If you pass the criteria, your lease qualifies as a true or Guidelines Lease, and you can take all tax benefits (such as depreciation for lessors and rent deductions for lessees) available for the leased property involved in your deal.

Lessors must shoulder the burden and receive the benefits of ownership to take the tax benefits of ownership. This theme, with different applicable rules, arises in accounting, tax, and legal areas throughout this book. Watch out for references in this book to a "true lease" that I use only to distinguish a lease from a loan transaction.

The operating lease

Unlike the finance lease, the *operating lease* extends for a relatively small portion of the useful life of the property (when new). Although such a lease can last for a day, like a rental truck or oil drilling field equipment, these leases often cover a period of three to ten years (and longer for certain assets). Lessors expect lessees to return the property at the end of the term and to put the property back out "on lease" to a new lessee. The property may even be sold at any point in time.

Lessors have become adept at managing equipment and risk. The lessor's goal is to lease an asset at substantial economic returns before the property becomes obsolete or worn out. Although *operating lessors* act like investors similar to their finance lease counterparts, they do not expect the lessee to pay most of their investment on the initial lease term. Commercial aircraft users, like airlines, commonly use operating leases to acquire needed "lift" and to finance the aircraft on a shorter term than a finance lease. As a consequence of this approach, lessors usually charge a higher rent for the risk taken and enter into several leases during the useful life of an item of leased property.

Similar to the finance lease, the operating lease can also be a net lease, a true lease, and a hell-or-high-water lease. During the lease term, the lessee will be obligated to all or most of the costs of operating the property without reduction, setoff, or abatement (the lessee's hell-or-high-water obligation at work). However, in these transactions, lessors may assume financial and other obligations to lessees. Such obligations may include paying a portion of the cost of maintenance, guaranteeing a delivery date from the manufacturer of the leased property if it is new, and sharing the cost of returning the property at the end of the lease term. Aircraft operating leases utilize these concepts. They may also be utilized in a negotiated transaction with many other types of leased property.

Depending on the negotiation and structure of an operating lease, a stipulated loss value or casualty value table may be used (similar to the value used in a finance lease). Operating leases can also use a single, agreed value during the lease term that must be paid if a casualty loss or default occurs. Chapters 7 and 8 talk about the stipulated loss and casualty value tables.

The Financial Accounting Standards Board in FAS No. 13 uses the term "operating lease" in the context of classifying and accounting for leases by lessees. That concept is not used for the same purpose as an operating lease in this section. There, the accountants draw a clear distinction (how clearly only they would know!) of an "operating lease" from a "capital lease." You should keep that term separate when considering the business aspects of an operating lease structure. See Chapter 15.

In short, the operating lease is designed to compensate a lessor for taking the risk of deploying property under the initial term of a lease for a shorter period of time than the useful life of the property. It also enables the lessee to use the property for the time period dictated by the lessee's needs in his business operations.

The service lease

The *service lease* is not as well defined as either the finance lease or the operating lease. By its name, it implies that the lessor may keep records, pay for maintenance and provide other services to a lessee.

For example, say that, as a lessor, you lease sound and audio equipment to a lessee under a service lease to use in Broadway shows. In that transaction, the lessee can ask you to perform numerous services, such as maintaining and upgrading the equipment. Unlike the net lease or hell-or-high-water lease, this transaction allows for certain financial offsets for the lessee's inability to use the equipment according to agreed standards. So how often do you think a Broadway show would allow a service provider to slack off and supply sound equipment that works just some of the time during a show? Is there ever a freezing day in July in New York City? In other words, service leases can impose high performance standards on the lessor.

Although lease terms vary, service leases tend to be shorter in duration than finance leases, and the rent should be higher to compensate for the services performed by the lessor. Beyond this point, these leases are highly customized, and the terms fit the particular transaction.

Common Lease Structures

Two primary leasing structures exist in the United States: the *single-investor lease,* a two-party transaction between a lessor and lessee, and *the leveraged lease,* a transaction with three or more parties including a lessor, lender and lessee. Chapter 5 provides figures of these structures and describes how they work.

You can create many variations of these two structures both in domestic and international transactions. Lenders and lessors often use one variation of single-investor leases that enables lessors to obtain loans from lenders by using the lease and/or leased property as collateral. The lessor and lender close these deals on or after the completion of a single-investor lease. They sometimes call this kind of deal a *back-leveraged lease.*

The names of leases may describe the type of lease transaction. For example, a lease agreement may be called a "Lease," a "Lease Agreement," a "Synthetic Lease," a "Bareboat Charter," an "Aircraft Lease Agreement," a "Master Lease Agreement," or a "Locomotive Lease," to name just a few. Labels depend on the function of the lease and do not determine how they may be classified by tax, accounting, legal, or other professionals or by various laws that apply to the leases.

Opinions vary about how to label or classify leases, but, functionally, you can, in substance, expect to see the types of leases described in the following sections.

Single-delivery lease

A *single-delivery lease* refers to equipment leases under which all property covered by the lease will, on the same day, be accepted by the lessee and placed in service. That event constitutes the *delivery* of the equipment and coincides with the day on which the lease term begins. This lease may often be a single-investor lease or leveraged lease of various types that I discuss throughout this book.

For example, suppose that you, as lessee, decide to lease a CT scanner from a lessor. You order the scanner from the manufacturer and install it in your medical facility. You complete the testing and prepare to start using it within a few days. You enter into a single-delivery lease with your lessor, and then, for all purposes, you accept the scanner under the lease. That day is the delivery date. The lease covers only the scanner and no other property. This lease provides for a single delivery.

Sale-leaseback

As a lessee, you can also enter into a sale-leaseback transaction. A *sale-leaseback* refers to a transaction in which the owner of property sells the property to a buyer who, immediately upon the purchase, changes his hat and becomes your lessor. The lessor (buyer) then immediately enters into a lease with seller who becomes the lessee. This transaction enables the seller/lessee to get cash out of property but retain control and possession of the property in exchange for paying rent to a lessor. Like the single-delivery lease, you can use this common structure in single-investor or leveraged leases.

This type of transaction may involve one item of property (such as a printing press) or many items of property (such as furniture). Chapters 13, 14, and 15 cover the tax and accounting aspects of these transactions, which can be used for both real estate and personal property.

Master lease for multiple deliveries of equipment

Lessors use *master leases* as a line of credit for equipment or personal property leasing. Lessors use master leases used frequently when lessees need multiple items of equipment over a period of time. If the lessee meets the credit and other criteria for a lessor's investment, a lessor commits to a master lease for specified period of time, often for up to a year. In some cases, depending on the credit of a lessee, a lessor can use a master lease to provide funding at his discretion for an open-ended period of time, during which the lessor has the capacity and discretion to accept or reject the credit risk of the particular lessee.

With this commitment in place, the lessee can then arrange for equipment deliveries over a period of time. Each time the lessee accepts equipment, a delivery date occurs under the lease. A schedule or supplement to a lease confirms the acceptance and delivery. A master lease can have many schedules over the period that the lessor commits to this agreement.

For example, say that a lessee needs a CT scanner in January, an X-ray machine in March, a conference room table and chairs in May, and a new computer system in October. Each item becomes subject to the lease as the lessee accepts the delivery of the equipment under the terms of the lease. The schedules or supplements are usually consecutively numbered and dated on the date of the delivery. This type of lease allows for lessees and lessors to develop relationships and a series of equipment leases all under one credit/lease arrangement. Vendors often use this arrangement for lessees who frequently acquire their products and need financing at the time. See the *Master Lease Agreement* in the Appendix.

Lease-in, lease-out (lease/sublease)

Some lessees lack the credit to convince people to lease to them. Some lessors will enter into international transactions that require a foreign lessor and a domestic lessee. A lessee may find that he cannot use equipment that he leased for a period of time, but does not want to terminate the lease. For these and other reasons, a lessee may enter into a head lease/sublease transaction. You can see other examples of this kind of lease throughout the book.

A basic head lease/sublease works in two steps:

- ✔ First, a lessor and lessee enter into a lease covering leased property ranging from a printing press to an aircraft. You can call that lease the *head lease*.
- ✔ Second, the lessee, who as a lessor is called a sublessor, enters into a second lease, called a sublease, with a new third party called the *sublessee*.

As a result, the head lessor leases to a lessee, followed by a lease by the lessee, as sublessor, to a new party, the sublessee.

Despite the existence of the sublease, the head lessor rules most of the time, depending on the credit of the sublessee and negotiating strength of the parties. A sublease often looks very similar to, or incorporates many of the terms of, the head lease. That arrangement allows the lessee/sublessor to transfer her obligations under the head lease to the sublessee who essentially does what the head lease requires.

For more on subleasing, read Chapter 8 where I include and discuss sublease provisions.

Common Market Segments

You should be aware of the terms that segment the leasing markets based on the amount of the *original cost* or *lessor's cost* or *equipment cost*. These costs refer to the total cost of the property paid by a lessor, including all fees, expenses, and installation and shipping charges to acquire the leased property. Three common market segments exist based on the cost of the leased property:

- Lessors commonly refer to the smallest leasing transactions as *small-ticket leases* because they fall within a market segment of the leasing industry where the lessor's cost is no more than $250,000. Some small-ticket deals start at $25,000, depending upon whom you ask. Below $25,000, some leasing professionals describe the deals as *micro-ticket* leases. Leases of computers, peripherals, office equipment, and telephone equipment are commonly financed in small-ticket transactions. See Chapter 21.

- Lessors refer to the next level up as *middle-ticket leases* because they fall within a market segment of the leasing industry where a lessor's cost is generally between $250,000 and $5,000,000. Lessors lease a huge variety of property in this segment, including (as a tiny sample) mainframes, enterprise networks, helicopters, equipment, and every other item listed in "Property You Can Lease" section earlier in this chapter.

- Lessors refer to the highest level as a *large-ticket* lease where a lessor's cost is more than $5,000,000. Examples of equipment include power plants, railroad equipment, commercial and corporate jets, vessels and other transportation equipment, and large mining and oil and gas exploration equipment.

Chapter 2

Appreciating the Benefits of Leasing

*W*hy do businesses lease property that they need instead of buying it with equity or debt? Fundamentally, leasing satisfies their financial or other business objectives. Leasing offers a flexible and powerful financial tool that not only benefits lessees but also provides advantages to lessors and lenders. Lessors and lenders have become increasingly sophisticated, competitive, and specialized in understanding the value and methods of leasing property and realizing the financial and tax benefits of their investments. Consequently, lessees benefit from their interests and skills.

In this chapter, I help you determine whether, as a lessee or a lessor, the benefits of leasing make leasing an attractive financial tool or investment for you. Consider Chapters 6 and 7 for the financial analysis of the benefits of leasing.

Lessee Benefits of Leasing

You can use leasing effectively for real and personal property. Depending upon the financial, credit, and tax posture of your enterprise, leasing can provide you many advantages in your business, which I outline in the following sections.

Financing 100 percent of costs

As a lessee, you can arrange 100 percent financing of property that you need. Think broadly about the costs of property that you want to lease because you can include more than just the price tag on the basic property (the *hard costs* by some descriptions). In addition, lessors pay certain *soft costs* such as interest incurred during construction of the leased property, design costs, installation costs, transportation fees, training, software, and service contract fees, and certain taxes.

For example, say that you need a specialized CT scanner installed in a clean room adjacent to a hospital. Lessors can lease the basic device and the real property. A lessor can also pay for the cost of the design of the room and the installation and shipping costs of the CT scanner from the manufacturer to you. In addition, the lessor can reimburse you for the installment payments on the CT scanner that your manufacturer requires you to make before the lessor ever enters the deal. All these costs become part of the lessor's cost and your financing.

A loan may fall short of this amount of financing because lenders usually avoid financing soft costs and require substantial down payments as equity paid under their loans. Here's a little nonleasing trick that you should know: Lessors, in addition to leasing, often loan money secured by equipment, and they can and will lend 100 percent of the hard costs (and even certain soft costs) if you, as a lessee, have good credit and pledge high collateral value equipment to attract them to your deal.

Creating a hedge against inflation

You create a hedge against inflation by leasing. Instead of paying the total cost of the property today and large down payments, you delay the use of your funds until the date on which you make your lease payment. The delay makes your cash worth less to the lessor because inflation, even at a rate of 3 percent per year, reduces the value of the payment by the same 3 percent per year (subject to adjustments for the timing of your payments). You also get to use your cash during the lease term instead of spending it up front on a purchase. In addition, your lease can lock in the rates that exist on the date that you close your lease and assure you that the lessor absorbs the devaluation of your payments over time due to inflation and other market factors. You should not incur increases in rent even if (as occurs with some property such as aircraft) your leased property retains much of its original value during the term of your lease. Your rent should be fixed at the inception of your lease, making you indifferent to changes in the value of the property upward or downward. The benefit or risk shifts to your lessor.

However, in case you think that you get a real deal, lessors make certain assumptions about inflation or rates of return over time and price that effect into your lease rates. See Chapters 6 and 7. Further, lessors, acting as lenders, fund fixed-rate loans (as disguised leases and directly), and they generally lock in a certain spread or profit to protect themselves from the effects of inflation and changes in interest rates. Finally, some lessors price your rent to float with interest rate indexes, such as the prime lending rate to maintain their spread or profit over the index rate regardless of changes in the prime rate (or other index).

Matching the lease term to the duration you need

Leases provide flexibility on the *duration,* or term, of use of property. Leases can and often do have longer terms than loans on the same property. Lessors can estimate with reasonable accuracy the value, estimated useful life, remaining useful life, utility, and marketability of leased property. Based on those and other criteria, lessors can set a longer lease term that matches the period during which you need to use the property. *Estimated useful life* refers to the period during which you can economically and functionally use an item of leased property. *Remaining useful life* means the period left from the date you consider its useful life until the date that you can no longer cost-effectively use the property. The *utility* of an item of property means the practical functionality of property for its intended purpose. *Marketability* of leased property refers to the attractiveness of the property to third parties in a market where one party is a willing buyer or user and the other party is a willing selling or lessor.

On the other hand, you may need an item of property for a short period of time. Lessors can accommodate shorter terms as well. For example, if you are a general contractor, you may find that, in the construction business, you need tractors, graders, and earth-moving equipment only for two years while you build a chemical manufacturing plant and related support facilities. Because you know your milestone payment schedule, you can lease the property for a period equal to the expected schedule. This flexibility provides the optimal availability of the property that matches your cash flow without ending up with a burdensome financing cost after the project ends.

Improving cash flow and lowering cost

When you analyze the benefits of leasing, you find that, in general, leasing usually costs less over the term of the lease than buying or borrowing to purchase real or personal property. Because leasing finances 100 percent of the purchase price of property, you will not drain off your cash flow or reserves to purchase the property or incur the significant down payment required by most lenders.

For example, assume that you need to acquire a new printing press for your factory at a cost of $1,200,000. If you borrow to purchase the press, your lender may insist that you invest equity into the transaction of 20 percent to 25 percent of the cost — cash out of your pocket of $240,000 to $300,000. If you lease the press, you retain that cash for use in your business and keep any borrowing facility free for other needs.

Leasing has become a very competitive business. If you have good credit, competition among lessors for your business can lower your cost. The larger your transaction and the more attractive the value of your leased property, the greater the competition and, correspondingly, in an efficient market, the lower your cost. You can access these markets and create competition to help your business to achieve savings and reduce cash flow. In a large-ticket transaction, you should seek bids from several lessors to minimize your lease payments. In most markets, creditworthy lessees, in larger deals, will attract more than one lessor. Chapter 4 describes the kinds of lessors who may be interested in your deal, how to negotiate with them, or how you get them bid for a lease that you want.

Getting the value from lessor's tax benefits

Taxes play a critical role in *tax-oriented* leasing transactions. Small-ticket, middle-ticket, and large-ticket "leasing" transactions may be disguised loans that do not transfer the benefits of lessor's taxpayer rates to you. However, middle- and large-ticket leases should produce lower rents if you structure a tax-oriented lease because your lessor uses tax benefits, in the form of depreciation deductions, to decrease its taxes and cost of owning the leased property. A *tax-oriented lease* refers to a lease in which the economics of the transaction include the value of tax benefits. The lessor should pass on most of the savings to you. You can inquire about the lessor's pricing to confirm the tax savings and compute the rates yourself. Without the tax savings (setting aside other pricing methods that lessors use), if you and your lessor borrow at the same cost of money, your cash flow and costs of leasing an asset would be nearly the same as a lessor's. To optimize the cost savings, your lessor should have a higher tax rate and greater capacity to use tax benefits than you do. Chapter 6 considers your decision to lease or buy property, and Chapter 13 describes the tax benefits and rules for tax-oriented leases. In other words, a lessor, in a tax-oriented lease, effectively transfers the benefit of its higher rates to you. The higher the lessor's overall tax rate (disregarding other factors), the lower the rent that you pay.

Look for the lessors with the highest tax rates. You can estimate these taxes based on how the aggregate tax rate in effect in federal, state, and local jurisdictions that impose tax liability on the lessor. For example, a large bank in New York City may have a tax rate in excess of 40 percent because of high combined state, city, and federal taxes that it must pay. Although a lessor's actual tax rate remains a closely guarded competitive secret, if the lessor's rates exceed yours, you can effectively arbitrage the tax rate difference to your advantage in your lease. The tax benefit to you, in theory, equals the excess of the lessor's tax rate over yours (subject to adjustments for state taxes and other factors). The lessor's higher tax rate provides a direct advantage to you by reducing your cost using property.

Most of the tax advantages of leasing result from the full and efficient use of tax benefits by a high tax rate lessor, together with the full and efficient use of rent deductions of rent by the lessee. You only get the advantage of the lessor's tax rate to the extent that the lessor passes on her tax attributes to your deal and uses her tax rate in calculations of your rent.

To illustrate the point, consider each of the following situations:

- If your company generates an excess of tax deductions, you may be subject to the *alternative minimum tax* (sometimes called the *AMT*). Your *alternative minimum tax* status results from a policy of the federal government that prevents companies with high deductions from wiping out income (where income minus tax deductions equals zero or even less than zero taxable income). If you have no taxable income, you pay no tax. To avoid this result, after corporations (or individuals) compute their tax obligations, they must apply the alternative minimum tax formula so that they pay at least 28.2 percent in taxes (subject to change in tax law). If a lessor has a tax rate of 40 percent, you gain a value from the difference between your two rates.

   A lessor with a very low cost of funds (assume 5 percent) can still compete for your business with a lower tax rate (assume 36 percent) than another lessor with a higher cost of funds (assume 7 percent) and a higher aggregate tax rate (assume 41 percent). You can judge each transaction based on the lowest rents and other factors. Lessors compute the rents using cost of funds sophisticated computer programs based on a variety of assumptions, all as discussed in Chapter 7.

   For example, a large specialty manufacturing business acquires millions of dollars of depreciable equipment, rail cars, trucks, production equipment, forklifts, and automobiles each year to operate and grow its business. The tax benefits of the depreciation would, if permitted by federal tax law, wipe out its taxable income. Leasing especially benefits this company, which faces the alternative minimum tax, by effectively utilizing the tax benefits against income tax at the 41 percent tax rate of its New York City lessor rather than against its own lower AMT rate of 28.2 percent. This difference allows for a significant transfer of tax benefits otherwise unavailable if the lessee purchases its equipment. In this company, the lessee experiences an immediate bottom line impact of increasing available cash flow, lowering the cost of funds (from borrowing or using equity capital), using tax benefits more efficiently, and reducing the use of capital from other sources for acquisition of the equipment.

   If you engage in business in foreign countries and generate significant foreign tax credits, you may not be able to claim all those benefits currently. Leasing helps mitigate the effect of deferring or losing those tax credits by arranging for a lessor to purchase and lease the property to you. As a result, the lessor uses the tax benefits and passes the value to you based on the lessor's tax rates and liability instead of your own.

- A company may find that it suffered so many tax losses that it cannot use them when created and has to carry them forward to future years as permitted by the Internal Revenue Code of 1986, as amended (referred to by most tax experts as the "*Code*"). Any deferral of tax benefits reduces their value. Leasing enables you to use current tax benefits available to your lessor where you otherwise would lose or defer the benefits from these losses.

For example, say that you have started a high-technology venture in telecommunications. The business requires massive investments in fiber-optic cable and related infrastructure equipment. By leasing your equipment you may receive the benefit of lessor's tax rates and avoid wasting tax benefits.

In addition to benefits that you can derive from lessors, as a lessee, you make rental payment with pretax dollars (say $10,000 per month). In a loan transaction, you can deduct the interest portion of the payment. For the loan, the interest payment may amount to a large portion of $10,000 per month at the beginning of the loan and decrease over the term of the loan (depending on the amortization schedule). In a lease, you benefit by deducting your entire lease rental payment as an expense ($10,000) every month. On balance, if you lease property and have tax liability, you do not receive depreciation deductions because that tax benefit shifts to your lessor.

Do not forget state taxes as an important element of leasing. You can defer sales taxes through leasing and pay taxes over the term of the lease in the form of an excise or rent tax in lieu of the sales tax. This tax deferral can be implemented as discussed in Chapter 14.

Managing equipment obsolescence

Have you worried that the technology equipment that you need will become obsolete before you have amortized your investment (or even put your property into operation for the first time)? Leasing provides you with the flexibility to cope with the incredibly fast technology product cycles that you now experience. If you structure a lease properly, your lessor will accept the obsolescence risk upon the return of property at the end of the lease. Although the property has remaining useful life, it may have little value. Your lessor may even allow you to update or upgrade the current technology as part of your lease to acquire newer technology. Computers and other high-technology assets often fall into this category. However, other property can become obsolete, such as medical equipment or other property subject to technology competition or regulatory restrictions.

For example, say that a lessor enters into a lease with a lessee using a $140,000 life-lung endoscopy system regulated by the Food and Drug Administration (FDA). During the second year of the term of the lease, the FDA changes the requirements for safety and technology of such devices resulting in an immediate 40 percent drop in market value of the device on lease to the lessee. Say that the lessee subsequently terminates the lease (as may be permitted in the lease) because the equipment becomes obsolete and surplus to his needs. The lessor takes the entire risk of the loss of value even though the lessor did not expect or plan for the law to change with such dramatic negative impact. As a lessee, you enjoy this downside protection where, as the owner, you would have the full risk. If, however, the lessor requires you in your lease to upgrade or update equipment to meet current regulatory standards as many lessors do, you can incur significant additional costs. However, as the lessee, you may be able to lease the upgrades or updated equipment from your lessor and thereby, once again, manage the obsolescence risk by transferring it to your lessor.

Despite this risk, lessors can and do take the obsolescence risk because they often (but not always) possess the knowledge and skill to remarket the property. *Remarketing* refers to the process of locating and closing a lease or sale of leased property that a lessor owns or controls after an existing lease ends. Lessors usually set your rent expecting to realize their planned investment return. Taking this obsolescence risk can raise your lease rates, but you may find comfort in the flexibility and predictability established at the beginning of your lease.

As a lessee, your right to return the property may allow you to keep pace with your competitors by leasing property that provides newest technology in the marketplace. You can also avoid the effort to resell the property to obtain proceeds for the down payment of the replacement property or to pay for other corporate costs.

Why burn management time when a lease imposes this remarketing burden on lessors? For many lessors, the resale or leasing to a third party plays a central part in their business plans. It also utilizes a lessor's marketing expertise to make a profit on the residual value of the equipment at the end of the lease term in excess of the residual value that the lessor assumes in his lease pricing, called the *residual upside*. *Residual value* refers to the value of a leased property at the end of the term of your lease. You can then focus more on the sale of your products or services rather than managing equipment obsolescence, marketing, and residual values.

Customizing the timing and amount of lease payments

Does your revenue swing higher at some point during the year (as opposed to staying level)? If you sell products at retail, for example, you probably experience significantly higher sales in the fourth quarter arising from the holiday buying. Leasing provides the advantage that the lease payments can, depending on the tax-orientation of the lease, increase during higher cash flow periods and reduce somewhat during slower times. Chapter 13 discusses some limitations on tax structuring payments arising under Section 467 of the Code.

Do you expect your revenue from your business to grow rapidly (a story that many businesses tell), but you really need a break on lease rates today? Alternatively, what if you win a major contract that won't pay you until a later date, but you need equipment now to perform under the contract? Could the opposite occur where cash flow is higher now, but will fall later because of anticipated capital investment planned after the start of the lease?

Lessors can structure payments that will be lower at one point during the lease term and then higher later and vice versa. Unlike a loan that will normally consist of level or reducing payments (on a mortgage amortization), lessors can customize lease payments to fit your cash flow needs. If your need dictates a level rent, a lessor can do that, too. To accommodate lower cash flow, lessors will even extend the term of your lease longer than the term of a comparable loan to reduce your individual rent payments. The willingness of lessors to allow such flexibility depends on many factors, including your creditworthiness, the value and residual value of the leased property, competition for your lease transaction, and the fundamental strength of the business environment in which you operate.

Such customization allows you to forecast more accurately your cash demands, time your lease payments to fit your business plan and model, maintain available capital for other obligations, and reserve your borrowing capacity for other needs.

Avoiding loan covenant restrictions

If you negotiate or have in place a loan agreement, it may contain *negative covenants* — promises to your lender that you will not permit certain negative results in your financial performance. For example, a negative covenant may restrict certain types of leases especially capital leases accounted for as a liability or debt on your balance sheet (with the property being treated as a corresponding asset). The trick for you is to exclude leases from the restriction, such as operating leases discussed in Chapter 15, and thereby expand your leasing options without breaching your loan agreement covenants. These leases, if properly structured, constitute off-balance sheet obligations under FAS 13, which is a very important benefit for public companies and private companies whose balance sheets may be scrutinized by investors and lenders. On the other hand, this off-balance sheet feature provides less benefit to smaller businesses or public entities that have little or no concern with their balance sheets or do not have investors or lenders looking over their shoulder.

Another approach to minimize the effect of negative covenants is to create a *basket,* or approved quantity, of leases that your lender will not restrict or include in negative financial covenant calculations.

Sidestepping budget restrictions

You can plan for the acquisition of any such item of property through a *capital budgeting process*. Capital budgeting refers to analyzing the acquisition of property that you expect to use for more than a year. By contrast, a wor*king* *capital* budget relates to acquisitions or investments that benefit your business for up to a year. Leasing may fall into a category of working capital that requires fewer approvals and flies under the radar of the capital budgeting process. Capital budgeting often involves detailed justification for acquisitions to senior management or the board of directors. Leasing may be viewed as a simple operating expense that midlevel managers and senior managers can approve and arrange as needed during any fiscal year. That alone can make leasing an attractive financing alternative to avoid the strains of annual budget planning for capital assets and big-ticket purchases. This budgeting process applies not only to private business but also to federal, state, and local government entities as well. See Chapter 19.

Easing documentation and legal concerns

Is your company or bank subject to regulation by someone? Is anyone free of regulation these days? Leasing carries the advantage that public disclosure to the Securities and Exchange Commission (SEC) and other regulatory agencies may be less burdensome or not even necessary. Regulatory approvals of leases may in some cases be limited. Competitive bidding may not be required by certain private or public entities.

In these areas, you must check with your legal and other advisors to properly structure leases to limit regulatory requirements and disclosure requirements arising in your business.

Even if you do cope with regulatory matters, leases, at least single-investor leases, in small-ticket or middle-ticket transactions, tend to involve less paper than their secured loan counterparts. Although lawyers may drive you crazy in a secured loan deal because of the complexity and detail of the documents, they can be almost manageable in small-ticket or middle-market leases. Many of these transactions use forms handled by administrators or paralegals instead of lawyers (at least in small-ticket deals). If you are a lawyer, you may be relieved to have one deal that someone else can do for you — so that creates a leasing advantage for you, too!

To avoid misleading you, forget what I just said when it comes to leveraged leases and other big-ticket deals. They present interesting challenges discussed in Chapter 5. Leveraged leases tend to be complex, highly negotiated, large-ticket transactions that create pounds of paper.

Receiving full service from lessors and other conveniences

You can enter into a *service lease,* where the lessor helps you with maintenance, insurance, administrative, and technical requirements.

In the fleet truck markets, for example, lessors will assist with identifying appropriate specifications for trucks and provide maintenance, fuel service, washing, administrative assistance such as payment and reporting on taxes, and disposal of used equipment.

By entering a service lease, you don't have to spend vital management time to arrange for or provide these services. You can focus on your core business, reallocate talent needed to build your enterprise, and increase productivity both from your staff and your leased equipment. You can find this kind of lease in office equipment, computers, rail cars, trucks, trailers, automobiles, and even aircraft. Loan transactions rarely, if ever, provide similar services.

Enjoying speed in completing deals

In the highly competitive environment for leases with good quality assets, lessors and their advisors often use their most diligent efforts to close and fund leases in very short periods of time. Loan transactions (particularly large secured loans) often include cumbersome and lengthy documentation requirements that result in more complicated and time-consuming legal process and expense.

Lessors tend to compete on speed when closing a deal. To close rapidly they may reduce cumbersome legal structures, and cast away extra documents. They want to win your business and meet deadlines that you request; so ask lessors, before you award a deal, how quickly they can close — and watch them scramble!

Lessor Benefits of Leasing

Lessors, too, have good business reasons to enter into leasing transactions and programs. Leasing property for many lessors constitutes very big business and an important part of a financial product line.

Tax-effective capital investments

As a lessor, you may develop leasing products and programs to gain tax shelter, mostly in the form of depreciation deductions, which reduce taxes on your income. See Chapter 13. By taking depreciation, you also lower the cost of owning property and can pass those benefits on to your lessees through lower rent described in Chapter 7. By owning more leased property, you can acquire more earning financial assets that produce income in the form of rent, residual income, and other compensation from lessees.

Residual value in leased property

Lessors develop expertise in determining the residual value of property. These lessors can, in pricing a lease, assume a value that they expect to equal or exceed on the sale or other remarketing proceeds of the leased property. As a result, if you, as a lessor, estimate correctly, you can realize a value greater than the amount assumed on your books and realize a profit from the lease transaction that may be very substantial relative to earnings derived from payments of rent. For this reason, some lessors expect to make their greatest return on, and develop strategies to take advantage of, residual value.

For example, say that you, as a lessor, assume that a $1,250,000 cement truck that you leased will retain 10 percent of its original value ($125,000) at the end of five years. Then, at the expiration of the lease, you sell the truck for 30 percent of its original value ($375,000). You have made a profit of $250,000 more than assumed in your original investment. That amounts to a 20 percent premium (without adjustment for the time value of money) over your original investment and represents the kind of success that makes residual value a key part of leasing for many lessors. The downside can also occur — a realization of 5 percent ($62,500), for example, on the truck means that you do not achieve your assumed residual and will not realize your basic investment return. You may even suffer a loss on the lease.

Profitable investments

As a lessor, you will be motivated to make the highest returns on your lease investments that you can relative to other types of investments or loans in your portfolio or available in the market.

You often earn higher returns by entering into tax-oriented lease structures that efficiently use your tax bill. You may also be able to obtain a higher lease rate depending on the credit story of your lessee. The residual value described in the preceding section may also boost your overall return.

You may find that, if you have a low cost of funds, you can win more than your share of deals. Conversely, if you have a higher cost of funds than other lessors, you may have difficulty winning business in an efficient market (that is, a market where lessees can find cheap money among lessors). Because the leasing market has become very competitive, squeezing down lease rates, you may have to take more risk in a transaction to achieve higher returns or even to win business. If you charge commitment or other fees, as may be possible in some transactions, you can boost your returns. One way to avoid eroding your returns is to impose on the lessee the obligation to include your out-of-pocket transaction expenses, such as legal fees and expenses, appraisal fees, inspection fees, and accounting or other professional fees as part of the lessor's cost. When you complete your pricing, you should find that what you can earn on a lease transaction provides a real economic benefit to you with some upside potential in true leases. Chapter 7 describes the economics for lessors in more detail.

Chapter 3

Facing the Risks in Leasing

. . . .

In This Chapter

▶ Identifying basic risks in leasing for lessees

▶ Listing potential risks and liabilities in the leasing business for lessors

▶ Receiving helpful hints to manage leasing challenges

. . . .

*W*hether you're the lessee, lessor, or lender, leasing involves risks like any other financial transaction. This chapter helps you evaluate some of the risks and business considerations in leasing. You weigh these risks against the benefits and lease economics to decide whether you want to enter into a lease on one hand or a debt or equity financing on the other hand (see Chapters 2, 6, and 7). This chapter speaks first to lessees and then lessors. You should each review the sections relating to the other so that you understand some of the risks of leasing from the other party's perspective.

Lessee Risks of Leasing

As a lessee, you accept many obligations to your lessor and, directly or indirectly, to any lender involved in your leasing transaction. This section discusses some of the risks that you should evaluate before you lease anything.

Potential loss of residual value

Before you lease, understand the risk that you give up of the residual value in the leased property. In true tax leases, as contrasted with leases disguised as secured loans or conditional sales, you generally return the leased property to the lessor at the end of the lease term (unless you purchase it under options that I discuss in the following paragraphs). When you return the leased property, your rights to and interest in the property ends. At that point, your lessor retains any residual value, and you do not.

If you purchase the property instead of leasing it, you enjoy continued use of the property without being forced to replace or purchase it at the end of a lease term. You own it; you can keep it or sell it; and you can, in short, do with the property as you see fit. If the property has substantial value, you retain that value or you can use it up or transfer it to someone else who pays *you,* and not a lessor, the residual value.

Lessors know all about these residual value considerations. Some lessors bank on residual value as an important part of their economic return in leasing. Lessors may, however, give you options at the end of the lease term to buy the leased property at a fixed price, called a *fixed price purchase option*, or an option to buy the leased property during your lease term, called an *early buyout option* (EBO). These options give you some control over when you choose to end your lease and buy the property. See Chapter 8 and the Master Lease Agreement in the Appendix.

For example, say that a lessor buys an aircraft for $2,000,000 and uses a residual value of 25 percent of the cost (which is $500,000) in calculating her expected return on the investment (without taking into account tax or other factors). Consider the risks that you each take and the potential benefits that you may each realize.

First, assume that you negotiate a fixed purchase option to buy the aircraft for 55 percent of the lessor's cost (which is $1,100,000) at the end of your seven-year lease term. You set this value because the aircraft could have a higher value at the end of the lease, so you limit your risk of paying that higher value by negotiating this fixed option price. Your lessor takes the risk that the price he negotiates will be about the same as fair market value so he does not leave any money on the table for you to keep.

Second, if at lease expiration the used aircraft market value offers 65 percent of lessor's cost (which is $1,300,000), you effectively share 10 percent ($200,000) of the residual value with the lessor ($1,300,000 minus $1,100,000 = $200,000) by purchasing the aircraft through this fixed price purchase option. You have controlled your risk of the price exceeding half of the original price when you want to buy the aircraft.

Third, your lessor keeps the required residual of $500,000 and also the $600,000 in residual upside (fixed purchase price of $1,100,000 minus assumed residual of $500,000 equals $600,000 in upside). Your lessor receives residual upside of $600,000, gaining much but not all of the value of the leased property.

As a lessee, you should accept only realistic purchase options and implicit residual values based on appraisals or the best market data that you can find when you close your lease. If the option price is too high, you may lose any opportunity to share the upside because you pay full value for the leased property. If the lessor sets the residual too low, your lessor may have to raise her rents (market conditions permitting) to make her economic returns. Although not always the case, the higher the residual assumed by your lessor, the lower the rent you pay. Lessors usually refuse to share their residual assumptions with you. You should plan to run pricing of leases yourself or with the help of a leasing professional to calculate approximate residuals that your lessor uses.

Maintenance, insurance, and tax risks

In most leases other than service leases you are responsible to maintain, insure, and pay taxes on your leased property in nearly the same manner as if you owned it. As noted in Chapter 1, lessors refer to this concept in leases as the *net lease* or *triple net lease provisions*. These costs can be significant, but should not be higher than if you owned the property. You take the risk of these costs escalating more rapidly than expected. For example, insurance costs can increase unexpectedly for certain types of coverage. Regardless of the amount, however, these costs and efforts provide no benefit to you once the lease term ends. They simply represent costs of using someone else's property. By contrast, as an owner, you keep the value, if any, that results from your expenditures. You may also be better able to limit these costs as an owner because your lease may impose more stringent (and costly) requirements than you would as the owner.

Usage of tax benefits

If, as a lessee, you have a federal and/or state taxable income, you can probably use the depreciation benefits derived from purchasing property. The depreciation benefits reduce your taxable income. If you lease, you don't use or you defer these write-offs. If you don't put these tax benefits to optimal use, you may experience a real economic loss because you do not purchase the property that enables you to use your current deductions to reduce taxes on your income today. However, if you have no taxable income when you lease, you gain from your lessor's taxable position and higher tax rate, and this risk is less relevant for you.

Evaluate your tax, business plan, and budget to determine if the cost of the lease merits the overall value of potential loss, deferral, or use of tax write-offs.

Loss of control of leased property: The lessor rules

Do you know how to maintain your property? Do you know how and when to upgrade it? Do you know when to trade or sell it? You undoubtedly say "yes" to these questions. However, when you lease, you may find that the manner in which you normally manage property differs from the approach required by your lessor. You can negotiate these terms, but as soon as you close, you no longer make the final decisions about many issues concerning the management or disposition of leased property. The lessor (or the lease itself) rules!

Indemnification risks

Leases impose some special risks on you. Finance lessors, the lessors who invest for the sake of deploying investment capital, are a risk-adverse crowd. They do not lease to you to manage property, like service lessors. Finance lessors lease to achieve a return on their capital. To avoid other costs and liabilities from undermining their return, they impose most risks on you in the indemnification provisions. See Chapter 8 on indemnification provisions.

As a lessee, you can think of *indemnification provisions* as a contractual safety net. You hold the net and catch most risks that can affect the lessor and lender relating to your lease or leased property, including the leasing, operation, maintenance, possession, or control of the leased property. Although you face some risks as an owner, you cover the lessor should anything go wrong, including your lessor's out-of-pocket legal fees and expenses of defense of any claim involving your lease.

Insurance obligations and the risk of loss

If personal or property injury occurs, your property or casualty insurance should pay for the damages. Unlike owning property, you face the risk that all of your insurance proceeds for the leased property will be paid to and retained by your lessor. In that event, you do not control or own the proceeds of a loss. In the case of a third-party injury or loss, you may also be required to reach into your pocket and pay for liability events if your insurance does not fully cover you and your lessor. Your lessor may require you to buy more insurance than you would buy for yourself (without a lease), adding to your total cost of leasing. See Chapter 9 on insurance.

Consider each of the risks of leasing individually and as a group. Not all risks deserve equal attention or importance. Weigh these risks (and others that you identify in your business that I don't mention) against the benefits of leasing described in Chapter 2. Then, if "you're good to go," look at Chapter 6 on the economics of leasing.

Lessor Risks of Leasing

As a lessor, you face a wide range of risks in leasing property. Fundamentally, your risk in leasing is whether you can make profitable investments in leased property. This section discusses some of the factors to consider in assessing the risks. Making the right decisions allows you to seize opportunities in leasing.

Credit risks

Will your lessee pay you what he owes under the lease when due or default in its obligations? Has the lessee demonstrated acceptable creditworthiness to lease from you as determined by your organizational standards? Regardless of how good a lessee looks in financial statements, does the lessee's overall credit history and prospects give you an objective basis to commit to make your investment in the leased property? Each of these issues (and others) helps analyze the credit risk of your prospective lessee.

Acceptable lessee profile

Before you start your credit analysis, ask yourself: Do I understand my prospective lessee's needs and expectations? Will the proposed transaction, including the proposed type of leased property, fit my business objectives (including economic return requirements) and business model? Does the leased property fit the requirements of my organization?

Answer these questions first. Then proceed with the other concerns that I discuss in the following sections. If the lessee, the leased property, or the proposed transaction doesn't fit your business model or organizational requirements, go on to the next deal.

Information needed to make a credit decision

Once a transaction looks feasible, you should gather (at a minimum) the following categories of information as part of approval of any transaction:

  ✔ **Financial statements and tax returns:** Request *consolidated* financial statements (which show the lessee and his subsidiary companies in one set of numbers) for the past three years, including statements audited by the lessee's accounting firm (if available). If available, ask for financial statements presented on a *consolidating* basis (that is, financial statements of lessee and his subsidiary companies presented individually in separate financial statements). These statements should help you determine the creditworthiness of the lessee and his affiliates, who may support the lessee's obligations to you (with guaranties, for example).

As a lessor, you should always require the lessee to demonstrate adequate credit strength. You can use you credit staff effectively by evaluating, among other issues, your prospective lessee's assets, tangible net worth, and cash flow. Look at the lessee's balance sheet for signs of financial growth, sound financial management, profitability, and stability. Read the notes to the financial statements to get the inside story. Request tax returns for the same period to confirm tax reporting and income that the lessee says that she earned and reported correctly where available for private (as contrasted with public) companies.

✔ **Information on the property:** Know your asset. You may or may not care about asset value to recover your investment. Some lessors rely primarily on the lessee's credit. If you do care, try to lease property that you understand thoroughly, including property with long useful lives, low obsolescence, or state-of-the-art technology that will last (for a little while at least) after your lease expires.

Whether you lease real estate or personal property, this property can save the day. If your lessee can't pay you, the collateral value of the leased property itself may.

Regardless of credit strength, you can keep your lessee's attention (and, more importantly, keep her money flowing) if the property you lease meets a critical need in the lessee's operations. A lessee will protect that property from your rights and remedies arising on default. As a priority, for those of you who rely on the residual value of leased property, select property to lease that, at the start of the lease or as soon thereafter as possible, has (or will have) sufficient value and marketability to salvage a high percentage of your investment should you have to sell, lease, or otherwise dispose of the leased property in a problem situation or at the end of the lease.

✔ **Industry information:** Know the industry in which your lessee competes. Study the industry to determine its current strength, prospects, and competition. Satisfy yourself that your lessee will flourish (or at least survive) for the term of your lease.

✔ **Determine how your lessee rates:** Does your lessee control a significant market share in her business segment or have a rating and ranking in her industry that you find worthy of considering? Has your prospective lessee competed effectively in the marketplace? Is the market prone to up and down cycles? Analyze whether your lessee can meet the obligations under the lease during those cycles. While you're doing this review, take a gander at reports from agencies in the know about the industry of your lessee. The rating agencies and financial information resources include Moody's Investors Service (`www.moodys.com/cust/default.asp`), Bloomberg L.P. (`www.bloomberg.com`), and Standard & Poor's (`www.standardpoor.com`). Consider their views about the industry and just how well your customer fits (to the extent available on your deal and lessee). Consider bank references — if the banks know your prospective customer.

✔ **Background on the management:** Know the senior management. Do they demonstrate the skill and capability to make money and grow their business? Have they developed a track record of success and integrity?

Satisfy yourself that you believe in the management. When all else fails, their integrity, experience, and skills may help you salvage a deal gone bad.

Residual value risk

In any lease that depends on the value of property to achieve an economic return, the lessor and lenders take residual value risk. If you assume that you will receive 20 percent for leased property and you get only 10 percent, you experience a 10 percent loss. To avoid such consequences, lessors and lenders should evaluate the following:

✔ **Quality, value, and useful life of the property:** Consider the quality, value, and the useful life of the prospective leased property. Experts, who buy, sell, and appraise or otherwise deal in markets of the same or similar property can determine the quality and value of the property you want to lease. They can evaluate the fundamental features, technological capability, and potential obsolescence of the property, among other factors. If you have equipment management personnel in your business, these experts can and do make these types of judgments.

You can manage this risk in several ways, including the following:

- First, you can make lower residual value assumptions on the value of the leased property. Taking such action makes sense when you don't have extensive knowledge about the leased property or how to remarket it, or lease high-technology equipment with high-obsolescence attributes, or have a strong lessee credit that mitigates the property value risk.

- Second, lease property that has a longer useful life, higher quality relative to similar assets in the market, low obsolescence, and retains its value.

- Third, hire experts outside of your organization to help you. You can lease almost any property where you value the property correctly. Look for specialists to help you. They exist for almost every type of asset.

Despite this analysis, you probably will still face the reality that, to put business "on the books," you may have to assume a higher residual value than a competitor to win the deal. Examine this risk closely before you hike your residual into unrecoverable territory!

✔ **Reliable delivery schedules:** You face the risk that a seller fails to deliver property on time. Suppose that you plan for certain periods during a tax year that you believe you can take the maximum tax benefits associated with a tax lease, which I discuss in Chapter 13. If the lease starts later, the tax benefits can be reduced (or increased depending on a variety of factors). You may expect to have the capital available to invest in such assets for a prescribed period of time. If the leased property delivers later, the capital may be used for other investments. If you have established a rent based on a certain cost of funds and such costs increase during a delay, your lease may become unattractive to a lessee even if you plan ahead and can adjust the rent upward to compensate for the rate increases. To manage these risks, the delivery schedule of the proposed lease property must be predictable and timely. You should, in any event, shift these risks to the lessee to maintain your expected economic return.

✓ **Maintenance and return of leased property:** Although you transfer possession and use of property that you own to your lessee, you should eventually get it back (if the lessee does not buy it). You encounter the risk of getting the leased property back, at all, and, if you do, getting it in the proper physical return condition.

If the lessee fails to return the leased property in the proper condition, the value of the property declines, and your investment assumptions and residual may be too high, resulting in a lower return or loss on your transaction. To mitigate this risk, know where your leased property is at all times and inspect it periodically.

✓ **Option to early terminate the lease:** Your lessee may negotiate a right to terminate the lease before the end of its term. Like a return of property, you assume a certain residual value that should exist on such termination. If the leased property has less value than you assumed, you could lose money on the deal. You mitigate this risk by including a termination value schedule in your lease that effectively requires your lessee to pay you any shortfall in value up to a predetermined amount in the schedule that preserves your investment return at the termination date.

Keep in touch with the lessee. Know his needs for the leased property. You may want to avert early terminations by offering upgrades or sublease rights.

Tax risk

Leasing is often a very tax-intensive method of financing. Chapters 13 and 14 discuss federal income tax and state taxes, respectively. Some tax risks may be uncontrollable or unpredictable. For example, say that you that you enter a tax lease of furniture and take the tax benefits of ownership on your tax return. You enter the transaction with a large tax bill in the first year of the lease, and you only too happily take the depreciation benefits from owing the furniture to cut down that tax bill. Unexpectedly, in the second year of the lease, you face a loss that wipes out your tax liability. In the same year, the IRS sends you an assessment notice because your lease fails to qualify as a true lease. In addition, the IRS selects a thorough (read zealous) agent to audit your books because several of your leases show signs of the same tax problems. One week after the IRS notifies you of an audit, the president signs a bill that reduces tax rates for you from 40 percent to 32 percent.

Ludicrous as these examples or timing may seem, every one of these circumstances can occur. So, what tax risks exist for you as the lessor?

- ✔ **Structuring risk:** The IRS can question that the terms of your deal do not qualify as a true lease, and you will not be treated as the owner entitled to the tax benefits. See Chapter 13.

- ✔ **Legislative risk:** The leasing industry has demonstrated its creativity and flexibility by coping with adverse legislative changes. Unfortunately, the change of tax rates can undermine assumptions that dramatically impact lease pricing as described in Chapter 7.

- ✔ **Audit risk:** If the IRS takes an interest in you, it can and will audit your books and records. You can incur substantial audit expenses for accounting, legal, and other professionals and can end up with adverse tax treatment of your leases.

- ✔ **Loss of tax appetite:** To make tax leasing attractive, you must have a "tax appetite" or a tax bill against which you can apply the tax benefits. If you have no appetite, well, tax benefits won't have that sweet taste of cutting your tax bill or help your after-tax returns!

Set your objectives regarding the use of your tax appetite at levels that you can justify based on past performance and future budgeted income taxes. Hire competent tax advisers who can help you create a transaction that passes muster under the applicable tax rules. Follow legislative developments and try to complete deals before changes in law occur that damage your economics (that is, don't go past "grandfathered" periods). Resist the temptation in the face of competition or credit constraints to agree to terms that defeat a solid tax position as the owner of the asset who is entitled to tax depreciation and any other tax benefits. If the competition can take more risk with its tax return, find another lease in which to invest. No single lease transaction should be so far off the beam as to interest the Internal Revenue Service in your whole lease portfolio, or otherwise adversely affect your financial results.

Accounting considerations

Accounting pervades leasing and decisions that you make to lease or not to lease. You consider the balance sheet and cash flow statement of the lessee as well as the notes to these statements to decide whether to proceed with a lease. Lessees can structure leases to appear on-balance sheets or off-balance sheets. Chapter 15 reviews many of these issues and others that help lessees and lessor classify and account for leases correctly.

Profit and funding challenges

For many years, I have heard the same old song from lessors: "A lot of money is chasing a few good deals." Nonetheless, the volume of leasing business has grown over the last decade to well over $200 billion dollars in 2001 (in the United States), according to the Equipment Leasing Association. Even though the leasing industry has experienced growth, you may also face some challenges that I want to mention briefly because they are important but demand more attention that I can provide here.

- **Funding shortfalls for lessors:** Despite economic growth, profits and funding risks remain a serious concern for smaller leasing companies. Funding sources seek stability, profits, and diversity in leasing companies and their portfolios. Lessors now more often cannot secure funding or their funding costs are much higher, for investment in leases, due to these constraints.

- **Consolidation and increased capital costs:** The funding shortfall arises in part from the consolidation of leasing, financing companies, and banks; and the withdrawal of those sources from the market of funding lessors, which need money to invest in leasing. Fewer (larger) lessors control more of the market and reduce the ability of smaller lessors to compete. To survive or grow despite these risks, many lessors have invited or succumbed to consolidations.

- **Profits tighten for lessors:** At the same time that funding falls short for lessors, margins and leasing volume of lessors has decreased as competitive pressures and costs of capital increase. *Margins* generally refer to rents minus the cost of funds. Not to be left out, even large lessors find that they must take higher risks to achieve higher margins/returns in their direct lease transactions.

Risk of loss

You experience a physical risk of loss of the leased property in every lease transaction. A *risk of loss* refers to the chance that property you own may be lost, damaged, stolen, or totally destroyed and impaired, wiping out the value of the property. See Chapter 10 on insurance and related issues.

Environmental liability risks

You may lease buildings, plants, or facilities, in addition to vessels and other assets that can create liability under state and federal environmental laws. You can protect yourself against those risks by acquiring proper insurance coverage and obtaining indemnities and other protections from your lessees.

If your lessee incurs liability for violations of any federal or state environmental law, the liability can be so large that your lessee may be unable to perform his obligations to you under your lease. You and your lessee may face civil and criminal penalties, as well as substantial environmental cleanup costs. You should identify and address these risks and find solutions at the beginning of your lease. Some lessors satisfy themselves with the lessee's indemnity alone.

Weigh carefully the strength of the lessee's credit against these potential environmental risks. You can mitigate these risks to some extent with pollution insurance, by restricting your leases to property that meets the highest standards of the environmental rules, and requiring and monitoring strict compliance by the lessee with applicable laws. Retain competent environmental counsel to interpret the environmental laws applicable to your proposed lease transaction and to help you write appropriate provisions of your lease agreement to protect you against potential liability or sanctions.

Management of a lease portfolio

Once you have signed a lease, the administration of the lease, including the review and reporting of the lessee's financial condition, becomes crucial. Neglected transactions can lead to unnecessary and avoidable problems with rent collection, credit issues, and other shortfalls by your lessees. Any and all of the shortcomings discussed in this section can cost you money.

Contract administration or *lease portfolio administration* is the group that you can form or use to assist you in completing lease transactions. Such a group can, among other services:

- ✔ Assure you that the lessee complies with the terms of the lease, including paying rent on time and complying with specific covenants

- ✔ Assist you with any administrative or service problem that may need to be resolved

- ✔ Keep your legal, credit, asset management, and business personnel informed of any early warning signs of potential credit problems

Usury risks for lenders in lessor's clothing

If a court treats your lease as a secured loan, as the lessor, you in effect become a lender. *Usury* is relevant to lenders in any deal and to you, as a lessor, when a court says that you are a lender, regardless of whether you label your main document a lease agreement or give it any similar name.

Generally, *usury* refers to requiring your lessee, in certain deals, to compensate you under your "lease" at rates in excess of the highest lawful rate. Usury can occur, for example, when you enter into an agreement to lend money or to refrain from collecting money for a period of time in exchange for compensation (including interest, fees, and other payments) that exceeds statutory limits as high as 18 to 26 percent in some cases.

This description generally summarizes the pattern of many usury laws. However, the specific statutes vary widely from state to state and apply differently to corporate borrowers in certain sizes of (loan) transactions than to consumers (who I do not consider here). The formulas or computations of usury limits are complex. The key issue is whether, as a lessor, your transactions become subject to usury statutes that limit the "rent" or "interest" or other fees that you can charge.

If you violate usury statutes, serious penalties apply ranging from fines to forfeiting collection of the loan to criminal penalties. Examine your leases closely. Make sure that if you intend to lend money through an agreement called a lease or a loan agreement that you comply with applicable usury laws. Usury laws generally don't affect true leases (or a similar concept as defined in each state). Consult legal counsel to be sure. You can violate usury limits by charging fees, interest, or other amounts or even taking an equity interest in your lessee or borrower.

Part II
How Leasing Works

The 5th Wave   By Rich Tennant

In This Part

In Part II, you start structuring, negotiating, proposing, and closing real deals. You can also find a discussion of the factors and calculations that provide meaningful evaluation of lease economics. In other words, you determine here whether the price of your lease as a lessee, or the economic return as a lessor, makes sense for you.

Chapter 4

Closing Your First Lease

*L*ike any business opportunity, getting started in a leasing transaction presents you with a series of questions and decisions. As a prospective lessee, ask yourself the following questions: Do I need additional property to operate my business? Should I lease the property? Who will provide the lease financing? How do I find the right lessor and complete the deal? Can I go it alone and get the best deal or should I hire professionals to help me? What terms should I negotiate in my lease? What costs do I incur to close this deal? What happens once I close the deal?

This chapter helps you answer these questions and provides you with some guidance about issues that you may encounter during the "proposal stage" or "commitment stage" of a lease transaction. These stages begin the process of financing property that you need to use in your business — something lessors hope that you do very often.

If you are a lessor (or even an intermediary), this chapter helps you understand (or refresh your understanding of) the needs of your lessees.

The Lessee Approach to Leasing

Regardless of how large or small your transaction may be, entering into a lease transaction involves a series of steps that enable you, as a lessee, to meet your financing objectives. Your analysis depends, in part, on the type of property you lease, the nature of your business, and the competition (if any) among lessors and lenders who try to "win" your deal.

Consider these basic steps of leasing, described in the following sections:

1. **Determine your need for additional property.**
2. **Decide whether you should lease that property.**
3. **Identify your financing source (that is, a lessor).**
4. **Create a lease proposal and/or commitment to lease.**
5. **Negotiate lease documentation.**
6. **Manage your relationship with your lessor and the requirements of your lease after closing.**

Determine your need for property

You have a business to run. In making your business successful, you determine your need for additional property based on your business model, business plan, and budget for revenue and expenses. You may, for example, provide home moving services and need to acquire five trucks this year to meet the demand. You may be a senior executive of a software business with customers around the globe whom you must "call on" every week. You can, therefore, justify obtaining a business aircraft to make these visits without the hassles of using traditional airlines. Finally, you may be a railroad with a need to acquire hundreds of covered hopper cars each year to replace your aging fleet. In each of these circumstances, your business presents a real need for property that you can lease. See Chapter 1 for a list of property you can lease.

On the other hand, you may want to expand your business and need to raise cash for the expansion. You may decide that you have valuable property that you don't need to own, so you can sell it to a lessor and lease it back from that lessor.

In each situation, as you plan for acquisitions or dispositions of your property, consider the following questions:

- ✔ Does your business plan and business model envision the need for additional property?
- ✔ Does the property make you or your business more productive and/or earn sufficient revenue to merit its cost?
- ✔ Do you expect to use the property for a period of several years (not just a short period of less than a year)?
- ✔ Is the property use critical to your operations or growth?
- ✔ Does your budget support the cost of the property?
- ✔ Will the property remain technologically useful for its intended purpose for all or most of its useful life?

If you answer "yes" to most of these questions, you have probably demonstrated a need to lease property. If the answer is "no," reconsider the business purpose and judgment for acquiring the property.

First, establish your need and plan for property based on the fundamentals of your business apart from how you may finance it. If acquiring the property furthers your business objectives, then decide how to best finance the property. If the property does not further these objectives, no matter how good the deal, neither leasing nor buying the property may be the right answer for you.

Decide whether you should lease that property

You should decide whether to lease the property based on a variety of criteria. In the market today, you may consider a low lease rate to be the most important feature. (Chapter 6 describes how to evaluate lease rates.) Or you may simply want to initiate a business relationship with skilled lessors and/or financial advisors, who can walk you through the process of successfully closing your deals. By weighing the benefits and risks, you can decide whether to proceed with leasing your property. See Chapters 2 and 3.

In making this decision, consider the following questions:

- Can your cash flow support rent payments at all times (whether your business is cyclical or steady)? See Chapter 2 on timing rent payments to cash flow.
- Does the leasing source you expect to use understand your business and financing needs? See Chapter 3 on lessor controls.
- Do you fully understand your responsibilities and liabilities in your lease? See Chapter 8 on indemnity and other lease obligations.
- Does your tax position make leasing a valuable financial alternative? See Chapters 1, 2, and 13 on tax benefits.
- Does the lease provide you with the rights and options that you need? See Chapter 8 and the Master Lease Agreement in the Appendix on lease options.

If you answer "yes" to all or most of these questions, leasing may work for you. If you answer "no," discuss these issues with a financial or legal advisor whom you trust to evaluate other financing in addition to leasing.

Identify your potential financing sources

After you decide that leasing makes sense, you then find a lessor and design a lease/rent structure that fits your budget and needs. Chapter 5 diagrams the parties and documents involved in a single-investor leases and leveraged leases. The size and nature of your financing dictates the type of lease that works best for you. With the right deal, you can access a variety of lessors.

You can make all the forays into the market, but lessors decide whether your deal interests them. Lessors consider many factors including those set forth in Chapters 2 and 3, to make that determination. For example, if you offer the lessor equipment with a long useful life and satisfactory residual value (that is, exceeding 20 percent or more of the lessor's cost at the end of the lease term), you have made a good start. Then, if you show a lessor a strong balance sheet, ample cash flow to pay your rent, and a strong management team, you should attract several lessors for your lease.

On the other hand, if you can't meet payroll, or you can't demonstrate predictable and substantial cash flow, or your management teams show pronounced weaknesses, you can expect less interest from lessors. In other words, if a lessor sees you as a *story credit,* you can expect to work hard to get your lease done. A *story credit* refers to a prospective lessee who has questionable financial results or other current weaknesses in his business, but can make a convincing presentation about his future prospects.

Lessors often understand and accept story credits. Don't shy away from telling your story, especially if you want to lease valuable property.

You can identify and arrange a lease with lessors in one of two ways. First, you can identify a few lessors who understand the property that you want to lease and negotiate terms of a lease directly with them. This kind of transaction may be referred to as a *negotiated deal.* As I discuss later in this chapter in the section "Prospective Lessors for You," vendors, banks, captive finance companies, and independent leasing companies can respond directly to your need for lease financing.

Secondly, you can make a *request for proposals* from lessors (sometimes called an *RFP*) to access a much wider range of potential lessors who will respond, if interested in your deal. Larger companies may be able to use this approach most effectively. In fact, this customized RFP process tends to appear mostly in large-ticket deals as contrasted with small-ticket and middle-ticket transactions.

A negotiated deal can save you time, but not necessarily money. It avoids drafting an RFP, sending the RFP to lessors, and negotiating terms of your deal in detail before you ever see a lease document. However, your lease rate and possibly your total costs to complete a negotiated transaction may be higher than what you can get from a widely circulated RFP. The RFP, on the other hand, lays out clearly the terms of your transaction so that, in negotiating documents, the lawyers and other professionals understand the "deal" terms clearly and can (in theory) minimize unnecessary and expensive negotiations. Because you and your advisors use substantial amounts of time in preparing the RFP and negotiating it with lessors, your initial transaction costs may be higher than a negotiated transaction. However, when (and if) you obtain a lease with lower rent and better terms than a negotiated deal, you can more than offset the transaction costs of the RFP.

Create a proposal or commitment to lease

After you identify lessors which have an interest in your deal, the lessors often submit a proposal to lease you the property that you need, and you may thereafter enter into a proposal or commitment with the lessor. A proposal and/or a commitment set forth the fundamentals, if not the details, of your lease transaction, from which lawyers draft your lease and related documentation.

Drafting and negotiating proposals and/or commitments can take several weeks to several months depending on the nature of the leased property and the complexity of the lease structure. Start your efforts with more than sufficient time before you, as lessee, intend to place the property in service, to preserve tax benefits and financing options. Add to the negotiating schedule the time you need to identify the best advisors and lessors to handle your business.

A proposal arises in a lease transaction during the so-called *proposal stage*, the point in time when a lessor whom you have identified sets out the terms and conditions (in writing) under which the lessor can provide lease financing to you. A proposal enables you and the lessor to have a "meeting of the minds," as lawyers like to say, or "to get onto the same page," as business people sometimes say. If a lessor responds to an RFP, the lessor should respond in the order and format that you establish and to the transaction elements that you requested (that is, the amount of rent, options to purchase, and risk of loss).

In a negotiated transaction, a lessor provides you a proposal containing the basic elements of the lease transaction. The lessor typically presents her proposal in the format that the lessor normally uses in the ordinary course of the lessor's business (so expect a variety of formats and content).

When you and your lessor determine that you have a "real deal" (that is, not just a discussion of possibilities but rather a deal that you both think can be completed), a proposal can (but doesn't always) move to the *commitment stage*. At this stage, a lessor either revises her proposal to turn into a commitment or makes a formal offer to lease property in a *commitment letter* for the first time.

A *commitment letter* refers to a document that you and the lessor sign indicating some level of agreement to complete a lease transaction. A commitment can take the form of a cover letter (generally containing legalese about the binding effect of the commitment, setting forth fees and expenses, and giving the lessor wiggle room to get out of the deal), together with a term sheet containing the substance of the deal. Alternatively, a commitment letter can take the form of a single letter signed by you and the lessor. In either case, a commitment letter can range in length from a few pages to dozens of pages for complex transactions.

Typical *binding provisions* (the promises that stick even if you don't close) include payment by you of nonrefundable "commitment fees" and an agreement by you to pay the out-of-pocket expenses of a lessor for legal, due diligence, appraisal, and other fees to complete the transaction. As a lessee, you should try to limit the conditions that you must satisfy to assure that, when the lessor makes a commitment to you, you can expect to complete the transaction without multiple escape hatches for the lessor. For example, once a lessor signs a commitment, he should generally not tell you that his commitment remains subject to approval by the Board of Directors of the lessor. Rather, a lessor should assure you that if you meet the requirements of the commitment letter, you will receive your financing without further approval. By contrast, you can expect an approval condition in a proposal letter (in addition to many other conditions that may be specified or not specified, in writing). In any case, you generally must close by a deadline date stated in the commitment or proposal. In short, these deals don't stay open forever.

Negotiate definitive lease documentation

No one seems thrilled to spend significant dollars on the documentation costs of lawyers. But whether you like lawyers or not, they can be your saving grace when it comes to lease negotiations.

The type of lease structure dictates how much lease documentation to expect. For smaller ticket and even some middle-ticket leases, you may simply sign lease forms without much negotiation. See Chapter 8. On the other hand, for leveraged leases or sophisticated single-investor leases, you can expect to negotiate extensively a variety of documents and terms that can impact your economic and business interests. See Chapter 8 for a discussion of a middle-market leases.

Find legal and other advisors with substantial experience in leasing transactions to help you (unless you are a leasing professional yourself, of course). They can add value by knowing, explaining, and negotiating the key issues that help you accomplish your financing objectives. Lawyers in other disciplines are not your best choice.

Manage your relationship with your lessor and the requirements of your lease after closing

Except in full-service leases, you encounter a wide range of obligations to your lessor that I discuss in Chapter 8. Your lessor expects you to pay your rent and meet your obligations to insure, maintain, and pay taxes on the property. In exchange, the lessor generally leaves you alone in what lessors call your right to quiet enjoyment and use of the property. In service leases, your lessor may undertake many of these obligations for you and charge you rent accordingly.

Prospective Lessors for You

The market holds a variety of lessors who may be interested in leasing to you. This section introduces some of those lessors and some aspects of their respective business models. You can begin to determine, based on your objectives, which type of lessor may work best for you and/or may have the interest to lease property to you.

Bank and bank-affiliated lessors

Banks of every conceivable size and location lease personal property (but most banks, for regulatory reasons, avoid real estate leases). Money center banks, regional banks, foreign banks, and even small-town banks may offer leasing products. Banks often, but not always, form leasing subsidiaries. To fund leases, these leasing companies may borrow from their parent holding companies or directly from third parties using bank loans, commercial paper, syndications of rents (selling portions of leases or financing lease payment streams), and *securitizations* (pooling of multiple leases and selling their payment streams as securities). See Chapter 23 on securitizations and syndications.

In larger banks, a strong credit position and substantial tax bill make them or their leasing affiliates very competitive in leasing transactions. In smaller banks, the banks can use deposits to fund leases within their regulatory restrictions as well as the other funding devices for other banks. Banks lease virtually any type of personal property from small-ticket office equipment to big-ticket vessels or aircraft.

Banks and bank-leasing companies almost all possess a range of documents from preprinted forms to lengthy leveraged leases. For larger deals, you can expect to see outside counsel and/or in-house counsel customize documents to fit your deal.

The life cycle of a lease: Negotiation to expiration

Each lease contains many similar phases or elements. After you sign a proposal and/or commitment to lease, you take the following steps starting at a lease negotiation and ending at the expiration of the lease:

1. **You negotiate and enter into lease documentation with the lessor.**

   These documents include the lease (the basic document for all leasing), purchase agreement assignments (which assigns your rights to the property to your lessor), a tax indemnity agreement which may also be included in your lease (where you protect the lessor against loss of assumed tax benefits in tax-oriented leases), bills of sale (that transfer title of the property to the lessor), schedules (setting forth specific economic terms of a lease and other details), and certificates of acceptance (to accept the property under the lease). Chapter 8 discusses the lease terms in more detail, and the Appendix sets forth a form of Master Lease Agreement.

2. **You assign to your lessor your rights to purchase property or sell the property to your lessor.**

   If you arranged a purchase from a third party, your lessor steps into your shoes to buy the property, which she then leases to you. If you want to sell property to your lessor and lease it back, then you transfer the property directly to your lessor.

3. **You formally accept the leased property under your lease.**

   When you accept the property, it becomes subject to the terms in the lease. Sometimes, the lease alone suffices to show your acceptance in a single-delivery type lease.

4. **Your lessor pays the seller for the property at such acceptance.**

   In most transactions, your lessor pays the seller and refunds to you any purchase deposits that you made to the seller. In a sale-leaseback transaction, your lessor buys the property from you and then leases it back to you under the lease documents.

5. **You start your lease term and assume most of the responsibilities for the leased property.**

   When you use and possess the leased property, you become responsible for insuring, maintaining, and paying taxes on the property in most leases called net leases. However, in a full-service lease, your lessor may cover some of these costs or provide services that help you meet your obligations and charge you for them.

6. **You may negotiate the right to terminate your lease or exercise an early buy-out option before the expiration of its term.**

   In each case, you may make payments to the lessor to end the lease early, to walk away (in the case of any early termination), or to buy the property (in the case of an early buyout).

7. **At the end of the lease, you may have options to renew your lease or purchase the property.**

   If you do not have or want to exercise either option, you return the property to your lessor (in tax-oriented leases and Article 2A finance leases, discussed in Chapters 13 and 16 respectively).

Independent leasing companies

As direct competitors of banks and bank-leasing companies, independent leasing companies can use creative structures and various funding mechanisms to compete effectively, as well as to offer products that banks may not. Leasing companies can lease virtually any asset that fits their business models and plans, including all property that a bank can lease.

They can also provide residual guarantees to other lessors that need such support to gain approval for the transaction or otherwise to give lessors confidence. A *residual guaranty* assures the lessor that he receives an expected value for the leased property at the end of the lease. See Chapter 15 for more on residual guarantees.

To fund their leases, large leasing companies may borrow from their parent companies or directly from third parties using bank loans, commercial paper, syndications, and securitizations. Some of these lessors may have somewhat higher cost of funds than banks, which means that they use their structuring skills and willingness to take residual risk to win your deal.

For small leasing companies, syndications of leasing transactions, bank lines of credit, and some securitization of leases remain a possibility. These companies face increasing pressure on finding funds for their deals.

Leasing companies almost all possess form documents for every deal — at least as a starting place for the lawyers. The range of documents can extend from preprinted forms to lengthy leveraged leases. For larger deals, expect to see outside counsel who customize documents to fit your deal.

Captive leasing companies

Large manufacturing companies can help their customers purchase their products by providing financing — generally dedicated to financing only their product. *Captive leasing* or *finance companies* play that role very effectively. For example, if a company manufacturers tractors, trailers, generators, and construction equipment for businesses around the world, the manufacturer can facilitate sales by having a related entity provide financing for those products as its sole mission in life — a *captive*. Captives often don't like that containment, so they begin to lease other property and grow into independent leasing companies, financing products of other manufacturers that fall within their knowledge, expertise, and business plan.

Captives receive all or most of their financing from their parent companies. If a parent is a large enterprise, its cost of capital may be very competitive with other lessors, making the captive's financing a simple, convenient, and less expensive alternative than seeking financing from independent lessors.

If a captive diversifies or seeks outside funding, bank loans, commercial paper, public equity, syndications, and securitizations all offer other reliable sources of capital.

Captives tend to offer you form documents for small-ticket transactions. You can expect to engage in little to no negotiation, unless your purchase/lease amounts to a large-ticket transaction. However, if a captive expands to other business outside of the parent, it, too, can customize documents for each deal.

Vendors

Some sales companies (vendors) simply skip the part of forming a leasing subsidiary and enter into leasing or financing arrangements directly with their customers. If you, for example, acquire computers from a significant (or even not-so-significant) company, it could lease the computers to you directly. Although this type of financing may be convenient, you may find that the lessor charges higher rents than independent or bank-leasing companies.

Vendors display a clear method in this practice. If they charge a higher rate, they can sell the lease to banks and other lessors (and show the deal as a "true sale" on their books), discount the stream of payments in syndications, or securitize a large pool of deals. They can also obtain other traditional loans and use commercial paper proceeds to fund these deals. In this manner, they not only receive payment for their goods and services (by creating a sale of their own goods and services) but also create a valuable financing business (that finances that sale). In effect, they get paid twice — first in the sale of their product and second in keeping a part of what you pay them for the financing. Vendors and captives share some similar approaches to financing products and services. For more on captive leasing companies, see the preceding section. For more on vendors, see Chapter 21.

Like captives, vendors often separate the manufacturing and selling part of their businesses from the financing. Such a separation helps distinguish legal rights and manage liabilities that each business may face. In Chapter 16, I discuss Article 2A of the Uniform Commercial Code, whose rules suggest that separating manufacturing from financing can help minimize liability of a financing party for manufacturer's defects or other problems with products and services.

Vendors tend to offer you their form documents — sign them and weep! You can expect to engage in little to no negotiation, unless your purchase/lease amounts to a large-ticket transaction, and, even then, vendors tend to stick to their knitting — one or two forms of documents fit all. If your deal involves big bucks, however, you may want to ask for a more customized approach and see what happens.

Leasing funds, financial advisors, and insurance companies

A variety of other companies recognize the potential of leasing or lending. A *leasing fund* consists of publicly or privately raised capital pool used for the purpose of buying and leasing equipment to lessees. A leasing organization forms around the pool of such funds. The lessor, who creates the fund, obtains attractive lease rates from lessees (compared to the fund's lower cost of money) for the fund investors, and in exchange receives payment for managing the fund, as well as a slice of the residual value at the end of the leases comprising the fund.

Insurance companies most often appear as lenders in leveraged leases. They lend in transactions where the lessee, the real source of credit, shows substantial strength to meet his obligations. They obtain their funding from policy premiums and earnings from premiums in search of an investment home. Regulatory restrictions and business models tend to push insurance companies toward debt products.

Brokers or financial advisors may acquire property and lease it for a period of time, but they generally buy with the intention of *flipping* or selling the lease or flow of rents to banks, leasing companies, or other financial institutions. The brokers create a temporary holding location for the leased property and act as intermediaries for the lessee or lessor in the basic leasing transaction, as I discuss in more detail in the next section.

Documentation of the insurance companies, brokers, and leasing funds tend to be customized because they often involve large-ticket deals. Lawyers abound, and lessees often pay for the privilege. Property that these entities lease all kinds of property, ranging from aircraft to power plants, fiber optic networks to industrial equipment, and furniture to computers, to name a few possibilities.

How to Select the Right Lessor

Selecting the right lessor may seem like a daunting task if you have not already developed relationships or know what sources to tap. With nearly 2000 lessors in the market, culling through them to find the best deal requires searching and due diligence, but your efforts may save you money and result in relationships that provide a valuable source of continuing leasing funding. This section suggests four approaches to finding the best lessor. After you (hopefully) find lessors in whom you have an interest and who show an interest in you, you can negotiate a lease or circulate an RFP for bids to identify the best deal for you, as discussed in the preceding section.

Your banker awaits you

You may need to go no further than calling your banker to start the ball rolling with lease financing. You should not, however, accept the first quote that you receive or anticipate that your bank represents the most knowledgeable or optimal source of financing. Instead, start with your banker but, at the same time, ask brokers, leasing companies, and other funding sources for competitive quotes on your lease. You may return to the bank, but in order to find the best deal, you need to explore at least a few other resources. The search may make your time worth its while in greenbacks!

Financial advisors

Banks, independent leasing companies, investment bankers, and brokers, may all act as intermediaries and help you find the right sources of funding. Many of them offer extensive databases and personal relationships built over a series of years in the leasing business. Often, these professionals can help you complete pricing analysis so that you can determine which deal offers the best economic terms for you. Some of these service providers even have legal teams available to you who can help assure that you negotiate a proposal or commitment, with the best terms for you. Banks and independent leasing companies and even some advisors may, to show their commitment to your deal, invest part of the lessor's cost in your leased property. Individuals can also act as brokers and often do; on occasion, they, too, invest in your property.

You can test the commitment of your advisors by asking them to invest. If they say no, perhaps you should consider those who say yes!

Investment bankers often provide the most sophisticated services and the largest transactions. Banks and other leasing companies can provide similar services. Individual brokers tend to focus on marketing your deals to sources of funding that they believe may accept your deal (whether or not these sources provide the optimal financing is another story).

Compensation most often takes the form of fees and residual sharing. Fees for brokerage or placement services range from ½ percent to 4 percent of the lessor's cost of the leased property. In addition, certain brokers may ask for additional compensation in the form of residual sharing with the lessor. See Chapter 15.

For taking this kind of risk or receiving these fees, can you assume that brokers and intermediaries add value and serve their purposes? No. You cannot safely reach that conclusion. Even though many quality intermediaries exist who can help you, the barriers to entry into this part of the leasing business can be so minimal that a wide variety of players may try to attract your business. You must exercise caution because brokers can make promises about who they know and what they can do, but may be mere dabblers (or less), not players in your type of leased property. They may quote you lease rates that they say they can secure for you, knowing that the market response will tend to be limited or non-existent. They may boast experience and results that they cannot demonstrate. Finally, they may spread around confidential or market information about your business so that lessors become skeptical of doing business with you or of giving you the best rates.

To select an intermediary properly, ask the following questions:

✔ **Structuring experience and market knowledge:** What comparable experience can you show me that you have in marketing, pricing, evaluating equipment choices, and structuring a lease deal similar to what I need? What structures do you recommend for my deal and why? What types of lessors may consider my deal? What rates can I expect to see and what terms? Is my choice of leased property the right one for my needs?

✔ **Marketing methods and materials:** How will you market my deal? Should this be a negotiated deal or should we send out an RFP? Will you arrange meetings with investors and provide comparative analysis of RFP responses? How will you protect my company's confidential information? Can you show me examples of offering materials (that is, a description of deals like mine) that you have presented to financing sources in three recent deals? How can we control transaction costs?

✔ **Time to close the deal and involvement in negotiations:** What timetable can I achieve to complete this deal? Do you participate in negotiating the documents, and, if not, why not?

✔ **The fees for services:** What fees will you charge and will they only be paid if and when my deal closes and I receive funding?

✔ **References:** Whom can I call to obtain references on your contributions in your last five deals of this type?

Your proposed intermediary should answer each of these questions fully before you enter into any agreement. In some cases, your prospective intermediary may not know the answer to questions regarding equipment, but the key is to look for the value that the intermediary can add based on the depth and quality of experience indicated by these responses. Don't proceed if you have any doubt about the intermediary's honesty or ethics in performing his or her obligations to you. Unfortunately, I have seen brokers pretend that they understand the deals only to cause costly delays. If you want to proceed, you can limit the time period during which you work with the intermediary. You should be able to terminate the relationship at will. In addition, make sure that you don't have an unintended and continuing liability for fees for a deal that you complete without the broker's assistance. (If a deal results from a broker's lead, get out your checkbook; that effort alone usually triggers broker's fees.)

You can find brokers by asking manufacturers, leasing companies, and professionals and by searching Web sites including those mentioned in the upcoming section, "Internet resources." Intermediaries also look for you, especially if you need significant financing.

Professionals in the business as referrals

Lawyers, accountants, tax advisors, appraisers, and even bankers may provide leads to financing sources because of the business they do. Explain to them the type of property that you want to lease and ask them for referrals to lessors or other funding sources. They may provide a referral in exchange for participating in a professional capacity in your deal. They may ask for a *success fee,* which is no more than a fancy term for a broker's fee that can range from ¼ percent to 4 percent (although professionals tend to negotiates these fees depending on the circumstances). In an altruistic moment (find one if you can!), a professional may help you without fees simply to create some goodwill because they value their relationship with you.

Internet resources

Every broker and service provider has, or soon will have, a Web site offering her services. You can find a variety of resources online, as I discuss in Chapter 21. Leasing organizations and publications, such as The Monitor Daily Funding Source Directory and the United Association of Equipment Leasing (UAEL), also offer resources to members. The UAEL provides information about many aspects of leasing, including a funding database, at www.elaonline.com. Look for the "Member Directory" and "FundingSource" for names of lessors and the types of leases they do. Almost every lessor has his own Web Site. Go to these sites and determine whether the lessor's financial product line matches your needs. If so, find the "Contact Us" icon (or equivalent) in the site and start asking the lessor some questions.

Chapter 5

Seeing the Picture: The Two Most Common Lease Structures

. . . .

In This Chapter

▶ Laying out the structure and cash flows of single-investor leases

▶ Illustrating how leveraged leases work

▶ Describing the parties and basic documents in single-investor and leveraged leases

. . . .

Although many leasing transactions involve two parties and one primary document, the lease, other deals are much more complex. To help you understand how the two most common lease structures work, I have applied that old adage that a picture says a thousand words. This chapter provides figures that depict the parties, the agreements, and the cash flows of a typical single-investor lease and leveraged lease. If you follow the lines along with my description, you can see and understand many aspects of leasing transactions, even if you are encountering leasing for the first time. When you complete this chapter, you should be able to structure the real deal.

You can then move on to many other types of leases that have evolved in both the domestic and international markets. See Chapters 10, 11, 12, 19 and 20. Most of the other deals possess some or all of the features described in this chapter. In short, the game on structuring starts here.

The Single-Investor or Nonleveraged Lease

A *single-investor lease*, a *nonleveraged lease,* and *single-source lease* are synonymous for a simple two-party financing transaction between a lessor and a lessee. In this transaction, a lessee is the end user of the leased property. The lessor buys the property with his own funds and enters into a lease in which the lessee agrees to take possession of and use the property for a period of time in exchange for a periodic payment of *rent.*

A lessee may acquire the leased property and place it under a lease in two fundamental ways:

- ✔ If the lessee identifies new or used property in the hands of the manufacturer or other vendor, the lessee can arrange for the manufacturer or vendor to sell the property to the lessor. The lessor then leases it to the lessee.

- ✔ If the lessee purchases the new property from the manufacturer or other vendor, she may thereafter sell it to her lessor, which then enters into a sale-leaseback transaction with the lessee.

To illustrate the concepts of a single-investor lease, assume the following transaction (see Figure 5-1):

- ✔ The lessee is engaged in the wireless telecommunications business and needs new computers and related servers to build a portion of his network.

- ✔ The equipment costs the lessor $1,000,000 (the *lessor's cost*).

- ✔ The lessee identifies the lessor without the assistance of a broker or other packager. The lessor and lessee enter into the lease for three years at a rent of $35,000 per month.

- ✔ Two manufacturers, Computer Co. and Server Co., have agreed to manufacturer the equipment and sell it to the lessee. The lessee has delivered a purchase order to the manufacturers specifying the type of equipment. The manufacturers plan to invoice the lessee for the purchase price of the property including shipping charges when the equipment is ready for delivery.

- ✔ To initiate the purchase, the lessee has made a deposit of $50,000 against the purchase price ($25,000 per manufacturer).

- ✔ The lessee is an operating subsidiary of a large parent company with substantial resources. The parent has agreed to guaranty the obligations of the lessee to the lessor.

This transaction, illustrated in Figure 5-1, is a middle-ticket lease. However, Figure 5-1 illustrates a common structure that you can use in most single-investor small-, middle-, and large-ticket transactions.

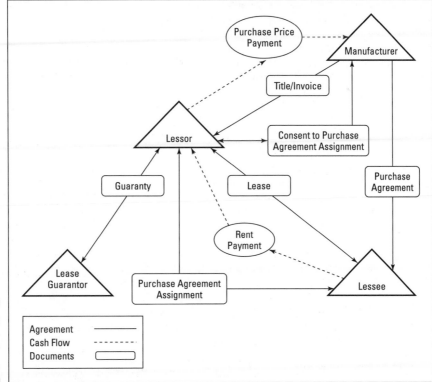

Figure 5-1:
The single-
investor
lease.

The parties to a single-investor transaction primarily include

- ✔ **Lessor:** The lessor owns and invests in the property to be leased. He purchases the property from the lessee or a third party. The property may be new or used. The lessor purchases the property entirely from his own funds. The lessor can obtain his funds from his internal cash flow, debt, equity capital or other financings, depending on the funding strategy used by the lessor.

- ✔ **Lessee:** The lessee selects and uses the telecommunications equipment or other property. She pays the rent and operates and maintains the property. She receives all income from the use of the property.

- ✔ **Guarantor:** The guarantor provides additional credit support to the lessor for the payment and performance by the lessee of the lessee's obligations under the lease. A *guarantor* acts as a *surety,* which means that she plays a secondary and supportive role for the performance by the lessee in her obligations to the lessor. A guarantor performs or pays for the lessee if the lessee fails to meet her obligations.

✔ **Manufacturer/vendor/seller:** The manufacturer/vendor/seller enters into the purchase agreements or purchase orders with the lessee and issues an invoice or bill of sale to the buyer on completion of a sale. The lessor leases the property to the lessee. The manufacturer probably requires at least a deposit or down payment from the lessee (such as the $50,000 deposit in the illustration in the preceding sections). In some cases, a lessor can enter into purchase agreements directly with the seller in connection with a lease of the equipment or other property.

The following points discuss the primary agreements used in single-investor lease transactions and the related cash flows:

✔ **The lease agreement:** The *lease agreement* is the basic financing arrangement between the lessor and the lessee. (Chapter 1 defines a lease. Chapter 8 discusses the terms of lease transactions. Chapter 16 discusses Article 2A of the UCC, which contains rules for leases.) In Figure 5-1, the solid line from the lessee to the lessor indicates the lease agreement between them. The dashed line indicates the cash flow, or rent and other payments under the lease. In most cases, if you are a lessee, you pay rent and other sums directly to lessor. If you are the lessor, you collect all amounts directly from the lessee. Unless the lease is a service lease or a certain type of operating lease, the lessor pays nothing to the lessee or anyone else other than to pay the purchase price for the leased property to the manufacturer/seller/vendor.

In the transaction in the preceding section, the lease agreement entitles the lessee to use the telecommunications equipment for three years at a rent of $35,000 per month. In that transaction, if you are the lessor in a tax-oriented lease (see Chapter 13), you reimburse the lessee for the $50,000 deposit in a lump sum at the start of the lease when you purchase the property to be leased from the manufacturer.

✔ **The guaranty agreement:** The guarantor enters into a separate guaranty agreement for the benefit of the lessor. He is not a cosigner on the lease. His obligations stand alone — to support the credit of the lessee when called upon by the lessor.

If you are the lessor, the guarantor generally promises you that he will pay or perform the obligations of the lessee under the lease. This agreement is called a *guaranty of payment*. As lessor, you should *not* typically have to pursue the lessee for payment before you can collect from the guarantor. If you do, this agreement is sometimes called a *guaranty of collection*. A guarantor only makes payments to the lessor if the lessor calls on the guaranty. A guarantor may provide a full guaranty of all obligations or place limits on the guaranty such as a percentage of what the lessee owes or a total dollar amount, or both.

In Figure 5-1, the solid line from the guarantor to the lessor indicates the guaranty agreement in favor of the lessor. Any cash payment by the guarantor to the lessor follows the same line.

✔ **The purchase agreement, invoice, and purchase agreement assignment:** As the lessor under this lease structure, you generally have no role in selecting the equipment (unless you are also the manufacturer or a vendor). As a lessee, when you select the equipment, you enter into a purchase agreement or purchase order and/or receive invoices for the purchase from the manufacturer or vendor. In some cases, you may also get a bill of sale (which transfers title to you). As a lessee you may receive warranties, training, or other valuable services from your manufacturer or vendor. Lessors generally want to obtain an assignment or transfer of those rights from you. But lessors want no part of your obligations other than to pay for the property sold by the manufacturer. The manufacturer or vendor, who really likes to get paid, should consent to the assignment or transfer and stand ready to perform for the lessor if you default under the lease. In effect, the purchase agreement assignment enables the lessor to pursue remedies directly against the manufacturer or vendor if you lose your rights under the lease.

In Figure 5-1, the solid line from the manufacturer to the lessee depicts the purchase agreement arrangement. The solid line (at the bottom of Figure 5-1) between the lessee and lessor shows the assignment of the purchase rights given by the manufacturer to the lessee. The solid line between the manufacturer and the lessor shows the consent to this assignment.

The Leveraged Lease

The word *leverage* derives from one of the oldest machines in history, the lever. The lever multiplies the force applied to a task, creating a much greater force. Similarly, in a leveraged lease, a lessor borrows money on a nonrecourse basis. *Nonrecourse debt* refers to a loan from a lender to the lessor for which the lender can seek repayment *solely* from the cash flow of the lease and the value of the leased property, but not personally from the lessor. As the lessor, you offer no personal credit support for the lease payments. Your lender must analyze and accept the creditworthiness of your lessee. This debt, which can equal or exceed 80 percent of the lessor's cost, increases the lessor's total cash available to pay for the leased property without the lessor using her own capital. The debt constitutes the leverage and enhances the economic benefits of the investment to the lessor and lessee because the lessor uses only a relative small portion of her own cash (for example, 20 percent), which is often called the lessor's *equity investment*. Chapter 7 examines the economics of leveraged leases.

In today's market, leveraged leases have become widely used to lease significant property, mostly in large-ticket transactions. Although many complex variations have been created, especially in cross-border financing (see Chapter 20), most leveraged transactions fundamentally contain the elements within the structure discussed in this section.

The leveraged lease involves at least three core parties: a lessee, a lessor, and a lender. Like the single-investor lease, the lessor enters into a lease with the lessee for a term in exchange for rent. Instead of repaying the lessor alone, the rent must service the debt incurred by the lessor. A lender insists that, regardless of the circumstances, the lessee must pay enough rent, at all times, to repay the loans that he has made to the lessor. That same rent should provide an investment return to the lessor.

To illustrate the concepts of a leveraged lease, assume the following:

1. The lessee is engaged in the wireless telecommunications business and needs new computers and servers to build a portion of her network, various communications towers bases, software and related equipment, trucks and other service vehicles, and other tools to install and service the items.

2. The property and other equipment have a lessor's cost of $30,000,000.

3. Two leasing companies each invest $3,000,000 or a total of $6,000,000 in equity, which equals 20 percent of the lessor's cost.

4. Three banks each lend the owner/lessor $8,000,000 of the balance of $24,000,000.

5. The lessors and lessee enter into the lease for five years at a rent of $700,000 per month.

6. The lessor pays principal and interest each month of $650,000. The lessor uses the tax benefits as the owner of the property.

7. Three manufacturers, Computer Co., Server Co., and Vehicle Co., produce most of the leased property. Each manufacturer enters into purchase agreements with the lessee.

8. The lessee has not paid for any of the property except for a $50,000 deposit to each manufacturer for a total of $150,000. Because the property is specially designed, the lessee has not taken delivery of it from the manufacturers, but will take delivery on the closing of the lease.

9. The lessee is an operating subsidiary of a parent company with substantial resources, which has agreed to guaranty the obligations of the lessee to the lessor. Given the complexity of the transaction, the lessee hires a lease broker/underwriter, Wall Street XYZ, Ltd., to help structure the transaction and locate the lessor and the lender.

This transaction is a large-ticket lease. Most leveraged leases involve big-ticket transactions because of the cost and complexity of the deals. Figure 5-2 illustrates a typical leveraged lease.

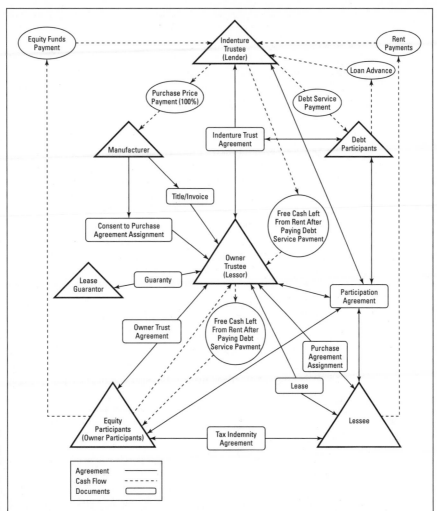

Figure 5-2:
The
leveraged
lease.

In a leveraged lease, as Figure 5-2 shows you, a larger group of parties exists, including the following parties:

✔ **The owner participant:** The equity investor in a leveraged lease is often called the *owner participant* or the *equity participant*. The owner partici-pant invests 15 to 50 percent of the necessary capital to purchase the leased property, which is often referred to as her *equity investment*. (In a single-investor lease, the lessor generally uses her own source of funds to purchase the property. In the leveraged lease, that is true only for the equity investment. The equity participant is comparable to a lessor in a single-investor lease, only one step removed. The owner trustee, as the lessor, represents the equity participant as discussed in the next section.) More than one owner participant may be involved in a leveraged lease. Owner participants tend to be leasing companies, banks, and other financial service companies, and as a group may sometimes be called *institutional investors*. Owner participants, as beneficial owners of a trust as described in the following sections, are also sometimes called the beneficial owners or trustors.

✔ **The lessor/owner trustee:** In a leveraged lease, the lessor performs similar functions to those of the lessor in the single-investor lease. He purchases and owns the leased property and enters into the lease with the lessee. However, unlike the single-investor lease, an owner trustee (instead of the lessor-investor) often acts as the lessor and owns the leased property in a grantor or other trust as the representative of the owner participant. He then leases the leased property to the lessee on behalf of the owner participant. An *owner trust* (also called a *grantor* trust) refers to an specific entity created under trust and other laws that can independently own legal title and other property rights granted to it by its beneficial owner (or *trustor*). The grantor trust can exercise all rights of an owner of property within certain contractual and statutory limits.

The owner participant owns a *beneficial interest* in the owner trust. Beneficial ownership means that the owner participant enjoys the benefits of the trust but does not own the legal title to the leased property. The seller or manufacturer transfers the legal title to the leased property to the owner trustee, which owns the property in an owner trust and can exercise the rights, enjoy the benefits, and accept the obligations of ownership.

An owner trustee is usually a commercial bank or trust company. A partnership, business trust or other entities may also be used in some circumstances to act as the trustee. The owner participant generally directs the owner trustee's actions and pays all costs of the trustee. The trustee forms the owner trust with the owner participant under a trust agreement and generally acts only on the orders from the owner participant. He has no independent discretion except in special cases and expects the owner participant to fully protect him against all risk and liability other than his own gross negligence or willful misconduct. An owner trust can shield the lessors from liability related to the lease transaction and create a separation from the lessor that protects lenders against the bankruptcy of the lessor. A trust may therefore be generally described as a *bankruptcy remote entity*.

Figure 5-2 sets forth the typical structure in which the owner trustee is designated as the lessor. Figure 5-2 shows a dashed line from the owner participant to trustee indicating the payment of fees and other cash needed to make the equity investment in the lease.

✔ **The lessee:** The lessee in a leveraged lease assumes the same responsibilities as the lessee in a single-investor lease and more. With a lender added to the parties in the deal, the lessee is also accountable directly or indirectly to the lender. Her payments will be structured so that the lessee pays enough rent to pay in full the debt service incurred by the lessor. Unlike the single-investor lease, Figure 5-2 shows that the lessee pays all rent and other sums directly to the lender (or her representative) called the *indenture trustee* (with the exception of certain indemnity and insurance payments).

✔ **The lender or debt participant:** The lender or *debt participant* generally loans a lessor from 50 to 85 percent of the necessary capital cost to acquire the leased property on a non-recourse basis. This loan is the balance needed to purchase the leased property. In the transaction described in the preceding section, the owner participants invest 20 percent or $6,000,000, and the lenders advance the balance of 80 percent of the lessor's cost or $24,000,000, for a lessor's cost of $30,000,000. Typical leveraged lease lenders include insurance companies, banks, and finance companies.

✔ **The indenture or security trustee:** The *indenture trustee* (also called the *security trustee*) represents and acts under the instructions of the lenders or debt participants. In the transaction described in the preceding section, the debt participants supply the indenture trustee with $24,000,000 to invest in the leased property. In addition, the owner participants, directly or through the owner trustee, will supply the equity investment to the indenture trustee, for total payment of $30,000,000 to the manufacturers.

Although the debt participants provide the loan itself, Figure 5-2 illustrates a truism in leveraged leasing: All cash, with few exceptions — including the initial equity investment — flows through the indenture trustee. The dashed line in Figure 5-2 shows that the indenture trustee pays the owner trustee any *free cash*. *Free cash* refers to the amount left after the indenture trustee subtracts out the debt due to the leveraged lease lenders. As the representative of the owner participant, the owner trustee, upon receipt of those excess funds, then pays the owner participant.

As is the case with the owner trust arrangement, debt participants may elect not to use a similar trust arrangement, called an *indenture trust*, in a leveraged lease. In that case, the debt participant (acting as the lender) will receive the equity investment from the owner participant, and advance the loan proceeds plus such equity directly to the manufacturer/vendor. If the owner participant elects not to use an owner trustee, the equity investor (acting as the lessor) will transfer his funds to the lender for further payment to the manufacturer or vendor. If more than one lender acts without an indenture trust, then one lender generally acts as the agent of the other lenders under a secured loan agreement with a lessor or his owner trustee. The owner trustee (or lessor, if no owner trustee exists) grants the indenture trustee (or lender, if no indenture trustee exists) security interest in the lease and the leased property as collateral or security. This collateral helps assure the lenders of repayment by the lessor. However, the lessee and the leased property itself, and not the lessor, serve as the real credit support for the payment of all debt service because the lessor has no personal credit obligations to the lenders (that is, his obligation is nonrecourse).

- ✔ **The manufacturer/vendor:** Like the single-investor lease, the manufacturer/vendor/seller enters into the purchase agreements or purchase order with the lessee. In the transaction described in the preceding section, the manufacturers or vendor typically sells the items and other property directly to the lessor (under a purchase agreement assignment or direct sale arrangement) for purposes of enabling the lessor to lease the property to the lessee.

- ✔ **The guarantor:** The guarantor plays almost the same role in the leveraged lease as in the single-investor lease. However, her liability is usually expanded to protect the credit risk of the lessor/owner trustee and of the debt participant/indenture trustee. She provides additional credit support to the lessor/owner trustee and the indenture trustee directly for the lessee's payment and obligations to the lessor and the debt participants.

- ✔ **The broker/underwriter:** A broker, packager, investment banker, or underwriter in a leveraged lease can provide a valuable service of structuring and finding or providing equity capital. These entities or individuals generally possess significant expertise in the market and know how to structure and price transactions based on specialized computer modeling created by and for the leasing industry. In the transaction described in the preceding section, Wall Street XYZ, Ltd., provides advisory services only to the lessee for which the lessee pays a fee.

The following points discuss the primary agreements used in leveraged lease transactions and the related cash flows:

- ✔ **The participation agreement:** The participation agreement (or PA) tells the story of the leveraged lease transaction. It also defines the common terms used in the lease, the indenture trust agreement, and the owner trust agreement. It contains various other agreements relating to all parts of the transaction including covenants, representations, and warranties that affect some or all of the parties. The solid line from most of the parties to the participation agreement shows how every one of the leasing players signs up for this one central agreement and undertakes obligations to (or makes agreements with) the other parties as set out in that agreement. Although not shown, a guarantor usually signs the participation agreement as well.

- ✔ **The lease:** The lease works in substantially the same way as the single-investor lease except the parties may be different. In Figure 5-2, one of the solid lines from the owner trustee to the lessee indicates the basic lease agreement. The owner trustee serves as the representative of the owner participant in the capacity of the owner-lessor where, in a single-investor lease, the owner of the leased property acts directly as the lessor.

The dashed line at the right side of Figure 5-2 from the lessee to the indenture trustee shows you that the lessee pays rent directly to the indenture trustee. The indenture trustee keeps its debt service (principal plus interest) and then sends the free cash to the owner trustee for the benefit of the owner participants. In the transaction described in the preceding section, the indenture trustee needs a total payment of $650,000 each month. Therefore, the $50,000 left would be paid to the owner trustee after the debt is paid as free cash.

✔ **The owner trust agreement:** An owner trustee enters into a trust agreement with one or more owner participants in which the owner participants specifically establish the trustee's duties and indemnify the owner trustee for acting within her duties. As a key part of her duties, the trustee acts as an owner of the leased property and monitors and reports to its beneficial owners on matters brought to her attention. The solid line from the owner participant to the owner trustee indicate the trust arrangement.

✔ **The trust indenture or the security agreement:** The debt participants establish an indenture trust for their benefit. They hire the indenture trustee, which enters into a trust indenture or security agreement among the debt participants, the indenture trustee, and the owner trustee relating to the debt portion of the leverage lease. The debt participants specifically establish the trustee's duties and indemnify the indenture trustee for acting within his duties. As a key part of his duties, the indenture trustee collects all rent, exercises remedies against the lessor if the lessor defaults on his obligations under the indenture, and monitors and reports to the debt participants on all activity brought to his attention.

In Figure 5-2, the dashed lines indicate cash flows into and out of the indenture trustee. First, the equity investment flows from the owner participant to the indenture trustee. The indenture trustee adds his loan (that he makes to the lessor/owner trustee) and pays the manufacturer the purchase price of the leased property. In the transaction described in the preceding section, the owner participants transfer $6,000,000 to the indenture trustee. The debt participants add their $24,000,000 for a total payment of $30,000,000 to Server Co., Computer Co. and Truck Co. (minus the lessee's $150,000 total deposit, in this deal, which the indenture trustee typically refunds in a lump sum to the lessee).

The indenture trustee usually controls the documentation process because he take the credit risk of the lessee supported by lessor only to the extent that the lessor invests his equity in the transaction.

✔ **The tax indemnity agreement:** Because leveraged lease pricing usually involves the use of tax benefits by a lessor, the lessee enters into tax indemnities (often in a separate agreement called the *tax indemnity agreement, or TIA)* to assure the owner participants that they will receive the anticipated tax benefits. In Figure 5-2, the solid line between the lessee and the owner participants indicates the TIA. The TIA generally remains confidential between the owner participants and the lessee. See Chapters 8 and 13 on indemnities.

- **The guaranty:** The guaranty agreement is substantially identical to the agreement in the single-source lease. It is made, however, directly by the guarantor not only for the benefit of the lessor but also (indirectly) as security for the benefit of the debt participants.

- **The broker's agreement:** The lessee, the owner participant, or the debt participant may enter into an agreement with a broker or intermediary. It provides for the payment of a fee by one of those parties to his advisor upon completion of the identified task (ranging from advising on structuring and closing a leveraged lease to investing debt or equity in the transaction).

- **The purchase agreement and purchase agreement assignment:** In Figure 5-1, the solid line from the lessee to the manufacturer depicts the purchase arrangement. A leveraged lease works in a similar manner (although the line is not shown in Figure 5-2). The solid line from lessee to lessor/owner trustee indicates the assignment of the purchase rights given by the manufacturer/vendor to the lessee; and the solid line between the manufacturer and the lessor shows the consent to this assignment. The lender will receive an assignment of these warranties as shown by the solid line from the owner trustee to the indenture. In most other respects, this arrangement works like a single-investor lease.

Although the single-investor and leveraged lease structure have some similarities, the legal rights, cash flows, and operation differ significantly. You can benefit from reviewing each figure line by line. First, trace the solid lines (representing the agreements) and then dashed lines (representing the cash flows). In addition, learn the players and what they do. By gaining an understanding of these figures, you can go a long way in applying the ideas covered throughout this book toward accomplishing your financing objectives through leasing.

Chapter 6

Figuring Out Lessee Economics

. . . .

In This Chapter

▶ Considering the time value of money in your business

▶ Deciding whether to use corporate cash or debt to purchase property

▶ Calculating the cost of leasing business property

▶ Making the lease versus buy decision

. . . .

*I*t's one issue to select the property you need for your business. It's another issue to decide how you pay for it. If you're like most lessees, you want to identify the least expensive way to get the business property that you need. In this chapter, I help you understand the bottom line cost of leasing or buying property for your business. I discuss buying with cash and debt first before turning to leasing and then compare leasing to buying property. I emphasize the idea that you present value cash flows before or after taxes to compare the real costs to buy or lease the property. When you finish this chapter, you should be able to make more informed decisions about whether you should lease or buy property each time you need it.

Acquiring Property — the Financial Approach

Regardless of the methods that you choose to acquire property, your analysis should include the key concept of the *time value of money*. This concept factors in the outflows and inflows of cash at various points in time during the term of your financing. Cash flows out of your business, for example, to pay for the property at one time (for example, a cash purchase) or over time (for example, the cost of making loan or lease payments). On the other hand, cash flows into your business from the revenue generated by the property itself (such as revenue from running a printing press) or from your business operations, all over a period of time. The *time value of money* refers to the value of money received at different times. The money that you receive today is worth more than money that you receive tomorrow, or over any other period of time. In short, getting more cash or other value in hand sooner is better. This section addresses the relatives of the time value of money concept, present value, and net present value and how they are important for you.

Defining your cost of capital and discount rate

To calculate the cost of your financing or leases, you need to calculate the present value or net present value of cash flows coming into and going out of your business. To perform those calculations, you need a *discount rate,* which is unique to your business or transaction. You can derive a discount from your *cost of capital,* which refers to the cost of money that you use in your business. It includes the cost to your company of any outstanding preferred and common stock, and various types of debt that you may incur such as your company's secured revolving loan facility or line of credit with your lender.

You can calculate the cost of capital on an *after-tax cost* or a *pre-tax basis.* The pre-tax cost of capital considers the cost of capital ignoring the benefits or burdens of taxes in acquiring the capital. You compute the after-tax cost of capital by determining the tax impact of each type of financing that you use, after considering taxes you pay on that money or taxes you save by using that money. For example, interest on debt is tax deductible (but dividends on stock are not). You often blend the amounts of each capital cost to derive your total cost of capital. Your chief financial officer or accountants can calculate these numbers and probably offer a healthy debate as to the proper criteria to establish the cost of capital of your company.

You can use that cost of capital as your discount rate. A *discount rate* is a factor, expressed as a percentage (for example, 10 percent), that you apply to a stream of cash flows, to determine the value of that cash as of a particular date. A discount rate can be computed before or after giving effect to taxes just like your cost of capital.

Figuring the present value of cash flows

Once you determine the appropriate discount rate, you can then calculate the *present value* of cash flows. *Present value* refers to the value today of a payment or stream of payments payable at one or more dates in the future. Using a discount rate of 10 percent, $10,000 received in three years has a present value of approximately $7,513. By doing this calculation, you have used the *discounted cash flow method* of financial analysis. This analysis gives you a way to compare apples-to-apples, one payment plan against another, regardless of the timing and amount of payments. It reflects the discount rate, the amount of payments, and the timing of payments. You reach one answer for each stream of payments; and you can compare the answers.

Risk-adjusted discount rates

In the context of a leasing or loan transactions, you may determine that your cost of capital alone does not capture all risks (or benefits) of the transaction. These risk factors may protect you against using unrealistic discount rates that ignore the real costs and risks you face in financing property. You reflect different risks by adjusting your rate upward for higher risk and downward for lower risk. For example, you may elect to increase your discount rate slightly if your existing lenders may, depending on certain performance of your business, increase your debt rate in part relating to your choice to borrow or lease to acquire more property. Risk adjusting discount rates is a subjective process that senior financial officers typically address. While adjusting rates may be prudent to reflect risk, it can be a very subjective process that may undermine the accuracy of computing your true cost of capital and present value of your cash flows.

The lower the discount rate, the higher the present value or net present value of a stream of cash flows. Conversely, the higher the discount rate, the lower the present value or net present value of a stream of cash flows. For example, say that you enter into the lease for the lathe with rents of $10,000 per year over a five-year term. If you discount that stream of rental at 5 percent, 10 percent, and 15 percent (with arrears payments), the present value of that stream equals $43,295, $37,908, and $33,522, respectively.

Buying Property with Cash or Debt

You can buy property using debt or equity (setting aside bartering, and other more creative means, of course). To determine your real cost, you can discount the cash flows of each deal and compare them.

Calculating the net present value of cash flows

The discounted cash flow method helps you determine whether acquiring property or borrowing to purchase property makes good economic sense for your business. It provides a fair comparison of costs that you pay (negative cash flow) and/or the net present value (NPV) of money that you realize on an income-generating (positive cash flowing) property. To illustrate, say that you have a rental business and you decide to buy a photocopy machine for an out-of-pocket cost of $5,000 today. You then agree with the end-user that the end-user will pay you $10,000 (ignoring taxes) to use the photocopy machine at the end of year three. What is the net present value of your $5,000 investment, assuming a 10 percent discount rate?

You can derive net present value in the context of buying property that generates revenue. You can also use the same approach with cash flows that you receive or pay in borrowing or leasing transactions:

1. **Establish the amount of money that you expect to receive in the future.**

   In the preceding example, you realize $10,000 at the end of year three (ignoring taxes).

2. **Figure the present value of the cash flows.**

   The $10,000 that you receive at the end of year three discounted at 10 percent equals $7,513.

3. **Determine what you invested to acquire the photocopy machine.**

   In this case, you invested $5,000 at once. You can also make a series of payments such as installment payments over time.

4. **Subtract the cost of your initial investment from the present value of the cash flow that you received from the investment (or series of payments) to derive the net present value.**

   In this case, you subtract your initial investment of $5,000 from the present value of the cash flow ($7,513) to end up with $2,513. You realize a positive value from the investment in the copy machine.

The calculation of net present value tells you whether the acquisition of revenue generating property makes good economic sense or is "attractive," as some financial types say.

- ✔ **An investment makes good economic sense or is "attractive" if the net present value exceeds the investment in the property.** The investment in the photocopy machine makes good economic sense because the net present value ($7,513) exceeds the investment in the photocopier ($5,000). You always shoot for a positive net present value because you make money over your investment even though you do not receive your return on the investment for a period of time (three years in this example).

- ✔ **An investment does not make good economic sense or is not "attractive" if the investment in the property exceeds the net present value of the cash flows received from the property.** If you get the opposite result, where the net present value of the cash flows does not exceed the initial cost of the photocopy machine, you should not make that investment without other very strong reasons unrelated to the economics of the deal. It generally does not make sense to lose money on a discounted cash flow basis or otherwise unless, for example, you cover the excess cost with other business revenue and need the property, such as a demonstration model of a machine, to help you build your business volume.

> ✔ **An investment is neutral if the net present value equals your invest-ment. You neither have a good economic reason to make the invest-ment nor a good economic reason to pass on the investment.** In this case other factors such as a strategic need for a certain type of property may determine whether you acquire property or decline to do so.

You may be tempted to say that you should ignore discounting to determine what you made on your acquisition of property or to overstate what you can make with the property. For example, you may conclude that you paid $5,000 for the photocopy machine and received $10,000 back and thus doubled your money. Actually, that conclusion misses the point that the present value of the $10,000 that you received equals $7,513, almost 25 percent less than the undiscounted or nominal amount ($10,000). If you fail to apply the dis-counted cash flow method, you get a false reading on value and can make serious misjudgments about the positive (or negative) value of acquisitions of property in your business. As another example, say that you pay $5,000 for a photocopy machine and you received back $5,000 at the end of year three. You broke even, right? No, you lost money because applying the discounted cash flow method, the $5,000 of cash flow has a real value, using a 10 percent discount rate over three years, of just $3,756, for a loss of $1,244 ($3,756 real-ized versus $5,000 spent = a $1,244 loss).

If one approach to your deal doesn't make economic sense, you can go back to the drawing board or sharpen your pencil, for example, to find property that costs less or a deal that produces higher revenues.

When you calculate the net present value of an investment in property, consider the probability of realizing different values for the various economic components. Also, substitute different values for your cost of capital, tax rates and other variables in your calculation. Create three variations, each of which may be referred to as a different economic case. First, determine the best case that you can imagine, called the *high case*. Then, consider the worst case imaginable, within reason of course, called the *low case*. Finally, shoot for the most likely case, called the *base case*. By testing various results, you perform a *sensitivity analysis*. Evaluate the net present value in each case and reach your best conclusion of whether the numbers justify your investment in property. You can also use this same approach to compare lease proposals to each other and to other financing of a particular item of property.

Realizing tax savings on purchases

The federal tax laws provide you a tax incentive to buy and use property in your business. When you buy property, the tax laws allow you to depreciate the *basis,* which is usually your cost of the purchase, under the Modified Accelerated Cost Recovery System, known as *MACRS.* See Chapter 13. The MACRS depreciation system allows you to reduce the effective cost of your purchase each year by a certain amount of tax deductions attributable to the depreciation of your property. For each purchase, you can determine the after-tax cost by applying those tax benefits to your cost basis. For example, if you buy a printing press for $2,000,000, then over a period of seven years, you write off 100 percent of $2,000,000. If in the first year of ownership, you can write off 15 percent against your taxable income, then in that year you reduce your taxable income by an amount equal to $2,000,000 x 0.15 = $300,000. Your after-tax cost takes that $300,000 deduction into account.

To determine whether this analysis is correct for you, however, you should run the numbers on your deal and look at the nominal and net present value results on an after-tax basis. Consider the following example of how you run the numbers. Say that you have cash reserves and elect to buy the printing press with an original cost of $2,000,000. For purpose of this analysis, you take the tax benefits under the Modified Accelerated Cost Recovery System as explained in Chapter 13. Using real MACRS percentages, say that the annual depreciation equals 14.29 percent of the lessor's cost in year 1 of your claim for tax benefits, and 24.49 percent, 17.49 percent, 12.49 percent, 8.93 percent, 8.92 percent, 8.93 percent and 4.46 percent. You currently pay state and federal taxes at a combined rate of 32 percent. The economics of owner-ship work as shown in Table 6-1.

Table 6-1		The After-Tax Cost of Purchasing with Cash			
Year Ending 12/31	Cash for Purchase of Property	Depreciation Deductions	Tax Savings From Depreciation Deductions	After-Tax Cost Per Year	Present Value of After-Tax Cost Per Year
1	Negative Negative	-$2,000,000 -$1,916,858	-$285,800	$91,456	-$1,908,544
2		-$489,800	$156,736	$156,736	$129,534
3		-$349,800	$111,936	$111,936	$84,099
4		-$249,800	$79,936	$79,936	$54,597
5		-$178,600	$57,152	$57,152	$35,487
6		-$178,400	$57,088	$57,088	$32,225
7		-$178,600	$57,152	$57,152	$29,238
8		-$89,200	$28,544	$28,544	$13,316
Purchase Totals		$2,000,000	$640,000	-$1,360,000	-$1,538,272

The economics of ownership with cash produces the following results:

- ✔ Tax savings from depreciation of $640,000 and depreciation of $2,000,000.

- ✔ An after-tax cost to purchase on over the write-off period of $1,360,000 on a nominal basis and $1,538,272 on a discounted basis (at a discount rate of 10 percent). Note how sensitive the timing is on value tax benefits. Taking tax benefits sooner is almost always better for your economics.

Buying property with debt

If you decide that you need to borrow money to acquire property, you receive the same depreciation tax benefits as you do when you buy with cash, plus an additional write-off for interest paid on the principal portion of your debt. The *principal* of your loan equals the sum loaned to you by your lender, and the *interest* on your loan refers to the compensation that your lender charges you for the use of the loan money. You can then calculate the present value of the stream of payments of your debt, on an after-tax basis, by reducing your payments by the amount you save in taxes each year from the depreciation and interest deductions.

To illustrate, say that you enter into a seven-year loan secured by a printing press with an original cost of $2,000,000. For the purpose of this analysis, you take the tax benefits under MACRS. Use the same depreciation deductions as the preceding purchase illustration and assume that you borrow $1,400,000. Your lender charges you 10 percent interest per annum and requires you to invest 30 percent of the purchase price (30 percent x $2,000,000 = $600,000) from your corporate cash. You currently pay state and federal taxes at a combined rate of 32 percent. (The value to you of the interest is 1.00 minus your tax rate (0.32) times the interest payment). The economics of ownership work with borrowed fund yield the following results:

- ✔ Tax savings from interest deductions of $223,799 representing the sum of interest deductions over the term of the loan (which does not occur when purchasing property with cash). Note: This element doesn't exist in Table 6-1 where you purchase for cash.

- ✔ Tax savings from depreciation of $640,000 and depreciation of $2,000,000 (which equals the benefit of an all cash purchase). Note: This element is the same as in Table 6-1.

- ✔ An after-tax cost to purchase over the term of the loan of $1,835,574 on a nominal and $1,375,181 discounted at a discount rate of 10 percent per annum. Note: The nominal and discounted cost here somewhat exceeds the values to purchase with cash. However, remember that you attribute no capital cost to using your cash to buy the property, which assumes that your cash has no value — a clearly erroneous approach.

Determining the Cost of Leasing Property

To compare the cost of leasing property and to the cost of purchasing the same property, you need to consider several factors: calculating the timing and amount of cash flows, analyzing the type of lease structure, and taking into account the impact of tax benefits.

Understanding leasing cash flows

When you enter a lease, you encounter a variety of cash flows, both incoming and outgoing. To analyze the cost of these cash flows, you calculate the present value of these cash flows from the date each occurs to the date your lease started. You can consider these cash flows on a nominal basis by just adding them up, but present value calculations offer a more accurate economic picture of the real cost of your lease.

On the incoming side of cash flows, if you own the property that you lease, when you sell your property to the lessor in a sale-leaseback transaction, your lessor pays you in cash for the amount of the purchase price. If you purchase property from a manufacturer or other vendor, you probably make a down payment on property that you intend to lease and your lessor reimburses you for the down payment.

On the outgoing side, you may pay fees and expenses of the transaction, often called *transaction expenses,* such as legal, accounting, and appraisal fees; and, of course, you also pay rent. You may pay rent starting on the day the lease begins or at the end of each *rent period,* which refers to the time elapsed between rent payments. Rent periods occur on a monthly, quarterly, semi-annual, or annual basis. Payments may be made at the beginning of the period, which is a payment *in advance,* or at the end of each period, which is a payment *in arrears.* These payments are not always the same amount in each rent period.

You may have one or more options or rights during the lease term that affects your cash flow (see Chapters 3, and 8): an early buy-out option, a fixed price purchase option, or at fair market value purchase option. Second, you may have the right to terminate your lease before the end of the term, called an *early termination option.* Third, you may be entitled to extend the term of your lease beyond the existing term, under a renewal option. These options require you to pay your lessor some extra cash during or after the end of the term. Each of these cash flows affects the ultimate cost of your lease. (However, you do not, in a tax-oriented lease, have to exercise any option and can return the leased property at the end of the term, which eliminates the extra cost.)

For example, say that you receive a lease proposal for a lathe with a lessor's cost of approximately $41,700 that requires you to pay rent annually in advance, in an amount of $10,000, over a five-year term. In other words you pay $50,000 total rent. By charging you rent in advance, your lessor makes more money than if it charged you in arrears because the lessor receives your installment one year earlier throughout the term. If a lease starts June 1, 2002, you pay rent on June 1, 2002 (in advance) instead of May 31, 2003 (in arrears). If that $10,000 earns 10 percent interest, your lessor earns an extra $1,000 ($10,000 at 10 percent interest equals $1,000) for five years merely because of the timing. If you apply a discount rate of 10 percent to the rent payments, the present value of the rent, payable in advance, is approximately $41,700. The present value of the rent, payable in arrears, is $37,908. This one cash flow term significantly affects your economics, making your lease more expensive by $3,792 in today's dollars ($41,700 minus $37,908). Each of the other payments also impacts the cash flow and economics of a lease based on the concept of the time value of money.

Add to this calculation a right to purchase the lathe at the end of the lease for $30,000 because of a fixed price purchase option that you negotiated. Now you calculate the present value of $30,000 and add that amount to the present value of rent in advance or arrears, and you get a more complete idea of what the lathe costs you to lease. The present value of $30,000 paid at the expiration of the lease (the end of year 5), equals $18,628 (at a 10 percent discount rate). The sum of the present values of $18,628 and $41,700 is $60,328. That amount represents your present value cost (without considering taxes or other factors) of leasing the lathe, assuming payments made in advance.

The impact of lease structure on pricing

In addition to the timing and amount of cash flows, the cost of your lease depends upon the structure of your lease and the discount rate that you use to determine the present value of the lease payments that you make. Consider the following aspects of a lease transaction:

✔ **Whether you enter a service lease or a net lease.** Each scenario alters the cost of your lease. For example, entering into a service contract to repair an item of equipment may be far less expensive than acquiring staff inside or outside of your company to do the same work, especially when you consider the management time you expend to find the help or get the job done. Include the fees or costs that you pay for service, including overhead allocable to the lease, to determine the cost of the lease. (The same idea applies to purchases.)

✔ **Whether your lease constitutes a true lease or a disguised security interest/loan.** If your lease constitutes a secured loan, your lessor cannot take depreciation benefits, and you cannot deduct your entire rent as discussed in the following section. If your lease constitutes a secured loan, you don't enjoy the same options to buy the leased property or terminate the lease, and you probably can expect to pay the full value of the leased property with interest or other payments on the amount of that value.

✔ **Whether you receive the anticipated tax benefits.** Related to the preceding structure point, your tax benefit primarily amounts to fully deducting your rent payment from your taxable income. In valuing those benefits, you calculate your combined federal and state tax rate. If your tax rate is lower than expected, your lease costs you more than if your tax rate remains at the expected level because you receive less value from your deductions in offsetting tax savings. (This concern also applies to buying property with cash or debt.)

✔ **Whether you use the appropriate discount rate to calculate the present value of your lease.** When selecting an appropriate discount rate, you can adjust the discount rate to a risk-adjusted discount rate that reflects the risks of the leasing transaction specifically and/or the risks of the additional lease financing on your company generally.

The impact of tax benefits on pricing

The availability of significant tax benefits for lessees and lessors distinguishes leases from buying with corporate cash or loans. See Chapter 7 for lessor pricing. If you cannot use tax benefits, or a lessor can gain greater value from tax benefits, that alone may push you toward leasing.

Imagine the following example. You enter into a seven-year net lease of a printing press with a lessor's cost of $2,000,000. You agree to pay rent of $30,000 per month in arrears for a total of $360,000 per year, before taking into account the lessor's tax benefits. You structure the lease as a true tax lease. Because the transaction has been structured to give the lessor tax ownership, the lessor takes depreciation deductions under MACRS. (See Chapter 13.)

You should get a lower rental rate because of the lessor's ability to claim these tax benefits. In any event, you, in turn, deduct 100 percent of your rent payment for income tax purposes. Say that you currently pay state and federal taxes at a combined rate of 32 percent. (The value of the deduction to you is 1.00 minus your tax rate [0.32] times the rent payment [$30,000] or $20,400.)

Say that you fully expect to purchase the printing press at the end of the lease and negotiate a 50 percent purchase option, protecting your economics because you believe that the market will be strong at the end of the lease, and the press could be worth 70 percent of its original cost. Here are the economics of that lease:

✔ **Rent payment:** $30,000/month x 12 months x 7 years = $2,520,000

✔ **Tax savings from rent deductions:** $9,600/ month x 12 months x 7 years =$806,400

✔ **After-tax cost:** $20,400/ month x 12 months x 7 years =$1,713,600

You can analyze these numbers as follows:

✔ **Each month you pay $20,400 of rent payments, on an *after-tax basis*, and $30,000 per month on a pre-tax basis.**

The *after-tax basis*, in this context, refers to the cost of your lease rent payments after taking into account the deduction that you receive for the full amount of your rent ($30,000 rent payment – $9,savings of the rent write-off at a 32 percent tax rate = $20,400 per month).

✔ **During the seven-year term, you pay a total after-tax cost of $1,713,600 as contrasted with a pre-tax rent amount of $2,520,000 (nominal tax savings: $2,520,000 – $1,713,600 = $806,400).**

A *pre-tax cost* refers to the cost of your lease rent payments *without* taking into account the deductions that you can claim for the full amount of your rent (that is, ignore $9,600 per month of deductions over seven years).

For purposes of a present value analysis, say that you only have a secured debt facility at a 10 percent rate, and you use that interest rate as your current cost of capital and discount rate in calculating the present value or net present value of your lease transactions.

Calculating the value of your write-offs

The value of your write-off of rent (or depreciation in a purchase) changes with your tax rate: the higher your rate, the more a valuable your tax deductions; and conversely, the lower your tax rate the less valuable your deductions.

For example, say that your rent payment equals $10,000 per year, and your tax rate is 35 percent. You can compute the after-tax cost of each rent payment using the following formula:

After-tax cost of rent = 1.00 – your tax rate of 35 percent expressed as a decimal (0.35) x the rent payment,

which is

$1.00 - 0.35 = 0.65 \times \$10,000$ rent per year = $6,500 after-tax cost of rent

If your tax rate decreases to 30 percent, look at the *increase* you experience (from $6,500 to $7,000) in your after-tax cost of the same rent payment:

$1.00 - 0.30 = 0.70 \times \$10,000$ rent per year = $7,000 after-tax-cost of rent

The present value of the lease payment, on an after-tax basis, in the preceding example, equals approximately $1,228,828 (the present value of the $20,400 after-tax monthly rent payments, in arrears over seven years at a 10 percent discount rate). If you exercise the fixed price purchase option of 50 percent of the lessor's cost of $2,000,000, you pay an extra $1,000,000 on the last day of the lease, which equals $498,028 discounted to the start of the lease at 10 percent. The total of the present value of the rent and of the purchase option represents the net present value on an after-tax basis of this lease: $1,228,828 (rent) plus $498,028 (purchase option) = $1,726,856. In addition, you also receive tax benefits from depreciating the amount of your fixed price purchase option of $1,000,000 under MACRS depreciation system after you exercise the purchase option.

When reviewing competing lease proposals, you (or your lease advisors) can complete a table similar to Table 6-1 and compare the pre-tax and after-tax values of the cash flows and of the present value of the lease streams to determine which one makes the most economic sense for you. Then, you compare those values against the after-tax cost to purchase including the cash flows involved in a purchase to determine which transaction proves to meet your objectives at the time. Your objectives may, for example, require that you preserve cash and therefore lease even though leasing may be more expensive overall or, alternatively, maintain control of residual value through purchasing as discussed more fully in the following sections. You don't make every decision based on the numbers alone. You may just emotionally prefer to control your property through purchasing, but before you take that route, do run the numbers so that you appreciate and calculate the real cost of your decisions.

Making the Lease-Buy Decision

In this section, I help you make the decision of whether you should lease or buy your property by comparing the cost of leasing against the cost of purchasing property with equity or other corporate cash or borrowed funds.

In making the lease/buy decision, if the net present value (NPV) that you calculate to buy property (by use of corporate cash or by borrowing) exceeds the NPV of the lease, then the lease makes good economic sense as a financing alternative. If the reverse is true and the NPV of the lease exceeds the NPV of your own investment (with corporate cash or debt), then your purchase makes more economic sense than the lease. Finally, if the NPV of each alternative is approximately the same, make your decision to lease or buy for other reasons because the economics remain neutral as to the best deal.

In each transaction, you can make the decision whether to lease or buy the property that you need in your business using the following four approaches (but the last of the four provides you the best answer):

✔ **Compare your actual lease versus loan payments on the same periodic basis (such as monthly or quarterly).**

You make this comparison without regard to present value or tax considerations. You simply compare the cost of a loan payment to a lease payment on a monthly, quarterly or other periodic basis and do not discount the cash flow (before and/or after-taxes). This method does show the cash drain on your business. However, this method does not work if you buy with cash or exercise options under your lease because you attribute no capital cost to your money, ignore the time value of money, and provide a limited comparison of the dollars that you spend when you spend them.

✔ **Compare all payments by adding up all the payments over the term of the loan or lease or the total purchase price for all cash purchases to calculate which alternative creates the lowest total payment amount.**

You total all payments on the basis of nominal cash flow alone and, similar to the first approach, ignore the time value of money and just compare the total dollars that you spend when you spend them without tax considerations. You should attribute some cost of capital to a direct purchase with cash when comparing cash purchases to leases or loans because money that you earn or borrow in your business can itself earn more money if you invest it or use it in your business operations.

✔ **Compare the cash flows of a loan to a lease discounted at an appropriate discount rate.**

You discount the cash flows but ignore any tax considerations. If you use this method with a cash purchase, you should first attribute a cost of capital to that money (to get a discount rate) to determine the total value of the money that you use. You do get a comparable cost of the two different financing methods, which helps you discern the cost in a discounted sum today of one type of method versus the other.

✔ **Calculate the cost of the after-tax cash flows discounted at an appropriate risk-adjusted discount rate (if appropriate).**

In this final approach, you use all the tools discussed in this chapter to calculate an after-tax value of leasing compared to borrowing or paying cash to buy property that you use in your business. This method allows you to make the truest comparison on an apples to apples approach, whereas each of the other alternatives does not.

Leasing should often cost you less than purchasing with cash or debt in tax-oriented (true) leases because of the cash flow timing and tax attributes of the lease transaction. If you don't get that result, recheck your numbers.

Note, however, that if you compare the after-tax cost of leasing with the cost of buying using the proceeds of a loan, your total rent payments may exceed your total loan payments of borrowing to purchase property. That result may occur because your lessor finances 100 percent of the lessor's cost and charges you rent based on that investment. By contrast, your lender may require you to invest 20 percent to 50 percent of the price of the property, and the lender advances only the balance of the purchase price (that is, 80 percent down to 50 percent). You should get depreciation deductions on the entire lessor's cost and interest deductions with respect to the interest portion of each debt payment relating to the loan, but you do not receive any tax benefit for your equity investment.

Regardless of the alternative selected or the cost described in the preceding discussion, the components of each alternative must be closely evaluated to determine which one results in the lowest cost. If you have a low tax rate and your lessor has a high tax rate, you may want to lease. If you need to preserve or raise cash, or your cost of borrowing remains high compared to the implicit cost of funds that the lessor charges in your rents, you may find that the after-tax cost of leasing compels you to lease. On the other hand, if your company has substantial cash reserves, a high tax rate, and low borrowing costs, you may, if you can spare cash, prefer to purchase the property. In the final analysis, your selection of the best alternative financing depends on more than the numbers presented in this chapter. See Chapters 2 and 3.

This chapter presents only a few of the important concepts and illustrations on pricing your transactions. No substitute exists, however, for completing pricing runs (that is, using computer programs that compare the cost of leasing to other financing) to test the financial viability of leasing or buying property. Find the right help if you need it, but do make this effort on any significant transaction for your business. See Chapter 7.

Chapter 7

Lessor Economics: Setting and Analyzing Lease Payments

• •

In This Chapter

▶ Understanding key factors that affect lease pricing

▶ Calculating yields in leases and loans

▶ Identifying some computer programs used in lease and loan pricing

• •

*I*n today's competitive market, winning a deal often boils down to offering your prospective lessee the lowest cost deal. With the trend toward greater sophistication in lease pricing, increasing competition, consolidation among lessors, and decreasing margins on your investments, knowing how to structure and analyze lease economics, as discussed here, can serve you well.

This chapter identifies some, but certainly not all, of the factors used in lease pricing. It discusses how to calculate your earnings and provides some information about lease pricing computer programs that can help you do your job more effectively.

Key Factors in Lease Pricing

As a lessor, you work in the business of making sound investments in property. Your decisions depend on many variables, including the type of property, the economic life and residual value of the property, and the competition to provide financing for that property. You determine (or, in many cases, someone higher up the corporate ladder determines) your target yields, investment criteria, and strategies to win deals. Not only do you face a competitive market, but you also cope with complicated pricing models that may have been created internally or that you have acquired from an outside source. You have to make the right assumptions to derive the right payments and structure for, and yields on, your leases. To meet these objectives, you need to understand lease pricing and methods of lease analysis.

You can measure your return on a lease investment in terms of its yield. *Yield*, in effect, refers to the value that you receive, expressed as a percentage of your investment, either on a before tax or after-tax basis, for risking your investment capital in a lease or loan on leased property. For example, you may, on an after-tax basis, realize a 12 percent yield on your investment from your lease in a printing press.

Lessors often refer to the process of determining the right payments and structure for, and earnings on, leases as the *pricing* of a lease transaction. The following sections discuss some factors used in lease pricing.

Your investment

You begin any lease analysis with your investment in leased property. In this section, I define and help you analyze the components of your investment with and without the effect of taxes.

The lessor's cost of leased property constitutes the primary component of your investment. You add to the lessor's cost the installation and other soft costs (and for some pricing programs, the transaction fees and expenses) as part of the amount that you fund or pay to start your lease. For example, assume that you want to provide lease financing for production equipment with a cost of $2,000,000 plus $25,000 of soft costs. Your investment equals $2,025,000 ($2,000,000 plus $25,000). That sum then also becomes your lessor's cost and your "investment" in your deal.

The preceding example applies to single-investor leases. In leveraged leases, you factor into the analysis the lessor's nonrecourse debt. For example, in the production equipment lease, say that you borrow 80 percent of the cost of the entire investment, which equals $1,620,000, and you provide the other 20 percent in equity, which equals $405,000. Have you invested $405,000 or $2,025,000? Your investment equals $405,000 provided the debt constitutes nonrecourse debt. If you don't use nonrecourse debt, your pricing and accounting changes dramatically because you have to account for and repay the debt personally. The leveraged portion, $1,625,000, however, counts in your economic analysis. Consequently, even though you invest only 20 percent ($405,000), you calculate your return on investment on the basis of $2,025,000. You can appreciate that power of leverage in the economics of leveraged leases because you benefit from a much larger lessor's cost than the cash you actually expend.

Investments also produce a series of cash flows, incoming and outgoing. Outgoing or negative cash flows start with the investment itself. You pay out $2,000,000 to the seller of the production equipment and you pay installation costs of $25,000. Your investment constitutes the first outgoing cash flow. That investment, in turn, produces incoming or positive cash flows in the form of rent, casualty loss value payments, fees, excess tax benefits (beyond current lease income), lease option payments, and residual value of the production equipment. You may have additional outflows for fees, maintenance, taxes, debt service (in leveraged leases only) or upgrade payments (in certain full service and other leases).

In addition, you can analyze cash flows on investments with or without considering taxes and residual value. The inclusion of taxes and residual value differentiates lease investments from loans. Loans generate interest-only income and perhaps some fees. Lessors who provide loan financing or lease financing in the nature of loans cannot claim depreciation benefits on the leased property. Therefore, they cannot enhance their returns or yield with tax benefits like tax-oriented lessors. They have no ownership right that entitles them to those benefits. However, lessees may, in those deals, claim the tax depreciation in those types of financings. Similarly, lenders do not assume residual value risk of property because they do not own and have no right in the property (other than a security interest).

Pretax cash flow refers to the cash flow, such as rent, that you receive from your lessee. *After-tax cash flow* refers to your pretax cash flows plus or minus taxes attributable to your investment. A significant component in the computation of your yield from the deal is the available tax benefits. The critical issues include the amount and timing of those tax benefits.

Tax considerations

Taxes constitute the magic in leasing for tax-oriented transactions more than any other single component of pricing (see Chapter 13), although many lessors find residual value to be even more important to their businesses.

If you want to play in the tax-oriented leasing game, go get a big tax rate. (This may be the first and last time that a high tax rate is a good thing!) If you find yourself making large amounts of taxable income in a state with high state and local taxes and you pay the top corporate rates to the federal government, you can compete effectively in tax-oriented leasing. For example, in New York or California, say the state income tax rate is 8 percent while the top federal income tax rate is 35 percent. The combined rate is about 43 percent. You deduct state income taxes from federal income to achieve a blended income tax rate. Say that your blended tax rate equals 40 percent. Although the 43 percent rate helps that lessor win over you, you can still offer better pricing than a lessor with a 35 percent rate can. These pricing advantages occur because the higher your tax rate, the greater tax benefits you receive, which may be the key to winning a deal and beating a lower rate taxpayer with lower lease pricing. See Chapter 6.

If your tax rate changes during the lease, you either experience an increased or decreased benefit of the transaction (assuming that all other pricing assumptions remain the same). Say that federal law changes or your income subject to taxation dramatically increases after the point that you no longer have any depreciation benefits left to take under your lease. At that point, sometimes called the *crossover point*, you start paying taxes on all taxable cash flow. You immediately experience a decrease in your yield and earnings because you pay more tax on your taxable income than planned in your original pricing. Conversely, if your tax rate declines after the crossover point, your yield and earnings increase because you keep more of the income than originally anticipated.

You experience a more pronounced effect of change in tax rates in leveraged leases than single-investor leases because you write off all the interest paid to your lender plus depreciation benefits on the entire lessor's cost and not just your investment.

When you enter into a lease as a tax lessor, you fully expect to continue paying taxes. As long as you pay taxes, your write-offs have value. However, if you experience a large loss, purchase a business that wipes out or reduces your tax liability or another event occurs such that you do not pay taxes as anticipated, then the benefits of the tax write-offs and the motivation to offer a leveraged lease disappear. You neither receive nor can pass through to the lessee the benefit of tax write-offs if you don't have enough taxable income to absorb the deductions arising from your lease.

You must price your leases to take into account the tax rules (see Chapter 13), which create constraints on how you price your deals. These rules create various constraints in pricing (the stuff you must do or not do as required by the tax laws) that dictate what pricing you can offer your lessee.

Residual value assumptions

Residual value upside motivates many lessors. As profitability of deals, based on the lease rate, trend down, some lessors rely on their skills in realizing residual value to make strong overall returns on their investments. Other lessors with less capability still expect to receive the residual value that they show on their books at the inception of the lease. Still others hope that lessees exercise purchase options and relieve them of the burden of remarketing leased property, which is not a real part of their business plan.

Residual value players do not fear the return of leased property. Rather, they understand the market for the property and probably do (or should) employ people who do nothing but value, inspect, and dispose of leased property.

Residual values can offer the big bang to your yield on a lease investment. By setting your booked residual below the amount you actually expect to realize, you effectively build in extra earnings at the end of the lease. Similarly, that extra residual may greatly improve your overall yield and make leasing a superior investment than any lease or loan in which residual plays no part. However, competition for deals may constrain your opportunity to create that residual upside.

As an illustration, say the yield on a 10-year production equipment lease is 10 percent, and you realize a 15 percent residual value in upside (over and above the 15 percent residual that you booked to meet your pricing objective). If you actually realize 30 percent residual, you receive on a nominal basis 15 percent in upside and 6 percent on a present value basis. That extra kick enhances your yield on investment (on a pretax basis) and makes that leasing deal an attractive use of your funds. Conversely, if you book 15 percent and receive a 5 percent residual, you may face a substantial loss.

If you rely on residual value to make your numbers, hire experts inside or outside your organization who can set values on leased property at the outset of your lease. Task your expert to set values each year of the lease showing the extent to which you face residual risk during the lease term and at expiration. Look for a negative spread between your booked residual value and the value you can realistically obtain in an orderly liquidation of the leased property. In other words, enter the lease understanding the downside (or potential losses) and upside (gain over your booked residual) during the lease, should the lessee default, or, at the end of the lease, should the lessee return the leased property. Resist the temptation to set residuals high at the outset of a deal simply to win the business, unless you have strategic reasons and a high level of comfort that you can actually realize the residual that you use in your pricing. This pricing parameter has been abused as a way to win deals without full analysis or capability to realize residual value. Such an approach can generate losses if residual values drop below expectations. You may protect your values with residual guaranty insurance where a third party effectively provides you a residual guaranty. (See Chapter 15 for more on residual value insurance and guarantees.)

Cost of funds of lessor

Lessors acquire their money to invest at a unique cost to them. No two have the same story to tell the financial markets including lenders.

As a lessor, your *cost of funds (COF)* may be the single most sensitive component of pricing next to your tax attributes and residual value. The *cost of funds* means how much your money costs you. For example, if you obtain funds at 6 percent from securitizations, you probably have a competitive advantage over a lessor that borrows from its bank line at 10 percent.

For most lessors, the market sets the price (COF) that they pay to obtain debt and equity financing. A lessor may, for example, issue short-term debt, medium-term debt, long-term debt, and/or preferred or common equity. For some lessors, commercial paper financing, bank deposits (for bank lessors), or a secured line of credit determines their cost of funds. Each lessor's financing rates are unique. Using its COF, a lessor then sets its minimum pricing level for leases and loans as a percentage amount in excess of its COF, called the *spread*. Most lessors find that if their spread is too high relative to other lessors, they have great difficulty in winning deals despite their tax or residual value assumptions.

The method of determining your COF may be too complicated to set daily or weekly. As a shorthand solution, you can instead use a publicly available index such as the prime rate, base rate, reference rate, Treasury Notes, or *LIBOR* (the London Interbank Offered Rate) that most closely approximates your true cost of funds. Then you set your spread (return) requirements over that rate. For example, you may express your spread requirements as 275 basis points over Treasury Notes with a maturity as close as possible to the date the lease expires.

Some lessors set forth a fixed rate in a lease proposal without the right to adjust rates for fluctuations in interest movements between the date of a proposal and a funding under a final lease agreement. Fix rates with caution. If possible, select a rate that protects your yield, so that the mere passage of time does not erode your yield. On the other hand, if rates drop during the interim, you probably don't mind a bit, but your lessee may care that it does not receive the benefit of a drop in rates where you receive protection to increase your rate if your cost of funds increases.

Timing of lease transaction

Your timing in lease transactions can affect your yield positively or negatively. You should be aware of a few examples of how this occurs:

- ✔ **The lessee's cost can, in some cases, be minimized the later in the year you close and fund a transaction**. When you fund a lease closer to the end of your tax year, you and your lessee can benefit. For every day that you fund closer to the realization of tax benefits (generally at yearend), the more value you (and therefore, your lessee) should receive from those benefits. See Chapter 13 concerning potential limitations on depreciation deductions in the fourth quarter of your tax year.

- ✔ **Timing of cash flows affects your yield.** The earlier that you receive cash from the lessee, the more it is worth to you. Conversely, the later that a lessee pays you cash, the lower the present value of the lease cost for the lessee. Subject to pricing constraints and competition, when you get paid can affect your yield and the lessee's desire to do business with you.

✔ **Timing of making tax payments.** Rents and other cash flows increase taxable income. Depreciation, interest payments, and expenses reduce taxable income. Generally, the sooner in time that you use deductions or other tax benefits to reduce taxable income, the higher you can push your yield. Most companies pay taxes quarterly. You can best analyze when to pay or defer taxes by using lease pricing programs described later in this chapter in "Pricing Software — You Must Have It."

Ending a lease before its time

A lease may end before its scheduled expiration date generally for three reasons. See Chapter 8. First, you grant your lessee a contractual right to end the lease earlier than the scheduled expiration date, either in the form of an early buy-out option or an early termination option. Lessees negotiate a right to end a lease early because the leased property becomes obsolete or surplus to their needs. Second, the leased property may be destroyed by some casualty event. Third, your lessee defaults, and you repossess the leased property. Each event triggers economic consequences for you.

This section briefly describes the economics of each and illustrates the components of the economic values that you should, or in the ideal world, would like, to recover in each case.

In leveraged and single-investor leases, you can grant your lessee one or more options to terminate the lease before the end of the scheduled lease term. The Internal Revenue Code imposes some constraints discussed in more detail in Chapter 13, but as a good rule of thumb, you can grant two or three options over a lease term of ten years.

On an early termination you need to recover your intended investment at the date on which the early termination occurs. To do so, you should receive a cash amount that enables you, in theory, to (at least) replace what you would have received on a present value basis had you completed the lease at its scheduled term. You call this payment the *early termination value*. Lessees and lessors negotiate these values, which, for you, should include the following components (and perhaps others in your financial modeling):

✔ Your basic investment that remains in the leased property

✔ A residual value upside payment sufficient to achieve your economic return or yield — an upside boost in your numbers

✔ In a leveraged lease, the outstanding debt that you borrowed from the lender

✔ Your tax liabilities because the IRS expects you to pay taxes on the taxable portions of the termination value just as it expects you to pay taxes during the lease term on rents and other taxable payments from the lessee

You can also agree that a lessee may buy the leased property during the term. Once again, expect your lessee to negotiate the price of the purchase. You should conform your pricing to the constraints of Revenue Procedure 75-21 discussed in Chapter 13.

You can calculate casualty loss values (also called stipulated loss values) in approximately the same manner as the early termination values and for similar reasons. These values protect you against the loss or destruction of your leased property. Your lessee pays you a lump sum equal to the amount you would have received if your lease expired on schedule, without incident, at the end of its term. If your lessee defaults, some leases also use the casualty value as a measure of the liquidated damages.

Selling, general, and administrative costs

Lessors sometimes understate (read omit!) in their pricing the proper amount of fees and expenses of closing a deal, administering the lease during its lifetime, and disposing of equipment. You overstate your yield by omitting or understating these costs, especially in middle- or small-ticket transactions. However, the larger a transaction, the less impact that fees and expenses tend to have.

To have pricing reflect the real cost of a transaction, include in your pricing a realistic cost of selling, general, and administrative expenses. If you want to avoid that drag on your yield, try to get the lessee to pay some or all of these costs (starting with legal, appraisal, and other fees and expenses at closing as a component of the lessor's cost).

Yield and Earnings Analysis of Leases

Once you consider the factors used in pricing leases and set your yield targets, you then use those factors and other methodologies to measure whether you achieve your yield or return on your investment.

If you like numbers, you can analyze yield and return on investment every which way. The complexity and debate on reliability and accuracy shows few limits for financial analysts. If, on the other hand, you need to understand the fundamental numbers and prefer to leave the tough stuff to the computer jockeys, stick around.

Yield on investment — internal rate of return (IRR)

Although you can measure yield in several ways, this chapter focuses on the *internal rate of return (IRR)* on investment. In this method, you base yield on your investment. IRR calculates the present value of cash flows in your lease using a discount rate that discounts the cash flows of your investment to $0.00. The discount rate is "internal" to the calculation because it constitutes your implicit yield (not an externally stated rate of return) that you calculate based on your investment assumptions such as the cost of the leased property, the term of the lease, and the available tax benefits.

Wouldn't it be great if the determination of yield and lease pricing stopped here? Unfortunately, IRR does not accurately produce yield when cash flow shifts more than once. Cash flow shifts in leveraged leases from negative cash flows to positive cash flows one or more times depending on your lease structure. As a result, you use computer-assisted pricing to determine your true yield before or after taxes to account for the timing and amount of these shifting cash flows.

Yield analysis of loans and disguised leases

If a lease does not include tax benefits, you price the deal like a secured loan. You can compute and express your yield before and after taxes on these "leases" in several ways. The methods include an IRR calculation, a return on equity (a ratio of the annual net cash flow to the equity invested in the transaction), or a return on assets (a ratio of the annual net cash flow to the lessor's cost of the leased property). However, you can simply take your cost of funds and add a spread, which constitutes the profit portion as a component of your total yield. For example, if you establish your cost of funds at 7 percent and charges the lessee a 10 percent lease rate, you achieve a 3 percent (or 300 *basis point*) spread over your cost of funds. (A basis point equals 1/100th of 1 percent.) The earnings on investment equals the spread times your investment balance outstanding at various dates during the lease term. In effect, you can determine your profit on a loan in a similar manner. If you use equity, you can treat the equity as borrowed funds and computes the yield in the same manner as a loan.

Yield analysis of single-investor and leveraged leases

Cash flows on leases that qualify for tax benefits under the Internal Revenue Code and Revenue Procedures require different (or additional) yield calculations from loans or disguised leases. The introduction of tax benefits means that you apply tax benefits derived from the leased property or financing costs to reduce your taxable income. If, for example, you have $100 in taxable income and a depreciation benefit this year of $20, then you report $80 in taxable income. The $20 reduction in taxable income actually saves you in real cash an amount equal to $20 x 1.00 minus your tax rate (for example 1.00 – 0.40 tax rate = 60% x $20 = $12) in savings, thanks to the depreciation write-off. Loans or disguised leases do not have a similar attribute.

The yield analysis of leveraged leases takes a quantum leap upward in complexity. The good news is that I don't do quantum here. The bad news is that you can't escape the complexity in leveraged lease pricing. In this section, I help you analyze the fundamentals of leveraged lease yields or returns on investment where IRR doesn't quite cut it. As an adjustment to IRR, most lessors use the *multiple investment sinking funds analysis* or *MISF*.

MISF yield analysis in general

The term MISF analysis derives in part from your investment in a leveraged lease on more than one occasion during the term of your lease term. You make investments on these occasions or separate investment phases because the pattern of cash flows in leveraged leases requires you to infuse cash during the lease term, not just at inception.

In the early years of a lease, you earn back most (or all) of your investment through payments of rent and positive inflows attributable to tax benefits. At that time, your investment balance becomes negative, and you enter the *sinking fund phase*. In the middle years of the lease term, after you use up your tax write-offs, you owe income taxes plus debt service payments that exceed your cash rent payments. Late in the lease term, the pattern shifts to a phase in which your cash flow again becomes a net positive. When your lease term ends, your investment balance equals zero on receipt of the assumed residual value.

In the initial phase of the lease, your tax benefits and other cash flow create positive cash flow in excess of your investment in the lease. At that juncture, under MISF, you set aside a fund (not real money but only as a factor in your pricing) called the *sinking fund*. In pricing, you use this fund to pay for taxes that you defer by using tax benefits in excess of your taxable income from this lease against other income unrelated to your lease. The value of the excess tax benefits lies in the assumption that you have other income subject to tax that you reduce by applying the excess write-offs from the lease. This extra benefit makes leveraged leasing an attractive tax-planning tool and investment.

The sinking fund builds up until the phase at which taxes and debt service exceed rent payments. The sinking fund, together with its earnings, pays this shortfall, or most of it. If the sinking fund falls short, dig into your jeans because you invest the extra (one of your multiple investments). The MISF analysis assumes that you earn a rate of interest, called the *sinking fund rate*, on the sinking fund that you use to pay taxes. The MISF method works like IRR except that it prescribes one rate for your investment in the lessor's cost (the *yield rate*) and another rate for the sinking fund phase (the *sinking fund rate*). The yield rate applies to the period when you have an investment outstanding in the leased property. The sinking fund rate applies when you don't have an investment balance outstanding (but still have to pay taxes and debt service). Usually, the sinking fund rate is a conservative one that represents a short-term investment rate, perhaps 3 to 4 percent. Depending on the pattern of cash flows in your lease, you may experience several different investment/sinking fund phases during the lease term.

Prudent lessors often use a zero sinking fund rate. If you take that approach and then do realize income from the sinking fund, you get some upside at the end of the lease.

Optimization of debt in leveraged leases

When you consider how much money to borrow, you *optimize* the proportion of debt to equity in any leveraged lease. Optimization involves the use of the amounts of debt that balance:

- ✔ Your required book yield (cash received net of debt service, and cash expenses); and
- ✔ Your economic yield (the yield produced by running computer models showing return on investment, which may be driven by noncash benefits such as tax benefits).

An unavoidable tension exists between achieving higher economic yields and higher book yields. Economic yields increase with more debt, while book yields decrease under the burden of that same debt. When combined with the tax constraints discussed in Chapter 13, you should let your computer programs find the right balance between debt and equity to meet your institutional yield and cash flow requirements for each leveraged lease.

Pricing Software — You Should Have It

Lease pricing can perplex even the best financial analysts. Under the tutelage of one very bright Socratic teacher, I attempted to learn how to do many of the calculations discussed in this chapter using a Hewlett-Packer 12c Calculator. To my amazement, I could get close or even, on rare occasion, hit the right answer to the economic problem. Today, with the level of competition and complexity of pricing combined, most lessors aim for a higher decree of precision and structuring than any handheld calculator can achieve.

You can produce many variations of leveraged lease analysis and related information from these programs. Well-designed programs can test all constraints and rules and optimize your pricing.

To help you respond to pricing challenges, here's a list of some, but certainly not all, of the better-known computer programs that can provide the level of lease and loan pricing and analysis that you may need. Their individual capabilities are far greater than my brief analysis of pricing. Use them (if you don't do so already) to help you price your deals. Don't get stuck on one approach as the different programs can help you "sharpen your pencil" and make more money from different structures based on your pricing and institutional restraints.

- ✔ **ABC:** You can use this program to perform pricing and financial modeling/analysis of domestic and international transactions. Contact Warren & Selbert Incorporated, 805-963-0776, www.warren-selbert.com

- ✔ **InfoAnalysis:** You can use this program to price, analyze, and structure leases, automate, track, and compare bids, and prepare a lease versus buy analysis. Contact International Decision Systems, Inc., 612-338-2585, www.decisionsys.com

- ✔ **SuperTRUMP:** You can use SuperTRUMP to perform financial modeling, pricing, reporting, and lease analysis as well as highly structured lease analysis and pricing for domestic and international transactions. Contact Ivory Consulting Corporation, 925-926-1100, www.supertrump.com

- ✔ **TValue:** You can use TValue for disguised or nontax-oriented leases and related pricing. It can calculate amortization schedules for mortgages and loans, yield on investments, present value, future value, interest rates, remaining balances, and down payments. Contact Time Value Software, 949-727-1800, info@timevalue.com

- ✔ **WinLease:** Created by Interet Corporation, you can use this program (often called "Interet") for complex and simple lease analysis, structuring, and pricing. Contact Interet Corporation, 973-912-7400, www.interet.com

Part III
Taking on Documentation and Insurance

The 5th Wave   By Rich Tennant

"We were leasing land to a guy running a truffle farm in France. He skipped out, but I understand we were able to recover some of his assets."

In this part . . .

You may never get a chance to do some real negotiating of a lease unless you do only small or micro-ticket deals. Every lease, without fail, needs proper insurance coverage. You may even lease specialized assets such as high-technology equipment, aircraft, and other transportation equipment like trucks and trailers, railroad rolling stock, and vessels. The chapters in this part show you how specialized assets create a need for unique types of documentation and insurance provisions, which protect lessors and impose responsibilities on lessees.

Chapter 8

Negotiating the Core Terms in Your Lease

In This Chapter

▶ Understanding your lease structure, documentation, and closing process

▶ Negotiating some important rights in your lease

▶ Knowing the meaning and consequences of an event of default

*J*udging from most lease documentation, it's easy to see why people think that lawyers get paid by the word or by the pound of paper they create. Leasing documentation can involve dozens of different documents, thousands of important words and concepts, and, yes, pounds and reams of paper. This chapter cannot discuss such a large subject in any really comprehensive way — as tempting as that may be for me, as a lawyer. However, it can and does cover the some of the most important provisions of a basic, single-investor lease.

As you read through this chapter, you may want to refer to the Master Lease Agreement in the Appendix (the "Lease"). I refer to sections in that lease as "Lease §xx."(The squiggle means "section.") Note that this chapter offers negotiating points and positions for both lessors and lessees that you can really use and may not find elsewhere. For more discussion of provisions of the Lease and how they change for specialized assets, review the lease documentation sections of Chapters 10, 11, and 12.

Documenting Your Deal

As discussed in Chapter 4, you complete the initial proposal stage of a transaction to set the fundamental terms of your deal. Then, the lessor typically prepares and sends her lessee the lessor's appropriate form of lease documentation for the transaction reflecting the terms of the proposal.

The weaker a lessee's creditworthiness, the more likely that a lessor expects the lessee just to sign on the line. In small-ticket deals, lessors often provide lessees with form documents to sign and permit little or no negotiation.

However, in most large-ticket transactions (and even in some smaller transactions), lessees can and often do demand that lessors negotiate the lease documents.

A lease transaction often involves several different documents. To keep track of all the pieces of a leasing puzzle, you can prepare a *closing checklist,* often created from closing conditions in a lease, to list all the documents, actions, and the parties involved in the closing. See Lease §15.

Before a lessee negotiates a lease, the lessee should establish the structure of the deal. This chapter and the Lease use a *master lease structure,* which includes a lease agreement and an attached form of *schedule.* The schedule allows lessees to accept, and lessors to fund, multiple deliveries of leased property over an extended period of time. Each schedule acts like a separate lease. It incorporates the terms of the master lease, and includes the key business terms. Most leases commence upon the delivery to, and the acceptance of the leased property by, the lessee.

For this book, the Lease contains the business options, but a Schedule often includes all or part of the option terms. Review the Schedule to the Lease for terms that typically appear in a schedule of a master lease.

As a lessee, you should ask your lessor to commit to provide lease funding for an extended period of time, such as a year, in a master lease structure, so that you can rely on the lessor's money to run your business. Realistically, however, you can virtually never get absolute commitments from lessors unless you have stellar credit or extraordinary market strength, or both. Consequently, negotiate hard elsewhere in your lease and be ready to accept conditions to funding that you cannot be in default or have any *material adverse change* in your business (a problem that may prevent you from performing your obligations under the lease).

Core Terms in Leases

This section describes some important terms of a tax-oriented single-investor lease for personal property.

The term of your lease and commencement date

The *lease term* for a lessee is the period or periods during which a lessee uses the leased property in exchange for rent. Many leases require a lessee to sign an *acceptance certificate* to commence the lease term and to confirm acceptance of the leased property under the lease. Acceptance means that the leased property operates properly and meets the requirements of the lease). Before lease commencement a lessee must satisfy *conditions precedent* for the lessor, the requirements that you satisfy to get the lessor's money invested in your deal. See Lease §15 for examples of conditions precedent.

Rent payments and lease terms

Lessors can charge rent on any periodic basis such as monthly, quarterly, semiannually, or annually. Most small-ticket and middle-market leases require monthly payments of rent. Leveraged leases and other large ticket leases use all different rent periods. See Lease §§1 and 4.

Some leases charge additional rent called *interim* rent. This rent covers the period from the delivery date of the leased property (that is, the date set forth in the schedule on which a lessee accepts the leased property under the lease) until a convenient starting date (for example, the first day of the next month). The start date is sometimes called the *rent commencement date*. See Lease §1. The period from the rent commencement date until the end of the initial lease term is often called the *base* or *basic term*. The corresponding rent payable during this term is often called *base rent* or *basic rent*. Finally, some leases grant the lessee the option to extend the lease term beyond the basic term. During the so-called *extended* or *renewal term*, the lessee pays another type of rent often called *renewal rent*.

Some leases require you, as the lessee, to pay interim rent equal to a daily portion of the annual basic rent payments based on a 360-day year (annual basic rent divided by 360 days). The interim term also extends the term of your lease (but usually not for long), during which you pay extra rent than you originally anticipated. However, like some lessees, you may want to use an interim term for administrative convenience to bridge the time period from the delivery date until the first or last day of the month as start date of the basic term (and rent payment date).

Although most lessors can invoice lessees for rental payments, the terms of most leases don't allow the lessee to use failure to receive an invoice as an excuse for not paying rent. See Lease §4(d).

You should therefore set up a system to pay rent on time even if you do not receive an invoice. In addition, you should carefully monitor the number of payments in the basic term. It is not uncommon for lessors to continue to bill for, and lessees to continue to pay, rental payments long after the basic term has expired.

Net lease; unconditional obligations

A net lease provision in a lease says that the lessee pays all insurance, mainte-nance, and taxes as if the lessee were the owner of the property. It also con-tains the infamous *hell-or-high-water* clause. This clause imposes on the lessee the obligation to pay rent and perform other obligations under the lease no matter what else happens, even if the leased property breaks or no one ever services it. In other words, the Lessee must perform "without abatement, reduction...recoupment," come hell or high water. See Lease §5 and Chapter 1.

 As a lessee, don't bother trying to negotiate the hell-or-high-water provision with the lessor. From a lessor's perspective, this provision is the most critical component of the lease. It enables the lessor to borrow against or sell your rent payments to manage his business (including cash flow and earnings). Therefore, the obligations that you accept under the lease are absolute and unconditional. If you do not pay rent on time or perform your other obliga-tions, the lessor loses the benefit of its bargain. However, not all is lost. If the lessor violates your rights, you can still sue the lessor for damages.

Lessee's representations, warranties, and covenants

Lessors typically ask lessees to make representations and warranties (statements of facts or of legal status) that:

- Lessees have the power, authority, and organizational approvals neces-sary to sign and perform the lease, and that the lessor can enforce the lease against the lessee.

- All information that the lessee provides, such as a credit application or financial statements, is true and accurate.

- The corporate or other kind of entity acting as the lessee exists and is in good standing (for example, the lessee has no tax liens from her state, or the state has not dissolved the lessee company).

- The lessee has no litigation pending or threatened that may interfere with his obligations or hurt his business in a big way.

A lessor may require a lessee to make continuous promises (called *covenants*) to comply with financial or other agreements in a lease. Leases tend to have few, if any, financial covenants like complex secured loan agree-ments, but some lessors insist upon financial and covenants to help manage their perceived credit risks of your lease.

Lessors generally do not make representations, warranties, or covenants to lessees. For lessors, "money talks." When they pay for the leased property, the money commits them to the deal, and, in their view, representations to a lessee have little value or purpose.

However, as a lessee, you can, and should, get a *covenant of quiet enjoyment* from the lessor (that is, the lessor agrees, that you can quietly enjoy the use and possession of the leased property without the lessor's interference unless an event of default occurs under the lease). You should also ask to qualify or limit your representations and warranties to what you actually know about your business activities and legal status. For any statement that sounds like something your lawyer should say, ask your lawyer to satisfy the lessor's concerns in your lawyer's written legal opinion addressed to the lessor, or in the lawyer to lawyer negotiations. A *legal opinion* is a letter by your lawyer addressed to the lessor, stating formally that, with qualifications and limitations, your lessor can enforce your lease and the related documents against you. It also says, among other things, that you have the power, authority, and approvals to close and perform your obligations under the lease.

Lessor's disclaimer of warranties

This section of a lease could be renamed "don't blame the lessor" because the lessor here says that she takes no responsibility for anything relating to the leased property. See Chapter 16 regarding Article 2A disclaimers of warranties and the limiting effects of "finance lease" on the lessee's rights. A lessor should not, and generally will not, in a tax-oriented (true) lease, as contrasted with a service lease, take responsibility for any malfunction or problem with the leased property.

The net lease requirements combined with the disclaimers of warranties by lessors in a lease means that lessees get recourse for equipment problems only against the supplier and not the lessor. See Lease §7.

As a lessee, you may understandably object to paying your lessor rent for leased property that doesn't work or has service problems, especially if your lessor or a related company sells you on the leased property. Some lessees simply refuse to pay rent and blame the lessor. This plan makes sense — don't pay for what you don't get.

However, save yourself some grief with your lessor. Seek your recourse against the supplier because your failure to pay rent leaves your lessor in a strong position to put you in default under your lease. Then, you can end up not only with operational problems with your leased property, but also with a potential losing and costly conflict. You may even lose possession of the leased property, which won't make your day.

Do you lose in every situation? Perhaps not, because you may prevail in your actions against the lessor if you can show that your lessor acted as the agent or representative of the supplier and/or made promises to you about the leased property.

Understanding this potential problem with lessees, as a lessor, here's a word to the wise: Don't become the agent of the supplier and don't confirm a supplier's warranties to your lessee. Unless you want enter into service leases, act like a finance lessor (see Chapter 16); stay in the money business only; and avoid selling or warranting leased property.

Lease indemnities

Most lessors lease property to end users to maximize their return on investment capital. To prevent unexpected liabilities from undermining these economic returns, lessors transfer most risks to lessees through indemnification provisions of the type described in this section.

General indemnification provisions

The general indemnification provision requires lessees to protect lessors from any cost or other problem regarding the purchase, sale, titling, transfer, leasing, operation, maintenance, storage, subleasing, or return of the leased property. See Lease §8. In effect, lessors make lessees pay any costs not included in the rent regardless of how or when the problem arises (even after the lease expires).

A more specialized category of indemnification relates to environmental risks. These provisions may appear in a separate environmental indemnity agreement that may help a lessor enforce the indemnities apart from other lessee obligations. If a lessor worries that leased property can create environmental liability risks, the lessor generally asks for environmental indemnification covering a broad array of risks. Environmental indemnification requires that the lessee protect the lessor against any loss, damage, claim, or expense, including attorneys fees and expenses, arising from any environmental hazard or material created by or involving the leased property.

As a lessee, you should not indemnify a lessor against problems that the lessor creates (for example, by acting carelessly during an inspection or creating liability to another lessor or lender involved in your deal). Most lessors don't expect you to indemnify them for their own gross negligence or willful misconduct. Otherwise, the lessor needs and deserves protection because you exercise care, custody, and control of the leased property, and can best manage the risks that you or the lessor encounters.

General tax indemnification and payment

Another type of indemnification flows from tax responsibilities arising from tax sale, leasing, possession, ownership, or use of the leased property. As discussed in Chapter 14, lessees in most leases pay state and local property tax, franchise tax, use tax, and other state taxes on the real or personal property that they lease. These provisions require the lessee to cover these costs, and handle any tax dispute in cooperation with the lessor, but at the lessee's expense. See Lease §9.

As the lessee, you should not indemnify a lessor for circumstances under your lessor's control (such as increases in the tax rate or state taxes incurred by a lessor when it transfers its interests in the lease or the leased property to investors), or for actions taken by a lessor after the lease expires. For the most part, you incur obligations in a general tax indemnity similar to those that you would incur if you purchased or owned the leased property. However, in certain jurisdictions, additional taxes arise that specifically apply to leased property, or to lessors. See Chapter 14.

Income tax indemnification

A lessee's rent should be somewhat lower than comparable loan payments because the lessor, in theory, passes through at least some of the lessor's depreciation benefits for buying the leased property, which reduces the rent payments. See Chapter 13. Lessees provide income tax indemnities covering federal and state income taxes of the lessor. The indemnity assures the lessor that she will receive the tax benefits that she assumes in her pricing or a payment from you in lieu of those benefits. See Lease §10. Lessors argue that lessees should pay for any loss of tax benefits regardless of fault (called an *all events* indemnity), but often accept indemnities based on some act or failure of the lessee to act affecting tax benefits (called an *acts and omissions indemnity*).

Tax indemnities can run from less than a page to many pages. They typically include provisions containing representations about tax benefits, tax assumptions, calculations for paying tax indemnities (in a lump sum or over time), contests provisions for dispute resolution with taxing jurisdictions, and appropriate exclusions from lessee liability.

As a lessee, you should try to negotiate several *exclusions* to tax indemnity provisions (exceptions to your liability) for the following reasons, among others, especially if you can not limit your indemnities to consequences of your acts or omissions (that is, you indemnify in all events):

✔ Acts, events, or circumstances relating to the lease and/or the leased property that occur after the end of the lease term, or as a result of the lessor's duties, negligence, or willful misconduct

✔ Insufficient tax liability on the lessor's part for him to use the anticipated tax benefits of your transaction, or a failure of the lessor to claim his tax benefits in a timely manner

✔ Any structural problem that exists with the lease (for example, if the lease does not constitute a "true lease" or violates Section 467 of the Internal Revenue Code, as discussed in Chapter 13)

Use and maintenance of leased property

Net leases require lessees to maintain their leased property as if they own it except that the lessees cannot make significant alterations or *non-severable improvements* without the lessor's prior written consent. Non-severable improvements are additions to leased property that can't be removed without damaging the leased property. See Lease §11.

As a lessee, you may have to meet higher or different standards of maintenance than you adopt for your own property. Lessors, who count on residual value as a meaningful part of their return, may impose rigorous maintenance standards on you. If the property that you lease requires significant maintenance, ask experts in the type of property to help you negotiate theses provisions and the *return* provisions as discussed later in this chapter under "Return of leased property" to avoid burdensome costs or unrealistic maintenance standards. See Lease §19.

Title to and location of leased property

Because lessees do not own the leased property, a provision often appears in leases that requires that they label the property as being owned by the lessor. Most leases also provide that lessees cannot relocate the leased property to a new state (or even a county in the case of fixtures) without lessor's prior written consent. See Lease §12.

Lessors periodically need to inspect the property that they lease and confirm that the property exists. Lessors really hate it if the property they own and lease doesn't exist or someone else claims an interest in the property. Generally, you can get the lessor to agree to permit you to move the leased property if you provide to the lessor advance notice of your intent to do so, and, perhaps, complete some documents that at least maintain all of the lessor's rights.

Risk of loss and insurance coverage

Chapters 9 through 12 discuss insurance provisions that illustrate how a lessee protects himself and his lessor from losses due to property damage and liability risks. Leases shift the risk of loss to lessees starting from the delivery of the leased property. Lessees remain liable for loss or damage to property during the lease term. Insurance coverage mitigates this economic risk. Lessors generally receive proceeds of total losses of leased property as measured by the stipulated loss value plus other outstanding obligations payable by the lessee under the lease. If a lessee is not in default, a lessor usually allows the lessee to obtain part or all of the proceeds of partial losses to make repairs. See Lease §§13 and 14.

As a lessee, you can negotiate the deductibles, types, insurance carrier, and amounts of insurance coverage. See Chapter 9 to understand how insurance helps you and the lessor from economic disasters.

Options during and at the end of the lease term

A lease typically provides options that provide lessees with flexibility to terminate or extend the lease term. Section 16(a)(i) to (iv) of the Lease, respectively, illustrate the following options:

✔ Terminate the lease before the end of the basic term

✔ Buy out the leased property before the end of the term

✔ Renew the lease at fair market rent or at a fixed rent

✔ Purchase the leased property at the end of the lease (or a renewal term) at fair market value or at a fixed price

Each of these options involves notice periods and payments. As a lessee, options can provide you with an opportunity to manage the cost of your leased property by setting specific purchase and renewal option prices. You can also control the timing of buying your leased property or terminating your lease by setting dates at which you can exercise options. Consider the costs of your options discussed in Chapter 6 and maximize your flexibility regarding your use and potential ownership of leased property. However, don't expect your lessor to give you every option. Many lessors really want you to buy the property at fair market value or to lease it at fair rental value to maximize their residual upside and/or to avoid your return of the leased property.

Right of first refusal and upgrades

Most lessors want to increase their volume of business with good lessees. What better way exists than to force lessees to give them the first shot at financing upgrades and improvements to the leased property? See Lease §17. Lessors want to finance upgrades for a good legal and practical reason, too: It avoids conflicts with other lessors over who owns what part of the leased property at the end of the lease term.

As a lessee, you should resist giving your lessor the right of first refusal because few other lessors will even make offers to lease to you if they know that their deal will be reviewed and perhaps replaced by an existing, competing lessor. You can protect your interests better if you give the lessor a limited time to make you the first offer to complete a financing. If you like the offer, you close; if not, you can freely elect any other deal within prescribed parameters and time periods.

Sublease and assignment

Lessors often limit subleasing by lessees to deals that the lessors approve. See Lease §18 and Chapter 1. Lessors also frequently prohibit transfers or assignments by lessees, although some mergers may be permitted. If a lessee needs to find a replacement lessee, the lessee looks for a replacement with equal or better credit than her own. Then, the lessee can make a reasonable request that the lessor allow her to assign the lease to the replacement lessee because the lessor faces the same or less risk. The lessee may also ask the lessor to release her from all obligations starting on the date of the sublease and assignment.

As a lessee, don't be surprised if the lessor refuses. The lessor may prefer to keep your deal active and enter into a different lease with your successor lessee. That approach builds leasing volume for the lessor even though you found the deal for the lessor.

By contrast, lessors retain the right to transfer or assign their interests freely, especially for sales of interests in a lease to other lessors or taking loans against rents from lenders. This kind of provision anticipates that if the lessor transfers all or a part of his interests, that the lessee will not make any claims against the new lessor that he had against the original lessor. In other words, the lessee's hell-or-high-water obligation extends to the lessor's transferees.

If your lessor wants to assign or transfer her rights under your lease, you should limit any liability that you may have to the new lessor to no more than the liability and indemnities that you gave to the transferring lessor. Watch out for requests from the new lessor or the lessor's lender for more terms that may impose more responsibility or liability on you.

For your part, you may anticipate some downtime in using your leased property. It may even become unnecessary for your operations. In this situation, your lessor may negotiate the right to sublease the leased property to qualified sublessees on lessor's "reasonable" consent or by standards set by your lessor. You likely will remain liable under your lease, so pick a good, creditworthy sublessee.

As to transfers by the lessor, as the lessee you can ask that, without your consent, your lessor will not transfer to a less creditworthy party or a direct competitor (who may value access to your secrets or lease).

Unfortunately, you can expect your lessor to resist such restrictions because your request limits the lessor's ability to freely transfer one of his financial assets — your lease. As an alternative, you can ask that your lessor always retains an interest in your deal and that you work only with the lessor. You can justify such a request because you chose the original lessor to lease to you — so why should that lessor transfer your leased property to a stranger with which you may choose (or have chosen) not to do business.

Return of leased property

When a lease expires or terminates, a lessee must "crate and freight" the leased property to the lessor. See Lease §19. Lessors often require that lessees return the leased property in proper condition to designated locations, and store the property there for a period of time at the lessee's expense. In many leases, lessees may incur significant costs to comply with the *return conditions*. Return conditions refer to physical maintenance, repair, and restoration of the leased property to specified standards before the lessee returns it to the lessor. The general standard requires that you return the leased property to the lessor in its original condition "normal wear and tear excepted." See Chapters 11 and 12 for a discussion of return conditions, for example, for aircraft, trucks, and railroad rolling stock.

As a lessee with responsibility to return leased property, negotiate for a return to a location within the same state or within a short mileage from your location of use, such as 250 to 750 miles away. Further, you should try to agree to pay for only a short storage period at your cost (for example, 30 to 60 days). Lessors may ask you for up to a year of free storage for some types of property (such as large immobile equipment). This time defrays a lessor's storage costs and facilitates remarketing to potential buyers or lessees who can inspect the property at your storage location. Your lessor also knows that if you have to incur expensive transportation and storage, you might buy the property to avoid the hassle. Unfortunately, you may then have to resell the property at a loss or with great effort. On the other hand, you may get the last profit (or laugh) in the deal if you sell the property at a price greater than you pay the lessor.

Events of default and remedies

If a lessee fails to comply with the lease, she commits a *default*. See Lease §§20 and 21. A default refers to a breach or violation of the lease, such as failing to pay rent when due. A default can immediately constitute an *Event of Default*, or a default can mature after a passage of time or occurrence of certain events into an Event of Default. An Event of Default provides a lessor the basis for exercising its remedies against her lessee.

As a lessee, once you default (or an Event of Default exists), all bets are off. *Don't* expect any sympathy from your lessor. *Do* expect to pay interest on late payments at a typical rate of 18 percent per year of the unpaid amount. You can occasionally negotiate these rates down, but lessors want rates that sting you. See Lease §4. *Do* expect your lessor to try to recover his property if you don't pay up quickly. *Do* expect to pay all of your lessor's expenses incurred after a default.

Remedies refer to the legal methods of recovering the possession of the leased property, and all amounts that a lessee owes under the lease. The lessor negotiates remedies in your lease terms and/or gets some extra help from applicable laws such as those set forth in Article 2A and Article 9 of the UCC. See Chapters 16 and 17. The remedies include potentially very significant money damages (payments) on top of surrendering the leased property, and interest for late payments.

You can sometimes negotiate *cure periods* (a fix it period) before an Event of Default occurs (which enables your lessor to start exercising remedies). For example, you can ask for three- to ten-day's *grace periods* (a breather) on rent due dates, and 30 days to cure covenant violations.

Most lessors do *not* give you time to cure breaches of your representations and warranties, or to reinstate canceled insurance. An insurance lapse puts your lessor's entire investment at risk. Once you breach a representation or warranty, you can't just say "oops" and take it back. The error sticks. Your lessor should not, in any event, have the right to put you in default for breaches of the small stuff (such as failing to send notices on time or other violations that have little or no impact on your key obligations like paying rent and insuring your leased property).

Chapter 9

Insuring Leased Property

*T*his chapter helps you appreciate what insurance can do for you. It also enables you to understand and evaluate whether the insurance coverage that you, as a lessee, maintain, or you, as the lessor, receive or buy, during a lease term adequately and properly covers your respective risks of loss and liability.

Insurance Basics: What It Is and Isn't

Insurance is a contract between one person or entity (the *insured*) and one or more insurance companies (the *insurer*). In an insurance contract, the insurer, for consideration (*insurance premiums*), agrees to reimburse you, as a lessee or a lessor, for the damage sustained to your property caused by an unexpected *peril* (such as fire or theft). Insurers also agree to pay a third person on your behalf certain amounts for which you become liable. In short, insurers accept and pay for risks of loss or liability to persons, properties, or businesses in consideration of your payment of insurance premiums. Otherwise, you would have to pay these losses and liabilities out of your pocket. Insurers have a duty not only to *indemnify* you (pay for losses covered by your policy), but also to defend you (hire lawyers who protect your interests when a claim arises).

Your insurance agreements include: *terms* (insuring agreements), *conditions* (duties that you owe to the insurance company in the event of a claim), *declarations* (underwriting information about the insured), *exclusions* (risks not covered), and *limitations* (limits on the amount of insurance provided as well as the scope of coverage) under which an insurance carrier agrees to assume the risks that you transfer to it.

Insurance of the type discussed in this chapter is not a financial guaranty of debt or of profit (lessor's or lessee's). A guaranty of payment requires the guarantor (a *surety*) to accept a secondary responsibility for the person or entity, such as a lessee, with the primary obligations. For example, a lease guarantor pays the rent if a lessee fails to do so. Insurance typically does not pay the rent. Insurance may pay the stipulated loss value, but, in general, only as a result of a total property loss.

Even though insurers have a duty to indemnify you, insurance is not an indemnity like you typically see in the lease provisions. Contrast Section 8 of the form of Master Lease Agreement in the Appendix and the related discussion in Chapter 8. An indemnity covers a broad range of risks and requires a payment by the lessee to the lessor or a third party for the benefit of the lessor (or lender in leveraged leases) with exceptions. The insurance policy is generally narrow in scope. It doesn't extend to every liability or risk arising out of the lease like a general indemnity provision in a lease. It responds to specific risks of loss and liability.

A *hold harmless* provision in a lease transfers risk to a lessee from a lessor. A hold harmless clause requires a lessee to keep a lessor out of harm's way financially and operationally with regard to the lease transaction and the leased property. In a similar manner, a lessee transfers risk to an insurer, except an insurer assumes and pays only for specific risks. In a general indemnity clause in a lease, the lessee pays for almost all non-investment risks of the lessor. For example, a hold harmless clause will require a lessee to pay any cost asserted by a third party resulting from the repair or maintenance of leased property. Insurance does not provide that protection.

You can and should expect your insurance to fall short of covering every risk of liability, loss, or expense that you face as a lessee or a lessor under your leases. Ask your insurance or risk management professionals to explain the scope of insurance so that you accurately assess the risk in your deals. See Chapter 3 on risks in leasing.

The Anatomy of a Lease Insurance Provision

As a lessee or a lessor, you can buy insurance for many types of risks. I primarily discuss property and liability insurance and related provisions in this section.

The insurance provision discussed in this section expands upon a short form of lease provision in the Master Lease Agreement in the Appendix (which is Section 13 there), and contains some specific elements that, as the lessor, you should include in your leases (negotiations permitting). Note in Section

13(a)(iii) of this insurance provision that the lessor leaves some room to add coverages that it did not require explicitly. As a lessor becomes more accustomed to a lessee's business or as coverage in the marketplace changes, a lessor may require additional or different protection for risks that it did not initially expect or fully appreciate.

As a lessee, you may want to delete or limit Section 13(a)(iii) that allows the lessor to require additional insurance. Because additional insurance costs you more money, this provision gives the lessor a blank check on your insurance account. On one hand, you can expect your lessor to resist, but, on the other, you can take some comfort that most lessors adapt their requirements to insurance available to you that you have evaluated and purchased for your business.

Almost every lease makes the failure to maintain insurance an immediate default. Lessors rarely allow lessees time to cure a default resulting from insurance terminating or lapsing. As a lessee, you must, for your own benefit (that is, your cash flow, budget, and business operations), make sure that insurance continues in full force and effect at all times and that you comply with your lessor's requests for coverage.

To show you how this sample provision works, consider the following illustration. Say that you, as lessee, enter into a true lease with the lessor. The lease finances 20 new tractor trailers with an invoice price of $100,000 each, for an aggregate lessor's cost of $2,000,000, and chemical processing equipment including a customized boiler and control equipment for an additional $8,000,000. The total lessor's cost equals $10,000,000. The lessor owns the equipment under a true lease. See Chapter 13 regarding true leases.

This insurance provision corresponds with, and can be dropped into, the Master Lease Agreement in the Appendix (called the "Lease") or in any similar lease (adjusted for the terms of that lease). To give some context for terms used in this provision, acceptance of the "Property" occurs on the execution and delivery of a "Schedule." The date of the Schedule and acceptance of the Property is called the "Delivery Date." See Chapter 1 for an explanation of a master lease structure. You negotiate the insurance coverage amounts set forth in square brackets.

As the lessee, you start with the basic premise that, under Section 13(a) of the Lease, a lessor requires you to obtain and maintain insurance throughout the lease term in form and substance satisfactory to the lessor. You presumably have instituted your own insurance coverage before the lessor ever appears on the scene. You expect your decisions on risk to prevail; after all, who knows your business better than you do?

Ask yourself, What does this insurance provision mean? Does it change my coverage? How do I respond to the lessor' requirements? What will this cost me?

Here is the sample insurance provision (called "Section 13 of the Lease"):

13. INSURANCE: (a) Lessee shall obtain and maintain for the Term, at its own expense, in form and substance reasonably satisfactory to Lessor: (i) "all risk" insurance against loss or damage to the Property, including automobile and boiler and machinery insurance; (ii) commercial general liability insurance, including contractual liability, products liability and completed operations, pollution liability and automobile insurance coverage; and (iii) such other insurance against such other risks of loss and with such terms as Lessor reasonably requires, including business interruption insurance with a waiting period of 60 days or less.

(b) The amount of the "all risk" insurance shall be the greater of the replacement value of the Property (as new) or the "Stipulated Loss Value" specified in the applicable Schedules, which amount shall be reasonably determined by Lessor as of each anniversary date of this Lease with the amount so determined being put into effect on the next succeeding renewal or inception date of such insurance.

(c) The deductible with respect to "all-risk" insurance required by clause (b) above and product liability insurance required by clause (a) above shall not exceed [$50,000 and $100,000, respectively]; otherwise there shall be no deductible with respect to any insurance required to be maintained hereunder.

(d) Each "all risk" policy shall: (i) name Lessor as the sole loss payee with respect to the Property, (ii) provide for each insurer's waiver of its right of subrogation against Lessor and Lessee, and (iii) provide that such insurance (A) shall not be invalidated by any action of Lessee, or any breach by Lessee of any provision of any of its insurance policies, and (B) shall waive set-off, counterclaim or offset against Lessor.

(e) The amount of commercial general liability insurance (other than products liability coverage and completed operations insurance) required by clause (a) above shall be at least [$10,000,000] per occurrence and automobile liability insurance shall be at least [$2,000,000] per occurrence. The amount of the products liability and completed operations insurance required by clause (a) above shall be at least [$5,000,000] per occurrence.

(f) Each liability policy shall (i) name Lessor as an additional insured and (ii) provide that such insurance shall have cross-liability and severability of interest endorsements (which shall not increase the aggregate policy limits of Lessee's insurance).

(g) All insurance policies shall: (i) provide that Lessee's insurance shall be primary without a right of contribution of Lessor's insurance, if any, or any obligation on the part of Lessor to pay premiums of Lessee; (ii) contain a clause requiring the insurer to give Lessor at least 30 days' prior written notice of its cancellation other than cancellation for non-payment for which 10 days' notice shall be sufficient; and (iii) be issued by insurers with a rating in Best's Insurance Reports of not less than A–FSC VIII (or an equivalent rating acceptable to Lessor if such insurers have not been rated in such reports).

(h) Lessee shall on or prior to the Delivery Date of each Schedule and prior to each policy renewal, furnish to Lessor certificates of insurance or other evidence satisfactory to Lessor that such insurance coverage is in effect, including property endorsements on the insurance policies of Lessee and an opinion of Lessee's broker, in form and substance satisfactory to Lessor, to the effect that the insurance coverage required by this section is in full force and effect and that all premiums due as of the date of such schedule have been paid in full.

The following sections explain the types of insurance coverage set forth in the preceding provision. Such coverage typifies most leases of personal property.

Physical damage insurance

Physical damage insurance protects property from damage (or *partial losses*) or destruction (a *total loss*). A loss can occur, for insurance purposes, as a result of a total actual loss (for example, a leased boiler blows up) or a *constructive total loss*. A constructive total loss occurs (and is often used with marine assets) when leased property suffers such extensive damage that the cost to repair it exceeds the value of the leased property after it is repaired.

All-risk coverage in general

Physical damage insurance can extend to *named perils* such as fire or floods or to *all risks* as required by Section 13(a)(i) of the Lease. Named perils coverage refers to the cause of a loss against insured property such as fire, flood, windstorm, earthquake, theft, and explosion.

In lieu of listing the perils covered, an all-risk policy covers losses arising from any cause except those specifically excluded. The excluded perils may be losses from flood or earthquake. If so, special amendments (*endorsements*) and additional premiums may be required to buy these coverages back from the insurer.

Because the chemical processing equipment in the illustrative lease involves real estate, the all-risk coverage creates the broadest coverage for a lessor both with respect to the personal and real property. In addition, boiler and machinery insurance, required by Section 13(a) of the Lease, protects from losses of boilers and pressure vessels or mechanical breakdown (for example, chemical processing equipment under a lease) and automobile damage (such as wrecks of the tractor-trailers on the roadways).

If you have several policies covering named perils, you may be able to buy a policy called a *difference in conditions policy,* which closes the gaps with coverage for the differences between an all-risk policy and your several named perils policies.

As a lessor you should have your own coverage. If for any reason your lessee's coverage fails or is inadequate, you should have contingent all risk coverage to pay for your exposure on such a failure or inadequacy.

Amount of all-risk coverage

Section 13(b) of the Lease establishes the amount of required all-risk coverage at the higher of the Stipulated Loss Value (an agreed value set forth in the lease that declines over the term) or the replacement value (as new). The reference to "as new" makes clear that the insurance for a similar item of used property in similar condition before a loss does not suffice. Only new property (or an equivalent cash payment) serves to replace the destroyed property.

As the lessee, you may object to a replacement of used property with property that is new. If the replacement occurs after leased property has depreciated and lost value, the replacement can occur with property of like value, utility, useful life and remaining useful life. If new, the lessor has a windfall from the increased value of leased property on the fortuitous occurrence of an insurable loss. For example, if a tractor-trailer burns up in a fire when it is 3 years old and worth $40,000, the lessor has a windfall if you have to replace it as new with a $100,000 tractor-trailer. You, as lessee, may also want the option to request that each insurance valuation of the leased property be made jointly by agreement or by appraisal. In any event, you should not raise insurance levels higher than the stipulated loss value (that protects your lessor's investment) without good reasons. This concern usually applies to property that appreciates or holds value such as aircraft and rail equipment.

Other methods on which insurers may calculate the value of losses include:

- ✔ *Actual cash value* (the value that reflects the depreciation as of the date of loss). If a tractor-trailer depreciates 20 percent per year over five years and suffers a total loss at the end of year three, it has depreciated 60 percent, and the value payable equals $40,000 ($100,000 x 3 years depreciation at 20 percent/ year = 60 percent x $100,000 = $60,000); $100,000 – $60,000 = $40,000 insurance payment

- ✔ *Replacement cost* (the cost in the market place for a similar tractor-trailer as of the date of the loss). If a $100,000 tractor-trailer increases in cost by 15 percent from the start of the lease until it suffers a total loss at the end of year three, the insurance should pay approximately $115,000 to replace the lost equipment.

> ✔ *Fair market value* (the value of property determined at arms-length as the amount a willing buyer would pay a willing seller for the tractor-trailer before the loss). If such fair market value of the $100,000 tractor-trailer decreases by 35 percent when it suffers a total loss at the end of year three, the insurance should pay approximately $65,000 as a result of the loss of the equipment ($100,000 x 0.35 = $65,000).

Stipulated loss value is the value that a lessor must recover to achieve its expected economic or book return on its investment in the leased property as of the date of the loss. Stipulated loss value therefore sets the minimum amount of insurance. For example, if a tractor-trailer with an original price of $100,000 blows up at the fourth month of a true lease when the stipulated loss value equals $102,750, the insurance should always be sufficient to pay $102,750 at that date of loss, even though the fair market value at that time equals $91,000).

Deductibles or self-insurance

Section 13(c) of the Lease establishes a maximum deductible at $50,000. Most physical damage insurance includes a deductible. A *deductible* refers to an amount that a lessee (or a lessor) pays for damage to or loss of leased property by agreement with the insurer that only pays for its share of the same loss. For example, if one of the leased tractor-trailers suffers $5,000 damage in a wreck under a policy with a $1,000 deductible, the lessee pays the first $1,000 damage. The insurance company pays the balance of $4,000.

In property insurance coverage, as a general rule, the higher the deductible an insured accepts, the lower the premiums the insured pays. A deductible can allow you, the lessee or the lessor, to control your costs. Before increasing your deductible, you should have adequate reserves for whatever deductible that you may incur as a result of the loss. For lessors, you depend on the lessee's coverage to protect you also before your policy responds a loss, which should reduce your premiums. See the section "Lessee's insurance as primary coverage," later in this chapter.

Loss payable clause

As the lessee, you can expect your lessor to ask your insurer to name the lessor as the sole loss payee in a loss payable clause, as required in Section 13(d)(i) of the Lease. The sole loss payee in theory means that the insurer issues a damage check directly and only to the lessor. However, insurers that allow you (as the lessee) to use the term sole loss payee in your lease usually make the check payable both to you and the lessor. The insurer avoids a fight regarding who gets the cash but honors the obligation, by paying the lessor the appropriate loss amount (in insurance lingo, as the interests of the lessor may appear) together with its named insured, the lessee. The named insured pays for and owns the policy in its name. The loss payee simply receives the proceeds of the policy when appropriate. Most lessors therefore accept insurance payable to the lessor "as a loss payee as its interests may appear."

Waiver of subrogation

When the insurer of the lessee waives its rights of subrogation, it agrees that it cannot step into your shoes, as the lessee, to sue the lessor or lenders to recover insurance payments made by the insurer to the lessor or lender. The right of *subrogation* allows an insurer to use the rights of its insured to seek indemnification from third parties whose wrongdoing has caused a loss for which the insurer is bound to pay insurance proceeds. A *waiver of subrogation* short-circuits this process because the insurer gives up the right to recover the insurance proceeds from the lessor and lender, which obviously lets these guys sleep at night.

Breach of warranty

Insurers should provide breach of warranty protection as illustrated in Section 13(d)(iii)(A) of the Lease. Although sometimes resisted by insurers, this coverage maintains protection for lessors and lenders even if the lessee (policyholder) breaches a condition or requirement in the policy. For example, to maintain coverage, a policy could require regular inspections of sprinkler systems. Even if lessee never inspects his sprinklers, lessors and lender should have protection in the event of a fire.

Waiver of set off and counterclaim

Section 13(d)(iii)(B) of the Lease provides for an insurer to waive any right of set off or counterclaim. This provision bars the insurer from using any payment obligation of its policyholder to reduce any payment under the insurance policy to a lessor or lender.

Liability insurance

Liability insurance (also called *casualty insurance*) protects lessors and lessees against certain claims of third parties. Such coverage can make payments for lessors to third parties that, if not insured, could more than spoil a lessor's investment return. For lessees, liability insurance not only mitigates the risk of out-of-pocket payments to third parties, but also can absorb the cost of painful and burdensome legal proceedings that can impair business operations and dominate management time.

Liability insurance provides protection for the lessor and lessee (and, in leveraged leases, the lender and indenture and owner trustees) for claims by third parties arising from bodily injury and property damage caused by negligence of the insured parties. See Chapter 5 for a description of the parties.

As an owner of leased property, a lessor can face liability in various ways such as the negligence by her lessee. Liability can also occur without fault under theories of strict liability.

As a lessor, you should consult your insurance brokers and lawyers if you lease complex property that can be defective or inherently dangerous so that you can assure that you receive adequate and proper insurance coverage.

Section 13(a)(ii) of the Lease requires that the lessee maintain commercial general liability insurance, including contractual liability insurance, products liability, completed operations insurance, pollution liability insurance, and automobile insurance. Pollution liability insurance generally requires the purchase of a separate policy (and premium). These coverages may be described as follows:

- **Contractual liability insurance** refers to coverage for liabilities that you, as a lessee, may assume via certain contracts to which you are a party, such as a lease. In that case, as a lessee, you assume the responsibility for liability losses to third parties that would otherwise be borne by the owner-lessor of the leased property. In addition to leases, insurance can cover several other contractual assumptions of liability of this type. You can find most of these liabilities in the general indemnity provisions of a lease (or other lease or financing documents). In essence, this insurance responds to (pays) losses for a covered liability under the indemnity or other liability generating provisions of a contract.

- **Automobile liability insurance** provides protection against liability imposed on any insured for bodily injury or property damage to others arising out of a use of a vehicle such as the tractor-trailer or a company car. Automobile insurance typically has two limits of liability: a limit of liability to any one person and another limit for any single accident. By contrast, property damage under automobile insurance has one limit or total amount that the insurance covers.

- **Products liability insurance** covers liability for damages caused by accidents that arise out of goods manufactured or sold or otherwise controlled or distributed by any person including a lessee. Typically, the accident must occur after the seller of the goods delivers them to a buyer. For a lessee, such protection helps, for example, if the chemicals produced by the leased property create a defective product that injures another person. The lessee's product liability coverage may pay for the loss suffered by that person.

- **Completed operations coverage** insures losses for bodily injury or property damage resulting from faults in work completed or abandoned by the insured (lessee) if the losses occur away from the premises owned, leased, or controlled by the insured. Contrast this coverage with premises and operations insurance that covers losses that take place while the work is being performed. For example, say that boiler repair guy fixes a gas-fired boiler built as part of a chemical plant leased by a lessee. After completion of the work, a nearby pipe connected to the boiler ruptures as a result of the repairs and hurts some plant visitors. Completed operations insurance covers for these damages. However, completed operations coverage does not insure against defects in goods or products manufactured, sold, handled, or distributed by the insured (which is the function of product liability insurance) or incidents involving premises and operations.

✔ **Pollution liability insurance** covers sudden and accidental discharges of pollutants that may, for example, occur if the chemical manufacturing property leased by a lessee suddenly and unexpectedly cracks and leaks a hazardous chemical at the lessee's plant. However, this coverage remains controversial and requires close consideration by knowledgeable brokers and underwriters so that lessees and lessors know what benefit you derive from the coverage.

Claims made versus occurrence coverage

Insurers issue two types of liability policies: claims-made insurance and occurrence-based policies. The less common type, *claims-made* policies, covers damage to third persons and injury to their property if and only if the damage or injury occurs and the claim is made and reported to the insurer during the effective period of the policy (called the *policy period*). Many policies remain in effect for a term of only one-year. You may have to buy claims-made insurance, for example, for hazardous products and pollution liability insurance coverages. An insured (like a lessee) may also purchase an optional extended reporting period called the *tail*. By purchasing the tail, the lessee has extra time to report losses that took place during the policy period but may not have been known until after the expiration of the policy period. The insured pays an additional premium for this coverage.

To emphasize a point: no tail, no coverage after the end of the policy period. Buy the tail coverage if you can for at least year if not two.

Occurrence coverage protects the named and additional insureds against covered losses that take place during the policy period. Unlike the claims-made form, the only reporting requirement with the occurrence form is that the insured (lessee) notify the insurer (or the agent) as soon as possible of the claim. When you put occurrence insurance in place today, the insurance responds to losses reported at any later time, even though the policy has expired. Section 13(e) of the Lease requires liability coverage on an occurrence basis.

You should try to acquire occurrence-based insurance, which is the usual and preferable coverage for lessees and lessors. Just because you have occurrence-based insurance does not mean that the insurance pays for a claim. A claimant must still prove a claim in accordance with substantive legal requirements and within the applicable *statutes of limitations* (which sets time periods during which claimants can assert claims). The insured must also meet insurance policy requirements.

Amount of liability coverage

Section 13(e) of the Lease requires coverage for liability in an amount of at least $10,000,000. Opinions differ with respect to how much coverage a lessee should carry on various leased properties. On a chemical plant, with potential for personal injury or product liability, for example, higher limits may be appropriate. Insurance brokers, risk manager, and industry practice can help you determine which coverage levels suffice.

Most insurance policies provide limits of liability for each occurrence. An *occurrence* refers to an accident or series of incidents occurring over a period of time that together result in personal injury or property damage. A fire or a broken water pipe at the chemical plant, for example, causing property damage to a neighboring property each constitutes an occurrence to which liability insurance responds.

In addition, insurers write commercial general liability insurance with an aggregate annual limit of liability. An *aggregate annual limit* refers to the total amount of losses for all occurrences in any policy period for which insurance may be paid. For example, say that a lessee has a $25,000,000 aggregate annual limit on products liability insurance with no deductible and that the lessee has a bad year with his chemical plant. On January 15, 2002, and July 2, 2002, the lessee and the lessor are sued for defective chemicals products manufactured at the chemical plant and lose on judgments of $26,000,000 and $21,000,000. The insurance pays $25,000,000 for the first claim, and the lessee pays the remaining $1,000,000, for a total of $26,000,000. Unfortunately, the lessee pays the second judgment of $21,000,000 entirely out of his pocket because it exceeded the per aggregate annual limit of $25,000,000 (after the first $26,000,000 judgment consumed its aggregate coverage limit for the year).

Commercial general liability insurance is usually written with two aggregate limits. One applies to product liability losses and the other (known as the *general aggregate*) applies to all other covered liability claims.

As a lessee, consider purchasing limits of liability in excess of the amounts required by your lease contract. To the extent economically feasible you should do so in order to avert high-award losses like the one described in the preceding example. If you, as lessee, purchased $25,000,000 of occurrence-based coverage with an aggregate limit of $75,000,000, you would have paid nothing other than deductibles, if any, applicable to that coverage, in the preceding cases.

Insurers can provide an initial amount of coverage called *primary insurance* and a second layer of insurance coverage providing insurance against specified risks in excess of the primary insurance, called *umbrella* or *excess insurance.* For example, say that, as the lessee with the chemical plant, you (being the prudent type) recognize the need for $75,000,000 of coverage. You can arrange a first level of coverage that responds first to claims in the amount of $10,000,000. Then you can usually purchase excess coverage in an amount of $65,000,000 (in excess of $10,000,000) for a total coverage of $75,000,000.

Check prices because the excess coverage should cost you less than a primary coverage of $75,000,000, but watch the terms on the excess.

Deductibles

Like property or physical damage coverage, a lessee may have a deductible with respect to liability insurance. Although less common than in physical damage policies, a lessor can permit deductibles of up to fairly high limits (for example, up to $2,000,000), depending on the quality of a lessee's creditworthiness. Section 13(c) of the Lease explicitly states that a lessee may have no deductible with respect to any coverage except property damage and product liability insurance. Lessors can negotiate this provision, like most others.

Named insured versus additional insured designations

Who is the *named insured* and who is the *additional insured* on the liability insurance policy? Watch these designations closely because they imply different rights and obligations. The lessee (for purposes of the Lease) is the named insured and must, as such, arrange and pay for all insurance coverage, renew policies, and interact with the insurers. The insurers issue the policy in the name of the lessee as the named insured.

As required by Section 13(f)(i) of the Lease, the liability policies should designate each of the other parties in a lease transaction such as the lessor (and in leveraged leases, the lenders and the indenture and owner trustees) as additional insureds. Additional insureds receive liability insurance (including legal defense protection) under the insurance contract arranged, evidenced, and paid for by the lessee as the named insured. However, the lessee pays for the coverage; the additional insureds don't.

Cross-liability and severability of interests endorsements

Section 13(f)(ii) of the Lease requires the lessee to obtain cross-liability and severability of interests endorsements. *Cross-liability endorsements* provide insurance against liability arising by and between the additional and/or the named insureds. A severability of interests endorsement treats the lessee's insurance policies that cover all those insured as separate insurance policies for each insured (as if each has his own policy). However, the limits of coverage stick as stated in the policy (for example, $10,000,000).

Other Insurance Coverage Requirements

Certain requirements of insurance regarding leases and leased property apply both to property and liability coverage. This section shows you how lessees must anticipate that their coverage stands up for losses before any insurance of lessors. It also indicates that lessees must prove that they have coverage in place with the help of their brokers in many cases.

Lessee's insurance as primary coverage

Section 13(g)(i) of the Lease requires that the lessee's policy be primary without right of contribution from the lessor. A lessor may (and probably does) carry her own separate contingent insurance coverage. This coverage is designed to respond on an excess basis for the lessor (that is, pay amounts not paid by the lessee's policy) as well as in the event of a lapse of the lessees coverage.

Without this requirement, a conflict between the insurance policies of the lessee and the lessor can arise. The lessee's insurers want the lessor's insurers to pay first for the lessor's losses. The lessor's insurers want to pay the lessor's losses only when the lessee coverage runs out. To avoid this conflict, the lessee acquires an endorsement on her policy stating that her coverage is primary. The lessee's coverage, whether liability, property, or other, responds first to any loss, damage, or injury without any demand against the lessor's coverage. The lessor's coverage responds independently and secondarily. Further, the lessor requires that the lessee pay all insurance premiums in Section 13(a) of the Lease without contribution (that is, a lessor does not chip in for the lessee's premiums even though the lessor is covered by the lessee's insurance). The lessor has no intention or economic incentive (absent a lessee default) to pay any part of the lessee's insurance, and this provision assures the lessor that she does not have to do so.

Notice of change or cancellation

Section 13(g)(ii) of the Lease requires that the insurers must give the lessor written 30-days notice of a cancellation or material change of insurance coverage. This time period allows the lessor time to make adjustments with the lessee or note changes for his records. A shorter ten-day period often applies to cancellation for nonpayment of premiums. During that ten-day period, lessors may, but do not have to, pay a missed premium to avoid a lapse in coverage.

Some brokers on their evidence of insurance certificate say that they will "endeavor to give notice" or similar words. The "endeavor to" language should be deleted so that notice must be given to the additional insureds and loss payees who depend on the protection afforded by insurance.

Quality of insurers

Section 13(g)(iii) of the Lease requires that insurance companies should have a rating by Best's Insurance Reports of at least A–FSC VIII. The letter A relates to A.M. Best's Financial Strength Rating. A "Secure Rating" applies when an insurance company rates A++ and A+ (Superior), A and A- (Excellent) and B++ and B+ (Very Good). Under B- means "Vulnerable Ratings." These ratings may be qualified or modified by A.M. Best.

The *FSC* designation means Financial Size Category and reflects the size of insurance companies based on capital, surplus, and conditional reserve funds, in millions in U.S. dollars. The range extends from FSC I of less than $1,000,000 to FSC XV of greater than $2 billion. I have selected FSC VIII for the sample Lease provision designating insurance companies with a size ranging from $100 million to $250 million.

Carefully considered and updated by A.M. Best, these ratings create objective standards for lessors to approve insurers without extensive due diligence. Not all insurers, such as Lloyds of London, receive (or have received) ratings from A.M Best. In that case lessors and lessees need to select other ratings or objective means to judge the acceptability of an insurer. For more information, see www.ambest.com.

Evidence of insurance and broker's letters

A lessee may *evidence* (prove the existence and compliance of) her insurance coverage to lessors and other additional insureds and loss payees in several ways.

> ✔ **Certificate of Insurance.** A lessee may cause her broker to issue a certificate of insurance that shows the following information: the types of coverages, the date of issuance, the effective date of the coverage and expiration dates of the policies, the locations of the leased property, the names of the insureds (including the lessor and lenders), the limits of liability, the numbers of the certificate and policies themselves, and certain terms of the underlying insurance. Often brokers evidence insurance on

an Acord form — an industry fill-in-the-blank and don't-say-much type of form. The Acord form has the "endeavor to give notice" language that should be stricken. Brokers with underwriting/binding authority can also produce evidence of insurance on custom certificates setting forth the details of coverage in the policy that correspond to the insurance provisions in a lease that requires the evidence of insurance.

✔ **Binder.** Before an insurer issues a policy of insurance, it can issue a written *binder* or promise that the insurance exists and you, as the additional insured or loss payee, as appropriate, receive the protections of the policy by virtue of the binder (whatever the form may say). A *binder* generally describes a definite time limit of effectiveness, the insurer's name, the insureds' names, the perils insured against, and the type of insurance. Usually, specimen forms of the policy to be written exist so that a lessee doesn't accept a policy without seeing the terms of its coverage.

✔ **Endorsements.** Both property and liability coverage ultimately must be endorsed on the actual policy of insurance to bind the insurer. The information contained on a certificate, plus actual details of the policy corresponding to the requirements of the lease, appear on the face of the endorsement or evidence of the endorsement on the policy.

Endorsements legally bind the insurer. Endorsement forms can be obtained from the insurer or may be manuscripted (created specially) by risk managers, brokers, and lawyers who practice insurance or leasing law. Provided that you can get the insurer to agree, I prefer and recommend that lessors and lessee obtain endorsements over the certificate of insurance.

✔ **Owner's and Contractors Protective Policy (OCP Policy).** A very conservative lessor may insist on an even stronger approach to liability coverage by requiring the lessee to obtain an OCP policy in favor of the lessor. Insurers issue this policy in the name of the lessor, effective for the term of the lease, with a limit of liability specifically related to the lease. The lessee, of course, pays for the policy in addition to its other insurance coverage.

As a lessee, you should resist providing this type of coverage unless you have very questionable ability to perform under the lease or under your other insurance policies. This somewhat infrequently used coverage disadvantages you because it may limit the liability coverage available under your other insurance and increase your cost.

✔ **Broker's Opinion and a Certificate, Binder, or Endorsement.** In larger transactions or in transactions in which the lessee's credit or knowledge of insurance seems adequate at best, a broker's opinion can help provide comfort of compliance with the lease. The opinion specifically states in detail that the lessee's insurance policy conform to all insurance requirements in the lease. The certificates, binders, or endorsement should accompany the opinion.

Chapter 10

Leasing High-Technology Assets

. . . .

In This Chapter

▶ Considering the economics of high-technology leasing

▶ Understanding the differences between financing hardware and software

▶ Describing some specialized provisions in high-technology leases

. . . .

According to the U.S. Department of Commerce in its June 1999 report, titled "The Emerging Digital Economy II," by 2006, almost half of the workforce in the United States will be employed by industries that are either intensive users or major producers of information technology products and services. (See www.ecommerce.gov/ede/summary.html.) The variety of benefits to producers, users, and consumers of technology assets have created new opportunities for vendors and financing institutions to help speed the pace of economic development and technological change.

This chapter focuses on some key issues that you encounter in leasing high-technology assets including information technology (IT) equipment. It distinguishes financing relating to hardware and software, briefly describes a uniform law, called UCITA, that may someday govern all computer information transactions, and reviews some of the substantive differences in technology leasing from the core terms of the lease discussed in Chapter 8. See Chapter 8 and the Master Lease Agreement in the Appendix.

Technology Equipment Leasing: An Overview

Leasing or financing high-technology assets, such as hardware and software, presents some special documentation, legal, and pricing challenges for lessors, lessees, and lenders. The operation, application, and the fundamental nature of the hardware and software differentiate these assets from other leased property.

Hardware refers to devices that can compute. Hardware comprises the part of a computer system that you can touch and see that performs functions using software. Hardware includes a huge array of equipment including personal computers (PCs), mainframe computers, workstations, point-of-sale equipment, local area network (LAN) devices (like routers, switches and servers), and modems (devices or programs that your computer uses to convert analog data transmitted over telephone lines into digital data that you can read). It does not include a toaster, refrigerator, or a CD player, for example, because these assets do not compute like a PC can (for now anyway). In this chapter, I use hardware somewhat more broadly to refer generally to equipment that uses computing technology and software. You can lease every one of these items of hardware.

Software refers to proprietary and other computer information, including source codes and programs, that provides functionality for technology equipment and other hardware. Software comes in a nearly unlimited variety of applications which, when made for specific business or other uses, is often called *application software.*

You can finance (and some say lease) application and other software separately or as an integral part of a lease of equipment (or other goods). For example, you can lease a truck containing onboard computers such as in the braking systems. When a computer program (software) becomes so associated with "goods" as to customarily be considered a part of the goods, Revised Article 9 of the UCC treats the *embedded* program as part of the goods (that is, a part of the leased property). See Chapter 17 on Revised Article 9.

Computers and other hardware

As computer and other high-technology evolves and expands at an ever more rapid pace, lessors often lease computers and related equipment under relatively short-term master leases of less than three years. Lessors attach *schedules* to the master leases (as discussed in the following sections on terms of technology leases) to reflect the delivery of multiple units of leased property at any particular date under the terms of the master lease. See Chapter 8 and the lease form in the Appendix. With such rapid changes occurring, lessors closely evaluate and often reduce their reliance on residual value of the leased property at the end of the lease term. Savvy lessors attribute greater value to computer, IT, and other technology equipment "in place, in use" (such as at a lessee's premises) than to equipment returned to a remote location. See similar issues in Chapter 21 on venture leasing.

Lenders participate in these transactions by lending to lessors. Lenders may place little or no value on the equipment as collateral because they enter into these technology loans as *cash-flow transactions.* Cash-flow transactions refer to loans made by lenders on the basis of the strength of a lessee's business to generate cash to pay debt service. This approach contrasts with *asset-based lenders* that rely on the value obtained from liquidating assets as the primary means to pay their loans. In most of these transactions, given the rapid obsolescence and decline in value and marketability of technology equipment, only the credit of the lessee really matters to most lessors and lenders.

Lessors try to stay competitive and manage the residual value by offering financing to lessees to pay for upgrades to the leased property. An upgrade offers a lessor additional investment opportunities and potentially improves residual values. Lessors may also try to secure a right of first refusal on upgrades to maintain ownership of the entire asset and impose limits on the rights of lessees to terminate their leases during the term. Lessors generally resist provisions that allow a lessee to displace the lessor's technology equipment with the next generation promoted by aggressive vendors. By doing so, the lessor can realize a return on his investment as planned without the burden of remarketing obsolete high-technology equipment in competition with advanced technologies in the market. Chapter 8 also discusses the right of first refusal.

High-technology leasing requires special expertise to understand the nature and value of, and market for, the leased property because of rapid technological changes and rapid obsolescence of equipment. If you, as a lessor, do not thoroughly understand these and other issues discussed in the following sections, find technology experts to advise you before you enter into a lease and again before lease termination. Such experts can help you establish appropriate lease pricing, residual values, and exit strategies in the event of default or other remarketing efforts.

Software

You often, if not always, need licensed software to operate high-technology equipment. Licensing fees for software can account for a substantial part of the lessor's cost of leased property. Yet the legal rights and remedies relating to software differ significantly from the equipment in which it may be used.

Economic concerns and other market realities

Technology lessors focus on the impact of *soft costs* in technology leases such as licensing, maintenance and servicing fees for the equipment that often must be included in the lessor's cost and paid at the inception of the lease. The combination or *bundling* of these soft costs, sometimes called *bundled costs,* raises important economic and pricing issues. For example, if a lessor pays the full cost of license fees at the inception of a lease term for the software, the inclusion of those fees as part of the lessor's cost dilutes the residual value as a percentage of lessor's cost of the leased property. That dilution occurs because the *licensor* usually grants a license to the lessee (and not the lessor) to use the software. A *licensor* refers to a person or entity that owns and grants a right of use, called a *license,* of intellectual property (such as the copyrighted software) to another person or entity, called a *licensee*. The licensee uses the software under a contractual arrangement with the licensor. Accordingly, the lessor generally has no expectation at the end of the lease term that she has rights to use the licensed software, and therefore assumes no residual value in the software.

As a lessor, your sale or transfer of the software to another party can lead to an action by a licensor/vendor for damages or other remedies. Determine whether any software is used with, or embedded in, your leased property and consult the licensor/vendor before you even attempt to transfer or use it. Don't expect to receive cooperation from the software vendors in all cases, especially without paying some fees or complying with license agreements.

Copyright law says that the ownership by a licensor of the copyright remains distinct from the ownership of the equipment in which it is embodied. Lessors do not gain rights to use and/or transfer licenses to the software without the permission of the copyright owner/licensor. A licensor retains his ownership and licenses (and some argue "leases") the software to a lessee. The lessee generally joins a large group of non-exclusive users of most application software products. As a result, paying bundled costs (for equipment and software together) can render the lessor's total investment potentially less valuable at the end of the lease term. The lessor may also find himself without the rights he needs to use or transfer to third parties the essential software for his leased equipment. Lessees have, for example, returned used computers to my clients stripped of software, and I can tell you that the client is not pleased when this occurs. The reduction in value of the leased property and the hassle of remarketing it becomes very evident, very quickly in such cases.

To address the dilutive effects of software costs, lessors can create separate financing rates for their investments in the hardware and for their payments of software costs. Within the same lease transaction, the lessor leases the hardware and, in effect, also makes an unsecured (or secured) loan equal to the amount of the software fees that it pays. As a result, lessors provide combined or *blended pricing* to a lessee where a portion of the costs attributable to software lack tax benefits and residual value, but the other portion relating to hardware can include tax benefits and residual value. In Chapter 7 on lessor pricing, you can see the potentially significant differences in the pricing between a lease or leveraged lease and a loan. In Chapter 1, you can evaluate how confusing a lease may be when, without saying so in many cases, it comprises two deals in one — a lease of hardware and a loan with respect to software. Some lessors create different schedules or separate the rents for hardware and software to protect their economics and to clearly distinguish their legal rights and remedies with respect to each type of "leased property."

Before entering into a technology lease, lessors and the lessee should determine whether the lessor (or another person that the lessor designates) can obtain rights to the licensed software. Software vendors follow a few approaches. They:

- Allow software transfers without additional fees, but keep track of the current user.

- Charge an additional fee if a lessor places the hardware with a new use.

- Insist that the old software be deleted from the hardware and that the new user obtains new software and a license.

The timing and costs of these requirements can hamper the lessor's remarketing efforts, reduce the value and residual value of the leased property, and increase the lessee's obligations to the lessor to replace or pay for the problem software.

Find out which of these scenarios applies to you. As an alternative, you may be able to become the original licensee or the first purchaser of the software (instead of your lessee) and may negotiate with the licensor to control the software by way of sublicensing it to your lessee. Before you, as the owner of the equipment and lessor, take on the obligations of the licensee, you should carefully evaluate the potential obligations that you assume to the licensor, the vendor or a distributor, by becoming the licensee, such as indemnification for infringement or misuse. You may also take on obligations to your lessee. In this case, your lessee enters into a license with you as the licensor and becomes your *sublicensee*.

Because you, as the lessor, remain a passive licensee from the vendor, you should protect yourself by requiring your lessee to indemnify you for these risks in your lease. This indemnity creates a full circle. As lessor and *sublicensor*, you assume obligations to your lessee, and then, as the lessee, you indemnify the lessor for taking on those obligations. By taking on the role of sublicensor, however, as the lessor, you can better control the software should you need to take possession of the equipment from the lessee and deploy it elsewhere with the licensed software included. As lessee, you still get the leased property that you want even though you do not control the software rights.

Installment payment agreements

One type of agreement that software vendors and distributors use to finance software license fees, separately or in connection with an equipment leasing transaction, is called an *installment payment agreement (IPA)*. An IPA provides for payment in installments of the amount of the software license fees. The IPA resembles a conditional sale of software, except that no sale occurs (that is, the lessee pays the full license costs, but no one transfers title to intellectual property that is licensed to the lessee).

An IPA could be called a "lease" because the end-user simply pays for using and possessing a copy of software. For example, if a software fee equals $240,000, a software vendor/licensor may agree to take two years of payments at a rate of $20,000 per month plus earnings (for example, 10 percent) on $240,000 to compensate the licensor for the payment of the fees over time. The lessor has no rights to the intellectual property, but the software probably provides essential operational or functional capability for the leased property.

Lenders can finance, or purchasers can buy, the cash flow stream from IPAs by advancing a discounted amount of the stream of payments to the vendor. The vendor in many cases structures a "true sale" instead of a financing so that he can account for the $240,000 software transaction as a sale on his books rather than a loan. The purchaser or lender takes an assignment of the rights to receive the cash flow in a "win-win" scenario — the lender/buyer gets a deal that he wants, and the vendor creates liquidity from, or a "sale" of the cash flow created by, his software.

Uniform Computer Information Transactions Act (UCITA)

In 1999, under the auspices of the National Conference of Commissioners on Uniform State Laws (NCCUSL), various industry groups proposed a new uniform law known as the *Uniform Computer Information Transactions Act* (*UCITA*). UCITA provides uniform and comprehensive rules for licensing "computer information." It governs a range of contract issues (but not intellectual property rights such as copyrights or patents) from the formation of an agreement to performance by the parties of their obligations. UCITA applies to computer software, storage devices, database access, Internet distribution of information, and other forms of computer information. It does not apply to licensing contracts for the newspapers, television, books, or movies. UCITA provides rules to fill a void where the parties to a contract do not otherwise make an agreement. It allows the parties to waive or vary any of their provisions by contract in the business context (with some limitations in the consumer arena).

Part 5 of UCITA contains provisions that address many of these issues raised in the preceding discussion. UCITA remains controversial and has only been adopted or introduced by legislatures in a few states. Virginia and Maryland enacted UCITA, and about eight states have introduced it. See `ucitaonline.com/whathap.html` for updates on those states.

UCITA is intended to fill gaps arising from the application of UCC Article 2A on leases (Chapter 16) and UCC Revised Article 9 on secured transactions (Chapters 17) with respect to computer information. Article 2A applies to tangible (moveable) personal property (such as equipment) and not software. Revised Article 9 treats embedded software as "goods" and licenses of software as "general intangibles." In both cases, a UCITA can fill gaps in the laws and provide uniform rules to govern contracts to license or buy software, create computer programs, distribute information, and gain access to databases. It does not apply to goods like Revised Article 9 or Article 2A (or Article 2 on sales) of the UCC. In short, UCITA picks up where Article 9 and Article 2A leave off.

UCITA creates a concept of a financial accommodation contract that can take the form of a lease of software or an installment payment agreement with remedies that a party providing the financing, called the *financier*, can enforce against the party accepting the financing. It provides for rights of a lessor under such a contract to cancel the contract and prevent the use of the software by a defaulting lessee. UCITA also entitles the financier to enforce the hell-or-high-water clause in non-consumer transactions.

UCITA differs from Uniform Electronic Transactions Act (UETA). UETA applies to all electronic records and authorizes the use of electronic signatures for "electronic transactions." An *electronic signature* refers to an electronic sound, symbol, or process attached to or logically associated with signing a record such as an agreement in a transaction. UETA has been enacted by more than 20 states. The drafters intend UCITA to be consistent with UETA. UCITA relates to substantive contract issues for computer information, but UETA does not. To read the model text of UETA and UCITA, see `www.law.upenn.edu/bll/ulc/ulc_frame.htm`.

Documentation Issues for Technology Equipment and Software

This section discusses lease provisions relating to high-technology equipment/hardware that differ from the provisions of the Master Lease Agreement form in the Appendix. See Chapter 8 for a discussion of the form. To help you refer to that lease, I refer to it here as "Section x of the Lease."

Agreement to lease property: Master leases and schedules

As a lessor, you can and probably commit to provide funding to your lessee for equipment delivering over a period of time under a master lease like the one set out in the Appendix. This type of commitment, referred to as a *lease line* or *lease line of credit*, enables your lessee to arrange for leases of groups of equipment that start on convenient delivery dates over the commitment period.

For example, as lessor, you can commit to fund up to $10 million dollars of computers and software licenses over a period of one year. During that year, your lessee can arrange for the purchase and delivery of the equipment (with the licenses) to her offices in multiple locations under a separate schedule for each delivery. See the Schedule illustrated at the back of the Master Lease Agreement in the Appendix.

Net lease; unconditional obligations

As a lessee, you probably can expect to adhere to net lease provisions that require you to maintain, insure, and pay taxes on your leased property. Unless you default on your obligations, you can also expect to have continuous use and quiet enjoyment of your leased property without interference by your lessor, especially when the high-technology equipment is critical to the operations of your business. If your lessor does not leave you alone and disturbs this *right of quiet enjoyment,* you can sue your lessor but, under your hell-or-high-water provisions in most leases, you must continue to pay rent.

In technology leasing lessors often finance leases by borrowing from lenders on a *nonrecourse basis* (that is, the lessor has no personal obligation to pay the debt service; and the lessee's rent alone pays the debt service directly or indirectly to the lender). As lessor, you grant to the lender a security interest in the lease and the equipment it covers to support your nonrecourse obligation to the lender.

As a lessee, you need to know that your lessor and her lenders depend on you meeting this hell-or-high-water payment obligation even if the lessor breaches your right of quiet enjoyment. If you contractually limit your hell-or-high-water obligation to pay rent, you may just shoot yourself in the foot. Your lessor, as a result, may have difficulty finding the lenders to finance your transaction or not be able to close your deal. Alternatively, the lessor may have to charge you rent that exceeds the financing rates commensurate with your creditworthiness to accommodate the perceived additional risk of an undermined hell-or-high-water obligation on your part.

Lessee's rights to vendor warranties

As a lessee, you make several representations and warranties to your lessor in completing a lease including representing that you selected the hardware or other equipment and satisfied the other requirements for your lease to constitute a finance lease under Article 2A. (See Chapter 16.) If your lease qualifies as a finance lease, the UCC automatically extends supplier's warranties to you from your lessor with respect to the hardware or other equipment (but not the software).

A vendor first provides all warranties and service contracts to you as the lessee for the hardware or other equipment. Then, you can assign those warranties and service contracts to the lessor during the lease term. As the end-user, you can utilize these rights and enforce them during the lease term directly against the manufacturer and vendor provided you comply with your lease. See Section 7 of the Lease. If you default on your obligations, however, your lessor can take over and use or transfer those rights (other than software rights) to a new end-user lessee.

Lessor's disclaimer of warranties

In a technology lease, your lessor disclaims warranties with respect to the equipment (including hardware) and software. In addition, it provides no warranties against infringement to avoid claims of licensors relating to software that you use. See Section 7 of the Lease.

Use, marking, and maintenance of leased property

Technology leases generally require that you, as lessee, use equipment manufacturers or independent service organizations to maintain your equipment in accordance with a manufacturer's maintenance requirements. Your lease may require service to be performed at the location of equipment to avoid repair or replacement with units of equipment that your lessor does not own. If the equipment service replaces your equipment, your lessor may be left without an item of equipment that he financed or a proper replacement. Some leases permit replacement of equipment provided that you amend your lease schedules and any UCC filings to reflect a replacement. In addition, you may be required to give tax indemnities for loss of tax benefits and general indemnities for copyright infringement relating to replacing like software and equipment resulting from a transfer to the lessor of replaced equipment by a vendor/repairer in place of the original equipment.

As the lessee, you may be required to mark all equipment to indicate that the lessor owns it. This concept applies to almost every lease. Lessor may prescribe the method of marking equipment.

Some lessees use bar coding tags or affix markers to the effect that the equipment is "Owned and leased by XYZ Leasing Co." or words to a similar effect. In a leveraged lease, lenders typically ask for additional words such as "and subject to the lien of DEF Bank" to evidence the debt advanced to lessor. In reality, many lessees don't mark equipment despite the lease requirement. As a result, a dispute may arise as to which lessor owns equipment after substitutions or replacements. These markings can provide helpful notice and confirmation of ownership, and avoid disputes among possible owners. Further, lenders can use the marking to aid in foreclosures or repossessions.

Insurance and risk of loss

Lessor and lessees in some technology leases provide different portions of the insurance coverage for the benefit of the other. Larger lessors in the high technology leasing business may provide property insurance coverage with respect to property in the hands of the lessee more cost-effectively than a lessee can provide it. In such cases, a lessee pays the lessor a fee for insurance coverage. The lessee provides the liability insurance in any event.

As a lessee with multiple offices and locations of equipment, you may negotiate with the lessor (and her lenders), and the lessor may accept high self-insurance levels in recognition of the relatively small per unit costs of equipment. As a result, most losses do not trigger insurance coverage like a single significant item of leased property such as an aircraft or vessel. If a loss occurs at a single location, the actual value of the loss may be small because equipment may be physically distributed at different sites and individually not amount to significant cost.

With many locations of the equipment and small amounts of equipment at each location, lessees may negotiate self-insurance on property loss up to a certain amount like $100,000 per loss (depending on the creditworthiness of the lessee). Liability insurance may not be affected by diverse locations. Risk managers and knowledgeable insurance agents should analyze these risks and set appropriate insurance levels with the approval of the lessor. See Chapter 9 on insuring leased property.

In technology leases, like other leases, the lessor may be repaid in a casualty in an amount equal to the present value of the remaining rents or the stipulated loss value. Alternatively, for conditional sales or loans, a lender should receive his remaining principal balance set forth on a schedule or in the lease. Some leases require a payment of all rent and debt payments due without discounting that number.

As a watchful lessee, you can question these nondiscounted numbers as a premium or penalty. You can also negotiate the right to receive all proceeds of a loss up to a negotiated level (depending on your creditworthiness and if you do not default on your lease obligations) to repair or replace equipment. If you replace equipment, you can expect your lessor to require documentation to convey rights to the replacement hardware to the lessor. In turn, lessors generally agree to convey any right they have in the salvaged/ replaced equipment to you or your insurance carrier and terminate the lease with respect to the damaged/destroyed unit.

Conditions a lessee must meet

In addition to meeting the typical conditions of the leases such as the ones in Section 15 of the Lease, as a lessee, you can expect your lessor to require you, as lessee, to provide:

- ✔ Copies of manufacturers' warranties and service programs (used by a lessor to monitor compliance and exercise rights on a lessee default)

- ✔ A purchase order or invoice/sale agreement assignment with the consent of the manufacturer (used to convey rights to service programs and hardware and software warranties)

Substitution

Substitutions may occur where a lessee exchanges one unit of equipment in one location for another unit of equipment in a second location. A lessee may then return the unit at the second location to the lessor. As a lessor, you may permit limited substitutions of equipment for administrative convenience. (Substitutions may also occur as in any other lease at a single location.)

As a lessee, you negotiate for the right to make substitutions in your lease to have operational flexibility. However, as a lessor, to avoid a lessee substituting an inferior unit of equipment and to minimize paperwork associated with swapping one serial numbered unit for another, you should maintain discretion of how much serial number swapping you permit. Further, you should avoid substitutions on significant leased property that may provide unique value to the lessee's enterprise. Here are some tests to determine whether allowing equipment substitutions makes sense for a particular lease:

- ✔ Is the substitution equipment made by the same manufacturer?

- ✔ Is the substitution equipment free of any lien, claim, or encumbrance of any person?

- ✔ Is the substitution equipment the same or higher model as the destroyed equipment?

- ✔ Can the lessee and lessor readily identify the equipment to be replaced (that is, the original leased property)?

- ✔ Is the substitution equipment in the same or better condition and in compliance with all maintenance requirements of the lease, service requirements of the manufacturers, and other standards as the original equipment?

- ✔ Does the substitution equipment have substantially the same useful life, remaining useful life, utility, and value as the original equipment?

If both the lessor and lessee answer these questions as "yes," then the substitution should generally work within the existing lease once you consider related issues such as the availability of tax benefits, documentation, and lease economics of the substitution.

Options during and at the end of the lease

Section 16 of the Master Lease Agreement in the Appendix sets forth several option provisions. Technology leases raise the following issues with respect to the indicated options.

Early termination

Some leases allow lessees to terminate early if the equipment becomes obsolete or surplus to their needs. Lessors, of course, strongly prefer that lessees keep paying rent for the entire term. Consequently, their interests differ. Lessees and lessors can balance their interests and allow the lessee to return a lessor's equipment in accordance with an early termination clause. In essence, a lessee can terminate the lease by paying the termination value. The termination value takes into account debt, tax, residual, and other economic benefits assumed by the lessor to achieve its anticipated returns. See Chapter 7 for a discussion of these values.

As a lessor, you may want to restrict a right of your lessee to terminate the lease until after a fixed period of the lease term elapses (for example, two years). See Chapter 8 and Section 16(a)(i) of the Lease for the procedures for early terminations. The fixed period provides you, as lessor, with the following benefits:

✔ A required financing period for the benefit of your lenders so that they can obtain the lowest cost funding available without concern about paying breakage fees or penalties if you prepay the loan before the end of the fixed period

✔ A return on your investment for a substantial part of the planned lease term (assuming the lease term lasts three to five years)

✔ An obligation of the lessee to pay for any investment losses that you may suffer from failing to replace the terminated lease with one of equal or higher economic value

Some lessors in an early termination may simply take back the equipment and demand payment in full of the termination value. As lessor, you can justify the payment because the lessee elects to terminate and should pay you what you would have received from rent had the lease not been terminated early.

However, as the lessee, you should ask for and receive credit for the value of the proceeds of a replacement lease or of a sale of the equipment that occurs prior to the termination date of the lease. The credit can take several negotiated

forms. For example, the credit may equal the present value of the rent payments from the replacement lease or a dollar for dollar credit for a cash sale
of the equipment to a third party.

Early buy-out options; upgrade financing

A lessor may allow a lessee to buy out a lease if a lessee needs financing to
upgrade hardware, but cannot reach agreement with lessor on the terms. To
facilitate upgrade financing, lessors may index rates or set interest rate caps
on upgrade financing. If a lessee refuses to accept financing for the upgrade
within these rates, the lease either continues as is, or the lessee may exercise
the buy-out. The option price varies and is determined based on stipulated
loss or termination values (or, if higher, the fair market value of the leased
property) plus additional costs and fees that help the lessor to maintain its
anticipated economic returns.

Renewal options

Leases may have continuous or *evergreen renewals.* These renewals occur
automatically at the end of an existing lease term until terminated by the
lessee. When equipment becomes obsolete or loses value rapidly when compared to newer technologies, lessors want to keep the equipment on lease for
as long as possible to avoid remarketing efforts and potential losses. Many
leases provide that, if the lessee not only fails to give proper notice to end
the lease, and either (a) fails to purchase the equipment or (b) fails to enter
into new lease arrangement for other equipment, then (c) the lease renews
automatically for a specified period until the lessee does give proper notice.
Lessee can and should resist these so-called *ABC clauses* (that is, if the lessee
fails to do (a) or (b) then (c) applies) because the lessee takes all, and the
lessor takes none of the technology or equipment downside risk. The lessor
(and perhaps its lender) assumes the lessee's credit risk only, leaving the
technology risk on the lessee.

Alternatively, the lessee can renew the lease at a fixed rent amount (for example, at 50 percent of the original rent as an estimate of the fair rental value at
lease expiration) or at a fair market value rent. Each lessee negotiates the
type of option at the lease negotiation stage depending on its economic perspective and expected needs for the technology assets at lease expiration.

Purchase options

At the end of the lease, lessees can purchase the equipment at a fixed or fair
market value price determined by the lessor, by agreement with the lessor, or
by an appraiser procedure. (See Section 16(a)(iv) of the Lease.) I'll give you
three guesses which approach lessors prefer. As always, lessors want to
decide purchaser prices in fair market value deals. To give lessors credit,
they can in many cases justify their numbers because of their expertise in
high-technology leases (and because they want the upside if they can get it).

Unless the lessor has a software vendor's/licensor's consent, the lessor does not have any right to sell or transfer software that has been licensed to the lessee. As lessee, a lessor should not charge you for an asset (the software) that he does not own. Because the software may be vital to the operation of the leased property, you should be aware of the potential negative impact on the value of the property without the software when negotiating your purchase options. You can tell the lessor that the leased property alone has little value and then watch the lessor's reaction as he evaluates the remarketability of the leased property absent the software. You might strike an attractive deal in the right circumstances if the lessor or next user/lessee can not readily replace the software to which you (but not the lessor) has the rights or obtain new software at a reasonable price and terms for the particular leased property continued use.

Lessor's rights of first refusal

If lessees upgrade computer equipment, the upgrades generally improve the performance and functionality of the original equipment. Lessees make these improvements by:

- ✔ Adding accessories (for example, add scanners or external zip drive) to a central processing unit, replacing components (for example, replacing a hard drive)

- ✔ *Swapping* entire units of equipment (for example, one point-of-sale unit for another newer one with a different serial number)

- ✔ Rebuilding parts or the whole of equipment (for example, rebuild a server) already subject to a lease

Some upgrades can be costly enough that both additional lenders and lessors provide the financing. The conflict of interests between the original lessor and lenders and the additional upgrade lenders or lessors require some understanding of whom has what rights with respect to the upgrades. Generally, improvements that cannot be removed without damage become the property of the original lessor (for example, the rebuilding of servers). However, the upgrade financing parties generally need to clear rights to the property that they own, in the case of upgrade lessors, or in which they have a security interest, in the case of upgrade lenders. To avoid potential conflict, the lessor can

- ✔ Enter into an *intercreditor agreement* or prohibit improvements that lessees cannot remove without damage to the original equipment. Intercreditor agreements refer to arrangements between upgrade and original lessors and lenders, and the lessee, regarding rights to ownership of the equipment and the order and priority of security interests and payments with respect to the upgraded equipment and the lease.

✔ Provide the original lessor a right of first refusal for all upgrades at prices and terms that match the competitive financing. See Section 17 of the Lease.

✔ Insist on a right to consent to upgrades and/or to the removal of parts of significant value. This consent requirement can help avoid a direct conflict between the rights of existing and new financing parties.

✔ Prohibit or limit a lessee from swapping parts for credit against new parts (sometimes called *net pricing*). Lessors can require that they automatically become the owners of all parts replaced and that the lessee can keep replaced parts and account for them to the lessor. Such an accounting can avoid dissipation of valuable parts by a lessee that diminishes the value of technology equipment.

The market reality and competition in high-technology leasing, however, generally requires some participation and cooperation by lessors in upgrades if they want to continue to finance the upgrading lessee; otherwise, lessees may terminate the leases and find more flexible players.

Lessee's sublease and assignment of leased property

Lessors can allow their lessees to sublease their equipment as an alternative to early termination rights or as a way to extend the earning period of their high-technology assets. A sublease often keeps the lessee "on the hook" for payments but minimizes the financial burden on the lessee of paying for unneeded or obsolete equipment. Lessors prefer to restrict or prohibit subleases without their consent to manage the documentation of a change of possession and credit risk of an unknown sublessee.

Dispute resolution

Lessees, lessors, and licensors can all use an alternative dispute resolution clause in the form of mediation or arbitration in connection with disputes relating to software and hardware.

Mediation involves a process where one neutral party works with two or more opposing parties to help them reach agreement. A mediator makes no binding decisions.

By contrast, *arbitration* involves a process in which one or more decision-makers (hopefully with high-technology and legal backgrounds) hear the arguments of the parties and make a binding and final decision in place of a court. Lessors often prefer the courtroom to arbitration, but arbitration clauses can produce a structure to end disputes more quickly and inexpensively, and with more knowledgeable decision-makers, than most courts. Mediation can precede arbitration and further minimize the cost in management time and legal resources to resolve disputes.

Confidentiality

Lessees often use hardware and software subject to a lease or financing to manage highly proprietary information. The technology itself may constitute a "mission critical" tool of a lessee's business operation. Lessors and lenders prefer that their collateral (both hardware and software) form a key part of their lessees operations. This situation keeps lessees focused on performing their obligations, and creates a need to maintain confidentiality. Accordingly, as a lessee in such a situation, your lease and software licenses should contain provisions that make all nonpublic information (that is, information of proprietary nature) confidential for a period of time (for example, a period of 12 to 18 months).

As a lessee, you can enter into a confidentiality or *nondisclosure agreement* (NDAs) with your lessor to protect your secrets. Note that these agreements do not require your lessor to keep all information secret. A lessor can disclose information that has been disclosed to a receiving person through no fault of that person and is therefore not confidential; exists publicly before signing the NDA; and a court or an administrative agency requires your lessor to disclose. Remember to protect your own secrets when you return your hardware to your lessor. Remove all confidential data that you do not want to share with your lessor or the next user of the hardware (as well as software for which no license has been arranged with the lessor). Discuss with your lessor and your software licensor well ahead of the lease expiration the retention of the software with, or the removal of software from, the hardware.

Chapter 11

Leasing and Financing Aircraft

· ·

In This Chapter

▶ Considering some differences between commercial and corporate aircraft

▶ Taking a glimpse at fractional share ownership

▶ Complying with federal and state laws involved in aircraft financing

▶ Recording and registering documents at the FAA

▶ Reviewing important principals of international conventions affecting aircraft

▶ Concentrating on special lease provisions for aircraft

· ·

I admit it. I love many of the toys involved in leasing, including aircraft. I spend a fair amount of my time on leasing and financing of aircraft, which tend to capture your imagination about travel and, for some people, luxury.

As you probably already know, the international and domestic aircraft business presents significant challenges and opportunities. You can encounter these challenges and opportunities in every aspect of buying, selling, managing, financing, and leasing aircraft.

This chapter helps you take on some of those challenges and seize some of the opportunities. It contains an overview of leasing and financing of commercial and business aircraft, as well as fractional share programs for business aircraft. It also covers some key registration and ownership rules that you must use when dealing with the Federal Aviation Administration (FAA).

In addition, you discover how international treaties can facilitate aircraft leasing and financing around the world, adding some order when you address foreign risk. Last but not least, this chapter describes certain important lease provisions that you negotiate in business and commercial aircraft transactions. You can review the basic provisions of a lease in Chapter 8 for comparison.

Overview of Aircraft Leasing and Financing

Although the government and the private sectors both use and lease aircraft, this chapter covers only the private/civil aircraft market. That market falls into two primary areas for leasing and financing purposes: commercial and business aircraft.

Perhaps the most significant use of aircraft involves commercial airlines registered with the FAA under Part 121 of the Federal Aviation Regulations (*FAR*). The second major area is business aircraft. Although I refer to business aircraft in this chapter, I use the term broadly to include business, personal, and corporate use of aircraft operating under Part 91 (private) or Part 135 (charter) of the FAR. According to the FAA, business transportation refers to the use of an aircraft by individuals for transportation required by their businesses. In contrast, the FAA says that *corporate/executive transportation* means any use of an aircraft by an organization for the purposes of transporting employees and/or property and employing professional pilots for the operation of the aircraft.

Leasing commercial aircraft

You see commercial aircraft at every international airport in scheduled passenger or cargo use — a Boeing 737, an MD-80, and an Airbus A-330, to name a few. These aircraft, when new, cost between approximately $40 to $150 million each, depending on the model and who buys them. Many companies lease these aircraft including commercial airlines, charter operators, and freight carriers.

Commuter aircraft, used primarily for transporting passengers and cargo between two relatively close points, constitute a cousin of commercial aircraft. Often used in commercial operation, commuter aircraft like the EMB 120 Brasilia (from Embraer) or the Beechcraft 1900C (from Raytheon Aircraft) can cost around $3 million and up. For purposes of this chapter, I group commuter aircraft in with commercial aircraft.

Leasing business aircraft

Business aircraft include helicopters (rotary wing aircraft) and piston or jet aircraft (fixed wing aircraft) with a cost ranging from $400,000 to $50 million.

According to the National Business Aviation Association (*NBAA*), during the 1990s, the number of business jets ("bizjets" for you jet aircraft fans) has more than doubled since 1980 to over 14,000 fixed wing aircraft in 2000. About 10,000 of these aircraft are registered at the FAA. As of 2001, the buying, selling, and leasing of business aircraft by some estimates reached a $10- to $12-billion annual market. For more background on business aircraft, see www.nbaa.org/data/.

Many companies and individuals lease business aircraft and purchase them with secured financing. These aircraft come in all sizes and configurations such as those described in the fractional shares discussion later in this chapter, the Pilatus PC-12, the Boeing 737BBJ, and the Airbus A319CJ.

Why do companies use business jets? Some executives say that their extensive travel justifies the price of an entire jet or helicopter. The NBAA says that using business aircraft:

 ✔ Saves employees time with efficient scheduling and minimum travel time away from home

 ✔ Increases productivity during aircraft travel with higher security and privacy onboard than on commercial transportation

 ✔ Projects a proper corporate image (you have to love this reason!)

When should you use business aircraft instead of commercial flights? Industry experts have their own spin on this issue, but as a general rule, if you travel by air:

 ✔ Less than 50 hours per year, use commercial or charter aircraft (that is, hire a whole aircraft on a trip-by-trip basis).

 ✔ More than 50 hours but less than 400 hours, charter an aircraft or enter a fractional share program (as described in the next section).

 ✔ More than 400 hours, purchase or lease a whole aircraft for your use (and you can charter it to others when you don't need it).

The wildcard, of course, depends on your personal decisions about the quality of your life, the management of your time, the safety and confidentiality of travel that you need, and, without a doubt, the size of your budget. This stuff is expensive. For example, a Gulfstream IV-SP can cost around $2,800 per hour to fly (subject to market changes). Of course, commercial air travel works in all events, but at some point in your analysis, business productivity and confidentiality, image, economics, and comfort may justify or at least motivate you to use business aircraft.

Fractional share programs of business aircraft

Deploying about 600 business aircraft worldwide (and increasing), *fractional share programs* have gained in popularity and practicality over the last 15 years. A fractional shares program allows you to acquire an undivided (fractional) interest in an aircraft (one-half to one-sixteenth for fixed wing aircraft) for a committed term of five years. A professional management company administers the program, involving at least two aircraft used by the shareowners. The management company handles all aircraft maintenance, flight, and business aspects of the program. As a shareowner, you:

- ✔ Enjoy co-ownership of an aircraft with the other fractional share owners.

- ✔ Agree with the shareowners in the program to exchange use of each other's aircraft in a pooled fleet to facilitate your travel (often with aircraft that look alike).

- ✔ Retain operational control by directing the manager of the aircraft.

- ✔ Bear the risk of loss or damage to the aircraft, as well as the potential increase or decrease in the value of your investment of the fractional share of an aircraft.

The price to play generally consists of paying your portion of the full aircraft cost plus various fees. For example, to acquire a one-fourth share of a $1,000,000 aircraft, you pay $250,000. For a one-sixteenth share (if offered), one-eighth share, and one-fourth share, you receive 50 hours, 100 hours, and 200 hours, respectively, of air travel, and so on. In addition, you pay a fixed management fee to cover the costs, such as maintenance, training, crew, and hangaring (storing) of the aircraft, plus a variable fee for actual usage costs (but not ground time or flight delays), including fuel, maintenance, engine reserves, and catering, often called the *occupied hourly charge.*

This travel product allows those who cannot or will not justify the expense of a lease or purchase of a whole aircraft to use a high-quality, well-maintained, private aircraft for transportation worldwide on demand at a fraction of the cost of a whole aircraft. The programs guarantee rapid availability of aircraft (for example, within four to six hours for some of the larger business aircraft). Such programs use a wide variety of aircraft, including the Gulfstream G-IV jet aircraft, Raytheon Hawkers, Dassault Falcons, Learjets, Cessna Citations, Bell helicopters, and Raytheon King Air turboprops.

You can purchase or lease shares in these programs, although purchases seem to be prevalent. The Business Aircraft Finance Division of The CIT Group has made significant inroads into financing fractional shares of owners. For more information, see www.cit.com/operatinggroups/

`equip_fin/industries/corp_air.asp`. In addition, the aircraft manufacturers and other finance companies offer financing for these shares. Ask your program manager for assistance with financing.

UAL Corporation, through new subsidiaries, has begun the development of a fractional shares "bizjets" program and plans to provide fractional shares and other business jet service to its customers (a first for a U.S. commercial air carrier). See `www.ual.com/site/primary/0,10017,3543,00.html`. United will join and compete with several other established programs, including the following:

✔ NetJets (the largest program in the world), operated by Executive Jets, Inc., a Berkshire Hathaway Inc. company. See `www.netjets.com`; 800-821-2299.

✔ Citation Shares by Tag Aviation, SA and the Cessna Aircraft Company. See `www.tagaviation.com/services/index-p.html`; 800-340-7767.

✔ FlexJet, a Bombardier Aerospace operation. See `www.bombardier.com/index.jsp?id=3_0&lang=en&file=/en/3_0/3_0_1_6_4_6.html`; 800-Flexjet.

✔ Flight Options. See `www.flightoptions.com/program/programsum.asp`; 877-703-2348.

✔ Raytheon Travel Air, a program of Raytheon Aircraft. See `www.raytheon.com/rac/companyinfo/aboutta.htm`. 316-676-5034.

For a good general article on some of these programs and more on how they work, go to `www.fool.com/community/pod/2000/000518.htm`.

The fractional share programs remain in their infancy despite being in existence as a concept since 1986. Other management companies continue to expand their programs and to enter the business. Check out the management companies closely. They provide the key to your service, safety, and the security of your financial interests (as well as those of the lenders and lessors that finance the shares). Also, for the legal eagles and regulatory types, you should understand the new (and developing) Subpart K of Part 91 of the FARs. This regulation creates a safe harbor from compliance with Part 135 regulations and constitutes a hybrid of regulation under Part 91 and Part 135 relating to the operation, maintenance and control of aircraft.

Techniques of leasing aircraft

Financial institutions, such as leasing companies, banks, manufacturers, and captive finance/leasing companies, among others, contribute billions of dollars of capital to the aircraft market worldwide. Various additional techniques exist to lease aircraft that you can use to secure the use (as lessee) or ownership (as lessor) of aircraft, including:

- ✔ Operating leases, a lease for a relatively small portion of the useful life of the aircraft, such as an operating lease for three to six years of a Boeing 737 aircraft or, less commonly, a three- to five-year operating lease of a business aircraft such as a Gulfstream V business jet

- ✔ Finance leases such as long-term leveraged leases and single-investor leases of a Boeing 747 aircraft

- ✔ Cross-border leases, which refer to leases of aircraft within one country with a funding source from another country

- ✔ Lease in-lease outs, which refer to leases by an owner-lessor to one entity, called a lessee/sublessor, who subleases to another entity, called a sublessee, where the sublessee may operate or register the aircraft in the same or a different country

- ✔ Off-balance sheet loans (such as synthetic leases) discussed in Chapter 15

As used here, the term *operating lease* refers to leases for a relatively short portion of the useful life of the aircraft and not the accounting concept of an off-balance sheet lease, also called an operating lease, discussed in Chapter 15. A *finance lease* refers to a lease under Article 2A of the UCC in which the lessor leases the aircraft for most of its useful life, but retains a substantial residual value risk. I describe these leases in Chapters 1, 15, and 16.

Recordation and Registration at the FAA

Unlike most other assets, aircraft leasing requires that you comply with both federal and state laws on filing or recording your interests in aircraft. Many laws apply to the ownership, leasing, financing, and operation of aircraft. This section focuses on federal preemption and special filings that you make in registering or recording interests in aircraft in leasing transactions.

Federal law preempts the UCC

The basic federal law of aviation, called the *Transportation Code*, 49 U.S.C. Section 44101, 44102 (and so on) is still commonly referred to as the Federal Aviation Act of 1958. The Transportation Code and its related federal aviation regulations, 14 CFR Parts 47 and 49 (*FARs*), create a national registration system for aircraft and a national lien recordation system for aircraft and certain engines, propellers, and spare parts. The Transportation Code and FARs play an important role in how you document leases and loans involving aircraft.

The Transportation Code controls the perfection of security interests in aircraft, engines, and propellers in the place of the UCC. See Chapter 17 for a description of perfecting a security interest. However, the UCC and other state laws govern other issues and property not covered by the Transportation Code. For example, state laws dictate whether a document between two parties is valid and enforceable, as well as the order of priority of rights in aircraft.

What does the FAA filing cover? Does it protect your interest in ancillary equipment, engines when not attached to an aircraft, and books, logs, and records pertaining to the aircraft? When dealing with aircraft, you may not find a bright line (that is, a clear distinction) between the application of federal law, the UCC, and other state laws. The Transportation Code defines the terms for aircraft, engines, and propellers, and many items do not fall within the scope of these terms. In this case, these items probably fall outside of the term *aircraft* under the Transportation Code, 49 U.S.C. Section 44102, which means "any contrivance invented, used, or designed to navigate, or fly in, the air." How clear do you find this description? When trying to decide what's covered and what's not, this definition doesn't help much, does it?

So what is a diligent person to do? When dealing with filings at the FAA versus the UCC, take the simple and cautious approach, as a lessor or a lessee, consult knowledgeable legal experts in these transactions to avoid mistakes that may undermine the rights and interests in the aircraft and related stuff. File at the FAA when you can under the Transportation Code and file a precautionary filing under the UCC as discussed at more length in Chapter 17.

Centralized filings at the FAA

The FAA maintains a centralized filing system for registering aircraft ownership and recording leases, security interests, and other *conveyances* affecting all aircraft and certain engines and propellers, which are rated at greater than 750 horsepower. A *conveyance* refers to an instrument, such as a bill of sale, conditional sale agreement, mortgage, lease, or equipment trust, affecting title to, or an interest in, an aircraft. All nonmilitary aircraft should be registered with a civil aviation authority of a country. For those registered in the United States, the FAA issues a unique "N" number (such as N123 ET), which is often referred to in the business as an *N number* or a *tail number*. To find out more about the FAA and its operations, see www.faa.gov.

If you sign a lease or grant a lien or security interest with regard to an aircraft and equipment related to an aircraft, you may record the leases, security agreements, lease assignments, and certain other conveyances at the FAA if and only if the interest meets certain technical requirements. For example, the filing may only relate to an aircraft or an aircraft engine or propeller with 750-rated takeoff horsepower or its equivalent, or certain spare parts. See Transportation Code Section 44705. To perfect your rights under the Transportation Code you must file the entire instrument or document that creates your rights. For example, if you want to perfect rights under a lease or security agreement, you must file the entire lease or security agreement — not just a notice or summary of the document. Remember these additional rules when you file at the FAA. Essentially all documents filed for recordation with the FAA are required by the FARs to have an original, ink signature — the FAA permits no electronic filing.

Ownership and registration of aircraft

The FAA also requires you to register ownership of aircraft at the FAA. Unlike recordation of conveyances, which covers certain parts, propellers and engines as well as all aircraft, registration relates *solely* to aircraft. You therefore *file for recordation* to perfect your interest in all aircraft, and certain parts, propellers, and engines (that is, you file and then the FAA records your documents in its system). However, you only *register* changes in ownership pertaining to aircraft (forgetting engines and propellers, which the FAA does not register).

When you change ownership of an aircraft, the FAA requires that you file a one-page document called the *AC Form 8050-1*, the Aircraft Registration Application. The white original and a green copy of the Application for Registration are filed at the FAA. You must place the pink copy of the Application for Registration onboard the aircraft, because it acts as your temporary authority to operate the aircraft in the United States only while it is being reregistered at the FAA. No other filing for registration is accepted or required by the FAA. As part of the registration process, you must also file an AC Form 8050-2, Aircraft Bill of Sale (or an equivalent) to transfer title to an aircraft at the FAA. Without giving you any more of the glorious details, just realize that the FAA has a series of arcane rules and forms used for registration and transfer of title to an aircraft. To see or download some forms used at the FAA, see www.faa.gov/aviation.htm. Look under "Aviation Forms."

If you are the buyer, you should always obtain a *warranty bill of sale*, which transfers title and includes a promise by the seller to make sure that you receive the entire interest in the aircraft without liens, claims, or challenges to the title. You get this bill of sale for a good reason that the pros sometimes forget. The FAA form bill of sale only includes a description of the airframe — no engines, propellers or parts. (Remember, only the airframes — and not engines, propellers, or parts — are registered at the FAA.) As a lessee or lessor, you should insist that the seller deliver to the buyer both the FAA bill of sale (for filing with the FAA) and a warranty bill of sale.

Who can register an aircraft at the FAA

Any aircraft operated in the United States must be registered at the FAA other than certain exempt aircraft, civil foreign aircraft, and military aircraft. To qualify for registration at the FAA, you must be a citizen of the United States or a resident alien (with exceptions).

Registration by U.S. citizens

As you probably guessed, the Federal Aviation Regulations define what a U.S. citizen means for purposes of registering aircraft at the FAA. Because citizenship applies to companies, individuals, and other organizations, citizenship is more complicated than just saying that you were born in the United States. Any business organization must meet the detailed citizenship rules or fall into one of the exceptions.

Although the citizenship rules qualify as another technical area of FAA requirements, you should be aware of certain key issues regarding registration. In general, any citizen of the United States can register at the FAA. Such a citizen includes an individual, a partnership (consisting solely of individuals who are U.S. citizens), and other registered entities such as corporations, limited liability companies, and trusts. For these entities, they must, generally speaking, demonstrate predominant U.S. ownership (75 percent by U.S. citizens), formation in the United States, and management/control of the entity (the president and two-thirds of the board of directors or equivalent must be U.S. citizens). To get the scoop with pinpoint accuracy, see the FARs or visit www.mcafeetaft.com (for papers on citizenship and other FAA issues).

Registration by non-U.S. citizens

Special tests exist that enable resident aliens and certain other noncitizens to register an aircraft at the FAA. As a noncitizen, you need to demonstrate, in essence, that a U.S. citizen controls the aircraft. In addition, if, as a foreign citizen, you want to register an aircraft at the FAA, you can register your aircraft in the United States if you, as owner, base and primarily use the aircraft in the United States (that is, at least 60 percent of your flight hours in any six-month period occur within the U.S.).

Given the complexity and technicality of these rules regarding perfection of interests in aircraft, engines, and propellers and the registration of aircraft, including citizenship issues, you should seek help from special counsel or title companies in Oklahoma City who work with the FAA daily. If you include Oklahoma City counsel at the beginning of a transaction, you may be able to avoid problems and structure your deal correctly. Also, they will be able to tell you exactly what documents you need to perfect your interests at the FAA. Finally, they can coordinate the escrowing of documents for filing at the FAA and issue a legal opinion that describes the filing of documents at the FAA and the legal effect of that FAA filing.

International Conventions Affecting Aircraft

In my aircraft practice, U.S. lessors express understandable concern about foreign registration of the aircraft, especially lessors of business aircraft. They worry that someone may claim that an aircraft that the lessor financed belongs to, or is subject to a lien of, a third party in a country in which the aircraft was once registered.

The section discusses some international conventions that mitigate these concerns and may help you to proceed with a good transaction that you, as a lessee or a lessor, might otherwise pass up. An *international convention* refers to an agreement on a specific subject signed by two or more contracting nations. Several international conventions affect rights with respect to aircraft.

Find out whether the country where an aircraft has been registered is a signer of the conventions discussed in the following sections, and confirm with local experts that the country's registry enforces the provisions of the particular convention.

Chicago Convention

Known technically as the Convention on International Civil Aviation, the contracting nations signed the Chicago Convention, as it is commonly called, on December 7, 1944, in Chicago, Illinois. In earlier sections of this chapter, I mention the FAA Aircraft Application Registration on AC Form 8050-1. The Chicago Convention provides that you may register an aircraft only in one jurisdiction at a time and that you must carry a certificate of registration onboard the aircraft. The concept supposedly protects lessors and lenders against registering, leasing, and financing of an aircraft in more than one country, and provides confidence for lessors and lenders who finance aircraft and expect to have an exclusive interest in the aircraft.

As part of your investigation of an aircraft, search the foreign records where it has been registered and obtain certified copies of the records from the appropriate agency that is the counterpart of the FAA. Do not rely solely on the Chicago Convention or any other convention to protect your interests. Do not buy from dealers or brokers who disregard this level of care unless you do the record search and satisfy yourself that you will not buy air (bad or no title to an aircraft) instead of an aircraft.

Geneva Convention

Known technically as the Convention on the International Recognition of Rights in Aircraft, the contracting nations signed the Geneva Convention, as it is commonly called (also the Mortgage Convention), on June 19, 1948, in Geneva, Switzerland. Its formal name explains its central purpose. The signers recognize and enforce each other's laws. Lessors and lenders take the most comfort in the provision in the Geneva Convention that when the registration of an aircraft changes from one signing nation to another. The Geneva Convention says that those parties with an interest in the aircraft must either consent to the transfer of registration subject to their interests such as a lien, or be paid in full (have their interests satisfied) before the transfer.

Rome Convention

Known technically as the Unification of Certain Rules Relating to the Precautionary Attachment of Aircraft, the contracting nations signed the Rome Convention, as it is commonly called, on May 29, 1933, in Rome, Italy. The Rome Convention establishes procedures for repossession (precautionary attachment) of aircraft that avoid disruption of commercial traffic or interference with government services.

UNIDROIT Convention

For many years, the International Institute for Unification of Private International Law has been developing the UNIDROIT Convention on International Interest in Mobile Equipment, known informally as the UNIDROIT Convention. This convention aircraft, railroad rolling stock, and property used or created in outerspace and contains an Aircraft Protocol specific to aircraft and engines.

This controversial document calls for the creation of one worldwide registry for the perfection of liens and interests in aircraft and engines. The Convention promotes centralization, uniformity, and certainty in filings. It also addresses and attempts to give uniformity to other matters relating to aircraft finance, including choice of law, default, remedies, and bankruptcy, in an effort to provide greater certainty to lenders and lessors involved in international transactions.

It says that a party who fails to file all security interests, leases, and other conveyances at the International Registry to be created under UNIDROIT would not be perfected and would lose its priority to a competing creditor or lienholder who did file under UNIDROIT. In other words, first to file wins: The time of the UNIDROIT filing would control the priorities of any competing claims irrespective of when the parties created their interests in the aircraft.

It is possible that the FAA and other registries would lose most, if not all, of their responsibilities, with regard to the filing of documents to perfect security and leasehold interests in aircraft and engines. However, the registration of ownership interests in aircraft would be unaffected and would continue to be the responsibility of the FAA and the registries of other governments. For more on the UNIDROIT Convention, see www.unidroit.org/ and click any reference to the draft Protocol on Matters specific to Aircraft Equipment.

Documentation Issues in Aircraft Leases

Leases of aircraft require customized provisions by aircraft type and use of the aircraft. Commercial aircraft require different provisions than business aircraft because of the nature of their use and the applicable Federal Aviation Regulations. This section briefly lists a few of the provisions that you negotiate in aircraft leases that differ from the master lease discussed in Chapter 8.

The following topics each require far more attention and detail that I can offer here, as much as I would like to do so. Take this list and use it to make sure that you understand and negotiate these points in your deals.

Maintenance and return of aircraft

Maintenance of an aircraft is expensive but critical to its safety and operation. Good maintenance can improve value while poor maintenance can cost hundreds of thousands of dollars to remedy.

Some lessors want to approve maintenance programs for aircraft encompassing scheduled maintenance and maintenance responsive to the condition of the airframe (the hull and all attached equipment), engines, propellers, and parts of an aircraft. Lessees may follow the manufacturer's approved program. They may also, in the case of airlines, have their own program approved by the FAA.

The FAA and/or manufacturer may issue various directives to aircraft owners and operators regarding safety. For example, the manufacturer may issue mandatory maintenance bulletins, advising users of required operational/ design corrections to be made to an aircraft during inspections or overhauls. In addition, the FAA may issue an Airworthiness Directive or AD, which constitutes a mandatory direction to effect certain repairs or modifications to an aircraft.

Engines represent a very high cost component of aircraft. One engine can cost many millions of dollars. For that reason, lessors require separate maintenance standards for engines. Engines must be maintained according to manufacturer's and FAA standards. If an engine is destroyed, that engine must be replaced with another engine of the same (or better) model. The replacement engine must have value and utility at least equal to, and be in as good operating condition as, the destroyed engine, assuming the engine being replaced was in good operating condition and repair as required by the terms of the lease immediately prior to such loss. The same kinds of rules apply to the return of any engine at the end of the lease. If an engine fails to meet the return standards, lessors almost always ask for a payment to put the engine in the condition it should have been had the lessee complied with the lease. That amount may be determined by a formula of paying the lessor cash that will enable the lessor to get the repair done, often to the half life point of the engine's repair cycle or overhaul (the midpoint between maintenance visits). You can and should negotiate this point because it potentially involves big bucks.

In operating leases of aircraft, lessors often require that lessees pay *reserves* to the lessor (in addition to rent) with respect to the airframe, engines and landing gear and other significant parts. The amount of these reserves may be based on cycles (the number of landings and takeoffs of the aircraft) and flight hours of operation. Lessors may even impose a minimum payment to the reserve regardless of hours or cycles. These reserves then defray the cost of the maintenance when performed. For very large airlines with strong creditworthiness, lessors may not require, or be able to obtain, these reserves.

At the end of the term, if the lessee does not exercise a purchase or renewal option, then as a lessee you return the aircraft to the lessor at a location designated by the lessor in the condition required by the lease. Lessors often hang tough in negotiations of return conditions because that value directly affects their profit in the deal.

Return conditions differ for the type of aircraft, the internal configuration of the aircraft required by lessor, and the results of testing and inspections prior to the return date. Lessees must adhere to these standards on return or pay to compensate the lessor for any shortfall in the condition and performance of the aircraft.

Setting maintenance and return requirements and monitoring maintenance requires a high level of expertise that you can resolve by obtaining expert assistance, especially if you are an aircraft lessor. As a lessee of business aircraft, if you do not have your own staff, find a competent repair facility and talented pilots or an aircraft management company to assist you.

Location and possession of aircraft and parts

As a lessee, your lessor allows you to establish a home base for aircraft. However, your lessor may establish some geographical limits on when and how you operate your aircraft. You can plan on giving your lessor access to the aircraft for inspection or repossession. Finally, your lessor expects you to take legal and tax compliance measures dictated by the selected location (payment of property, sales and use taxes as discussed in Chapter 14 for U.S. aircraft).

For business aircraft, a lessee frequently needs a maintenance service and professional operator to fly and maintain the aircraft. The lessor prefers to approve these arrangements because of the high value of the aircraft and desire to know who has possession of it at all times. Lessors can specifically approve management or operations agreements in the lease.

For commercial aircraft, airlines often pool engines and interchange parts. A *pool* may be a physical location from which a part or engine is taken or simply a contractual relationship among airlines. Lessors must allow lessees to remove parts and engines and send them off-site to approved repair facilities. To keep an aircraft operating, engines may be removed, and different engines may replace them.

Most lessors prefer to avoid conflict or confusion over ownership of any engine. Consequently, lessors often prefer, if possible, that their lessee repair and put the original engine back on the airframe rather than attach any other engine.

In the case of parts, the approach differs. If parts become worn out, destroyed, damaged, or seized, lessees remove them. In performing normal maintenance, lessees may not reinstall every part. Recognizing reality, lessors may allow a certain value of parts up to a dollar amount not to be reinstalled (just disappear from the maintenance effort). In any event, the aircraft must still be properly maintained.

Insurance

Chapter 9 discusses insurance in some detail. Aircraft finance requires some special types of insurance coverage. Domestic U.S. carriers as well as the London Market have provided insurance for the aviation industry.

Physical damage insurance

Aircraft may be covered by an all risk hull insurance coverage. *Hull insurance* protects against physical loss or damage to aircraft or engines. If an aircraft suffers a total loss, but engines survive, the underwriter still pays the policy amount and then salvages and sells the engines to recover a part of the insurance payment. Insurance coverage also covers engines when not attached to an airframe.

The aviation underwriters accept a value for such losses at the *agreed value* of the parties in lease transactions. The agreed value refers to a level of insurance negotiated by the parties that may equal or exceed the stipulated loss value in the lease or the fair market value of the aircraft.

Liability insurance

Aircraft can cause huge losses or liability that you have seen chronicled in the newspapers. To address this risk, liability policy levels for business aircraft may range from less than $10 million to $300 million, while commercial aircraft insurance may range from $300 million to a billion dollars in coverage for large airlines.

Political risk insurance

Because aircraft can go places that may involve political instability, lessors generally require a special coverage to guard against confiscation, seizure, appropriation, and other detention by or in a foreign country that prevents a lessor from repossessing an aircraft. See Chapter 20 regarding insurance in international transactions.

The insurance usually requires a waiting period of 180 days before it pays. However, the insurance does not cover mere delays, despite the aggravation and uncertainty that delay may cause. It responds when an affirmative act prevents a lessor from realizing its rights (for example, when a government changes or enforces its laws to prevent the release of the aircraft).

War risk and allied perils coverage

Aircraft can get in harm's way. Recently, I worked on a deal in which a lessee planned to fly her aircraft into Israel during the height of one of the armed conflicts. Although such risks may be excluded from hull and liability insurance, underwriters may put them back (in a write-back provision) and cover confiscation, sabotage, nationalization, riots, civil commotion, detonation of atomic weapons, and other similar fun events. War risk coverage may also be available but essentially is underwritten by the United States to encourage the use of civilian aircraft in war time conditions under The War Risk Insurance Act, 49 U.S.C. Section 1531-1542.

Title insurance

Title insurance is a relatively new product on the market for business aircraft (primarily), and it insures title to aircraft and other rights. The concept of aircraft title insurance, and the policy itself, is very similar to real estate title insurance. You can use aircraft title insurance to insure that validity, priority and enforceability of a security agreement or lease assignment, as well as to protect against conflicting liens and claims of others in an aircraft. For more information about aircraft title insurance, see www.firstam.com/faf/html/corpdir/html/titti.html.

Other unique aircraft insurance coverage

As a lessee or a lessor, you should at least be aware of, and ask your risk managers about, two other types of coverage (among the many others that exist for aircraft):

- **Diminution of Value Coverage,** which provides coverage for the reduction in the value of an aircraft after it sustains major airframe damage.

- **Pollution Legal Liability Coverage,** which responds to liability arising out of environmental liability at or around airports where landlord's don't pay for a pollution incident.

Subleasing

If lessors generally had their way, they probably would not allow subleases without their consent.

In business aviation, lessors can often refuse to allow subleases. In commercial aviation, however, airlines need the flexibility to sublease aircraft to manage their fleet without giving up needed lift or incurring large payments to the lessor to terminate a lease. If an airline has substantial creditworthiness or a compelling operation rationale, lessors usually permit them to sublease. These subleases may occur domestically or internationally. A few (but certainly not all) of the typical requirements to sublease include the following:

- Any sublease should be subject and subordinate to the lease (if a problem occurs under the lease, the lessor can sweep away the sublease). Sublessees despise this provision because a lessee default can disrupt the sublessee's quiet enjoyment and use of the aircraft. This point often draws heavy negotiation from lessees.

- The sublease should ideally be in substantially identical form as the lease and have a term that ends on or before the end of the term of the head lease.

- The sublessor may sublease only to acceptable sublessees and appropriate insurance must be maintained at all times.

✔ In an international sublease, the registration of the aircraft may be changed to comply with the laws of the sublessee's country. However, all maintenance and return standards in the head lease must be met (the FAA standards that may be more demanding than the foreign standards).

✔ The head lessor, at his option, may take an assignment of the sublease for security for the performance by the lessee of his obligations. The lessee remains fully liable to comply with the lease.

If you change the aircraft registration for a sublease, as a lessor or a lessee, consult with your domestic and foreign counsel to assure that your interests remain valid and effective during a sublease.

FAA scrutiny of purchase options

For registration purposes, the FAA determines whether the lessee or the lessor is the owner of the aircraft.

The FAA uses fairly technical requirements from the *Leiter Letter* (issued September 24, 1990) in analyzing who should register an aircraft at the FAA as its owner. It looks at the lessee's purchase options. For example, a purchase option of less than 10 percent of lessor's cost is a red flag indicating that the lessee should be the registrant. The FAA also examines the lessee's cost of perform under the lease to determine whether that cost exceeds the purchase option price. If so, the FAA tends to conclude that the lease constitutes a financing, which requires registration of the aircraft in the name of the lessee the registrant (but note that who holds title to the aircraft is a separate issue that the FAA does not determine).

The FAA allows a lessor to be the registered owner of the aircraft when it finds evidence (which may, in part, be a statement in the lease) that any purchase option is at fair market value or equals or exceeds the expected value of the aircraft at the expiration of the lease. The other question is whether the lessor has not transferred substantially all of the economic risks of ownership to the lessee. If not, the FAA registers the lessor of the aircraft as its owner. If so, the FAA registers the lessee of the aircraft as its the registered owner.

Truth in leasing

The FAA regulations provide that all leases and conditional sale contracts covering large aircraft (greater than 12,500 pounds) must include *truth-in-leasing provisions.* The FAA requires this special language so that all parties to the lease clearly understand their responsibilities under the lease with regard to maintenance and operations of the aircraft, thus assuring truth in leasing.

This requirement does not apply to foreign air carriers or domestic air carriers holding an operating certificate issued by the FAA. They presumably understand their obligations.

The truth-in-leasing section of the lease must be in large print and be located in the last section of the lease immediately preceding the signatures of the parties to the lease. The lease must be filed at the local FAA Flight Standards Office at least 48 hours before takeoff and disclose the location of departure, the departure time, and the registration number of the aircraft. A copy of the lease must be placed on the aircraft.

Chapter 12

Leasing Railroad Rolling Stock, Vehicles, and Vessels

*T*he industries and assets covered in this chapter each need and deserve more attention than I can provide here. Consequently, this chapter highlights some key issues involved in leasing railroad rolling stock, vessels, and vehicles.

In this chapter, I also discuss some of the common issues and documentation provisions that you may see in leasing each type of asset. Understanding these issues enables you to structure and negotiate documentation more effectively. The basic provisions of leases appear in Chapter 8 on the core terms of leases.

Leasing Railroad Rolling Stock

Railroad operations connect businesses with each other across the country and with foreign markets. They also contribute billions of dollars to the U.S. economy through investments, wages, purchases, and taxes.

Lessors own and actively lease railroad rolling stock used in the interchange system of the United States. Rolling stock refers to all the different kinds of railroad vehicles with wheels operating on railroad tracks throughout the United States (as well as Canada, Mexico, and other parts of the world). The United States has an interchange system that allows railroads to use railroad tracks anywhere in the United States and to have their rolling stock pulled by locomotives of other railroads. To place a unit of railroad rolling stock into interchange service, a railroad becomes a member of the Association of American Railroads (AAR), a well-known trade association for railroads in the United States.

The AAR has a membership that includes large national railroads as well as regional railroads. For any member to place its rolling stock in interchange service, it must agree to be bound by uniform Interchange Rules under a simple Interchange Agreement. Lessors usually refer to the AAR for a variety of compliance requirements under railroad leases, including maintenance, repair, return, interchange, and other obligations of their lessees as discussed in the following sections. A Field Manual, published by the AAR, establishes rules that these items, and lessors often refer to this manual and other AAR rules collectively as the AAR Rules or AAR Interchange Rules.

Many types of rolling stock exist with potentially high residual value, low obsolescence, and long useful lives. This rolling stock may consist of tank cars, locomotives, covered hopper cars, gondola cars, cattle cars, and other freight cars of wide use and description. Because of the diversity and value of these assets, many techniques exist for leasing them. To illustrate, for lessees, consider a few approaches:

- ✓ You can enter into a long-term leveraged lease (say, for up to 20 years) for locomotives (often using a conditional sale agreement or security agreement to evidence the debt portion of the transaction).

- ✓ You can enter into an operating lease (say, for three years) for the same locomotives. This arrangement allows you to fill a relatively short-term need for capacity that a lessor can accommodate.

- ✓ You can enter into a "car service contract" in which you pay "service charges" (such as rent) at a certain rate (say, $2 per $100 of cost) per railroad car, for the actual use of the cars. As lessee, you may agree to limits on mileage, reporting obligations, and charges for miles of use. If the car becomes damaged other than because of your responsibility, rent should abate (stop) during repairs.

- ✓ Lessors can enter into single-investor leases with you for various periods of time, which may range from seven to 20 years.

Each technique has different economic, equipment residual, credit, and other issues that lessors and lessees negotiate as part of the deal. These techniques may be used with variations worldwide on all types of railroad equipment.

Federal law preemption and regulation

After many years of heavy regulation under the control of the Interstate Commerce Commission (ICC), Congress backed off and passed the Staggers Act in 1980. The Staggers Act encourages competition and allows management to establish market rates. In 1996, Congress abolished the ICC under the ICC Termination Act of 1995 and replaced it with the Surface Transportation Board (STB). Owner-lessors today remain free of regulation by the STB because, as passive investors, they do not constitute "railcarriers" or "common carriers" (entities exercising direction and control over railroad cars).

The UCC governs security interests in goods, including equipment. Although rolling stock constitutes equipment, Section 9-109(c) of UCC Revised Article 9 specifically recognizes that federal law preempts the UCC. In this instance, federal law preempts the UCC as it relates to filings at the STB giving notice of liens on rolling stock. The UCC says that a UCC financing statement, the form filed in the states to perfect a security interest in property, is not necessary or effective to perfect security interests in property subject to a federal statute. See Chapter 17 for more on Revised Article 9.

The ICC Termination Act of 1995 generally controls the perfection of security interests in place of the UCC. However, the UCC and other state laws govern other issues not covered by that act. The state or foreign law that you select generally governs substantive rights such as who has priority to a railroad car. Further, loose equipment or spare parts not used on rolling stock may only be subject to the UCC. Superstructures and racks that are attached to or used on railroad cars are subject to the STB filings. You should consider both state and federal law in almost every rail financing or sale transaction. Consult knowledgeable legal experts in these transactions to avoid mistakes that may undermine your interest in the rolling stock.

In Chapter 11, I discuss the central filing system for aircraft. The STB, like the FAA, also provides one central filing system to record all encumbrances against rolling stock in the United States. Lessors and lenders can file many types of documents at the STB including equipment trusts, conditional sale agreements, and other instruments evidencing mortgages, leases, and conditional sales of railroad cars, locomotives, and other rolling stock.

The STB takes only filings of liens and other interests in rolling stock. It is not a title registry for bills of sale or similar instruments. The STB maintains these filings with a consecutive number and the date and hour of their recordation. The filings remain open for public inspections and describe the parties and other identifying information. Any assignment of these interests should be filed at the STB also.

To identify interests that exist in rolling stock, lessors and lenders should search the STB (and UCC) records for any evidence of liens or other interests in the rolling stock that they want to finance or lease. Unfortunately, record searches at the STB do not always produce a reliable or accurate picture. The value of the information, of course, depends on the record reflecting the identification number, type, and ownership/lien chain with respect to the rolling stock in which you have an interest. Lessors and lenders should file entire leases or conditional sale agreements or memoranda describing these documents in connection with every leasing and financing transaction.

Documentation issues in leases of rolling stock

Leases of rolling stock require customized provisions by type and use of the rolling stock. The following list mentions provisions that you negotiate in rolling stock leases that differ from the standard lease provisions discussed in Chapter 8 (which relate to the lease set forth in the Appendix).

- ✔ **General and environmental indemnities:** Railroad assets can carry all kinds of freight and substances. Most of these railroad assets can lead to environmental liability for a lessor and lessee. Spills, releases, or discharges of oil, fuel, or other hazardous substances used in maintenance or carried as cargo can create potential environmental and other liability for lessors and lessees. On January 1, 2000, the U.S. Environmental Protection Agency (EPA) published its final regulations concerning emissions of locomotives. Lessors respond to these regulations, whenever possible, by imposing an obligation on lessees to protect the lessors, as passive investors, from liability for failing to comply with environmental laws or any other event relating to the railroad asset that may create liability. In addition, lessors usually require lessees to maintain and alter their locomotives and other rolling stock to comply with changes in law.

  As a lessor, you should draft your leases to include protection from changes in law that create new obligations with respect to equipment that you own. As a lessee, you should anticipate before entering into a lease that you may have to pay all those costs as part of the lease. If that obligation rests on you, negotiate for options to terminate the lease for obsolescence or to purchase the railroad asset at a fixed price. If the investment is significant, as a lessee, you should consult with your lessor about sharing or investing the cost to upgrade the rolling stock to comply with changes in laws.

- ✔ **Maintenance and use of rolling stock:** Lessees should anticipate that they have to maintain their rolling stock in good order and repair, normal wear and tear excepted, in compliance with all applicable laws and the AAR Interchange Rules. In addition, savvy lessors may impose very specific maintenance requirements for the type of railroad rolling stock and require lessees to comply with manufacturer's specifications and repair regimes.

- ✔ **Location of use of rolling stock:** Railcars originating in the United States routinely cross the border to Mexico and Canada in normal use. Incidental crossings from the United States occur in the ordinary course of operations. Lessors generally have to permit such usage. However, many lessors prohibit any use of rolling stock in Mexico because the country does not have a central filing system. Keeping track (no pun intended!) of locations of rolling stock can be difficult. Securing the return of equipment from, and maintenance of equipment in good condition in, Mexico can challenge the most skillful equipment managers and create significant credit risk. Canada does have a central filing system in which a lease may be deposited (filed of record) with the Registrar General of Canada. The existence of this lease then must be published in the Canada Gazette (the official newspaper of the Government of Canada). These actions, if done correctly, perfect the security interest for purposes of the recording system in Canada and for the United States recordation system.

✔ **Return of rolling stock:** Lessors pay attention to the return provisions in a big way. Getting equipment back at the right location, in the proper condition, and on the required date affects residual value and a lessor's overall yield and cash flow. Return provisions say that lessees must return rolling stock to a designated location or locations (including a limited number of units returnable at a location) designated by the lessor. The rolling stock must be in the proper condition for return to the lessor — which includes being clean of commodities and in good repair in accordance with the maintenance provisions of the lease. For more complex assets like locomotives, lessors may require detailed return conditions that its lessee must meet or pay for any deficiencies. Lessors often attempt to impose on lessees the whole cost to return, store, and insure rolling stock, at least for a period of time of up to 180 days after the lease terms ends. If a lessee fails to return an item of rolling stock, the lessor will require that the lessee pay for it as if that item were a total loss at the applicable stipulated loss value as to the end of the lease.

As a lessee, you should plan to return your equipment on time and in the proper condition. However, the return condition and the period of free storage, location of return, and insurance obligations (among others issues) remain open for negotiation. If you believe that you cannot or may not return rolling stock on time at the end of the term of your lease, negotiate for options to purchase or renew your lease or lower holdover rentals. Keep up with maintenance, as lessors often charge you to put the rolling stock in the condition required for its return.

✔ **Marking rolling stock:** If you see any railroad rolling stock anywhere, look for its markings indicating the ownership of and liens on the railroad rolling stock. The STB also requires the markings, as does the lessor, to show the filing at the STB.

✔ **Insurance:** Railroad-lessees often self-insure their leased property. Railroads rationalize their action because an individual unit of rolling stock, except a locomotive, has a relatively low value compared to their entire fleet. The railroad would often rather repair or replace units at their various shops along the road (railroad, that is) than pay for insurance premiums. Railroads also may collect some contribution for the damage under the AAR Rules if another railroad causes the damage. Lessees should in all events carry significant liability insurance, but such insurance may have high deductibles.

Lessors should carry insurance for catastrophic liability, particularly personal injury and pollution liability, if you can purchase the coverage. Credit managers should assess the credit worthiness of the railroad before accepting self-insurance, and risk managers should have contingent property damage coverage to fill gaps where a lessee fails to make good on damage or loss.

✔ **Subleasing:** Lessors prefer that lessees do not sublease without consent. However, through negotiation, lessors may allow subleases to a group of "permitted sublessees" whom they may list as part of the lease or to which they give their "consent not to be unreasonably withheld." Limited exceptions may be permitted for single trips to customers or suppliers in accordance with applicable tariffs. Violations of this provision can result in defaults and/or penalty payments.

✔ **Remedies for bankruptcy and other defaults:** Locating railroad assets can challenge the best of lessors. Remedies include an obligation to return rolling stock on demand or to allow lessors to repossess the rolling stock — if they can find the cars, of course. For bankruptcy aspects or railroad leasing, see Chapter 18.

Leasing Trucks, Tractors, and Trailers

According to the Survey of Industry Activity 2000 created by the Equipment Leasing Association, the annual volume of trucking and trailer leasing constitutes more than 20 percent (or approximately $45 billion dollars in 2000) of the total volume of leasing ($226 billion dollars in 2000). This section discusses briefly some of the key issues that you face in leasing these assets.

Unlike railroad rolling stock, trucks, tractors, and trailers do not enjoy long asset lives and high residual value. Consequently, lessors often structure leases of these assets as security agreements or sales with the price paid for over time in installment payments. A few, but certainly not all, methods of leasing these assets appear in the following list.

✔ **Conditional sales agreements:** Not really a lease at all, a conditional sales agreement enables a "lessor" to retain title to the trucks and trailers but effectively receive full payment of a loan equal to 100 percent of the cost of the equipment over time.

✔ **Fleet service contracts:** Lessors that lease large groups of trucks to a lessee, called fleets, impose various fees on top of rent payments so that, by the end of the term, the lessor has been paid in full. These deals basically work like loans with payment of the depreciated value of the truck or trailer to assure that the lessor at the end of the lease, in addition to rent payments, receives payment for her residual risk. Typically, a lessor may sell the equipment for a nominal price to the lessee when all of these payments have been made.

✔ **Single-investor leases and leveraged leases:** The term of a single-investor and a leveraged lease can extend for generally three to seven years, depending on market conditions, the type of equipment, and the creditworthiness of a lessee. These leases contain many of the features discussed in Chapters 5 and 8.

✔ **TRAC leases:** A TRAC lease refers to a lease that contains a terminal rental adjustment clause. That clause makes adjustments in the final rent payment owed by a lessee. The lessee pays for any shortfall in the resale price of a vehicle, determined at the end of the lease, from the antici-pated amount needed to payoff the "lessor." This TRAC payment amount effectively equals the stipulated loss value minus proceeds of sale.

To some, it is a balloon loan payoff amount. TRAC leases are called "open-end" leases to signal a lessee's unlimited rental obligation to make up any shortfall in the vehicle's value at the end of the lease. If, on the other hand, a lessee is so lucky as to get a resale price/value that exceeds the TRAC amount, the lessee can keep all (or at least) most of the excess through a downward adjustment of last rent payment under the TRAC lease. See Chapter 22 for a discussion of the benefits of TRAC leases for lessees.

A TRAC lease provides a type of "lease" financing for motor vehicles includ-ing trucks, tractors and trailers, and automobiles. (It excludes farm tractors, forklifts, construction equipment, or certain other off-road equipment.) Although TRAC leases don't look like true tax leases, Congress fixed that conclusion by enacting Section 7701(h) of the Internal Revenue Code, making a TRAC lease a true lease for tax purposes under the Code. Score one for the motor vehicle industry and vehicle lessors! Lessors structure TRAC leases as single-investor leases because TRAC provisions do not permit lessors to use nonrecourse debt like in traditional leveraged leases.

✔ **Synthetic leases:** Synthetic leases may be used in leasing trucks, tractors, and trailers. You can read about them in Chapter 15.

Many lease provisions in the Appendix and the insurance provisions in Chapter 9 relating to automobile insurance apply when leasing vehicles. Two specialized variations merit your review:

✔ **Titling, licensing, and registration:** The titling of motor vehicles by a certificate of title differentiates leases of motor vehicles from most other types of assets. Title to other assets pass to the owner with a bill of sale or invoice. Generally, a lessor requires that his name appear on the cer-tificate of title as the owner of the vehicle. Then, as owner, he leases the vehicle to you, as the lessee.

In some large-ticket leveraged or single-investor leases of a large number of trucks, tractors, or trailers (say, 250 tractors and trailers), the lessor may appoint you, as the lessee, as his agent. As agent, you obtain the titles to each vehicle in your name and hold all titles for the benefit of the lessor. For some lessors, the administrative aspects of dealing with a high volume of vehicle titles can create a substantial and costly burden on the lessor's administrative staff. By contrast, you may regularly manage vehicle fleets and have substantially greater expertise and back room capability to handle title problems and administration.

✔ **Return of the truck, tractors, and trailers:** Lessors of railroad rolling stock and lessors of trucks, tractors, and trailers share similar return conditions applied to the particular asset. Where the rubber hits the road, so to speak, with trucks, tractors, and trailers, is in the often-detailed terms of the physical return condition. For example, as the lessee, you can expect to satisfy requirements regarding the vehicle including its general appearance, tire tread depth, minimum engine operation and capability, safety equipment, cargo area cleanliness, brake condition, and other maintenance records.

As a lessee, unless your maintenance standards have been extremely rigorous, these high standards effectively require that you buy the vehicle rather than return it. The lessor uses these standards, in part, to achieve that result. Otherwise, the lessor insists that your truck, tractor, or trailer must meet these standards; and if not, that you must pay for the repairs to hit the standards. As the lessee, you can

✔ Plan to buy the vehicle rather than worry about these return conditions.

✔ Plan your maintenance around meeting these standards.

✔ Negotiate standards that reflect your normal maintenance practices so that complying does not create a financial or maintenance burden on you.

Leasing Vessels

When you discuss leasing vessels, you have already missed the boat! Vessel financing sports a lexicon all its own. For example, you charter a vessel instead of leasing it. You do not sublease a vessel; you subcharter it.

While many similarities exist between financing vessels and other equipment, the vessel-financing world offers you a deep and long history of regulation and commerce, with a strong and vibrant international presence. Shipping, fishing, and other commercial uses of many vessels occur at every moment of the day throughout the world. Yachting, the high-end sport, provides yet another aspect of the use of vessels worldwide. In many areas of vessel use, you find lessors, called owners, providing financing in various forms that look and act like leases and secured loans.

What is a vessel?

A vessel can be a huge tanker or a small yacht, a container ship or river barge, a floating casino that tours into international waters, a shallow water jack-up oil rig or a cargo ship, a passenger ship, or a fishing boat. Vessels come in many shapes and sizes. They share the simple attributes that they generally float and can move across the surface of water. The U.S. Coast Guard (also called the Coast Guard in this section) defines vessels in Title 46 of the Code of Federal Regulations Section 67.1, includes "every description of watercraft or other contrivance used or capable of being used as a means of transportation on water, but does not include aircraft." How's that for a nice clear definition? (Not!) Is anything that that floats a vessel? Of course, you have other features discussed in the next sections.

What is a vessel classification?

Vessels in most cases are built to classification society standards. If they comply, they are "in class" with that society. Vessel classification refers to the published rules regarding the structural strength and integrity of all essential parts of the hull as well as the safety and reliability of the propulsion, electrical, pneumatic, steering, and other systems aboard the vessel. These rules and regulations help establish and maintain basic conditions onboard, so that a ship operates properly in its intended service.

What is a classification society?

A classification society refers to a private authority with special maritime and engineering expertise that establishes classification and certification requirements to verify the vessel's fitness for intended purpose throughout its useful life. The International Association of Classification Societies (IASC), for example, says that it dedicates its services to safe ships and clean seas. Accordingly to IASC, more than 90 percent of the world's cargo carrying tonnage is "entered" with one its ten Member Societies and two Associates of IACS. See www.iacs.org.uk for a listing of the member organizations and information about the regulatory and organizational aspects of IASC's classification functions. Lloyds Register of Shipping is one of the largest classification societies. Lloyds says that nearly a quarter of the world's merchant fleet is classed by it in accordance with its own rules for the construction and maintenance of ships. Lloyds surveys ships on behalf of more than 135 governments to ensure that they meet national and international safety standards for ships and shipping. See www.bmec.org.uk. The American Bureau of Shipping is the only classification society based in the United States. Owners of U.S. flag tonnage often enter their vessels with ABS. In certain circumstances, the Coast Guard delegates its function to inspect vessels to ABS. See www.eagle.org/.

Vessels and shipping involve international issues. Although I discuss some aspects of American vessel financing, you must view the entire subject of vessel finance from an international perspective.

Registration of vessels

You may register vessels with a ship registry in various countries throughout the world, such as the United States.

In the United States, the Coast Guard can register many (but not all) vessels. Before registration and trading under the United States flag, however, the Coast Guard inspects the vessel (or delegates that function to ABS). In most cases, a vessel (generally of significant size and international use) must possess a number of internationally required trading certificates dependent on the classification of the vessel. Classification societies establish and attempt to enforce those standards.

Documentation and registration in the United States

If, as discussed in the following section, you are a citizen of the United States, you may initially document or register a vessel flying the U.S. flag by filing a Coast Guard Form CG-1258, Application For Initial Issue, Exchange, or Replacement of Certificate of Documentation; Redocumentation. This form requires that you provide information about the vessel and its owner(s) necessary for registration and documentation. The Coast Guard issues a Certificate of Documentation to evidence that you have successfully registered a vessel in the United States. Vessels below certain tonnage limits, depending upon the use of the vessel, may be "uninspected." Virtually every ocean-going cargo vessel must, in addition to a Certificate of Documentation, obtain a Certificate of Inspection. The same requirement can apply to inland vessels, especially those carrying passengers or used to haul hazardous materials.

Each vessel appears of record under its own documented name. To distinguish vessels with similar or even identical names, the Coast Guard's National Documentation Center assigns a unique "official number" to each documented vessel. A vessel retains its official number so long as it remains documented with the Coast Guard, even after sale or name change. The records also show any hull identification number, The records also show any hull identification number, any official number awarded by the Coast Guard, and the hailing port.

Previously when the Coast Guard maintained separate documentation offices around the United States, it used detailed rules regarding hailing ports and "home ports." The National Documentation Center in Falling Waters, West Virginia, now administers the documentation of vessels nationwide. A U.S.-flag vessel need show as a hailing port only a proper postal address within the United States. A Miami harbor tug may show its hailing port to be Nome, AK. The Center's address is: National Vessel Documentation Center (NVDC), 792 T J Jackson Drive, Falling Waters, West Virginia 25419-9502 (800) 799-8362 or (304) 271-2400. Fax: Main: (304) 271-2405 Credit Card: (304) 271-2415. Also, see www.uscg.mil/hq/g-m/vdoc/Poc.htm. The Center has adopted innovative "fax filing" of documents relating to vessels, which enables transactions to close thousands of miles from the Center, but to take effect as if filed with the Center immediately.

If you own a registered vessel, you must renew the endorsement(s) on Certificates of Documentation each year. Failure to renew the endorsement(s) may result in the vessel being removed from documentation. Operation of a vessel with expired endorsements may result in a civil penalty. If your vessel has been lost, sold, abandoned, destroyed, or placed under state numbering, you must notify the National Vessel Documentation Center in writing. If the Certificate of Documentation is available, it must be surrendered to the Coast Guard.

Once you establish the record, you file documents to show various events. A Coast Guard Form CG-1340 Bill of Sale provides a record, available for public inspection and copying, of the sale or other change in ownership of a vessel, which is documented, will be documented, or has been documented pursuant to Chapter 121of Title 46 of the United States Code. The Bill of Sale remains on the books of the Coast Guard for examination by governmental authorities and members of the general public.

The record can also show a grant of various rights affecting a vessel on Coast Guard Form CG-5542, Optional Application for Filing, including a mortgage, assumption, subordination or amendment to a mortgage or chattel mortgage. Each filing is listed by date, book, and page.

Citizenship and other standards for U.S. vessel registration

Similar to the registration of aircraft in the United States, the Coast Guard enforces statutory standards that a vessel must be owned by a citizen of the United States. Generally speaking, the citizenship rules say that a corporation, trust, partnership or other registered entity constitutes a U.S. citizen if it senior managers, partners, members, and owners are citizens. If the vessel carries cargo or passengers between points in the United States (including to and from Puerto Rico), the vessel must be built in the United States (to the degree and in way required by U.S. law). An owner may register and document a vessel (file registration form CG-1258) with the Coast Guard if a vessel weighs at least five tons and is registered under the laws of a foreign country. A citizen of the United States must own the vessel. For Coast Guard forms that you can download, see www.uscg.mil/hq/g-m/vdoc/instr.htm.

Many other qualifications and technical requirements exist for United States registration. These rules do not apply to the same extent, however, if a vessel engages in foreign trade (outside the waters of the United States).

Certain other registries around the world do not impose such strict rules. These registries, called open registries or flags of convenience, allow anyone to register ships under their flag. Some, like Liberia, have a requirement (which can be waived) that a Liberian citizen owns the vessel. Owners can satisfy this requirement by having the legal owner be a Liberian company. Panama, another large open registry, allows anyone, whether Panamanian or not, to register ships there. Following the lead of Panama and Liberia, a number of countries have adopted laws allowing for open registries, including the Bahamas, Luxembourg Cyprus, Malta, the Marshall Islands, Vanuatu, St. Vincent and the Grenadines, and Antigua. Each county charges certain fees for registration, periodic filings, and annual taxes.

Regardless of where you register a vessel, expect to encounter various types of forms to complete. Each registry has its own process. Before you buy or charter a vessel, you should check the records for registration of title or lien in the name of other individuals or entities to ensure clear rights to the vessel. As a lessee, you, too, want to avoid conflicts with others who purport to have rights against the vessel. You should be aware that unlike other assets, maritime liens can be secret or recorded. You must therefore allow time to check the maintenance, crew, and supply payment history of the current owner to try to find liens or unpaid bills. If these costs exist, they can attach directly to the vessel. The person holding those rights can enforce rights against the vessel like the vessel itself is a person responsible for payment.

Federal law preemption in vessel financing

The UCC often governs security interests in goods, including equipment (with exceptions). Although vessels constitute equipment, the UCC specifically recognizes that federal law preempts the UCC as it relates to filings for notice of liens on vessels under registries established by federal law, such as the registry of vessels with the Coast Guard. See Chapter 17 on Revised Article 9 to the UCC.

Special lien and lender issues

Maritime law allows for the creation of liens on vessels that may not appear in the maritime records of the applicable registry. As noted in the preceding sections, certain liens, such as those that the suppliers of goods and services to the vessel ordered by an authorized person (called necessaries) and its crew, have a special priority. These liens may be imposed without any filing in the maritime records. However, secured lenders holding preferred ship mortgages may be entitled to priority over supply liens that accrue after filing of the preferred ship mortgage. A preferred ship mortgage that meets certain requirements wins if valid under substantive law. However, crew wages, salvage, necessaries, and tort claims (personal injury relating to the vessel), which may not appear in any record relating to the vessel, take the top spot in priority.

If you buy or charter a used vessel, conduct extensive due diligence to determine whether any liens or nonpayments exist and require the seller to indemnify you for those liens. You may be wise to hold back some cash to pay liens or claims that arise for up to a year or 18 months after a sale to avoid unanticipated cost. As an owner (lessor) or charterer (lessee), you should have the same concerns. If the vessel is new, maritime liens do not exist until a vessel has been launched; so file your documents before or concurrent with the launch and confirm that the shipyard and its subcontractors have been paid in full.

Documentation issues in charters

In many respects, the provisions in Chapter 8, in substance, cover many issues in vessel financing. This list highlights a few (but certainly not all) differences between the specialized leases for vessels and leases of other assets.

✔ **Charters and more charters:** In vessel financing, you can enter into a bareboat charter or a time charter or contract of affreightment among other types of arrangements. A bareboat charter refers to a long-term net lease of a vessel in which the charterer (lessee) takes possession and uses the vessel. These charters typically contain a hell-or-high-water clause that precludes nonpayment of charter hire (rent) without any reduction or abatement of rent for any reason, such as a problem with trading, detention of the vessel, or requisition of the vessel by a foreign government. A time charter refers to a lease in which the owner provides the crew and remains in possession of the vessel for the benefit of the user for a particular time period. A voyage charter, as the name indicates, is a lease agreement for a single voyage, usually between a cargo owner, as lessee, and a vessel operator, either the owner or a time or bareboat charterer, as lessor. A contract of affreightment is an agreement between a charterer/cargo owner with long-term needs and a vessel operator who agrees to furnish ships for future voyages. It often does not even specify a particular vessel. Various forms of documents exist for these charters such as Barcon 89, a commercial form published by the Baltic and International Maritime Counsel (BIMCO) — see www.bimco.dk. You can draft customized charters for vessels ranging from tankers to yachts.

✔ **Maintenance of vessels:** In order for registration of a vessel to occur in a particular registry, the vessel must remain in the condition required by the registry. An owner of vessels on bareboat charters (but not time or voyage charters who have crew onboard) do, and should, insist on the right to inspect vessels to confirm compliance with these requirements.

Classification societies set standards for a vessel to remain "in class," and lessors who lease out on a "bareboat" basis should require lessees to adhere to those standards. Lessees, on the other hand, need to know those standards well so that they properly assess the costs of chartering the vessel from the lessor. Lessors often survey vessels at the beginning of a charter, periodically during, and at the return of the vessel at the end of a charter to ensure that these and other standards for maintenance and return have been met.

✔ **Insurance:** Insurance provisions pull in the lexicon once again. Property damage insurance takes on the name hull and machinery insurance. Comprehensive commercial liability is called protection and indemnity insurance. The terms vary somewhat because of the nature of the asset that requires real insurance expertise of specialized brokers and underwriters.

Underwriters in the maritime liability insurance area often consist of protection and indemnity clubs. These "clubs" are actual mutual insurance companies, owned by their "member" policyholders. They provide a spreading of risk of liability among many the members. Except for pollution liability coverage, the liability coverage these clubs offer may not have prescribed limits.

Property damage coverage responds to damage to a vessel's machinery or hull as a result of perils of the sea. The insurance payable for a total loss equals the agreed value. That value may be more or less than the value of the vessel at the date of the loss. As in other leases, a charter may contain a set of values, called stipulated loss values or casualty loss values that set the amount of coverage payable in a total loss by the charterer or its insurance carrier.

Part IV
Going by the Book: Tax, Legal, and Accounting Rules

The 5th Wave   By Rich Tennant

"I'm sorry, we can't draw up a variable lease on the Blues Bar based on when you think you'll get your mojo back."

In this part . . .

Taxation motivates leasing. It's crucial, period! This part explains the critical subjects of Federal income tax and state sales, use, and property taxes in a useful and friendly way, but with enough detail to help you actually do deals with the knowledge of many key issues. You also won't want to miss my discussion of the Revised Article 9 of the Uniform Commercial Code. This law, effective in all but a handful of states on July 1, 2001, impacts every lease and changes significantly the prior law, now aptly known by many as Former Article 9. In addition, you find a discussion on bankruptcy from the point of view of how lessees can use bankruptcy laws to their advantage and how lessors can cope with the related events.

Chapter 13

Considering Federal Taxes

. . . .

In This Chapter

▶ Structuring a true lease instead of a conditional sale

▶ Listing the criteria to qualify as a true lease under federal tax law

▶ Describing the tax benefits for lessees and lessors in leasing

. . . .

*T*o get the real bang for your buck in leasing, read this chapter. It presents some key tax concepts that you need to understand. Tax benefits drive the economics of leases that qualify under federal income tax laws as true leases, and tax benefits add significant value to such leases over other types financing or leasing.

This chapter explores true tax leases that may be structured as leveraged leases or single-investor leases. In this chapter, I help you identify and apply the criteria to qualify your lease as a true lease rather than a security agreement or conditional sale. This chapter also describes the tax benefits that you can claim, as the lessee or the lessor, depending on how you structure your lease.

When you read this chapter together with the Chapters 6, 7, and 20, you can understand why and how tax structuring has propelled leasing forward as a viable and creative economic tool in expanding the capital expenditures for businesses in the United States and around the world.

Understanding a True Lease

In 1975, the Internal Revenue Service (*IRS*) issued Revenue Procedure 75-21, 1975-1 C.B. 715 as guidelines to determine whether a proposed leveraged lease constitutes a true lease (sometimes called the *Guidelines* in this chapter). Originally, if a leveraged lease fit the true lease criteria, the IRS could issue a revenue ruling that the proposed transaction constituted a true lease for federal income tax purposes. Revenue Procedure 75-28, 1975-1, C.B. 752 tells you what information and representations you must include in a request for private ruling. A *private ruling* expresses the decision by the IRS, in response to the request of a taxpayer, of how the IRS will treat a specific transaction as a true lease or a conditional sale.

Today, you can ask for a ruling, but you can generally apply the Guidelines yourself without a request for such a ruling from the IRS, to help you structure a true lease of single-investor leases and leverage leases. However, note that you have no legal protection if you rely upon the Guidelines without obtaining a private ruling, but you can still do what most lessors do — figure it out with the help of knowledgeable tax counsel. Although a single-investor lease technically lies outside of the Guidelines, the relevant Guidelines also help you create a valid, true lease in a single-investor transaction. Lessors in single-investor leases can ignore the aspects of the Guidelines relating to non-recourse debt because lessors in those deals don't use such debt.

A true lease is sometimes called a *Guidelines Lease.* A true lease takes the synonymous name of a Guidelines Lease because the Guidelines provide the best statement of the meaning of a true tax lease. A *true lease* refers to a lease of property in which the lessor demonstrates that it has assumed the benefits and burdens of ownership of the property in a manner that entitles the lessor alone to claim all applicable benefits of a tax owner of property under Federal tax law. You can determine whether a true lease exists based on all the facts and circumstances of a transaction, legal precedent from applicable case law, and Revenue Rulings issued by the IRS. A true lease is not a conditional sale or security agreement.

Creating a True Lease

To claim the economic benefits derived from tax benefits, you must structure your lease as a true lease and not a conditional sale or other financing.

Tax consequences if you do create a true lease

If a lessor succeeds in structuring a lease as a true lease, then the lessor becomes the tax owner of the property. Tax owners may claim depreciation deductions and, in leveraged leases, the interest deductions on the debt portion of the transaction. Those deductions shelter income from the lessor's lease rents until later tax years and, in leveraged leases, defer tax payments on other income unrelated to the lease transaction until later years. See Chapters 6 and 7 on after-tax economics for lessees and lessors.

Tax consequences if you don't create a true lease

If a lessor fails to structure a lease as a true lease, the tax law treats the lease as a conditional sale or other financing or secured loan. The lessee's payments break into components of imputed principal and interest instead of rent. The lessee becomes the tax owner of the property. As a secured party and not the lessor, the lessor receives no depreciation benefits or interest deductions. Economically, the lessor may not be entitled to the residual value because the lessee is treated as the tax owner. If a lessor prices her lease as a true lease, but the IRS says that the lessor's lease constitutes a conditional sale, the lessor may experience a steep drop in her yield on the lease. Depending on the lessor's arrangement, a lessee may have to indemnify the lessor for loss of those tax benefits, but often, the lessor's failure to structure a lease as a true lease becomes the lessor's own tax loss (the lessee provides no indemnification for that goof). See "Income tax indemnification" in Chapter 8.

Original tests of a true lease

The IRS issued Revenue Ruling 55-540, 1955-2 C.B. 39 in 1955 long before the Guidelines. This ruling sets forth some general criteria to determine whether an agreement constitutes a lease. This ruling says that whether you structure a true lease or a conditional sale depends on the intent of the parties with no single test or any special combination of tests absolutely determining the answer.

Be clear about your intent. State it in your lease. For example, say

"Lessor and Lessee intend that for United States Federal income tax purposes (i) this Lease shall constitute a true lease and not a loan, conditional sale agreement, or financing agreement; and (ii) Lessor shall be considered the owner and Lessee shall be considered the lessee for all purposes."

Structure your lease to carry out your intent. If you intend to create a true lease, the lessor should act like an owner and be entitled alone to take the benefits of the tax owner. The lessee should act like a user of property only without ownership or equity but with responsibilities to the lessor to possess the leased property, and pay rent, maintain, and pay the costs related to the normal use of the property.

Criteria for a true lease

The Guidelines provide most of the essential criteria to establish a true lease. This section asks you a series of questions to help you determine whether your lease constitutes, or proposed lease structure will constitute, a true lease or other financing arrangement for tax purposes. Although this section asks black-and-white questions, the entire area is painted with many shades of gray. If you meet all the criteria, you establish a true lease. If you fail any of the criteria, you may end up with a financing (but in this chapter, I mostly refer the term conditional sales instead of financings).

As you read this chapter, keep in mind that the criteria do not all carry the same weight in the eyes of the IRS. Stay focused on three points. First, look for the economic substance in every "true lease." Enter into a transaction only if it makes a profit apart from the tax benefits. Second, make sure that your lease has a meaningful residual value in it at all times. Third, the IRS and courts weigh and balance the true lease criteria in great depth, so don't go through a tax lease without the help of a leasing lawyer or other tax professional trained in these matters. Failing one or more of the criteria may not prevent you, on balance, from achieving true lease treatment.

Twenty percent unconditional investment by the lessor

Question: Does the lessor make a 20 percent unconditional investment in the cost of the leased property and maintain that investment "at risk" throughout the lease term? Would you believe that this is a basic question? Tax lawyers love this stuff! If your answer is yes, the answer indicates a true lease. If your answer is no, the answer indicates a conditional sale. This section shows you how to reach your answer.

First, the Guidelines require that lessors make, or unconditionally commit to make, an investment of at least 20 percent of the cost of the leased property at the start of the lease and maintain that 20 percent investment "at risk" throughout the lease term. A lessor may provide the investment either by:

- Paying with his own cash (not cash acquired from a "limited recourse" or nonrecourse lender)

- Committing to buy the leased property without any condition that even remotely may occur to terminate a lessor's obligation to pay for leased property

Despite the 20 percent guideline, lessors may still achieve true lease status if they invest as little as 13 percent of the cost of certain leased assets. In high technology and real estate leases, some lessors invest as little as 10 percent and 6 percent, respectively. However, to stay on the safe side, when you can, as the lessor, shoot for 20 percent. In a leveraged lease, you can use non-recourse debt to pay the balance of the cost for the leased property but should not include that debt in determining the amount of the lessor's investment.

Second, the Guidelines require that a lessor keep a continuing investment in the transaction throughout the lease term in a minimum amount of at least 20 percent of the cost of the leased property. The Guidelines determine whether a lessor maintains the investment by applying a mathematical formula. The formula is applied as of the inception of the lease based on projected cash flows. It includes an estimate of realizing a residual value of at least 20 percent of the lessor's cost. In essence, the formula determines whether a lessor cashes out too early in the lease term. In other words, a lessor must not receive his anticipated profit and cash any faster than pro rata over the lease term; otherwise, the lessor has little or no risk late in the lease term (see Section 4(1)(C) of the Rev. Proc. 75-21). If the risk doesn't exist, the lease fails under this part of the Guidelines and may not be treated as a true lease.

Finally, a lessor may not receive the funds used to make his qualifying investment from any member of the *Lessee Group*. The *Lessee Group* includes the lessee and any party related to the lessee within the meaning of Section 318 of the Internal Revenue Code of 1986, as amended (called the "Code" in this chapter). As interpreted by the IRS, a related party refers generally to corporations and other entities subject to 50 percent or more common ownership with the lessee.

Although a lessee can elect to terminate a lease early, for example, based on the obsolescence of the leased property, the lessor can't use a contingency to extract funds from the Lessee Group and thereby get her investment back during the term. Similarly, a lessor can't *unwind* (end) a deal during the term due to some contingency so as to recoup its investment early from the Lessee Group.

The 20/20 tests

The *20/20 tests* refer to a determination that 20 percent of the original value and 20 percent of the original useful life of the leased property remain at the end of the lease term.

First Question: Estimating at the start of the lease, will the leased property have a fair market value at the end of the lease term equal to at least 20 percent of the original lessor's cost? In answering this question, you do not consider inflation or deflation during the lease term or, typically, the costs to dismantle or remove the leased property. If your answer is yes, the answer indicates a true lease. If your answer is no, the answer indicates a conditional sale.

You exclude costs of removal only if the net lease obligations of the lease require this removal to occur at the lessee's cost. In that case, a lessor may determine the value of the leased property "in place, in use" (which means the value working at the lessee's location for the purposes for which the lessee uses the leased property). For example, if, as a lessor, you lease a printing press to a lessee with a lessor's cost of $2,000,000, the press must, at the end of the lease term, still be worth $400,000 (without considering the costs of removal to a new location).

Inflation may not be considered. The Guidelines seek to create a "snapshot" at closing date of the value of the leased property without considering future increases in value attributable to inflation. Some of the decided cases appear to reject this limitation.

If the lessor and/or the lessee have the option to renew their lease at a fixed rental rate, the lease term must be extended to the end of the potential renewal term, whether or not the parties exercise a renewal option. See Section 4(2) of the Rev. Proc 75-21. To illustrate, say a lessor and lessee enter into a five-year lease in which the lessor can require a lessee at the end of the lease to renew for one two-year period. The lease term should be considered to be seven years. Say that a lessee can elect a fixed-price renewal option at 50 percent of the original rent for three additional years. The lease term should be considered to be eight years. See Section 4(1)(C) of the Rev. Proc 75-21.

Second Question: Estimating at the start of the lease, will the leased property have remaining useful life at the end of the lease term equal to at least 20 percent of the original useful life? In answering this question, your remaining useful life must be at least one year at the end of the lease. If your answer is yes, the answer indicates a true lease. If your answer is no, the answer indicates a conditional sale.

Useful life refers to the economic life of the leased property rather than its physical life. As a result, you consider not only the wear and tear on the leased property, but also its obsolescence, in determining useful life.

The lease term may only extend for 80 percent of the originally estimated useful life of the leased property. In other words, the useful life must always extend at least 125 percent of the original lease term. For example, say that you lease a printing press on a ten-year lease, the printing press must have an estimated useful life equal to 10 years x 125 percent = 12.5 years. Alternatively, 80 percent of 12.5 years = 10 years.

In each of these tests, the determination of value and useful life should, at least in large ticket transactions, be supported by a written appraisal from an independent appraisal firm that provides support for compliance with these tests.

No payment by lessee of the lessor's cost

Question: Did the lessee directly or indirectly pay any part of the cost of the leased property? If your answer is no, the answer indicates a true lease. If your answer is yes, the answer indicates a conditional sale.

The Guidelines say that no member of the Lessee Group may pay any of the cost of the leased property. See Section 4(4) of the Rev. Proc 75-21. If the lessee, through no fault of her own, experiences cost overruns that exceed the lessor's commitment, the lessee must either exclude portions of the leased property from the lease or obtain the lessor's investment in the full cost. For example, if the lessor commits to $2 million for a lease of printing press, but additional costs push the cost to $2.6 million, the lessee must drop at least $600,000 of equipment from the lease transaction or the lessor must increase her commitment to $2.6 million. The lessee may not simply sell the lease asset to the lessor for less than its value (costs).

A lessee may be able to incur some soft costs where he constructs or initially purchases the leased property. He can call these costs overhead. The better approach, however, requires the lessee to include these costs (that is, allocate them to the lessor's cost) that he would not otherwise incur if he did not acquire and lease the leased property.

No lessee loans or guarantees of debt

Question: Does the lessee provide any direct or indirect guaranty or loan to the lessor or a lender to pay for the leased property? Does the lessee incur any debt itself in the leveraged lease? If your answers to both questions are no, the answers indicate a true lease. If your answer to either question is yes, the answer indicates a conditional sale.

Section 4(5) of the Rev. Proc. 75-21 says that no member of the Lessee Group may lend the lessor any money to purchase the leased property or guaranty any loan incurred by the lessor to purchase the leased property. Case law differs from this guideline, but the best approach requires that the lessor alone repay the leveraged lease debt. In any event, rent in most leases, and especially in leveraged leases, includes the amount that the lessor needs to pay for the debt service. Consequently, the lessor should not ask the lessee to cover debt service through a guaranty or a promise to pay the lender.

The Rev. Proc. 75-21 do not prevent someone outside the Lessee Group from providing credit support in the form of a letter of credit, residual value guaranty, credit insurance, or government guaranty. A member of the Lessee Group can also guaranty to the lessor the obligations of the lessee under the lease.

No lessee payment of transaction costs

Question: Is the lessee required to pay at closing from her own resources the transaction costs incurred by the lessor and/or lender to close the lease transaction (the transaction costs)? If your answer is no, the answer indicates a true lease. If your answer is yes, the answer indicates a conditional sale.

In structuring leases, determine whether the lessee directly pays transaction costs at closing, such as legal fees, appraisal fees and professional fees and expenses, printing, escrow, title insurance, and other fees and expenses of closing a leveraged lease transaction. You should note, however, that Section 4(4) of the Rev. Proc. 75-21 says that lessors and not lessees must pay fees and expenses that don't clearly pertain exclusively to the lessee's own transaction costs. These costs must be allocated to the lease property, as part of the cost of the leased property and included in rent, payable by the lessee over the lease term. Lessors can, of course, increase the rent to cover paying the expenses. The lessee can pay her out-of-pocket expenses, such as attorneys' fees.

At closing, you may not know, or have bills for, the total amount of transaction costs. Lessees can generally pay these costs as "supplemental rent" (which is an extra rent payment for unknown expenses). The parties reasonably estimate these expenses at the time of closing). The lessor typically pays the expenses out of this supplemental rent within six to eight weeks after closing when final expenses are submitted to the lessor for payment. See Rev. Ruling 79-13-094, Dec. 28, 1978.

No lessor puts or rights to abandon property

Question: Did the lessor include in his lease documents any right to abandon the leased property where it sits or any right to require the lessee to buy the leased property? If your answer is no, the answer indicates a true lease. If your answer is yes, the answer indicates a conditional sale. If the lessor can force a lessee to buy the leased property, the lessee agrees to repay the lessor's remaining investment, which alleviates the risk to the lessor of loss that an owner bears. Any such requirement shows that the lessor does not carry the burden of the residual risk. See Section 4(3) of the Rev. Proc. 75-21.

No lessee bargain purchase options

Question: If the lessor grants a purchase option for the leased property during a lease term (an *early buyout option* or *EBO*) or at the end of the lease term, did the lessor require the lessee to pay the fair market value determined at the date of the option? If your answer is yes, the answer indicates a true lease. If your answer is no, the answer indicates a conditional sale. In considering this answer, the lessor may establish at the start of the lease term a reasonable estimate of fair market value and fix the price of the EBO or of the purchase option at the start of the lease term.

A *bargain purchase option* essentially refers to an offer to purchase that a reasonable lessee can't refuse. A lessor may certainly offer the lessee an option to purchase the leased property at its fair market value (or higher) determined at the end of the lease term under Section 4(3) of the Rev. Proc. 75-21. Although the Guidelines do not permit it, the courts have determined that a lessor may even offer a lessee a *fixed-price purchase option,* for tax purposes, if the price is a reasonable estimate of the fair market value. A fixed rate purchase option means a right to buy the leased property, at a price set at the start of the lease that the lessee pays during or at the end of the lease. The price should equal or exceed the estimated fair market value of the leased property.

Take a conservative approach on purchase options. Fix your price at the expected fair market value as of the end of the lease. Avoid bargains. The more the lessor gives up in the value of the property to the lessee (actual fair market value minus the fixed option price of lessee), the more the IRS may consider that the lessee has "equity" in the deal inconsistent with Rev. Proc. 75-21 and applicable case law.

By contrast to purchase options, an option to renew the lease at a nominal or fair value amount does not stop you from qualifying your transaction as a true lease under the Guidelines, with one catch. You must, at the beginning of the lease, satisfy the 20/20 tests, and you must include all renewals as part of the lease term when you figure out the 20/20 calculation. However, you do not have to include renewals at fair rental value determined at the time of the renewal.

Early buyout options (EBOs) present a different analysis than renewals. If the EBO price is less than the fair market value of the leased property, the lessee has an incentive to end the lease early to capture that value for itself, even though the price may be very substantial.

You determine whether this right creates a problem by asking whether the lessee is economically compelled to exercise the EBO. If, based on economics, the lessee comes out way ahead by purchasing rather than staying in the lease, you may face a true lease issue. In practice, lessors price early buyout options either at an estimate of (or more than) fair market value, taking away a compelling economic reason for the lessee to exit the lease. This approach by lessors helps structure the lease within the true lease requirements.

Lessor must make a profit apart from tax benefits

Question: Does the lessor expect to make a profit on the lease apart from the value of the tax benefits of owning and leasing the leased property? If your answer is yes, the answer indicates a true lease. If your answer is no, the answer indicates a conditional sale. This test (called the *profit test*) is imposed by the IRS to prevent leases that are based solely to the tax savings to the lessor.

Lessor must receive free cash from the rents

Question: Does the lessor expect to receive annual free cash of at least 2 percent of the lessor's cost as a result of owning and leasing the leased property? If your answer is yes, the answer indicates a true lease. If the answer is no, the answer indicates a conditional sale. This test requires the lessor to show that the aggregate of his cash receipts under the lease will exceed the aggregate cash disbursements by a reasonable amount. Disbursements include costs incurred by lessor to finance his equity investment. The IRS has accepted 2 percent annual return on the equity investment of a lessor as satisfactory.

Special Rules and Requirements for Tax Leases

As if the Guidelines aren't enough aggravation, this section presents a few more concepts that you must follow in pricing and negotiating the terms of your tax leases. These concepts do not determine whether your lease qualifies as a true lease. Rather, these concepts represent limitations or constraints imposed by Congress and the IRS on the tax benefits that lessors can structure into a lease transaction. In other words, these constraints may affect whether a lessor achieves the overall tax benefits of the lease.

Uneven rents and the saga of Section 467

Section 467 of the Code challenges even the most knowledgeable tax lawyers and accountants. The Section 467 accounting rules generally do not apply to (among others) rents payable in equal amounts over a lease term or to leases involving aggregate rent payments of less than $250,000. If you do not pay or charge level rents in your lease or use the cash method of accounting for rent payments, read the following sections.

Lessors must generate rent to repay and earn a return on their investments. For tax purposes, the later in the lease term that a lessor reports income, the later the date on which a lessor pays taxes. The later a lessor pays taxes, the more cash he keeps and the higher yield he achieves. The IRS really likes to get paid its taxes and really hates it when taxpayers try to avoid paying their taxes when the IRS thinks that the taxes are due. As a result, Section 4(1)(B) of Rev. Proc. 75-21 includes the 90/110 rules, which try to prevent lessors from avoiding taxes by sophisticated lease structuring aimed at deferring tax payments until a later time during the lease term.

Under the 90/110 rules in the Guidelines, the IRS can refuse to give a private ruling under the Guidelines if the annual rent for any year of a lease amounted to more than 10 percent above or below the average annual rent for the lease term. For example, in general, if rent on average equals $100,000 per year, the rent could neither exceed $110,000 nor fall below $90,000 in any year to obtain a ruling that a lease qualifies as a true lease.

Section 467 effectively displaces the 90/110 test with stronger and far more complex rules and regulations on tax deferrals that extend way beyond the scope of this discussion. Section 467 addresses how rent must be allocated to lease periods under a lease for tax purposes. It says that if rent payments in the early years of a lease are too high and lease payments in later years of the lease are consequently too low, the excess rents constitute prepaid rents. These prepaid rents must be leveled out according to Section 467. As a result, the lessee cannot take rent deductions as early as planned (that is, the deductions must be allocated to later periods), and the lessor must recognize income allocated to the earlier periods in which the lessor actually received the income. This result can really spoil your day if your economics rely on the deferral of income as a lessor or the early deductions of rent by the lessee.

The IRS wants to constrain rent payments other than level rents. Watch out for uneven rents (rent in unequal amounts). Any significant deferral of rent payments may trigger Section 467 and result in a costly reallocation of rent under complex reallocation rules. Consult tax practitioners who understand Section 467 to try to structure your lease correctly.

Permitted lessee improvements to leased property

Lessees may make improvements or upgrades to leased property during a lease term. They occur in two types: severable *improvements* (improvements that can be removed without damage to the leased property) and *nonseverable improvements* (improvements that can't be removed without damage to the leased property). Lessees can generally make severable improvements without tax consequences unless the lessor realizes income on a sale of the property including the improvement or compensates the lessee by giving the lessee a share of the value of the property attributable to the improvement. A lessor can realize income if the improvement increases the productivity or capacity of leased property by more than 25 percent of the original capacity or costs more than 10 percent (adjusted for inflation) of the original lessor's cost of the original leased property. (You don't consider improvements to comply with health, safety and environmental standards required by governmental regulation.)

No limited use property in true leases

Revenue Procedure 76-30, 1976-2 C.B. 647 says that at the end of the lease term, a third person (outside the Lessee Group) must be able to use the leased property based on present knowledge and engineering standards. In other words, if the lessee alone can use the leased property at the end of the lease term, and no one else will buy it, rent it, or can feasibly use the leased property, then the property has limited use. In that case, it may be treated as *limited use property,* such as a unique or custom-made pollution equipment or a smokestack attached to a masonry warehouse.

If your transaction involves limited use property, take a hard look at whether you can still achieve true lease treatment on that property.

Tax Benefits in True Leases

Once you qualify your lease transaction as a true lease, as a lessor, you become entitled to the tax benefits as the tax owner of the property. This section briefly describes the current depreciation and interest deductions available to lessors.

Although I address this section primarily to lessors, lessees can take the same tax benefits in any purchase or conditional sale of property. Consequently, as a lessee, in reading this section, you can gain an understanding of benefits potentially available to you and to your lessor. Tax law regarding depreciation, a key tax benefit, has been relatively stable for almost a decade. However, you should keep an eye on Congress for changes that may occur to spur capital investment in a slowing economy or recession and adjust your pricing accordingly.

Depreciation benefits and systems

The value of tax deductions for depreciation provides the incentive to enter into tax-oriented single-investor and leveraged leases. These deductions enable lessors to price tax-oriented leasing cheaper than other kinds of financing as covered in Chapter 7. The allowance for depreciation motivates capital investment by lessors with a tax bill.

Depreciation refers to the decline in value of property through its use and the passage of time, wear and tear, technological change, and obsolescence. Under Federal income tax law, as the owner of income producing property, you can take a deduction from your income for depreciation of property because the property depreciates during the lease term. Section 167 of the Code allows you to deduct certain amounts from your income for exhaustion, wear, and tear (including a reasonable obsolescence) of property.

Depreciation deductions are specified by the Code and the related regulations. They are based on the cost of the property, the depreciable life (the "recovery period" set by law) of the property, and the method of depreciation used by the owner of the property.

The straight-line method of depreciation

Straight-line depreciation is the slowest method applicable to new and used property. It refers to depreciation deductions equal to the *tax basis* of the property divided by the number of years of useful life of the property. For example, say that manufacturing equipment has a useful life of five years and a basis of $100,000 (cost). The write-off each year is $100,000 divided by 5 years = $20,000 per year in write off, or 20 percent per year over five years. *Basis* refers to an amount, subject to complex adjustments, that is generally equal to the cost of the property and expenses to acquire it. Your initial basis is the amount that the IRS allows you to write off through depreciation deductions. Your *adjusted basis* (original cost minus the depreciation deductions taken in prior years) determines your gain or loss on a sale or other taxable disposition of your property. You may not depreciate all costs that you incur because they may not qualify as a part of the basis of leased property under applicable laws and regulations.

The declining balance method of depreciation

The *declining balance method* allows the lessor to take deductions determined by multiplying the adjusted basis of the property by a declining balance rate. As characterized in Section 168 of the Code, you can use the *200 percent declining balance method* for recovery periods of ten years or less and the *150 percent declining balance method* for other property. Both methods allow you to write off the tax basis of the property faster than straight-line. Both switch to straight-line when you can maximize the deduction using straight-line depreciation.

The declining balance rate equals two times the straight-line depreciation rate each year in the case of 200 percent declining balance and one and one-half times the straight-line depreciation rate each year in the case of the one and the 150 percent declining balance method. In essence, you apply 200 or 150 percent of the straight-line rate to the depreciation left each year after you subtract all prior year's depreciation. For example, say that you are leasing the same manufacturing equipment with a $100,000 basis and a five-year recovery period. In the first year, ignoring first-year conventions, you can write off $100,000 x 20 percent (the straight line write off) x 2 (the 200 percent) = $40,000. In year two, start by subtracting the write-off from year one from $100,000 and do the same calculation: $100,000 minus $40,000 = $60,000 x 20 percent (the straight-line write off) x 2 (the 200 percent) = $24,000. Use this approach each of the other three years until straight-line write-off exceeds the 200 percent, and then switch to straight line to write off the balance.

The Modified Accelerated Cost Recovery System

The *Modified Accelerated Cost Recovery System* (MACRS) refers to the latest and greatest depreciation system in the Code that allows you to recover the cost of income-producing property over specific recovery periods. It establishes an accelerated system of allowing you to take deductions faster than a straight-line basis.

MACRS provides six recovery periods based on class life:

- Three years (for example, special handling devices for rubber manufacturing)
- Five years (for example, light general-purpose trucks, semiconductor manufacturing equipment, computer-based central office switching equipment, and automobiles)

✔ Seven years (for example, certain aircraft, office furniture, fixtures, and equipment, and railroad tracks)

✔ Ten years (for example, grain and sugar mill equipment and refining equipment)

✔ Fifteen years (for example, municipal sewage plants and telephone distribution plants)

✔ Twenty years (for example, municipal sewers)

See Section 168 of the Code and the related regulations to find the type of leased property involved in your deal.

In MACRS depreciation, you have to adjust your depreciation depending on when during the year you place property in service. You can generally depreciate most property according to the *half-year convention,* which gives you depreciation deductions starting at the midpoint of the taxable year regardless of when you place the property in service.

Talk to your tax advisors about the concentration of property in the last quarter of the year to assess the impact of the midquarter convention. The midquarter convention applies if you invest more than 40 percent of the aggregate basis of your property in the last three months of the year (October 1 to December 31 for calendar year taxpayers). You must then determine your depreciation (excluding Section 1250 real property) by treating property placed in service during any quarter as being placed in service at the midpoint of that quarter. This convention, when applied, can reduce depreciation otherwise available under the half-year convention.

Also try to structure your deals to avoid placing property in service during a short taxable year (resulting, for example, from forming a new partnership of equity participants midyear). Otherwise, in short tax years, you suffer further reductions in your first-year depreciation deductions.

To use MACRS, follow these steps.

1. **Find your property type in the recovery periods described in the Code, and select the recovery period for your type of property.**

2. **Determine the basis of the property, which generally equals the lessor's cost of the property.**

3. **Apply the appropriate depreciation rate to the basis of the property for each year of the lease.**

   You can most easily accomplish this step by reviewing tables provided by the IRS in Revenue Procedure 89-15, 1989-1 C.B. 816.

4. **Determine the effect of the first-year conventions and adjust these deductions each year.**

With property that you can depreciate over five years, for example, this adjustment causes you to take the benefits for a total of six years because you do not receive a full-year deduction in year one. Here is how it works. Say that you place the manufacturing property in service in the fourth quarter under a five-year recovery period, using the mid-quarter convention, and 200 percent declining balance method. That timing produces deductions during the recovery period at the following actual rates: Year 1: 5.00 percent, Year 2: 38 percent, Year 3: 22.8 percent, Year 4: 13.68 percent, Year 5: 10.94 percent, and Year 6: 9.58 percent.

5. **Use the computer programs discussed in Chapter 7 to run the numbers to determine the economic effects of the preceding steps.**

The alternative depreciation system (ADS)

MACRS doesn't apply to all property or circumstances. The *alternative depreciation system (ADS)*, created under Section 168(g) of the Code, provides a slower depreciation schedule than MACRS. ADS applies to property used predominately outside the United States during a tax year (see Chapter 20), certain tax-exempt use property (such as property used by tax-exempt entities described in Chapter 19), tax-exempt bond financed property, certain imported property, and property to which the taxpayer elects to apply ADS. Generally, ADS applies the straight-line method of depreciation, using the half-year or midquarter convention, over a period of the class life of the property. The IRS doesn't afford these taxpayers the same tax benefits as entities that use MACRS because of policy reasons. In particular, in case of property leased to tax-exempt entities, generally the depreciation period is no less that 125 percent of the lease term. Under Section 168(g)(4) of the Code, you can still use MACRS for aircraft, railroad rolling stock, vessels, motor vehicles, satellites, and containers that maintain a certain contact with the United States.

Interest expense deductions in leveraged leases

Once you qualify your transaction as a true lease, you can also deduct interest payments under Section 163(d) of the Code for funds that you borrow to purchase the property. To get the advantage of leveraged leasing, you must deduct the interest on the non-recourse debt.

Discuss the limitations on interest deductions with your tax advisors to assure full deductibility of interest on your leveraged lease debt.

Lessee Tax Benefits

As a lessee, you generally enter a tax lease to receive the benefits that the lessor can transfer to you through lower rent generated from the value of tax benefits that the lessor receives. You structure your leases, therefore, to assure that you and your lessor create a true lease. If you do create a true lease, you receive rent deductions. If, however, you structure a conditional sale instead of a true lease, you receive the same tax benefits as the lessor. Because you may not be able to use the tax benefits or want to use them as the tax, the economics of your lease may drop significantly, through paying higher rent, for example.

Work with your lessor to achieve a true lease or a conditional sale, as the case may be, to preserve your economics and business intent.

If you do succeed in creating a true lease, you can deduct the full amount of your rent. As described in Chapter 6, the economic benefit of that deduction exceeds the benefit of deducting interest payments. Interest constitutes only a portion of a debt payment, while rent amounts to the entire payment to your lessor. Watch out for changes in tax law that may make leasing or borrowing more attractive for you, especially if you expect to make capital expenditures in your business.

Chapter 14

Dealing with State Sales, Use, and Property Taxes

*W*henever I start a new leasing transaction, I sometimes post a note on my computer screen that says, "Sales and property tax issues" to remind me to deal with state property and sales tax before closing. It's a subject you must consider in every leasing or sale transaction.

Complex and varied rules exist on state taxes for leases of real and personal property. You must comply with these rules. As a lessee, you often pay high taxes to the state and local governments in addition to your lease payment. As a lessor, these taxes combined, as a percentage of your lessor's cost, may far exceed your yield. Sales and property taxes generate a crucial source of revenue for state and local governments. Whether you buy or lease, government gets its share of the action. In short, you can't ignore or overstate the importance of state and local taxes, although a little complaining is certainly understandable!

In this chapter, I discuss some common principles of state sales and property taxation affecting your purchase or sale of real or personal property. These principles affect the economics of your deals and potentially the rights of taxing jurisdictions to impose liens on property that you lease or own.

Paying Sales Tax: The Name Game

You usually pay sales tax when you buy something, whether it's on a shirt at a retail store or a printing press from the manufacturer. These rates range from 3 percent to 10 percent of the purchase price for example, with an average national rate of about 6 to 7 percent.

How do you know when a tax is sales tax? You look for several fancy names used by the states that, unfortunately, do not tell you clearly what the tax is. You'll love these examples. Some states, such as California, Kentucky, and Minnesota, say that they grant a seller of property the privilege to sell products in their states. Consequently, each state imposes a *privilege tax* on the seller. Other states, such as New York, North Carolina, and Ohio, say that consumers enjoy the right to buy goods in their states, and impose a *consumer tax* on the consumer (which the seller must collect). Some states, such as in Florida and Texas, use a *transaction tax,* which is collected and paid by seller on each sale. Still other states, such as Arizona, New Mexico, and Hawaii, say that the seller must pay a tax on all gross receipts from sales. New Mexico calls it sales tax a *gross receipts tax,* Arizona refers to it as a *transaction privilege tax,* and Hawaii prefers the name *general excise tax.* And then there is the State of Illinois, which imposes *occupation taxes* on retailers and persons providing services.

These taxes look and act like a sales tax, so why don't the states just call them sales taxes? You can find the answer in the language of a state's constitution. In some states, the constitution mandates a particular type of tax while in other states the name amounts only to a matter of semantics. The difference goes beyond what you need to understand to get through your day-to-day business. Therefore, for simplicity, I just refer to these various taxes as *sales taxes*.

Regardless of what states call sales tax, as a seller or buyer, depending on the state, you pay taxes on sales or leases of property in most, but not all, states. Alaska, Delaware, Montana, New Hampshire, and Oregon, for example, charge no sales or use taxes on the sale of personal property. Although the state of Alaska doesn't impose a sales tax, some localities within Alaska do have a sales tax. Delaware has a license tax that is imposed at different rates on sellers, lessors, and lessees.

Paying "Use" Taxes

Use tax complements sales taxes. *Use tax* compensates for sales taxes that you do not pay when you purchase property. When you purchase property from an out-of-state seller, you pay a use tax. Use tax picks up where a state can't impose a sales tax. Generally, when you make a purchase across state borders, you do not pay sales tax in the seller's state. However, you may be subject to a use tax based on the storage, use, or consumption of your purchase in your own state. Consumers generally pay the use tax, although the states require many sellers and all lessors to collect use taxes. If you pay use tax, you usually do not pay sales tax. If you pay sales tax, you usually do not pay use tax. In short, together sales and use taxes constitute one tax, a mirror image obligation in most jurisdictions. You pay one or the other, but generally not both.

As a lessee, you may not care much about the difference between sales or use tax unless your state has local jurisdictions with no (or lower) use taxes. Some states, such as Colorado, Iowa, Kansas, Missouri, and New Mexico, have local sales tax, but no local use tax. For lessees, the lack of a local use tax results in a lower tax rate when the seller or lessor is out of state.

As a lessor, you must correctly apply sales or use tax rates to collect the correct amount of taxes. You must be especially careful to use the correct local tax rates in a particular state in which several different local tax rates exist.

As an out-of-state lessor, watch out for states in which you may claim certain exemptions or tax reductions under sales tax laws but not under complementary use tax laws. For example, you may claim bad debt exclusions from sales tax, tax discounts for timely filing of vendor returns, and other exemptions under sales tax laws but not under use tax laws in the same state. As unfair and potentially unconstitutional as this result may seem, as the lessor you must plan for potentially higher tax rates as an out-of-state company than an in-state company when you collect sales and/or use taxes from your lessee. You should check your tax indemnification agreement with your lessee to make sure that your lessee pays whatever rates affect your lease or purchase.

The streamlined sales tax project

The National Conference of State Legislatures (NCSL) is developing a new software system for the collection of sales and use taxes on electronic and virtually all other commerce. The NCSL is sponsoring the Streamlined Sales Tax Project. It constitutes an effort by certain states, with input from local government and the private sector, to design, test, and implement a simplified sales and use tax collection and administration system. In December 2000, the Project approved a Uniform Act and Uniform Agreement that provides the basis for state legislatures to debate and enact legislation to implement a more simplified system in their states. Following approval, the NCSL forwarded the Project's Act and Agreement to the states, the National Governors' Association, and the NCSL. This project may radically change how sales and use taxes apply to leasing property in every one of the 32 (or more) participating states. As of the writing of this book, the issues remain unresolved, including definitions of leases or rental and software. Once decided, leases, rental, and software may become subject to a uniform sales and use tax. For further information on the Streamlined Sales Tax Project and to download a copy of the Uniform Act and Uniform Agreement, click the Project's Web site at www.streamlinedsalestax.org.

For every rule or concept that I discuss in this chapter, exceptions, often complex or politically motivated, may exist. Consequently, you must consult with your state tax advisors or lawyers to identify the tax treatment of any lease or purchase transaction of significance for you. If you sell products or services, learn the sale tax rules and comply strictly with them.

Sales and Use Taxes in Leasing Transactions

States impose sales or use taxes on leasing transactions. At the inception of the leasing transaction, a lessor may purchase property from the manufacturer or from the prospective lessee (in a sale-leaseback transaction). A lessor then enters into a lease and collects rent. The following sections address how sales and use taxes apply to these transactions.

Sales or use tax basis

The *tax basis* refers to the amount or price of property on which states charge the sales or use tax. It usually includes the rent and other amounts paid by a lessee. Basis often excludes the amount or price for transactions that become worthless, such as when a lessee files bankruptcy and liquidates without paying rent or use tax on the rent. As a lessor and lessee, you must determine the basis under the state law applicable to your transaction. Generally, you look at the state law where the lessee takes delivery of the property being purchased or leased.

In Texas, for example, the sales tax applies based on the sales price of the property. The sales price does not include such items as cash discounts, refunds to the customers of the sales price, or the value of property taken in trade for a sale of taxable property of a like kind or nature. For example, if you trade your old car in for a new one, you pay sales tax only on the net amount paid for the new car after subtracting the value of the old car used in trade. You should be aware that other states don't give you this credit, and you should negotiate your purchase price accordingly.

The impact of a conditional sale versus a true lease

As a lessee or a lessor you also should determine whether the state law treats your "lease" as a true lease or a conditional sale. I discuss the distinctions between a true lease and a conditional sale or security interest in

Chapters 1 and 17. That distinction becomes crucial in many areas, including states sales and use taxes. The states adopt all kinds of definitions of a conditional sale versus leases to help make the decision of who pays the sales/use tax and when that person pays the tax. And yet many states do not make a distinction and treat all leases the same and tax the rent as it is due.

As a general principle, if your lease transaction is treated as a sale (sometimes called a finance lease, a credit sale, or conditional sale), the tax is due on the purchase or at the start of the lease. In this case, the state assumes that the seller (lessor) will transfer title to the purchaser (lessee) at the end of the lease. For example, if your lease contains a purchase option of $1, Texas treats the lease as a conditional sale and collects the tax at the start of the lease (subject to exemptions and exceptions) rather than on each rent payment. If, on the other hand, the state treats your deal as a true lease (sometimes called an *operating lease*), taxes are paid on each rent payment. Do not confuse the term operating lease here with the accounting term described in Chapter 15.

Whether you're a lessee or lessor, review the state sales tax rules on leases in each state where the property will be located. Analyze whether you should treat your lease as a true lease. If a lessor characterizes the transaction as a true lease when the applicable state views it as a conditional sale or a financing, the lessor may be caught short on her tax payments. The shortfall occurs because the lessor collects tax on rents rather than on the cost or basis of the property at the start of the lease. Lessees ultimately pay these taxes because most lessors charge the taxes to lessees under their leases. A lump sum payment to make up a shortfall between the rent and sales calculations may come as a rude awakening to a lessee during the lease. This payment may be an even a more bitter pill for the lessor if the lessee fails to pay it when charged. Consider an appropriate strategy with the states in which you do business to avoid these surprises. If the lessor buys the property and leases it out on a $1 purchase option lease, you can state the interest separately from the lessor's cost (the principal portion of the financing) to avoid sales tax on the interest portion of the "rent."

Lessor and lessee options to pay sales or use tax

In a few states, such as California and Michigan, the lessor has the option to pay the sales tax when he purchases the property for leasing or rental or charge the lessee tax on his lease payments. In these option states, lessors often purchase property under a resale certificate and collect taxes measured by rental receipts.

Rental receipts include rent payments, late charges, property tax reimbursements, and insurance payments. Rental receipts exclude collection costs, costs of court actions for tort actions and the cost of judgments, late charges, and certain other fees. In other words, sales or use tax applies to the sales price or similar costs paid to the lessor.

Collecting tax on rentals is generally easier for lessors because it makes collection of tax uniform with the other states that do not have options. Collection of tax on rent also reduces exposure for additional sales or use tax in another state if the lessee relocates the property because the lessor continues its collection of tax adjusted for each location.

Taxable events subject to sales and use tax

On the sale and/or on the subsequent rent collection, a taxable event may occur. Each sale, purchase, and lease is a separate event for sales and use tax, even though it involves the same property. States generally impose sale or use tax on the purchase transaction (generally and as a part of a leasing deal) unless:

✔ A retailer or lessor buys the property for resale or lease.

✔ The lessee pays a sales or use tax on rentals.

✔ The state has no sales or use tax.

✔ The transaction, property, or lessee has an exemption from tax.

A *retail sale* generally consists of any sale of tangible personal property other than a sale for resale. A *sale for resale* refers to a transaction in which the buyer, such as a lessor, buys with the intent to resell or lease the property to a buyer or lessee. Generally, as the buyer-lessor, you don't pay tax on the purchase if you intend to immediately lease the property and collect the appropriate tax from a lessee. Not all states allow this approach.

Sale taxes in sale-leaseback transactions

Unfavorable sales and use tax consequences arise on sale-leaseback transactions in several states. The following separate events, related to property involved in a sale-leaseback, show the effect of sales tax impositions and exemptions.

✔ **Sales tax event #1:** The prospective lessee purchases a printing press. Unless the lessee is a sales tax-exempt organization or the printing press is exempt from sales tax for other reasons, the prospective lessee pays sales tax on the original purchase of the printing press (that is, the tangible personal property is taxable).

✔ **Sales tax event #2:** The prospective lessee identifies its prospective lessor and sells the printing press to the lessor. This transaction is the sale that occurs before the leaseback. Any subsequent sale to a lessor by a lessee, which immediately leases the property back from the lessor, is treated as a sale for resale and is not subject to tax on the sale.

✔ **Sales tax event #3:** The lessor leases the equipment back to the lessee. This transaction is the leaseback. As in event #1, unless the lessee is a sales tax-exempt organization or the printing press is exempt for another reason, the lessee pays sales/use tax on the rental stream under the lease.

Here's the point. Sales and use tax law refers to each individual event of sale or lease. States generally don't consider tax previously paid on the property as a basis for exemption. Does this mean that states slam lessees with double taxation or pyramiding sales taxes? In short, yes, it happens. Without adequate knowledge of the applicable sale tax law (for example, finding a good exemption and properly structuring your leases), you do encounter potential double taxation. Note that California has written an exemption for the illustrated sales event # 2 (sale to the lessor) and event # 3 (leaseback to the lessee). The lessee pays tax only once when it purchases the equipment (sales tax event #1) if the leaseback occurs within 90 days of the original purchase (or first functional use of the leased property). If the leaseback occurs after 90 days, the exemption ends, and the leaseback is taxable. California aggressively enforces state taxation. It likes your cash, but cuts you a small break here!

Take the tax officials seriously. Stay within time limits and make sure that you learn and comply with the tax system as it applies to you.

Taxes at the end of the lease term

At the end of a lease, a lessee may have an option to return the leased property to the lessor or purchase it. On a return, when the lessor leases the leased property to a new lessee, guess what happens? You've got it: The states magically restart taxes on the new lease with the new lessee. On a purchase by a lessee or a third party, the states generally treat transaction as a sale and impose tax. Well, someone has to pay for all those wonderful state services!

Exemptions from Sales and Use Taxes

Even though these tax obligations seem like they blanket the universe of deals, there's hope. You need to determine whether a sales/use tax exemption exists for your deal.

One or more exemptions may apply. Exemptions commonly include the following categories:

- Purchases of equipment for re-sale, lease, or re-lease (often used by lessors)
- Purchases of property or materials used in manufacturing, fabricating, or processing tangible personal property
- Purchases or leases to tax-exempt organizations, such as religious organizations, health-care organizations, charitable organizations, government entities, or other favored organizations in a state (such as community theaters, symphonies, art galleries, libraries, and credit unions)
- Purchases of aircraft for use as common carriers, or by a foreign government or for nonresident for use outside the state
- Occasional or isolated sales (such as the yard sale or other sales not in the ordinary course of business)
- Purchases of property used in favored applications such as research and development
- Property used in agriculture
- Purchases of vessels and rail equipment used in interstate commerce

Exemptions just don't happen without jumping through a few hoops. Lessors and other retailers or persons engaging in business in a state generally issue an exemption or *resale certificate* in the form prescribed by that state. Lessees may likewise be able to claim exemptions based on their use or exempt status. To obtain a right to issue these certificates, lessors, lessees, and certain exempt organizations must file or register with the applicable state taxing authority (such as, the Department of Taxation and Finance in New York). States may require that lessors or exempt entities post a bond to cover potential tax liability and sometimes charge nominal licensing/registration fees.

A *resale certificate*, for example, typically requires that a lessor provide her name and address, the name and address of her vendor, a certificate number showing her authority to do business or collect sales or use tax in the state, a description of the nature of her business, and her signature. Some resale certificates offer blanket exemptions and apply to all purchases during the period that the certificate remains effective. In that case, as the appropriate issuer (lessor or lessor), you don't need to complete certificates for each purchase.

After the state issues a sales tax license to a lessor, the lessor must provide an originally signed resale or other exemption certificate to the seller and include the lessor's sales tax license number. This certificate works like an affidavit to assure the seller that the lessor does not have to charge the lessor sales or use tax. The inclusion of the license number establishes that the lessor is registered to collect tax on rent when she leases the property.

Thereafter, the lessor charges her lessee use taxes on the lessor's rental receipts.

Similarly, in the case of a lessee that can claim an exemption, the lessee issues his exemption certificate to the lessor to assure the lessor that the lessor does not have to collect sales tax on each lease payment. If a state exempts a lessee organization or purchase transaction from paying sales taxes, the good faith acceptance of the completed certificate ends the obligation of the lessor to collect taxes.

In short, as a lessor or lessee, if you claim an exemption from sale or use taxes, you generally issue the exemption certificate and apply to a state for the right to do so.

The preceding discussion illustrates some of the approaches taken by states. States vary the approaches to sale/use taxation based on their own revenue, political and process goals, and objectives. Lessors and lessees should carefully scrutinize exemptions to avoid the underpayment or nonpayment of sale or use taxes based on a faulty exemption. Exemptions may have time limits or restrictions. Look for those limits before you accept or use an exemption.

The Multistate Tax Commission (MTC) has developed a Uniform Sales and Use Tax Certificate that at least 38 states accept for use as a blanket resale certificate and for similar purposes on purchases of goods and services including leasing transactions. You may download a copy of the form from the Taxpayer Services section of the MTC site at www.mtc.gov/TXPYRSVS/Services.htm#Registration. It includes instructions and specific exceptions by state after the first page. The form, when properly completed, allows a general type of transaction to avoid or defer sales tax.

Taxing Mobile Equipment

Mobile equipment presents a special and complicated sales tax challenge. Tax may be imposed where title passes and where a lessee uses the property. You determine whether the initial sale requires payment of a sales tax. As discussed in preceding sections, you may purchase leased property in a state that has no sales or use tax. However, except for aircraft, you may be stuck with a sales tax in the state in which the manufacturer or seller does business.

In addition, states impose sales and use tax on equipment where the lessee locates it. Because lessees can locate leased property, such as aircraft, trucks and trailers, in several states, lessors may be subject to tax in each state. In that case, lessors pass that tax on to the lessee through provisions in the lease that make the lessee responsible to pay the taxes. Lessees select the states where they use the property, so they should pay the freight — the tax, for the particular state, that is, or so that's how lessors see it.

Aircraft, for example, can land in one state for lease closing and hours later set down in the state that the lessee uses as the home base or airport for the aircraft with very different tax impact. To illustrate, say that a lessee enters into an aircraft lease. If the lessor purchases the aircraft while it sits in Oregon, he pays no sales tax because that state has no sales or use tax. If the lessee then flies to New Hampshire and bases the aircraft there, he faces no use tax on the rentals in that state. The story would be entirely different if the lessee takes delivery of the aircraft in New York and then immediately based it in California. New York imposes a sales tax and California imposes a use tax on the rental receipts.

The key to handling sales/use tax when leasing mobile property is plan, plan, and plan some more. If you have a choice, plan where to take delivery of the property and where to use the property. Check the sales tax statutes in each state where you may use the property for any significant period of time. Look for reduced rates or exemptions from tax. You may be able to use an exemption arising from keeping property outside of a state for a certain period of time (for example, California has such rules regarding aircraft). Alternatively, the nature of your business or of your type of transaction or leased property may allow you to claim or use an exemption in the relevant states.

Understanding Property or Ad Valorem Tax

Property tax refers generally to tax on physical or intangible property that you own as of a certain date located in a particular place. These taxes fund local and state government costs, such as police, fire services, schools, recreational areas, and other public services. The term *ad valorem tax* simply refers to taxation according to the value of the property, whether the value goes up or down from time to time. As a contrast, you determine sales tax based on the price or basis of the property when you purchase it and use tax based on the amount of the rental stream.

Would you believe that many (but not all) of your friendly state and local governments tax almost every kind of property that you own or lease? In fact, you pay tax on real, personal, and even intangible property. You may or may not be aware that you do or should pay these taxes. If you transfer title to a printing press and lease it on real property located in Florida, for example, you probably pay all these taxes on the both on the press and the property on which it sits, as well as the transfer of title and purchase.

Whether you are a lessor or lessee, you can count on every state and most localities imposing property taxes on your real property and its *appurtenances* (such as buildings, structures, and improvements including fencing, storage buildings, or walkways) affixed or attached permanently to the land. If you lease any real estate, including a building and leasehold improvements, such as new counters or carpeting, you pay tax on that property. You even pay taxes on personal property constituting leasehold improvements such as air-conditioning systems and wiring.

You may also pay taxes on personal property that you lease. You can distinguish personal property from real property because you do not permanently attach personal property to or intend to make it a permanent part of real property. You can see, weigh, measure, or touch this property, but it excludes real property. Chapter 1 lists some of the personal and real property that may be taxed. Personal property taxation covers most every item of leased property that I discuss in this book, such as machinery and equipment, vehicles, hardware, office equipment, and production equipment.

Can you always clearly distinguish between real and personal property? No, you can't always draw a bright line between personal and real property, and that decision can change what property tax you pay. You may pay no tax at all if you own or lease personal property instead of real property. So you should focus on this issue.

How can you distinguish real property from personal property? You can generally remove personal property from its location without material damage to the property on which it sits or to which it is attached. Personal property is not adapted to the use of the real property. Personal property does not rise to the level of a fixture, which refers to property so affixed to real property as to effectively become a part of it (such as, a chimney).

At least 38 states impose property taxes on tangible personal property. If you locate personal property in the following states, you may luck out and avoid personal property taxation: Delaware, Hawaii, Illinois, Iowa, Minnesota, New Hampshire, New Jersey, New York, North Dakota, Pennsylvania, South Dakota, and Vermont. Although less relevant here, note that if you transfer title intangible property (such as, stocks, bonds, patents, and so on), watch out for taxes on this *intangible property* in Alabama, D.C., Florida, Kentucky, Louisiana, Maryland, Minnesota, Mississippi, Oklahoma, and Tennessee.

Taxing your property

By some estimates, more than 80,000 state or local authorities with taxing power (which I call *taxing jurisdictions* in this chapter) exist around the country. The ones with jurisdiction over you and your property, including states, counties, special taxing districts, and cites, tax some or all of your real and/or personal property. Some states, such as Illinois and New York, tax you only on real property. Other states, such as Florida, impose taxes on personal and intangible property. Oregon taxes real and personal property. If you have business property located in any jurisdiction, you determine whether one or more (and often more than one) taxing jurisdiction exists to tax your property.

Lessors, by law, are obligated to file and pay the property tax. Many lessors do file and pass the tax charge back to lessee. Some lessors appoint their lessees as the responsible party to file and pay property tax. If the lessee files and pays property tax, then the lessee should check the property tax laws and assessment practices in his state. Some states, such as Ohio, may ignore the fact that a lessee files tax returns and impose a double assessment on the lessor. The state then forces the lessee to file for refund (unless as the lessee you really like to pay a double tax!). Other states may require an appointment of agent form to be filed with the assessor. Some lessees prefer to file the property tax when they can provide market data on the property and potentially reduce the assessed value.

Paying taxes

Lessees and lessors pay property taxes. Taxing jurisdictions impose the tax liability on the taxpayer whose personal or real property is located in their jurisdiction at the time that they assess the taxes. If you own property, you pay the tax each year. Depending on the type of lease and state, the lessee or the lessor may be treated as the owner. California, for example, considers the lessee in conditional sale leases (a lease with a $1 purchase option lease) to be the taxpayer for property taxes.

Owner-lessors often pass on this tax payment obligation to lessees, if permitted by the laws of the taxing jurisdiction. If the lessee cannot pay the taxes directly, then the lessor charges the taxes in addition to the rent and should send the payment to the taxing jurisdiction when due.

Although as a lessor, you may want your lessee to prepare and file these returns, you and your lessee may reconsider that approach so that as a lessor, your tax returns remain consistent in form and approach in each taxing jurisdiction.

The total amount that a taxpayer pays in taxes equals the sum of all lawful state levies. In other words, every taxing jurisdiction takes a piece out of the taxpayer, which together add up to the total property tax liability. For example, if you live in a city, you probably pay taxes to the city and the county in which your property is located.

You should make your tax payments when due or at least before you get into a collection fight with the tax jurisdiction. If you don't pay on time, the tax jurisdictions have the power to place a lien on your property and impose stiff penalties, which is not a good thing. Creditors hate tax liens, and trust me when I tell you that you don't improve your credit record or borrowing capability by allowing property tax liens to show up there.

However, do watch out for excessive tax assessments and do fight assessments that you feel do not fairly value your property. Experts exist to assist you in these fights. As a lessee, you must fight assessments within strict time limits relating to your protest and on appeals. These fights generally occur long before the bill becomes due and long before you may even see the bill. Know the timetable for property tax appeals. If you're not comfortable with property tax appeals, by all means seek out assistance from others with experience in such matters and check their references.

As the taxpayer, you pay taxes based on the fair market value and the assessed value of the personal or real property located in a particular taxing jurisdiction.

- ✔ **Fair market value:** States generally impose tax on all or a portion of the fair market value of property. *Fair market value*, in the property tax context, has some pretty fancy definitions, but generally refers to the most probable price that a knowledgeable seller can sell property to a buyer in competitive market.

  Appraisers acting on behalf of an assessor help establish fair market value of real estate in accordance with the cost approach, the income approach, and the sales comparison approach. For more information about appraisers and their qualifications and training, see the Web site of the American Societies of Appraisers at `www.appraisers.org/disciplines/real.htm`. The Web site of The Appraisal Foundation at `www.appraisalfoundation.org/default.asp` discusses the Uniform Standards of Professional Appraisal Practice (USPAP), widely used in real estate appraisals to apply similar tests and factors to an appraisal in every location.

- ✔ **Assessed value:** *Assessed value* refers to the value, established by the tax jurisdiction, to which you apply the applicable tax rate in that jurisdiction. The rate may be the 100 percent of fair market value, sometimes called a *full assessment*, or less than 100 percent of the fair market value, sometimes called a *fractional assessment*. For example, say that you own or lease a vessel with a hailing port in Oregon with a fair market value of $1,000,000. In Oregon, say the assessed value set by the taxing jurisdiction equals 40 percent of $1,000,000 or $400,000. Oregon therefore imposes the property tax rate on $400,000. Say that the annual tax rate totals 3 percent. As the taxpayer, you pay $12,000 per year in property tax on the vessel. The 40 percent figure (4/10s) represents the *assessment ratio,* which refers to the percentage of fair market value against which taxing jurisdictions apply their tax rates.

Assessing property

The process of determining the value of property is referred to as *property tax assessment*. Taxing jurisdictions establish their own assessment procedures and timing. They usually focus on property that sits in their jurisdiction as of January 1 of each year, although some states focus on different dates (Indiana's date is March 1). This annual property tax day is generally referred to as the *assessment or lien date*. Say that, as lessor, your leased (real) property sits in Dallas, Texas. The taxing jurisdictions assess your leased property on January 1. Following January 1, the taxing jurisdiction goes through a review of all property within its jurisdiction and places a value on the property. This process can take several months to notify taxpayers of assessed value and allow a time period for taxpayers to contest values that, from the taxpayer's view, fail to represent fair market value. Following the process of valuation, the taxing jurisdiction applies a property tax rate (commonly referred to as *millage rate*) to the value and issues a tax bill. In Texas, the tax bill is due on receipt of the tax bill but becomes delinquent if not paid before February 1 of the year following the assessment. Most states follow a similar approach.

In general, the local assessor leads the charge on assessing your property. The *assessor* is the elected or appointed official who arranges for assessments of all property in his or her jurisdiction so that, as a property owner, you get the privilege of paying taxes on your property. The assessor's staff and its consultants locate and identify your property, develop a record of what you own, determine its taxability and classification, and then determine the value of your property. The assessor determines fair market value through appraisal or other information that the assessor asks you to provide.

For personal property, as the taxpayer, you file a tax return listing the original cost of personal property owned or in your possession as of the assessment date, which is the date when the assessor assesses and taxes property based on its ownership and value as of that date. With that information, the assessor determines the assessed value, and the treasurer issues a notice of taxes due to you as the taxpayer.

For real estate, the assessor determines the assessed value of a your property without any required annual real property tax return or input from you. See www.iaao.org/1234.htm for a selected list of the offices of property tax assessors and appraisers, and examine some of the sites for a description of how they do their jobs.

Assessors often prefer that you help provide information on which to establish fair market value of real property, and personal property. However, assessors can and do determine fair market value of property without your input. Some level of cooperation on your part may help you predict the ultimate value or at least contribute to a realistic appraisal. An appraiser in doubt (such as one who gets no help from you) may use higher numbers for fair market value and force you to contest the value.

Claiming exemptions

Like sales taxes, exemptions in property tax exist for the claiming. Creativity and politics produce a raft of exemptions that may reduce, *abate* (reduce for a certain amount or time), or eliminate taxation on your property. One or more exemptions may apply to your property. Exemptions commonly include the following categories:

- State and local government-owned property (other than use or leasing for private interests)

- Federal government and foreign government-owned property or property exempt under federal law

- Property used in interstate commerce and certain exports and imports

- Religious, educational use property (used for the public good or in religious activities)

- Charitable and nonprofit use property

- Favored business property by jurisdiction in the form of permanent exemptions (for example, software or pollution equipment) or temporary exemptions such as tax abatements (such as, reductions in tax for specific development in a specific of cost for a specific period of time) to help projects that encourage development and/or produce new local jobs

- Business inventories, property in transit, aircraft, motor vehicles, and certain vessels (such as watercraft not used for hire)

- Personal property not held for sale or use in the ordinary course of business

- Your local political favorite such as cotton stored in a warehouse in Texas (to get one call your local politician for some help!).

Because property tax is generally imposed directly on the owner, some exemptions may be lost on leased property, particularly when the lessee is an exempt government or charitable organization. Check the state law and with local government in advance to determine whether an exemption will be recognized. In some states, such as Oklahoma, you must file special applications and paperwork to gain exemption from the assessment process.

Getting More Help on State Taxes

Because state taxation presents an extremely complex and diverse subject, this section offers you Web sites for most of the states in the United States where you can review the laws and rules that may apply to you or your business and contact the tax jurisdictions for assistance. While these sites don't replace hitting the books, they can help you identify areas in which you may pay or save on property, sales, and use taxes as well as keep you current on changes in law and procedures, and property tax contacts. You can also contact the Equipment Leasing Association at `www.elaonline.com` and request the annual ELA Tax Manual, which lists the Web site of most every state taxing authority and summarizes the sale and property tax rules of each state.

Try the following site for more information on sale, use, and property taxes: `www.piperinfo.com/state/index.cfm` (search under Department of Taxation, State Comptroller, and Department of Revenue for direct hits); and `www.taxadmin.org/fta/link/link.html` (for current state tax home pages, forms, facts, and issues for each state).

Chapter 15

Accounting Meets Leases

● ●

In This Chapter

▶ Focusing on the risks and benefits approach of FAS 13

▶ Classifying leases by lessees and lessors under FAS 13

▶ Understanding the importance of lease classifications

▶ Accounting for leases under FAS 13 by lessees and lessors

▶ Creating a synthetic lease to optimize accounting and tax benefits for lessees

▶ Using residual guarantees to meet accounting and other objectives

● ●

*I*n November 1976, the Financial Standards Accounting Board (FASB) issued its Statement of Financial Accounting Standards No. 13 (sometimes called "FAS 13" in this book). FAS 13 establishes standards for lease accounting. FAS 13 has been extensively amended and interpreted by FASB and its Emerging Issues Task Force (EITF). The EITF receives, analyzes, and responds to emerging issues in accounting for approval by the FASB. See the Web site `accounting.rutgers.edu/raw/fasb/public/index.html` for a detailed history and status of FAS 13.

Despite its complexity, however, FAS 13 simply provides you, as a lessee, with the opportunity to keep leases off your balance sheet, one very important benefit of leasing. As a lessor, FAS 13 provides you with a viable and somewhat flexible alternative to account for and build your leasing business.

This chapter addresses some key issues in lease accounting, including the classification and accounting for leases from the lessee's and the lessor's perspectives. It does not cover many other issues in FAS 13 relating to real estate leases, subleases, and business combinations that may affect your business.

The Benefits and Risks Approach

The fundamental objective of FAS 13 is to determine whether a lease "transfers substantially all of the benefits and risks incident to the ownership of property" to the lessee. As the lessee, if your lease transfers substantially all the benefits and risks of ownership to you, then you capitalize your lease under FAS 13 because in substance you appear to be the owner of the property.

If the opposite is the case (your lease does not transfer substantially all the benefits and risks of ownership to you), then you treat your lease as an operating lease under FAS 13. In substance, you do not appear to be the owner because you do not pay as much of the cost of the property as in a capitalized lease. You treat an operating lease as a current expense. Generally, you try to achieve operating lease treatment because that enables you to keep the lease off of your balance sheet. For more detailed discussion see "Accounting for leases by lessees" later in this chapter.

As the lessor, if your lease transfers substantially all of the risks and benefits of ownership to the lessee, then you account for the lease as a sale of property to your lessee (which is called a sales-type lease) or as a financing or loan (which is called a direct financing lease). You become a seller or lender instead of a lessor for accounting purposes. Otherwise, you can treat your lease as an operating lease. For more detailed discussion, see "Accounting for leases by lessors" later in this chapter.

Classifications and Symmetry in Lease Accounting

To help classify your lease, as a lessor or a lessee, FASB has come to your rescue (not!) and provided an elaborate set of criteria for you to apply to your lease transactions. FASB designed FAS 13, in theory, so that, as a lessor or a lessee, each of you accounts for your lease in a way that corresponds to, or is symmetrical with, the accounting for the same lease by the other. In other words, if the lessee classifies his lease as an operating lease under FAS 13, the lessor correspondingly accounts for the same lease as an asset. If, on the other hand, the lessee classifies his lease as a capital lease, the lessor correspondingly classifies the lease as a direct finance lease or a sales-type lease (sometimes called a capital lease by lessors). In practice, the classifications don't always correspond.

Is that a problem for you as lessors and lessees? No. While the symmetry objective of FAS 13 sounds good, and you can often achieve it, FASB understands and expressly permits different interpretations and applications of FAS 13 criteria by each of you, which results in apparently conflicting classifications. So, don't worry if that result occurs in your deal when you apply the FAS 13 criteria discussed in the following sections.

Some accounting terms used in FAS 13

The following definitions may help you apply the concepts that I discuss in this chapter. You can use them in all of accounting, including in FAS 13, as generally defined here.

Assets refer to things that usually have some lasting economic benefit to you that you realize or claim as a result of your past transactions, activities, or events in business. For example, a tractor purchased last month by a lessor and leased to an agricultural business constitutes an asset of the lessor.

Balance sheet refers to a financial statement of your assets, liabilities, and shareholder's equity.

Expenses refer to a cost of doing business that you incur when you spend cash, incur liabilities

or use up your assets. You incur expenses in connection with delivering or creating goods and/or rendering services in the course of your business operations. For example, as a lessee, when you buy fuel for the tractor or pay rent, you pay an expense item.

Liabilities refer to your future obligations in business that you create from today's business activities. You can have short-term or long-term liabilities. For example, a maintenance bill incurred and payable in 30 days by a lessee to tune up the engine on the tractor used in his farming business constitutes a short-term liability (that is, an account payable).

The Lessee Approach to FAS 13

This section speaks to lessees and discusses the criteria that you use to classify a lease, the accounting for your lease once you (or your accountant) pick its classification, and certain reporting and disclosures regarding your leases that FAS 13 requires. Finally, I suggest to you why you should care about this stuff — saving the best for last, I guess.

Classifying your lease-operating versus capital lease

As the lessee, when you structure your leases for accounting purposes, you initially determine whether you want to create a capital lease or an operating lease. If you satisfy or meet any one of the criteria of a capital lease in FAS 13, your lease constitutes a capital lease. In all other cases, your lease constitutes an operating lease. That's it! You now know the basic rule to classification under FAS 13 on your side of the deal. The trick is determining whether or not you satisfy or meet capital lease criteria. See Figure 15-1 for a flowchart depicting the classifications.

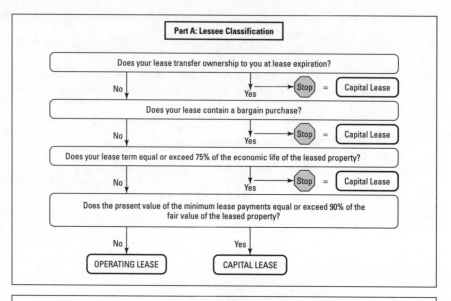

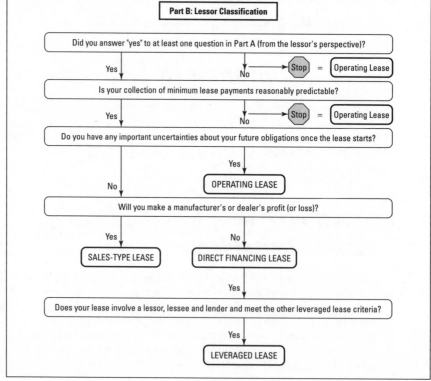

Figure 15-1:
The core
questions
that you ask
to classify
leases
under
FAS 13.

The term operating lease as used in FAS 13 does not have the same meaning as the term operating lease in a general business or state tax sense. See Chapters 1 and 14.

FASB helps you make your determination by providing four criteria to decide whether your lease constitutes a capital lease.

Defining and implementing the four FAS 13 criteria

Your lease constitutes a capital lease if, as lessee, you meet or satisfy *any* of the following four criteria:

- ✔ Under Paragraph 7a of FAS, if your lease transfers ownership of the leased property to you, at the end of the lease term, that lease constitutes a capital lease.

- ✔ Under Paragraph 7b of FAS, if your lease contains an option that allows you to purchase the leased property at a bargain price, that lease constitutes a capital lease.

- ✔ Under Paragraph 7c of FAS, if the lease term in your lease equals or exceeds 75 percent of the estimated economic life of the leased property, that lease constitutes a capital lease. You can refer to this criteria as the *75 percent economic life test*.

- ✔ Under Paragraph 7d of FAS, if the present value of the rentals or other minimum lease payments equals or exceeds 90 percent of the fair value of the leased property, that lease constitutes a capital lease. You can refer to this criteria as the *90 percent recovery test*.

If your lease doesn't meet or satisfy any of these criteria, then your lease constitutes an operating lease. Each criteria uses terms defined in FAS 13. The terms remain subject to wide interpretation despite FASB's goal to make FAS 13 a "cookbook" approach to achieving consistent treatment and reporting of leases by lessors and lessees.

The FASB criteria have created numerous implementation problems. So, which do you want first — the good news or the bad news? Here's the good news.

Criteria 7a is a snap to determine and criteria 7b and 7c (the 75 percent economic life test) seem manageable. However, here's the bad news: Criteria 7d (the 90 percent recovery test) presents the real challenge to structuring and achieving operating lease treatment.

When in doubt, begin your classification effort with the 90 percent recovery test first. If you pass that test, don't bother with the rest. In other words, if you do meet or satisfy the criteria by having a present value of your minimum lease payments that equals or exceeds 90 percent of fair value of the leased property, you account for your lease as a capital lease. If, on the other hand, you fail the 90 percent recovery test (that is, the present value of your minimum payments falls under 90 percent of the fair value of the leased property), apply the other criteria.

You determine the classification at the inception of the lease only once, which is the earlier of the date of the start of your lease term or the date on which you receive a commitment from your lessor.

Note that I use *fair value* in this chapter (because FAS 13 uses that term) where it often has the same meaning as fair market value as used throughout this book.

Criteria 7a: Lease transfers ownership

To determine whether your lease transfers ownership to you at the end of the lease, open your lease or commitment and look for any provision to that effect. It may say, for example, that title to the leased property transfers automatically to you for free or for nominal amount such as a $1 at the end of the lease term. If you find any such transfer provision, stop, you have a capital lease. The provisions effectively mean that you full pay lessor's investment in the leased property with your rent (the equivalent of debt service payments) during the lease term. You clearly have all the benefits of ownership (and presumably the risks, too) if you own the property at the end of the day.

Criteria 7b: Lease contains a bargain purchase option

To determine whether you receive a bargain purchase option, open your lease or commitment and look for any provisions in which your lessor transfers ownership to you at the end of the lease for a bargain price. The easiest and most frequent example of a bargain price occurs in the so-called *dollar-out leases* in which you pay a buck at the end of the lease and walk away with title to the leased property. For any higher price, you and your accountants need to make a judgment at inception as to whether you receive a *bargain purchase option*. A bargain purchase option exists when the price that you pay to purchase the leased property during or at the end of the lease falls so far short of fair value that you and your lessor can be reasonably assured that you will exercise your option. In other words, the price is too good to refuse.

Should you, as a lessee, just avoid this issue and not put options in your lease? No. You should almost always ask for options to control and predict the total cost of the lease. You just need to decide, at lease inception, whether the option amount looks like a bargain — option that you know that you'll exercise because it's way cheap for the leased property. For example, a 40 percent purchase option (that is, 40 percent of lessor's cost) on a tractor, at lease inception, may not then look less than fair market value. However, that option may turn out to be a really good deal if at lease termination the tractor is worth 50 percent of the lessor's cost. Your end-of-lease hindsight does not convert the 40 percent option into a bargain.

Criteria 7c: The 75 percent economic life test

Criteria 7c, the 75 percent economic life test, requires that you and your accountants once again exercise some judgment at lease inception (which means that you try to persuade your accountant to accept your conclusion) about the economic life of the leased property. Then you simply try to structure a lease term to equal less than 75 percent of that life for operating lease treatment or to exceed 75 percent of that life for capital lease treatment. For example, if you lease an aircraft for 10 years, and that aircraft has economic life of 20 years, your lease term equals 50 percent of the economic life (a 10-year lease term divided by a 20-year economic life = 50 percent). Result: You do not meet or satisfy the 75 percent economic life test and, if you fail the other tests, achieve operating lease treatment. Conversely, if you lease that same aircraft for 18 years, you pass the 75 percent economic life test (that is, meet or satisfy its criteria) and have created a capital lease, calculated as follows: 18-year lease term divided by 20-year useful life = 90 percent, which exceeds the 75 percent economic life test.

For purposes of the 75 percent economic life test, consider the following:

- ✔ *Economic life* refers to the estimated period during which leased property can be expected to remain economically useful.

- ✔ *Lease term* refers to the fixed noncancelable period during which your lessor requires you to pay all lease payments, come hell or high water, plus the following:

  - Any periods in which you have a bargain renewal option (that is, a right to renew that's too good to refuse) such as a $1 payment to renew your lease

  - All periods before the date of a bargain purchase option

  - All periods during which you feel compelled to renew because of significant termination penalties imposed on you by your lessor or because you can't terminate without an interruption of your business

  - Any period during which you effectively promise to pay a lessor's debt

The 75 percent economic life test does not apply at all for leases that commence within the last 25 percent of the estimated economic life of the leased property. For example, if a truck has a 10-year economic life, you can eliminate the 75 percent test if the lease term starts after the middle of the seventh year of its economic life (10 years x 75 percent = 7.5 years).

Criteria 7d: The 90 percent recovery test

The 90 percent recovery test requires that you identify and calculate your minimum lease payments and then discount them to present value, as of the date of lease or commitment, at the appropriate discount rate discussed later in the section "Interest rate for present value calculation."

Taking a closer look at minimum lease payments in the 90 percent recovery test

To calculate minimum lease payments, you include and exclude certain payments as described in this section.

Amounts to include in minimum lease payments

Your minimum lease payments include all of the following:

- **Payments that your lessor can make you pay during the lease term.** You must pay basic rent, residual guarantees, redelivery costs, and fees.

- **Penalties that you pay for failing to renew or extend your lease.** A *penalty* refers to any obligation that interrupts your business or forces you to forgo an economic benefit or suffer an economic cost. For example, your lessor offers you only a short initial term and a long renewal term for a MRI machine that you installed at high cost. You really can't remove or return the machine after the initial term without losing money and business and suffering great inconvenience of tearing down walls to get it out. Therefore, you must include the renewal rents in your minimum lease payments.

- **Amounts that you guaranty to your lessor (that is, a residual guarantee) up to the specified maximum deficiency that the lessor can make you pay (unless you buy a residual guarantee from a third party and the lessor explicitly releases you from all obligations).** For example, say that your lessor assumes a residual value of $25,000 on a tractor-trailer. The lessor estimates that she should receive at least $20,000 at the end of the lease term. You agree to guarantee your lessor up to $15,000 of deficiency on a sale of the tractor-trailer at the end of the lease. The lessor in effect takes the risk that the tractor-trailer will be worth less than $10,000 ($25,000 minus your $15,000 residual guarantee = $10,000 lessor risk). You include the $15,000 in your calculation of minimum lease payments (not the estimated $5,000 deficiency calculated as follows: $25,000 assumed value – $20,000 estimated residual recovery = $5,000). For more fun on residual guarantees, see Financial Accounting Board Standards Interpretation No. 19, Lessee Guaranty of the Residual Value of Leased Property (1977). For more discussion, see the section titled "Using Residual Guarantees in Leasing" later in this chapter.

Remember that lessees may not guaranty the residual value of a lease and obtain true (tax) lease treatment under Revenue Procedure 75-21. See Chapter 13. However, if the lessee does provide a residual guarantee as described in the preceding paragraph, he may still achieve off-balance sheet accounting treatment. This hybrid situation creates a *synthetic lease* or *off-balance sheet loan* where the lessee not only gets the tax benefits but also keep the lease off of his balance sheet. For more discussion of synthetic leases, see the section titled "Creating a Synthetic Lease" near the end of this chapter.

✔ **Contingent rentals computed on the basis of index rates in effect when your lease term starts.** Your lessor may calculate your rent, in part, on the basis of a floating interest rate index in effect when your lease term starts, such as the prime rate. You include the rent based on that index rate on the date you do the classification as if it were a fixed rate.

Amounts to exclude from minimum lease payments

Your minimum lease payments exclude all of the following:

✔ **Payment for extraordinary wear and tear on the leased property.** For example, damage to a vehicle that you do not repair during normal maintenance visits. You and your accountant must exercise some judgment as to excluding this type of payment.

✔ **Residual value guarantees by a third party unrelated to the lessee.** You do not include residual guarantee payments of third parties because lessees do not recognize these payments under FAS 13 as their own money. (Remember: Lessors *do* include residual guarantee payments in calculating their minimum lease payments (which can lead to nonsymmetrical classifications of a lease.)

✔ **Contingent rents.** *Contingent rents* refer to rent amounts that you do not fix in your lease like base rent, but depend on other factors or changes (other than the mere passage of time) that occur after your lease term starts. Contingent rent does not include changes in construction or acquisition costs. For example, you may pay contingent rent based on a specified volume of sales (for example, sales each year of a 10-year lease based on the use of a leased printing press or sales at a leased retail store), the actual usage of the leased property (for example, payment by the hour for use of an aircraft sometimes called "power by the hour") or the changes in a floating rate of interest after your lease term starts. You expense contingent rents as you incur them. For more fun on contingent rents, see Financial Accounting Standards No. 29, Determining Contingent Rentals (1979).

Before you exclude contingent rents from your calculation of minimum lease payments, make sure that your transaction makes economic sense based on the other fixed rents alone. Contingent rents must relate to the use of the leased property. Otherwise, your accountant may challenge your proposed exclusion of contingent rent.

> ✔ **Executory costs.** *Executory costs* include insurance, maintenance, and property taxes that you pay to your lessor. If the lessor pays any of these costs, you must estimate your lessor's cost and the profit the lessor includes on top of the cost. Then you exclude that total amount from minimum lease payments.

As a lessee, if you want to achieve operating lease classification, you try to exclude as much in payments from the calculation of minimum lease payment as possible. The less the rent and other amounts that you include in your present value calculation of "minimum lease payments," the less chance that you have to pass (that is, satisfy or meet) the 90 percent recovery test (which turns your lease into a capital lease).

Interest rate for present value calculation

Once you identify your minimum lease payments, you can use the lower of two interest rates to discount them to present value. If known to you, you must use your lessor's *implicit interest rate*. If you don't know that rate, you use your *incremental borrowing rate*. The lessor's implicit interest rate or yield equals the interest rate that discounts the minimum lease payments and unguaranteed residual value (minus any amounts required to pay debt service on any nonrecourse borrowing in a leveraged lease) to the lessor's net investment (that is, equity). See Chapters 6 and 7 for more information on yield and discount rates.

You can ask your lessor for her implicit interest rate, but don't be surprised if you receive a polite "No way!" or "Why do you want to know?" Unless that rate appears in your lease, lessors tend to guard their yields, cost of fund, and other similar economic. In any event, perhaps you don't want to know your lessor's implicit interest rate. "Why not," you ask? The lessor almost always has a lower implicit interest rate than your incremental borrowing rate because that rate reflects the lessor's tax benefits, and her (potentially lower) cost of capital. Using a lower discount (that is, interest) rate increases the present value of the minimum lease payments, which is exactly the opposite of your goal if you want to keep your lease off your balance sheet. Lessors, however, should work with you to keep your lease off your balance sheet (that is, as an operating lease) if practical.

As a general rule, you (as the lessee) use your incremental borrowing rate to discount minimum lease payments. To determine that rate, you and your accountants may need to exercise some judgment about the appropriate rate if you engage in several different types of borrowing facilities or no borrowing facilities. Your *incremental borrowing rate* may equal the loan rates for recent loans, a blended rate of your cost of borrowing over a recent period of time, or a rate based on the rate that financial institutions would, on your application, extend to you at the time of the lease. Remember to add fees or other costs of issuing your debt that your total cost includes (for example, like points on a mortgage).

The higher the discount rate, the lower the present value of minimum lease payments. Don't use your lessor's lower rate if you can avoid it.

If all these variations seem a bit daunting (in which case I feel your pain!), take heart as most lessors have lease pricing programs on their computers (see Chapter 7) that can calculate these tests and variations of the tests in excruciating detail. Ask your lessor or your lease advisor for assistance!

Accounting for leases by lessees

Keep in mind that you account differently for capital leases and operating leases.

If you (and your accountants) classify your lease as a capital lease, you record the leased property as an asset and the related lease obligations as a liability on your balance sheet. You record the lease as the lower of (1) the present value of the minimum lease payments during the term or (2) the fair value of the leased property. You account for leased property by amortizing the leased property consistent with your normal depreciation policy for assets that you own if you satisfy or meet criteria 7a and 7b. In all other cases, you amortize the leased property over the lease term. You allocate the lease payment between a reduction in the principal portion of your rent payment and interest on that principal (that is, your imputed interest rate used to discount minimum lease payments). You allocate in this manner so that you pay a constant periodic interest rate (for example, 10 percent) on the declining principal amount of your investment.

If you score an operating lease, you don't show the leased property as an asset or a liability on your balance sheet. Instead, you write off rent payments over the term as an expense. Even if you do not make level rent payments because you pay rents that increase or decrease during the term of the lease or prepay rent, you still expense rent on a straight-line basis (that is, in equal amounts in each rent period) over the term of your lease. You can use a different write-off if you can demonstrate that your proposed rent expense matches the time pattern in which you benefit from the leased property.

If you think that the accounting treatment means that you say nothing about operating leases in your financial statements, stop right there. You must disclose information in your footnotes for any off-balance sheet sublease describing the deals, residual guarantees, the future minimum rent payments, and the rent for the reporting period.

For capital leases, in addition to showing the asset and liability, you also footnote

✔ The gross amount of assets presented by major classes according to nature or function of the assets

✔ Minimum lease payments in the aggregate for the next five years (net of executory costs) and the amount of imputed interest calculated in reducing minimum lease payments to present value

✔ Total contingent lease payments actually incurred for the period in which you present the income statement

Keeping leases off your balance sheet is a key benefit of leasing. The effect of this accounting means that when you calculate your *debt-to-equity ratio* for your lenders, your balance sheet looks stronger because your lease payments don't show up as debt. Your debt-to-equity ratio measures how efficiently you use debt or if you have been prudent in the amount of debt that you have incurred relative to your equity.

The changing views of accounting for leases

The entire approach of the FAS 13 covered in this chapter focuses on a risk and benefits approach to determine how to classify and account for leases. Now, lenders, credit agencies, and accountants around the world continue to increase their sophistication in analyzing the true nature of leasing. Some accounting authorities such as FASB and the Accounting Standards Board in the United Kingdom (FASB's counterpart) have begun to consider different approaches to the real liabilities evident in leasing. Strikingly, they both have started considering replacing the risks and benefits approach with an asset/liability approach to accounting for all leases. That approach would require capitalization of *all* material leases, a dramatic change in FASB 13.

Under this new approach, lessees would have to record the value of the right to use leased property and the value of purchase options and renewal options as assets on their balance sheets. Lessees would also have to show minimum lease payments and residual guarantees as liabilities. Lessors would correspondingly account for rent receivables and residuals as assets.

The asset/liability approach, in theory, would enhance the symmetry in accounting for leases that FASB intends to achieve under FAS 13. Lessees would have to capitalize all material leases. All immaterial leases would be disregarded for capitalization purposes and treated as operating leases. Lessors would account for all leases as finance leases. The concept of accounting for operating leases (for lessees and lessors), and perhaps even leveraged leases, for lessors would therefore end.

Any change could take several years to occur at FASB, but you should keep a watchful eye on the development of the asset/liability approach. Without a doubt, that approach could significantly impact the acquisition and financing in the air, rail, banking, energy and telecommunications industries in general and leasing and lease accounting in particular (for example, with drastic changes to financial covenant calculations and little or no more off-balance sheet leases). For updates and summaries of FAS 13 and other accounting statements, see accounting.rutgers.edu/raw/fasb/tech/index.html.

In addition, your loan agreements often contain financial covenants restricting debt (including capital leases), but the covenants may *not* limit off-balance sheet leases. If the covenants do limit these leases, the limits may be somewhat more liberal depending on how sophisticated a lender you have. In other words, lenders may create limits, or *baskets*, that allow you to incur obligations for more leases than a corresponding amount of debt.

The Lessor Approach to FAS 13

FAS 13 requires that you, as a lessor, classify your leases as *sales-type leases, direct financing leases, leveraged leases,* and *operating leases.*

You classify a lease as a sales-type if the transaction gives rise to a manufacturer's or dealer's profit (or loss) and meets all of the following tests:

- ✔ Your lease meets or satisfies at least one of the four criteria under Paragraph 7 of FAS 13.

- ✔ Under Paragraph 8a of FAS 13, you can reasonably predict that you will collect the minimum lease payments.

- ✔ Under Paragraph 8b of FAS 13, you have no important uncertainties about the amount of unreimbursable costs (future obligations) that you may incur once your lease term starts.

You should meet these criteria when you lease instead of sell the property. When you do meet the criteria, you realize a manufacturer's or dealer's or manufacturer's profit (or loss) explained as follows:

A *dealer's* or *manufacturer's profit* refers to the amount of profit that you receive at the start of the lease term. Usually (but not always) you make this profit in the role of a dealer or manufacturer marketing your products. Your profit typically results from charging rent and figuring your residual on the sale of leased property at a price in excess of the amount of your lessor's cost of the leased property. If different than the lessor's cost, use the amount that you show on your books as the cost of the property.

A *dealer's* or *manufacturer's loss* occurs when the carrying amount on your books exceeds the fair value or lessor's cost of the leased property. The lessor's cost/fair value equals the amount that you receive from charging rent to your lessee including your residual on the leased property at the start of the lease term.

You classify your lease as a *direct financing lease* if:

- ✔ Your transaction satisfies the first three criteria under the sales-type lease (see preceding list).
- ✔ Your transaction does not give rise to a dealer's or manufacturer's profit.
- ✔ You do not classify your lease as a leveraged lease (see next list).

Your transaction constitutes a *leveraged lease* if your deal meets the direct financing lease criteria in the preceding section (but doesn't constitute a sales-type lease), and you also meet or satisfy the following additional criteria:

- ✔ Under Paragraph 42b of FAS 13, your lease involves three parties: a lessee, a long-term lender, and a lessor.
- ✔ Under Paragraph 42c of FAS 13, you take on substantial leverage (generally 50 percent of debt is considered minimum leverage) from the lender on a nonrecourse basis (that is, you agree to repay debt solely from the lessee's lease payments and the value of the leased property).
- ✔ Under Paragraph 42d of FAS 13, your net investment (as described in the following sections) declines in the early years of your lease and increases in later years of your lease before you eliminate your investment at the end of the lease.

You classify your lease as an *operating lease* if you cannot meet or satisfy the criteria set forth for a sales-type lease, a direct financing lease, or a leveraged lease.

Accounting for leases by lessors

As a lessor, you account differently for sales-type leases, direct financing leases, leveraged leases, and operating leases. More than a brief discussion of these complex rules extends beyond the scope of this book — much as I would like to discuss these rules in all of their glorious detail!

In a sales-type lease, you report your sales revenue in an amount equal to the present value of the minimum lease payments and the residual value of the leased property. For you, minimum lease payments have the same meaning as for lessees, except that you also include any guaranty of residual value payments beyond the end of the lease term by an unrelated, creditworthy third party.

You charge sales revenue with your *cost of sales*. *Cost of sales* equals the carrying amount of the leased property (that is, its cost), plus *initial direct costs* (legal fees, credit evaluation, and other documentation costs directly and solely related to making the sale and entering the lease) minus the unguaranteed residual value of the leased property. You defer and amortize initial direct costs over the lease term and record unearned income so as to produce a constant rate of return on your net investment over the lease term.

Unearned income equals the sum of the minimum lease payments and the unguaranteed residual value minus the cost of the leased property, the initial direct costs, and other transaction costs (for example, credit evaluation and documentation costs). Your implicit interest rate is the internal rate of return (IRR) calculated in the lease, and it is the rate at which you recognize earnings — just like interest earnings on a loan. You can run the IRR on a financial calculator. You include the number of periods in the lease term and lessor's cost (as outflows) and fees, rent, residual, and other minimum lease payments (as in flows). In other words, the calculation of lessor's cost versus cash inflows creates the IRR. Residual values must be reviewed annually under Paragraph 17d of FAS 13. You can adjust them downward but not upward.

You account for a direct financing lease in a manner similar to the sales-type lease. Your unearned income equals the sum of the minimum lease payments and the unguaranteed residual value of the leased property minus the cost of the leased property. Like the sales-type lease, you record unearned income so as to produce a constant rate of return on your net investment over the lease term using the rate implicit in the lease. Like sales-type leases, residual values must be reviewed annually. You can adjust them downward but not upward.

For leveraged leases, you record your *net investment*. Your net investment refers to your rent plus residual minus unearned income minus nonrecourse debt service that you will realize in the transaction.

You compute your net income by subtracting your original investment from the after-tax cash receipts. As discussed in Chapter 7, FASB recognizes the *separate phases* or multiple-investment sinking fund method of reflecting income during the lease. Phasing is caused by the tax benefits to the lessors that result in cash savings in the early years of a lease and payment of those savings in the later years. You compute your net investment in a lease on a net after-tax basis. Then, you allocate that income throughout the lease term.

Residual values must be reviewed annually under Paragraph 46 of FAS 13. You can adjust them downward but not upward.

You account for operating leases as the lessor by recording rent as income over the lease term. You depreciate the leased property over its economic life. You defer any initial direct costs and amortize them over the lease term.

Sale Leasebacks

Lessors and lessees often enter into transactions called sale-leasebacks, which I cover in Chapters 1 and 5.

As a lessor or lessee, your accounting for sale-leasebacks works about the same way as I have discussed for other leases. However, you need to consider three other key issues:

- ✓ FAS 13 establishes special accounting rules for real estate and integrated personal property subject to leases, such as equipment attached to, and/or costly to remove from, real estate.

- ✓ A lessee amortizes the gain (or loss) on the sale of the property over the lease term and in proportion to rents paid (that is, expensed).

- ✓ A lessee may have a federal and state income tax liability for the gain on the sale of the property to the buyer/lessor. A lessee may also have to pay state sales tax on that sale even though the seller/lessee has already paid sales or use tax on the property. Exemptions may exist from sale or use taxes (see Chapter 14). Lessees with net operating losses under federal and state income tax rules make good candidates for these deals because their losses shelter their gain (if any) on sale of their property to the buyer/lessor.

You should note that if a sale has taken place for accounting purposes, the leaseback *must* be an operating lease.

Using Residual Guarantees in Leasing

Residual guarantees or *residual value insurance* refer to arrangements by which lessors or lessees can transfer a portion of their risk of a drop (from expected levels) in value of leased property to a third party (sometimes called a *residual value guarantor* or *insurer*). In exchange for taking this risk, the guarantor (or insurer) charges fees and/or shares residual upside (if any) in excess of the guaranteed (or insured) amount. The guarantor (insurer) can issue residual guarantees (or insurance) for a wide variety of assets such as aircraft, railroad rolling stock, vehicles, construction equipment, and even real estate.

As a lessee or a lessor, you can enter into a residual guarantee agreement (or receive an insurance policy) that provides this residual value protection. Each document requires that you maintain the leased property in accordance with standards acceptable to the residual value guarantor (or insurer). Assuming that you meet your obligations, then, typically, the agreement (or policy) should say that your residual value guarantor shares your pain (or downside), and perhaps a part of your gain (residual upside), if any.

As the purchaser of this product, you should carefully confirm the creditworthiness of your insurer or guarantor to assure that if you face a loss of residual value, you can reasonably expect these guys to exist and meet their obligations to you.

You can use residual guarantees or residual value insurance to:

- ✔ Increase your earnings (taking into earnings the guaranteed residual)
- ✔ Enhance your yields (by having assurance of a particular residual value and perhaps more)
- ✔ Secure the remarketing expertise of the guarantor (and perhaps the insurer)
- ✔ Achieve the desired accounting treatments as the lessor for your lease/portfolio (that is, book a lease as a direct-finance lease, permitting you to accelerate earnings into the early years of the lease)
- ✔ Manage your exposure to a particular class of assets (by keeping your residual risk to a desired level)
- ✔ Meet your internal underwriting/approval requirements for your particular lease or lessee

To illustrate, say that, as a lessor, you want to lease a tractor trailer fleet for a total of $5,000,000, and take a 30 percent residual value risk ($1,500,000) in your pricing. However, you feel that some risk exists that you may not be able to sell the items for that much at lease expiration. You buy residual guarantee insurance to protect any residual value risk between 20 percent and 30 percent of lessor's cost (that is, for any residual value amount that you do *not* receive in the range from $1,000,000 to $1,500,000). The guaranteed residual value is 30 percent.

Here's how the guarantee works for deficiencies or shortfalls in the guaranteed residual. Say that you realize proceeds of 10 percent of lessor's cost ($500,000) on the sale of the trailers. Your residual guarantor pays you the 10 percent ($500,000) shortfall from the guaranteed residual value between 20 percent ($1,000,000) and 30 percent ($1,500,000). Note that you would still not recover the 10 percent between the first 10 percent ($500,000) and 20 percent ($1,000,000) of the lessor's cost.

Here's how the guarantee works when you have upside. Say that you realize 40 percent of the lessor's cost ($2,000,000): Your insurance provider or guarantor has no payment obligation because you exceeded the guaranteed amount of $1,500,000. In fact, you may have to share the residual upside at the time of the realization above the 30 percent guaranteed residual value (which equals a sharing of $500,000 or 10 percent of the lessor's cost). In a typical sharing arrangement, you may give your guarantor (or insurer) up to 50 percent of your residual above 30 percent guaranteed residual value. In this case, that amount equals a *residual share* of 5 percent of lessor's cost (50 percent of 10 percent upside over 30 percent = 5 percent of lessor's cost of $5,000,000 = $250,000). Ouch! This is the moment at which you realize the potential cost of residual value protection. However, as lessor, you can stop complaining because the upside represents found money that you didn't expect; otherwise, why would you buy the residual value insurance?

As a lessor you may re-lease your property instead of selling it for cash. In that case, your residual value guarantor (or insurer) shares with you all proceeds of a lease in excess of your guaranteed residual value (30 percent/$1,500,000) once the present value of the new lease payments exceeds that same guaranteed residual value level.

Residual value sharing agreements vary significantly in their complexity, and the levels and timing of each guaranty. As a lessor, you can negotiate a guarantee or an insurance policy to assure that the price that you pay meets your economic, tax and accounting objectives. Insurance companies, manufacturers, and leasing companies can provide versions of these products that suit their particular expertise and appetite for equipment risk. Lease advisors often can suggest sources to provide these guarantees. For an illustration of available product for residual guarantor, you can contact GATX Capital Corporation at (415) 955-3200, E-mail: info@gatxcapital.com, and for an example of a residual value insurer you can contact RVI Group at (203) 975-2100, E-mail: info@rvigroup.com.

Although I address this discussion primarily to lessors, lessees with residual value guarantees to their lessors can use guarantees in a similar manner to protect their downside risk. The upside sharing may change based on the extent to which the lessee is entitled to upside in his arrangement with its lessor.

Creating a Synthetic Lease

A synthetic lease combines the best of both the accounting and tax benefits affecting leasing. A *synthetic lease* is also called an *off-balance sheet loan*. If this description seem contrary to my attempts throughout this book to distinguish secured loans from leases, you're right. However, the two types of deals have been intentionally and cleverly "synthesized" to create a valuable hybrid transaction. You can use this popular lease product to finance real estate and a wide variety of personal property such as turbine generators, power plants, aircraft, machinery, and equipment.

For accounting purposes, as the lessee, you treat a synthetic lease as an operating lease. For federal income tax purposes, you treat a synthetic lease as a secured loan or conditional sale. Synthetic leases take advantage of inconsistencies between accounting rules under FAS 13, and tax rules under Revenue Procedure 75-21 (and the related case law). You may encounter higher transaction costs and lease rates because of the complexity in the lease terms. However, you can get the best of both worlds:

- ✔ You keep the tax benefits (depreciation) related to the "leased property" and thereby reduce your tax liability.

- ✔ You neither show the leased property as an asset or the lease obligations as a corresponding liability on your balance sheet.

To qualify your deal as a synthetic lease, you must not satisfy or meet the FAS 13 criteria (so you do *not* create a capital lease), and you must not comply with Revenue Procedure 75-21 (and related case law requirements) so that you *do not* create a true lease.

To structure a synthetic lease, your lease must qualify as an operating lease under FAS as follows:

✔ **The lease must *not* transfer the leased property to the lessee by the end of the lease term for free or a nominal amount.** In a synthetic lease structure, as lessee, you have an option (but not the automatic right for free or for a nominal amount) at the end of the term either to:

- Purchase the property for an amount equal to the outstanding "lease" balance (which equals the remaining principal and interest amount of the off-balance sheet loan)

- Return the leased property to the lessor

Consequently, the lessor takes some residual risk with respect to the leased property (that is, the lessor has downside risk of not recovering his risk capital invested in the leased property when he remarkets the leased property after you return it).

To protect the lessor's investment (the principal portion of the off-balance sheet loan), a lessor in a synthetic lease typically charges you a *guaranteed residual amount,* which far exceeds a nominal amount. The *guaranteed residual amount* typically equals the highest amount that you, as lessee, can pay under the lease and retain the lease's classification as an operating lease under FAS 13. In other words, the present value of minimum lease payments is equal to or less than 89.9 percent of the fair value of the leased property at the start of the lease (so as not to exceed the 90 percent recovery test).

If you return the leased property at the end of the term, the lessor typically sells it to a third party to recover her remaining principal balance. The sales proceeds reduce the amount of the guaranteed residual amount that you may have to pay. For example, say that you lease a tractor that you don't buy at the end of your lease, but you have a guaranteed residual amount of $10,000. Your lessor has to recover her remaining "principal" balance of $12,000. If the tractor sells for $13,000, you generally (but not always) receive the amount in excess of your guaranteed residual amount (in this case, the extra $1,000). You pay nothing more to the lessor because your lessor recovers her outstanding principal balance of $12,000 out of the sale proceeds. If, by contrast, your lessor recovers only $1,000, you pay your full guaranteed residual amount of $10,000, and your lessor absorbs a loss of $1,000 to total the $12,000 principal balance.

✔ **The lease must *not* contain a bargain purchase option.**

✔ **The lease term must last for *less* than 75 percent of the useful life of the leased property.** Typical synthetic lease terms will last for less than half the useful life of the leased property (including any renewals), and in any event, will always be less than 75 percent of the estimated economic life of the leased property. For example, if the useful life of tractor is 10 years, then the lease term must be less than 7.5 years for FAS 13 purposes, and probably 5 years for synthetic lease purposes.

✔ **The present value of the minimum lease payments must be *less* than 90 percent of the fair value of the leased property.** This rule results in lessors often assuming approximately 10.1 percent residual risk, and the lessee being responsible for a guaranteed residual amount of up to 89.9 percent of the residual value risk.

Keep in mind that the key tax issue in synthetic leases is whether the lessor or the lessee is treated as the owner of the leased property for tax purposes. In a synthetic lease, as the lessee, you must be treated as the tax owner. In a typical synthetic lease the assumed residual value risk is approximately 10.1 percent, well short of the 20 percent minimum value that a lessor must maintain under the tax requirements to achieve true lease treatment. See Chapter 13. Because your lease fails these tests, even though you are the lessee in a synthetic lease, you are still considered the tax owner.

In addition, a lessee may not guarantee the residual value of a lease and obtain true (tax) lease treatment under Revenue Procedure 75-21 as discussed in Chapter 13. However, the lessee does guarantee a significant portion of the residual value in a synthetic lease, by agreeing to pay a guaranteed residual amount. The lease therefore fails this true lease test. Consequently, you are treated as the tax owner for federal income tax purposes.

To slam home the characterization of the synthetic lease, synthetic leases explicitly state that you and the lessor intend that the transaction should be treated as a loan for federal income tax purposes. You grant a security interest to the lessor, and the lessor perfects his security interest like a secured lender. In the end, you achieve a synthetic lease.

The Grand Flow Chart of Lease Classifications

If a picture says a thousand words, refer to Figure 15-1, which depicts the core questions that you ask to classify leases under FAS 13 from the lessor's and the lessee's perspectives.

Chapter 16

Rules for Leasing: Article 2A of the UCC

- -

In This Chapter

▶ Identifying three key points in Article 2A of the Uniform Commercial Code

▶ Describing a finance lease

▶ Making and disclaiming warranties

▶ Examining some rights and remedies of lessees

▶ Considering your freedom of contract and lease assignments

- -

*T*his chapter introduces you to the law of leases under Article 2A of the Uniform Commercial Code (UCC). Unfortunately, in my view, Article 2A is the Rodney Dangerfield of the UCC: It gets no respect. Many lessors simply don't include references to Article 2A in their leases or don't consider it significant in their deals.

Perhaps lessors have a point. Article 2A, by design, just fills gaps in your lease. If you don't fully cover an issue in your lease within the scope of Article 2A, Article 2A responds and completes or clarifies the terms in your lease. If a lease contains your complete agreement, who cares, right? Before you say "not me," read this chapter because provisions lurking in Article 2A can give or take away important rights and remedies for both lessors and lessees that may help or hurt you in your lease transactions.

Scoping Out Article 2A of the UCC

Article 2A of the UCC provides rules exclusively for leases. Modeled in many respects on Article 2 of the UCC, a chapter that relates to the sale of goods, Article 2A sets out the rules of leasing that often sound like a sale transaction under Article 2. But don't be deceived. This law is different. Article 2A attempts to provide rules that, in theory, if not in practice, uniformly and consistently advance the best of commercial law applicable only to leases. As you read this chapter, to give you reference points, I sometimes refer to sections in Article 2A as "*2A-xxx*".

Regardless of the form, Article 2A applies to every lease of *goods*. Article 2A doesn't cover real estate or intangible property. The term *goods* refers to tangible personal property, including fixtures. See 2A-103(1)(j) (goods) and 2A-309 (fixtures). The term goods often means all things that are moveable at the date of your lease.

When I talk about equipment or leased property in this book, I almost always mean goods as used in Article 2A. Chapter 17 talks more about goods within the context of secured transactions.

In effect, Article 2A covers transactions involving personal property ranging from a lease of a hand tool for a day to a leveraged lease of a power plant for 20 years. In fact, Article 2A applies to almost all the tangible personal property listed in Chapter 1 that you can lease — but not your office building or garage (that you can lease, of course, but not under Article 2A). So, if the leased property can be moved and you can touch and feel it, or it constitutes a fixture that you can lease, Article 2A probably applies to it.

Knowing the Parts of Article 2A

Article 2A consists of five parts or subchapters. Part 1 establishes the scope of the law, some of the definitions, and other general information, such as using digital signatures.

Part 2 talks about forming a lease contract (closing your deal). A *lease contract* refers to all the legal obligations affected by Article 2A that result from the lease agreement (which means the bargain struck by a lessee and a lessor). See 2A-103(1)(l). This part includes warranties that you can make as a lessor or receive as a lessee.

Part 3 covers the effect of the lease contract, such as enforcing the lease, or your rights (both lessees and lessors) to use or transfer the leased property or the lease itself to someone else.

Part 4 covers how you perform, or more to the point, fail to perform, the lease contract. Article 2A sets forth warning signs that your deal is going bad.

Finally, it's curtains in Part 5. In that part, you find a discussion of defaults and remedies of lessees or lessors under a lease, such as figuring damages if the lessee defaults or addressing a lessor's failure to deliver leased property as required by the lease.

Article 2A contains many important provisions, but consider the following key points:

 ✔ Article 2A fundamentally covers leases and not secured transactions such as security agreements disguised as leases.

 ✔ Article 2A allows you to create a *finance lease* that can provide certain benefits for lessors and place some limitations on the rights on lessees.

 ✔ Article 2A gives you freedom to make your own deal, but fills gaps in your lease contract with rights and remedies that can significantly affect your transactions.

To decide whether Article 2A applies to your deal, you must first decide whether your agreement constitutes a lease governed by Article 2A or a security agreement governed by Article 9 of the UCC. In Chapters 1 and 17, I help you distinguish a lease from a security agreement.

Article 2A of the UCC defines a *lease* as a transfer of the right to possession and use of goods for a term in return for consideration. A lease is not a sale of goods. See UCC Article 2-106(1). A lease does not involve deals where a lessor or lender retains or creates a security interest under Article 9. Generally, the term lease includes a *sublease,* which refers to a transfer of the right to possession and use of leased property by a lessee under an existing lease, as a lessor (the sublessor), to a third party, as the lessee (the sublessee). A sublessee gets her rights from the lessee (the sublessor) to the extent of the lessee's rights under lease with her lessor. See 2A-103(w); 2A-305.

From here on, if you decide that your agreement doesn't constitute a lease go to Chapter 17 for a discussion of Article 9. Article 2A does not apply to your deal. If you don't know for sure whether your deal is subject to Article 2A or Article 9 of the UCC, stick around and, just for grins, read Chapter 17, too.

Figuring Out Your Rights and Remedies

As a lessor or a lessee, Article 2A offers you both some valuable rights and remedies. In this section, I talk about Article 2A from the separate perspectives of the lessee and the lessor. You should read about the other's rights and remedies to understand how to best negotiate and enforce the terms in your lease under Article 2A.

A lessor's perspective

As a lessor, you can gain or lose valuable rights under Article 2A. Like other lessors, you may shudder at the idea that a lessee can exercise rights against you for your breach of a lease. Take a deep breath! Lessees can and do have rights and remedies against you. You can, however, shape a lessee's rights if you take certain actions. Your starting point is to qualify your lease as a finance lease if you can.

If you are a lessee, beware of the finance lease! It limits your rights against your lessor.

A *finance lease* refers to a lease (as defined in Article 2A) involving three parties: you, your lessee, and the supplier of the leased property who generally manufactures or sells the property that your lessee orders. Article 2A defines a *supplier* as a person who sells or leases goods under a finance lease.

Avoid confusion of terms.

✔ A finance lease in Article 2A does not necessarily have the same meaning as the common usage of the term finance lease as described in Chapter 1. The business usage there refers to a lease that lasts for most of the life of leased property (that is, at least 75 percent of the useful life of the leased property). That finance lease may or may not constitute a finance lease under Article 2A.

✔ Many people refer to a lease that disguises a security agreement as a finance lease transaction or lease financings. I even refer to leases from time to time as lease financings. A disguised security agreement (labeled a lease) does not even fall within the scope of Article 2A. Article 9 and other laws claim that territory.

Examine each lease separately for its substance under Article 2A to avoid confusion about which kind of finance lease that you want to describe or understand. Your deal must first constitute a lease under Article 2A before it can qualify as a finance lease.

You can and should (if possible) structure a finance lease in the most typical way: Require your lessee alone to select the supplier of the property, order the property, and/or know all about the warranties and uses of the property. Otherwise, unless you manufacture or sell the property, tell your lessee in writing to work with the manufacturer or seller directly on warranty issues and require your lessee to approve, in writing, the property that you will lease and the contract to buy it. As lessor in a finance lease, you do not select, manufacture, or supply the leased property. See 2A103(a)(7) for the details.

Because the finance lease criteria focus on the deal and not the lessor or lessee, a wide variety of institutional and other lessors can take advantage of the rules.

If you are a dealer or a manufacturer, your leases don't qualify for finance lease treatment. However, if you form a separate finance company, which many manufacturers do, sometimes called a captive finance company, you can legally separate that company from the manufacturer/seller and argue, successfully in most cases, that your leases constitute finance leases. Then, you can get the benefits of finance leases under Article 2A.

To meet the criteria for a finance lease, you can use the following common approach: Ask your lessee to enter into a purchase contract or purchase order assignment (see Chapter 5) with the manufacturer or supplier. That party is not you, of course. In that assignment, your lessee assigns all its rights to you under the purchase contract for leased property. You assume no obligations other than to pay for the property once the lessee satisfies the conditions to start the lease, but you do not act as the lessee's agent in selecting the property. Ask the supplier to consent to this arrangement in writing. Attach a complete copy of the purchase contract to the assignment and require the lessee to confirm that it has read and understands the warranties, indemnities, and other provisions and that the document is complete and up to date. By taking these steps, your deal should meet the finance lease criteria.

As the lessor, you gain several protections and benefits when your deal qualifies as a finance lease, including the following:

✔ In effect, you do not break the relationship between the lessee and the supplier. You simply get out of the way of your lessee who can make all warranty claims on the leased property directly against the supplier. See 2A-209.

✔ The seller/supplier warranties automatically extend to the lessee. You do not make warranties to the lessee about the leased property. You have no warranty liability to your lessee. See 2A-209 to 2A-213. You act as a passive source of money only. In theory, only the supplier provides warranties and responds to your lessee's gripes when leased property doesn't work. I say, in theory, because lessees often complain to their lessors about performance or maintenance problems with their leased property, even when the lease requires the lessee or others to maintain it.

✔ After your lessee has accepted the leased property under a finance lease, the lessee in effect has no right to revoke the lease because the leased property did not conform to the requirements in the lease. See 2A-103(5), 2A-516 and 2A-517.

✔ You can treat your lessee's obligations as absolute and unconditional. The lessee's obligations stand independent of any deficiency in the leased property or any failure on your part to perform in accordance with your lease. (This statutory version of the hell-or-high-water clause automatically applies.) See 2A-407; _Colonial Pacific Leasing v. McNatt, et al,_ 268 Ga. 265, 486 S.E. 2D 804 (Georgia 1997).

Be sure to include the net lease provision (that a lessee pays all taxes, maintenance, and insurance), and hell-or-high-water provisions in your lease to avoid relying on this statutory provision. See Section 5 of the lease form in the Appendix (sometimes called the "Lease" in this book) for an illustration of such a provision.

✔ You can pass the risk of loss of the leased property to your lessee (that is, if the leased property is destroyed, the lessee pays for it). See 2A-219.

If your transaction doesn't qualify as a finance lease, you must comply with all the warranty rules under Article 2A (which are similar to rules under Article 2 relating to sales of goods). Under Article 2A, you may make a variety of express and implied warranties (promises) about the leased property without intending to do so, and you don't have to say, "I 'guarantee you' or 'warrant to you,' Mr. Lessee." Bragging or expressing an opinion doesn't usually constitute a warranty. However, you can create a warranty by promising, for example, that a machine tool will work correctly for a year or confirm a supplier's warranty.

Finance lessors rarely make warranties on purpose. However, even if you do, you can also take them away or disclaim them in writing in your lease contract. In effect, you take away the basis for your lessee to make warranty claims against you. See 2A-214. You can also exclude implied warranties (that is, negate or, you know, nuke them!). However, you do give your lessee a warranty of quiet enjoyment. To see an illustration of these disclaimers and exclusions, look at the lease provisions in Sections 7 and 14 of the Lease. See 2A-211.

Your lease should say what *events constitute defaults* by your lessee in some detail, such as your lessee's failure to pay rent or insure the leased property and what remedies that you can exercise after an event of default occurs. See Sections 20 and 21 of the Lease. By doing so, Article 2A may not come into play. See 2A-503. However, if, in your lease, you don't specify your remedies, or you say that you have all rights and remedies permitted by law, or a court decides that you can't enforce your chosen remedies for an event of default, Part 5 of Article 2A provides some rights and remedies. Under Article 2A, a lessee in default is often not entitled to notice of default or notice of enforcement from the other party to the lease agreement. See 2A-502.

Save yourself some aggravation in a fight; give notice to your lessee of an event of default to avoid questions that may delay getting a solution to the problem. Article 2A allows you to create and limit remedies. Ask your counsel to help you fashion the rights and remedies for your deal. Most lessors establish a core set of remedies, and then negotiate them.

Under Article 2A, you can exercise remedies stated there (unless you say otherwise in your lease). They focus on getting back lost rent payments, residual, and tax benefits. Here is a short list:

✔ You can sue your lessee for liquidated damages. You can use liquidated damages in those cases when you cannot, with certainty, calculate actual damages during the lease term. Figure out what you stand to lose at any particular date during the lease term. A stipulated loss table often serves this purpose because it says what money you need to recover your investment with a return as of any particular date during the lease term. See 2A-504.

Courts have invalidated liquidated damages provisions against a lessee whenever they seem unreasonable and punitive (that is, excessive relative to the lessor's probable loss). Structure liquidated damages provisions in reasonable amounts that you can justify as fairly representing the harm that you may suffer on an event of default. You should be able to recover past due rents, discounted remaining lease payments (using a reasonable discount rate based on market rates at the start of your lease, such as 6 percent or so in 2001), residual value in the leased property, and tax benefits, plus incidental costs that you can prove that you incurred in exercising your remedies (for example, legal fees, commissions, refurbishment costs and appraisal fees). See 2A-530.

✔ You can, without giving up other rights against the lessee, cancel and terminate the lease (2A-505), or repossess the leased property; then you can sell or re-lease the leased property to someone else. See 2A-525. You can't breach the peace (for example, start fights and break stuff), however, when repossessing your leased property. See 2A-525(3).

✔ You can recover damages. You can measure damages by figuring the present value of the rent under your lease minus market rent for substantially similar transactions (if one exists) or the sales proceeds of the leased property. See 2A-507, 2A-528(1). You can, in any event, also claim past due rent and incidental costs. You generally do not have to sell or re-release the property to mitigate damages (that is, minimize damages that a lessee may have to pay you). As the owner of the leased property, you make commercial judgments of the best way to protect your interests.

A lessee's perspective

As a lessee you need to understand and use the ideas described in the preceding sections for your lessor because that enables you to negotiate a better deal and protect yourself against the exercise of remedies in a default (which you should try to avoid, of course). In addition, you, too, have some arrows in your own quiver under Article 2A to deal with defaults by your lessor (though your lessor will ask you to waive these rights).

As the lessee, Article 2A says that you have remedies for lessor defaults. You can try to fashion default provisions in your lease, but you can expect heavy, if not total resistance, from lessors. Lessors in finance leases (and most other leases) believe that they just finance your property and can't default because they do nothing else. They will say that you identify and arrange the purchase of the leased property. They just pay for it and lease to you. In any event, if you don't describe defaults, Article 2A will. The defaults by your lessor include a lessor failing to deliver the leased property in conformity with the lease contract (for example, your leased property doesn't arrive on time or doesn't work right) or repudiating (that is, not performing) the lease contract (especially in nonfinance leases). See 2A-401.

If you don't negotiate, Article 2A may fill the gap with some lessee remedies provisions that may enable you to cancel the lease contract and recover rent and security from the lessor. You can and should try to create your own remedies including the following (see Sections 2A-508 to 2A-522):

- ✔ Cancel the lease or revoke your acceptance of the lease

- ✔ Reject or revoke acceptance of the leased property

- ✔ Recover damages from the lessor for breach of warranty or for any other reason

- ✔ Deduct from rent all or any part of any claimed damages resulting from lessor's default under the lease

- ✔ Accept partial delivery of the property

- ✔ *Cover* by making any purchase or lease of other property in substitution for property due from the lessor (with any losses to be paid by the lessor)

- ✔ Seek specific performance (that is, force your lessor by court order to fulfill its agreements to you)

You can try to negotiate remedies against your lessor, such as the ones listed, but lessors almost always require you to waive all or most of your remedies (and rights), as illustrated in the Section 22(a) of the Lease. They also insist almost without exception that you sign up for the hell-or-high-water obligation that you can't offset, abate, or reduce rent. In a pinch, you can argue that your lessor's rights and remedies established when you signed the lease are unconscionable, unreasonable, and unenforceable. See 2A-108. However, the bottom line here, and perhaps the reason that Article 2A gets no respect is this: These rights and remedies almost never survive, and the lease provides most of the rights that favor lessors to the exclusion of Article 2A.

General Provisions

The point for you to take in this section is this: Although you have the freedom to cut your own deals, if you want to transfer any rights or obligations under your lease as a lessee, or any interest in the residual or rents as a lessor, consult your counsel. The transfer provisions contained in Articles 2A and 9 of the UCC, as discussed briefly in the following sections, present some difficult legal issues and limitations on your rights and interests.

Freedom of contract reigns

Article 2A preserves (and you can't waive) your freedom of contract. In other words, you can do a deal your way (for most stuff). The Lease contains many of the terms that Article 2A addresses. See Article 1-102(3); Comments to 2A-102 and 503. The lease contract that you negotiate, using your freedom of contract, is generally effective and enforceable as against third parties such as purchasers of the leased property and creditors of the lessee and the lessor. See 2A-301.

Limits on assignments and subleases

Your lease may contain anti-assignment provisions, which say that, as a lessor or a lessee, you can't assign or transfer any rights in your lease or for lessees, sublease, the leased property.

For lessors, these anti-assignment provisions may attempt to limit your transfer of the residual value of leased property, or the rent/cash flows under the lease.

These provisions can create serious problems for lessors who need to assign leases to obtain financing from lenders, or for lessees who may have to sublease their leased property to cut rent expense during periods when they don't need the leased property.

Article 2A and Revised Article 9 provide some rules that make some of these transfers effective while others are not. See 2A-303; RA9-407. For example, regardless of the terms in a lease, a lessor can create a security interest in the rents the lessor receives from the lessee. See RA9-407(a). On the other hand, the lessor can effectively forbid a lessee from transferring leased property, or his obligations under the lease to someone else. See RA9-407(b).

However, if such a transfer occurs despite a restriction in a lease, the transfer may entitle the lessor or the lessee (the one who doesn't make the transfer) to sue the other for money damages, or to exercise other remedies under the lease.

For lessors, you may or may not be able to make transfers of your interests in the lease or the cash flows, or residual without the consent of the other party (for example, the lessee consents to a lessor transfer). You should (and most lessors do) obtain the lessee's consent in your lease for any transfers that you might want to make to others (for example, to buyers of your leases or lenders against your leases as collateral). You may want to sell or finance the entire lease or the residual value or the rent stream to raise capital or increase earnings. You should insist that the hell-or-high-water protection applies for the benefit of your lender or buyer so that the lessee has to perform under the lease without abatement or setoff. Without this assurance, you may have difficulty in selling or financing your leases; or if you can sell or finance your lease, the loan rates may be higher or the purchase price correspondingly lower to reflect the added risk of lessee defenses to performing for your transferee.

For lessees, you can expect your lessor to limit any transfers such as a right to sublease or delegate (that is, unload) your obligations, so discuss those issues when you negotiate your lease. In addition, as a lessee/sublessor, you generally remain responsible for complying with the lease. See 2A-9-303(7). As the lessee, you should discuss whether your lessor intends to sell your lease to another investor/lessor quite apart from your ability to prevent that sale. Even though you usually can't stop a sale, you can Negotiate some requirements applicable to the lessor's transferee. For example, you can require that the lessor and its transferee keep your secrets confidential and not be direct competitors.

For both lessors and lessees, each should waive defenses against any transferee of the other so that any dispute before the transfer date does not affect the new guy. Article 2A and Article 9 of the UCC affect these rights, but don't prevent either of you from negotiating appropriate agreements to protect and enhance your interests. Just be sure to ask your lawyers to help you create enforceable restrictions in your lease.

Chapter 17

UCC Article 9 Affects Leasing

● ●

● ●

*W*hile true leases differ from secured transactions, some leases may just be secured transactions in disguise. Sometimes you can easily distinguish a lease from a secured transaction, and other times you can't. So take your pick at the threshold of your deal — it's one or the other. Whatever you decide, Article 9 applies. This chapter shows you how to use Revised Article 9 to enhance and protect your transactions.

An Overview of Revised Article 9

Effective July 1, 2001, almost all states and the District of Columbia adopted a new and improved Article 9 of the UCC, which I call *Revised Article 9 or RA9,* replacing the old Article 9, which I call Former Article 9 or FA9. Alabama, Florida, and Mississippi delayed their effective date of RA9 until January 1, 2002, and Connecticut delayed its effective date until October 1, 2001. To give you reference points to these laws, I sometimes refer to sections in the Former Article 9 as "*FA9-xxx*" and sections in Revised Article 9 as "*RA9-xxx.*" To review the "Pre-Official Draft" of the text of Revised Article 9, see the Web site of the National Conference of Commissioners on Uniform State Laws (NCCUSL), which organized the drafting of Revised Article 9, at `www.law.upenn.edu/bll/ulc/ucc9/ucc9woc.htm`.

Revised Article 9 governs many (but not all) secured transactions. A *secured transaction* refers to an arrangement in which a debtor grants a secured party a security interest in property to secure the debtor's payment or performance of an obligation. It also covers deals where a seller retains title to property until the purchaser pays for it. In other words, a lessee/borrower generally puts up collateral to support her promise to repay money to a lessor/lender.

Revised Article 9 also provides rules regarding the creation, perfection, and enforcement of consensual security interests in personal property (such as a printing press) and fixtures (such as air-conditioners on top of a building). A *fixture* means goods that become so attached to real property that an interest in them arises under the real estate law of the state where the fixture is situated. See RA9-102(a)(41).

Revised Article 9 does not apply to secured transactions to the extent that, for example, foreign and federal laws preempt Revised Article 9 or other state laws govern a secured transaction such as vehicle titling statutes (like when a bank puts its lien on your car title). See RA9-109(c).

Ask your counsel whether Article 9 alone applies to your deal. For most leases, the answer will be "yes." However, in addition to Revised Article 9, you may need to make filings at the FAA, the STB or the Coast Guard to perfect a security interest in or lien on aircraft, railroad rolling stock, and vessels. See Chapters 11 and 12 regarding the extent to which federal law preempts the UCC regarding these assets.

Although Revised Article 9 governs many different types of transactions, a typical one starts with a secured party, as lender, extending credit to a debtor. A *debtor* (as the borrower) generally incurs obligations to a secured party and grants a security interest in his property (such as a printing press), called the *collateral*, to secure his obligations to the secured party. See RA9-102(a)(28). A *secured party* receives the benefit of a security interest in the collateral and his proceeds. See RA9-102(a)(72). The term *proceeds* includes (among other things) cash and other property acquired on the sale, lease, exchange, or other disposition of the collateral, such as a foreclosure sale of a printing press after a default. See RA9-102(a)(64) and 9-315; FA9-105.

The debtor and the secured party typically enter into a *security agreement* (and related financing documents), which sets out the terms of their deal. See RA9-102(a)(73). A *security agreement* refers to the document that creates or provides for a security interest in certain personal property (such as a printing press), including fixtures. See RA9-201; RA9-102(a)(73). It contains a grant by a debtor of a security interest in favor of the secured party in the collateral, and must "reasonably identify the collateral." See 9-108. It also describes the obligations of the parties, actions that constitute "defaults," and the rights and remedies of the secured party arising from a default by the debtor (such as failing to make loan payments). See RA9-201-210. If a debtor defaults in performing her obligations to the secured party, the security agreement (and Revised Article 9) gives the secured party rights and remedies against the debtor and the collateral to repay the secured party for the obligations incurred by the debtor. See RA9-601-628.

The secured party perfects her security interest in the collateral. This crucial step ultimately establishes the priorities among competing creditors and among parties who claim rights or interests in the same collateral, including other secured lenders to, and holders of liens and judgments against, the debtor. See RA9 9-301-343.

Classifying Your Lease

If your lease constitutes a lease under Article 2A of the UCC, you can, in theory, ignore most of Revised Article 9. Chapter 1616 describes the rules just for leases under Article 2A. See RA9-102(b); Article 2A-103.

If, on the other hand, your lease creates a security interest, Revised Article 9 treats your deal as a secured transaction in which the lessee (as the debtor) grants a security interest to its lessor (as the secured party) regardless of its intent to create a lease under Article 2A. The economic substance of your transaction counts, not the labels for the parties or their documents, such as "lessor" versus "secured party;" "lessee" versus "borrower;" or "lease" versus "security agreement" or "conditional sale agreement."

For lessors, you may get a rude awakening in your lessee's bankruptcy if the lessee persuades the Bankruptcy Court that you never entered into a lease under Article 2A. At the moment of such a court ruling, your deal takes on the character of a secured transaction under Revised Article 9, and, like it or not, you begin a "zero sum game" — what you lose as owner/lessor of the "leased property"(collateral), the other creditors of the "lessee" gain. See Chapter 18 on bankruptcy. You may also potentially face usury and residual value risks discussed in Chapter 3.

Criteria for security interests

Revised Article 9 refers you to rules that establish a bright line (not!) between leases and secured transactions. See revised Sections 1-201(37)(B); 2A-103(10) (effective for Revised Article 9 states).

If, at the beginning of the lease term, you answer "yes" to any of the following questions about your "lease," then your lease is deemed to create a security interest to which Revised Article 9 applies:

- ✔ Does the original term of your lease equal or exceed the remaining economic life of the leased property?

- ✔ Is the lessee bound to renew the lease for the remaining economic life of the leased property?

- ✔ Is the lessee bound to become the owner of the leased property?

✔ Does the lessee have the option to renew the lease for the remaining economic life of the leased property for no or nominal consideration (for example, for free or a $1 per year renewal rent) upon complying with the lease agreement?

✔ Does the lessee have the option to become the owner of the leased property for no or nominal consideration (for example, for free or for a $1 purchase price) upon complying with the lease agreement?

To illustrate how these concepts apply to your lease, say that you enter into a ten-year lease transaction with the lessor of the printing press with a lessor's cost of $1,000,000. The remaining economic life of the printing press on the day that you start the lease term equals ten years. The total rentals exceed $1,000,000. The lease contains a purchase option to buy the press for $1. The agreement is called an Equipment Lease.

What did you create — a lease or a secured interest? Answer: Your lease created a security interest because you agreed to a term of the lease (ten years) equal the remaining economic life of the printing press (ten years), and a bargain purchase option (the $1 payment). In effect, you entered into a conditional sale where the total payments made by the lessee over time entitle the lessee to obtain the title to the press for a buck. See Section 1-201(37)(B)(i) and (iv). Your deal looks like a secured loan because your lessor has no risk of ownership. The lessor receives full repayment of its $1,000,000 of lessor's cost plus implicit interest on that cost (that is, interest buried in the rent). Revised Article 9 therefore treats the lessor as the secured party and the lessee as the debtor. All appropriate provisions of Revised Article 9 apply to the transaction because it falls within the scope of Revised Article 9 and possesses the characteristics of a security agreement rather than a lease under Section 1-201(37) of the UCC.

Criteria for leases

The UCC establishes criteria that, if present in your lease at the beginning of your lease term, do not indicate that you have created a secured interest. See UCC Section 1-201(37)(B). In other words, you can include the following features in your lease, and they alone do not convert your lease into a secured transaction.

✔ At the time that you, as a lessee, enter into the lease, the present value of the rent and other amounts that you pay equals or exceeds the fair market value of the leased property.

✔ You assume the risk of loss and agree to pay taxes, insurance, filing, recording or registration fees, or the maintenance costs for the leased property.

✔ You have the option to renew the lease or to become the owner of the leased property (but not for free or nominal consideration).

> ✔ You have the option to renew the lease at a fixed fair market value rent or to become the owner of the leased property for a fixed fair market value price.

Although you can't rely entirely on these features as a cookbook to creating a lease, leases commonly contain terms that track these features. See the Master Lease Agreement in the Appendix. These features allow you, as the lessee, to control property under your lease and accept certain risks of using and possessing the property. At the same time, the lessor retains some of the important risks and benefits of ownership. In short, the economic realities of these features, if properly structured, can distinguish your lease from a secured transaction from a lease.

So what do you do, as a lessee or a lessor, when you don't know for sure what you've created? You can restructure your transaction to create a lease based on the preceding criteria if that is your goal. Alternatively, you can do what almost everyone does — proceed with your deal, your way, regardless of whether you are a lessee or a lessor, or even a secured lender, and take some precautions to protect your interests as discussed in the next section.

Precautions to Take with Your Leases

The decision of whether you created a lease or a security interest may challenge the best of you (count me in!). To address the uncertainty, you should, at a minimum, take two steps routinely in almost every lease transaction (just in case some court disagrees with you when you want to treat your deal as a lease).

First, you should insert in your leases a precautionary grant of a security interest in case the lease constitutes a secured transaction. While technically such a grant may not be necessary, it is common practice. A simple version of such a grant may read as follows:

Notwithstanding the express intent of the parties, should a court of competent jurisdiction determine that this Lease is not a (true) lease, but rather a lease intended as security or a security agreement, then Lessee shall be deemed, as of the date of this Lease, to have hereby granted to Lessor a security interest the property subject to this Lease and all proceeds thereof.

Beware that even this approach is no substitute for properly structuring a transaction. Pick your deal type, be it a lease or secured transaction, and comply with the appropriate provisions of Revised Article 9 and Article 2A of the UCC discussed in Chapter 16. Lessees can and do challenge their lessor's rights. Note that the language suggested above often varies depending on the complexity of the transaction. Consult your legal advisors for the specific language for your deal.

Second, as a lessor, you should file a precautionary financing statement. See RA9-505. This financing statement (described in the section, "Perfection of a security interest," later in this chapter) says that if a lease constitutes a security agreement, the financing statement perfects a security interest granted by the lessee (as debtor). By taking this action, as a lessor (secured party), you can create and preserve a first priority security interest in the leased property and the proceeds should a court treat the lease as a security agreement. The financing statement contains language that mirrors the "precautionary grant" of a security interest. You can, and should, insert the term "lessor" near "Secured Party" and "lessee" near "Debtor" in the financing statement to make clear the relationship that you intend to create.

If you file a precautionary financing statement, do you admit that your lease constitutes security agreement? No. Article 9 recognizes that you can, at your option, file the financing statement to protect your deal against the possible decision by a court that your lease constitutes a security agreement or a lease intended for security. The mere filing has no substantive impact on the true lease characterization of your transaction.

Selected Aspects of Revised Article 9

This section discusses some parts of Revised Article 9 relevant to leasing personal property. In this section, I assume that your lease creates a security interest, and that these provisions therefore apply to your "lease" transaction. As a result, view every lessor as a secured party, and every lessee as a debtor under Revised Article 9.

Categories of collateral

Revised Article 9 classifies collateral (that is, your leased property) into several categories that expand and alter the categories used in Former Article 9.

My descriptions of collateral categories do not, intentionally, include all of their subcategories or details. Note that each category exists on its own, exclusive of any other category. Consult your legal advisor to identify the category and specific rights, remedies, and procedures that apply to your leased property.

✔ **Goods.** *Goods* refer to tangible personal property and exclude other kinds of collateral, such as money, documents (contracts), or instruments (such as negotiable promissory notes). See RA9-102(a)(44); FA9-105(1)(h). Under Revised Article 9 software embedded in goods becomes part of the goods (such as computer chips installed in cars). Goods include four mutually exclusive subcategories: inventory, consumer goods, farm products, and equipment. Equipment constitutes one of the most important subcategories of goods in personal property leasing and in this book. RA9-102(a)(33). It covers a huge variety of property (for example, a printing press, lathe, or computer) and, as a category, captures goods that don't fit in one of the other three categories. Equipment typically can last a long time. Inventory includes goods that a lessor leases to another person or holds for sale or lease such as a rental truck or a copier machine. See RA9-102(a)(48). Inventory, however, is in general held or used up in a short period of time.

A secured party can make a loan to a lessor and take a security interest in a lessor's goods/inventory (equipment) as collateral. This type of transaction is vital to some lessors in raising capital and increasing volume in their leasing business.

✔ **Chattel paper.** *Chattel paper* refers to any record that evidences both a monetary obligation and either a security interest in or license or lease of *specific* goods. RA9-102(a)(11). Chattel paper includes leases, conditional sale agreements, and security agreements plus a related promissory note covering specific goods (as contrasted, for example, with all equipment combined with other assets of a debtor like inventory or receivables).

Chattel paper comes in two forms: electronic chattel and tangible chattel paper. *Electronic chattel paper* refers to chattel paper stored in electronic medium. This concept is new in Revised Article 9. It includes, in theory, an authenticated, computerized record of a lease created in a transaction completed entirely on the Internet. See RA9-102(a)(31). *Tangible chattel paper* means chattel paper evidenced in a tangible form (that is, a lease written on paper and signed, with pen in hand, by the parties). See RA9-102(a)(78).

✔ **General intangibles.** Revised Article 9 includes a catchall category that modifies Former Article 9, called *general intangibles*. This category of collateral picks up intangible property interests that the other categories of collateral do not. However, it also excludes some types of collateral such as deposit accounts (for example, bank accounts). See RA9-102(a)(29); 9-104. Equipment sellers often provide performance warranties to buyers/lessors in leasing transactions, and these warranties constitute a *general intangible*.

General intangibles include two subcategories: payment intangibles and software. A *payment intangible* refers to personal property where the principal obligation of the account debtor is the payment of money (for example, an unsecured loan agreement that isn't represented by a promissory note). See RA9-102(a)(61); RA9-109(a)(3). Software refers to a computer program, informational content in a program, and supporting information. A computer program in a laptop constitutes software and not goods because it is separate from the computer. A secured party (lessor) can take an interest in software. See RA9-102(a)(75). If, however, software is embedded in goods, it becomes a part of the goods, and not a general intangible. For example, software embedded in printing press controls constitutes a part of the press, which is categorized as goods and equipment.

When in doubt, describe your "leased property" (collateral) as equipment and software in any filing of a financing statement (precautionary and true ones) under the UCC. Your classification of collateral determines significant rights and remedies and establishes methods to create and perfect your security interest covered by Article 9.

Creation of a security interest

How do you create a security interest? Three factors must exist for a security interest to come alive legally and be enforceable. When these factors all occur, the security interest attaches (with exceptions, of course). A security interest attaches when:

- ✔ The parties *authenticate* (that is, sign or encrypt for electronic transactions) the security agreement in which the debtor grants a security interest to the secured party (lessor) and reasonably identifies the collateral. See RA9-102(a)(7) and 9-108.

- ✔ The debtor has rights in the collateral or power to transfer it.

- ✔ Value has been given (for example, the secured party (lessor) pays the seller the purchase price for the leased property in connection with entering into a conditional sale, lease, or disguised security agreement, or advances a loan). See RA9-203.

Perfection of a security interest

A secured party (including a lessor under a lease intended as security) can perfect his security interest by filing a financing statement or by other methods prescribed by Revised Article 9. See RA9-501-527.

A security interest in collateral must attach as a totally separate and necessary act from perfecting your interest. Further, if the secured party fails to perfect properly, other creditors, including other secured parties, the debtor's trustee in bankruptcy, and subsequent purchasers of collateral, can take priority to the collateral.

A secured party can perfect his interests in property in one or more ways depending on the type of collateral. It can perfect security interests by taking possession of collateral or, for certain collateral, by exercising control over the collateral. For example, for electronic chattel paper, you perfect by control or filing a financing statement. RA9-105. You must also comply with special rules for electronic identification of the secured party on the electronic copy of the lease or other electronic chattel paper (that is, the lender (lessor) puts an indelible mark on the electronic image and also marks it as the original).

See RA9-314(a); RA9-312(a). However, a secured party can perfect in a deposit account only by taking control of the account. See RA9-102(a)(31); RA9-104; RA9-312(b); RA9-314. Control or possession often wins over filing to perfect a security interest.

One way to take a first priority security interest in tangible chattel paper is to take possession of the only executed original. See RA9-313(a); 9-330. Tangible chattel paper (such as a lease) should be marked with words such as "lessor's original" or a legend indicating that the counterpart of the lease in possession of a secured party (lessor) constitutes the only original under the UCC. See RA9-330. Such marking assures the lessor that she possesses the original in which she alone can grant a first priority security interest to her secured lenders.

In addition, you can automatically perfect a security interest on attachment without filing a financing statement for certain collateral (for example, the sale of payment intangibles or a promissory note). See RA9-309.

This rule facilitates sales of payment intangibles or promissory notes by lenders or lessors (subject to Revised Article 9), and enables them more easily to record immediate sales of those transactions to increase earnings.

Lastly, filing a financing statement is probably the most common method to perfect your security interest in leased property as a lessor. RA9 501-522. Revised Article 9 makes extensive changes with regard to filing financing statements under the UCC. A *financing statement* refers to a record of the security interest that a secured party files on a prescribed form in an appropriate governmental office to perfect, and to give notice to others, of his security interest in the collateral. See RA9-102(a)(39). For example, you can perfect a security interest in equipment by filing a financing statement. See RA9-301, RA9-307 and RA9-316. For fixtures, a secured party perfects by making a *fixture filing* (a financing statement filed in the records related to the real property on which the leased property is located). See RA9-501(a).

The following points acquaint you with the new UCC filing system under Revised Article 9 (but you should hit the books for more details):

- ✔ **New filing system — media neutrality.** Moving into the electronic era, Revised Article 9 allows for filing of financing statements in any format or by any media including electronic filings on tendering the financing statement (that is, presentation). See RA9-102(a)(39). This change can save you time and money in completing your transactions (with a few less documents to sign for closing).

- ✔ **Duration, lapse, and termination.** Filings of financing statements generally last five years, and you must continue (extend) them within six months prior to the date they lapse (expire) using a prescribed form of *continuation statement.* See RA9-515.

✔ **Contents of a financing statement (called a UCC-1).** Revised Article 9 requires only three essential items of information that you must communicate to the appropriate filing office in your financing statement: the exact registered name of the debtor, the name of the secured party or his representative, and a description of the collateral.

By using strict rules, Revised Article 9 provides searchers of the UCC records a predictable and dependable method of finding UCC financing statements and other filings. Former Article 9 requires a signature on the financing statement. Revised Article 9 dumps that requirement and allows the debtor/lessee to file the financing statement without further approvals or signatures once the lessee (debtor) signs the security agreement or a lease intended for security (that is, a secured loan). If a secured party (lessor) wants to file financing statements before signing, she must obtain debtor's (lessee's) written permission separate from the security agreement before the closing (for example, by a separate agreement or even in a lease proposal or commitment). See RA-509(a) and (b).

If, as the secured party, you don't state the exact name of the debtor (lessee), you have one safe harbor, but you should not depend on it. If the search logic of the state in which you file picks up your filing in a search under debtor's name that you use, your filing keeps priority over conflicting lenders or lessors. See RA9-503 and 506(b).

✔ **How you describe collateral.** Revised Article 9 allows you to describe collateral in a financing statement by category (such as, equipment), by specific listing (for example, "printing press, serial no. 123"), by quantity, by formula, or by procedure. Secured parties can even use generic words to describe collateral such as "all assets" or "all property" (not useful in most leasing deals because they involve specific property). However, a security agreement must describe collateral by category or specifically. See RA9-504(2); RA9-108.

✔ **Where to file.** Filing under Revised Article 9 is like picking real estate: It's "location, location, location." Revised Article 9 requires (in a change from Former Article 9) that, except for fixtures, , a secured party needs only to make central filings in the location of the debtor (lessee). The *location* of the debtor for filing changes for different types of debtors such as individuals or registered organizations (limited partnerships, corporations, limited liability companies, and so on). See RA9-301, 307, 501 and 502(a)(1). For example, for corporate debtors, you only file a financing statement in the office of the Secretary of State where the corporate debtor is registered. Revised Article 9 ends the so-called dual-filing requirement, which requires a secured party to file in the county where the property is located and at the central location, such as the Secretary of State. See RA9-301, RA9-307 and RA9-316. For fixtures, however, a secured party perfects by making a fixture filing. See RA9-501(a).

✔ **Filing official national forms, indexing, and timing.** Revised Article 9 mandates that filing offices accept a national form of financing statement and amendments. This change improves uniformity and objectivity by filing offices when accepting and rejecting filings. See RA9-521. Filers index alphabetically by the name of the debtor (lessee). See RA9-519(c)(1). Revised Article 9 also requires acceptance, rejection, and indexing of filings within specific time frames. See RA9-520. I won't hold my breath waiting for this change to happen as required!

After you close your lease/secured loan, the lender (lessor) can't just snooze and wait to file a continuation statement. Certain events trigger a requirement to make new filings of financing statements within four months to one year after the event (with exceptions) to maintain a perfected security interest in collateral. For example, the time allotted is

✔ Four months if a debtor (lessee) changes its location to another jurisdiction (see RA9-316(a)(2)).

✔ One year if a debtor (lessee) merges with another entity and that entity is located in another jurisdiction, or the debtor (lessee) transfers collateral to another person that becomes the debtor and is located in another jurisdiction. See RA9-316(a)(3).

Lessees should inform lessors of such changes, and lessors should immediately check with their counsel to determine what new filings, if any, may be required.

Priority of security interests

Even though your security interest becomes enforceable, you still need to go an extra step to achieve the first priority security interest in the collateral. Revised Article 9 creates rules to establish the winners in a contest for priority in collateral. The general rule says that if you perfect by filing a financing statement first, you win in a contest for first rights in the affected collateral perfected by filing. See RA9 322(a)(1). However, many exceptions exist to this general rule (a discussion beyond the scope of this book). See RA9-322. To determine who wins after you perfect, look to the law where the leased property is located. See RA9-301.

You should note one extremely important exception. A *purchase money security interest* refers to a security interest in collateral that arises when a supplier or lender (lessor) with respect to that collateral provides the financing enabling the debtor (lessee) to purchase that collateral. For example, if, as a lender (lessor), you provide your debtor money to buy a printing press, your security interest may have a super priority in the printing press. To get that priority, you must file a financing statement within 20 days of the date that the debtor (lessee) first obtains possession of the printing press. See

RA9-324(a); FA9-312(4). During that 20-day grace period, as secured party, you can perfect your interest without concern that another secured creditor of the buyer (debtor [lessee]) can jump ahead of you. You get that special grace period because you provide the cash to buy the property. Such a priority encourages lessors to make investments in goods (such as equipment) without concern that a pre-existing secured lender may take prior rights in those goods.

Enforcement of security interests

Part 6 of Revised Article 9 extensively revises enforcement rights by a secured party against its debtor's collateral. The provisions give the debtor and certain other interested parties, such as the guarantors, minimum legal protections (many of which they can't waive even though lenders [lessors] often want them to give up these rights). The secured party (lessor) enjoys a variety of rights and remedies on a default by a debtor (lessee), but must always act in a commercially reasonable manner. See RA9-607(c), 610, 608(a)(3). The parties define a debtor's default in their security agreement/lease which include, for example, nonpayment, misrepresentations, failure to maintain insurance, and breaches of covenants such as maintaining property.

Debtors/lessees should work hard to avoid defaults because once a secured party starts remedies, as debtor (lessee), you can bet that you face an expensive and probably losing battle. However, if the secured party (lessor) doesn't play by the rules, Revised Article 9 gives you, as the debtor (lessee), the right to recover actual damages from the secured party (lessor). See RA9-625(b).

After a default, a secured party can exercise extensive remedies, such as:

- ✔ Collecting on or taking possession of the collateral under RA9-607 and RA9-609

- ✔ Selling or keeping the collateral in satisfaction of the obligations owned by the debtor (lessee) under RA9-610(f)

- ✔ Demanding payments directly from guarantors under RA9-607(a)

- ✔ Applying proceeds of collateral collected by secured party (lessor) under RA9-608; RA9-615

- ✔ Seeking a deficiency from the debtor (lessee) under RA9-608 (with exceptions of course)

The secured party must give notices to secondary obligors (such as, guarantors) and other secured parties when he disposes of collateral. See RA9-611(c) and RA9-624(a). In a secured transaction, the secured party must return any excess proceeds from collateral (as if this ever really happens in most cases!) over the debt obligation to the debtor. See RA-608(b) and RA9-615(e).

Chapter 18

Bankruptcy Hits Leasing: Lessee Tools and Lessor Consequences

• •

In This Chapter

▶ Reviewing the basics in bankruptcy for leases

▶ Preventing creditor actions with the automatic stay

▶ Dealing with troubled lessees

▶ Working through a lessee's bankruptcy

▶ Understanding special bankruptcy rules for aircraft, vessels, and railroad rolling stock

• •

*U*nfortunately, not every one succeeds in business. Whether you're a lessee or a lessor, you probably know when you're heading for bankruptcy. Perhaps you can't pay your debts as they become due, or your obligations exceed your assets. You may have taken over advances on your bank revolving line of credit or blown your financial covenants. Your trade creditors demand payments in cash on delivery.

For some troubled lessees and lessors, you can work out your financial problems with your lenders and lessors. For others, you have go into bankruptcy — a time-consuming and expensive process. Although bankruptcy law applies equally to lessors and lessees, this chapter approaches bankruptcy primarily from the view that lessees file bankruptcy. Lessors, as creditors, then have to cope with the consequences and plan for the possibilities.

To help you understand bankruptcy for leases, whether you are a lessee, a lessor, or a lender, I introduce you to the basics and describe the lessee's and lessor's perspective of a lessee's bankruptcy primarily involving business reorganizations. To give you some reference, I refer to some specific sections in the Federal Bankruptcy Code (sometimes called the "Code" in this chapter) as "BC xxxx." You can find the full Code in Title 11 of the United States Code (USC) at www4.law.cornell.edu/uscode/11/index.html.

Bankruptcy Basics for Leasing

The Code provides debtors protection from creditors. Debtors refer to those with the debts that file under the Code, including lessees (a different debtor than the one covered in Chapter 17). See BC 101(13). Creditors refer to those who have claims against the debtors, including lessors. See BC 101(10). The Code also establishes relative priorities among creditors to assets of the debtor.

In this chapter, I assume that a lessee, as the debtor in bankruptcy, wants to reorganize her business under Chapter 11 of the Code rather than liquidate her assets under Chapter 7 of the Code. See BC 109(b), 701, 702 and 726. I do not consider other chapters in the Code.

Starting bankruptcy proceedings

Any company, partnership, or other business organization (or individual) can voluntarily commence a case in bankruptcy by filing a petition with the Federal Bankruptcy Court. See BC 109(d). In addition, any three creditors, acting together (or one creditor where fewer than 12 creditors exist), can file a bankruptcy petition against a debtor and start an involuntary bankruptcy case if the debtor has not been paying his undisputed debts as they become due (with some other requirements of course). See BC 303(b) and (h).

Filing voluntarily

The filing of a voluntary bankruptcy petition automatically constitutes an *order for relief* (see BC 301) and places the property of the debtor/lessee into a bankruptcy estate, a new and separate legal entity from the lessee. The bankruptcy estate holds the lessee's assets and is responsible for his liabilities. It possesses new powers and gains new protections to deal with the debtor/lessee's assets and creditors, such as lessors. It is, in effect, the lessee in protective clothing. The entry of the order for relief also triggers the automatic stay (discussed in the next section). See BC 362.

Managing the business after filing

A debtor under Chapter 11 generally continues to manage her business as the *debtor in possession*. See BC 1101(1). However, the creditors (and others) may request that the Bankruptcy Court appoint a trustee to manage the business of the debtor/lessee. See BC 1104(a). The creditors must show cause for displacing the lessee's management with a trustee, who is often an independent expert in the lessee's field of business. Such cause includes fraud, dishonesty, or gross incompetence on the part of the existing management of the debtor/lessee. (Ordinary incompetence is not enough!)

Overview of a bankruptcy reorganization

During the case, the creditors, including lessors, make claims and exercise their unique rights against the debtor under the powerful jurisdiction of the Bankruptcy Court. Because Chapter 11 allows a debtor to reorganize his business, a debtor's goal is to eventually prepare a *plan of reorganization,* which describes how the debtor plans to restructure his obligations to all his various creditors and operate a viable business outside of bankruptcy. See BC 1123. At the same time that the debtor/lessee files his plan, he is required to file a *disclosure statement* that describes the financial and historical basis for the plan and contains "adequate information" necessary for creditors to vote intelligently on the plan. See BC 1125(b).

The plan must designate classes of claims including secured claims, unsecured claims, and tax claims. See BC 1122. Voting on the plan is done by class of creditors and occurs after the Bankruptcy Court has approved and ordered the distribution of the disclosure statement, the plan, and the ballots to all creditors. See BC 1126. Each class must vote in favor of the plan, or the Court must determine that the plan is fair and equitable (without discrimination against claimants) and then force the plan of reorganization on the creditors called the *cram down.* For the Bankruptcy Court to cram down a plan, at least one group of creditors that sacrificed rights must approve the plan. BC 1129(b)(1). Ultimately, a plan must satisfy an extensive list of requirements and gain acceptance by holders of claims and the Bankruptcy Court. See BC 1129(a) and (b).

If all goes well, the Bankruptcy Court enters an order that confirms the debtor/lessee's plan of reorganization, and the lessee emerges from bankruptcy. A new lessee entity then exists with reduced/reorganized obligations and with a shot at the success in business that eluded her before filing bankruptcy. If no confirmation occurs, however, a debtor may have to convert her case to Chapter 7. See BC 1112. Then it's curtains, because the business in Chapter 7 liquidates its assets (if it has any) and ends its business operations over time. Creditors receive a distribution of property or money (they hope!), usually amounting to a fraction of what the debtor owed them, and that's it — game over. Alternatively, the Bankruptcy Court may dismiss the case. See BC 1112. The debtor re-enters the world without the protective cloak of the bankruptcy laws, and the creditors can move in on the debtor.

The Lessee's Approach in Bankruptcy

As a bankruptcy case proceeds, certain differences between leases and secured loans become evident. See Chapters 1 and 17. The Bankruptcy Court can reduce and/or delay payment to a secured creditor under a plan of reorganization, but, with court approval, you, as the debtor/lessee, must either assume or reject your lease in its entirety unless you otherwise agree with your lessor. See BC 365. If you reject a lease, the lessor can recover her leased property and make a claim for prepetition damages (that is, damages arising before your filing in bankruptcy), such as unpaid rent. If you assume the lease, you have to pay your contractual rent, generally cure your defaults, and otherwise comply with the terms of the lease. See 365(b). On filing the bankruptcy, however, both your lessors and secured creditors (and all other creditors) must face the impact of the automatic stay in bankruptcy. See BC 362. The following sections explain these concepts.

The big freeze: The automatic stay

On filing of a voluntary petition in bankruptcy, federal law immediately erects a shield (that is, a sort of court injunction) around you and your bankruptcy estate called the *automatic stay*, which prohibits creditors from taking any action against you or your property. See BC 362(a). The stay gives you time to address your financial problems without the immediate pressure of creditors' demands. Protected property in your estate includes your estate's leasehold rights in a true lease and property that your estate owns. See BC 541(a)(1). For example, creditors must immediately and completely stop

- ✔ All collection activity and legal proceedings to recover any debt or other claim arising before you filed your petition in bankruptcy, called *prepetition claims*

- ✔ Any attempt to repossess or control leased property, such as taking back or holding onto a tractor in the midst of a repossession leased from a lessor

- ✔ Any attempt to create, perfect, or enforce any lien against leased property, terminate the lease, or take extra collateral

Any attempt by your creditors to take any action against you to collect a debt as the debtor, for example, violates the automatic stay and provides the Bankruptcy Court grounds on which to hold your creditors in contempt — potentially resulting in fines, penalties, and other sanctions. Your creditors, including lessors, must understand that violating the automatic stay is really a foolish thing to do! Courts have been known even to scold the IRS and state court judges for violating the stay.

Your creditors can obtain relief from the automatic stay by seeking an order from the Bankruptcy Court. To get that order, the creditor must show

- ✔ Good reasons to lift the automatic stay, such as lack *of adequate protection* of an interest in property of such party (for example, showing that you don't have the ability to pay rent or operate and maintain the leased property according to the terms of the lease). See BC 362(d)(1).

- ✔ You lack any equity in the leased property and that you do not need the leased property for an effective reorganization of your business. See BC 362(d)(2).

Lessee choices: To assume or to reject

With an automatic stay in effect, as the debtor/lessee, you (or your trustee) then have some choices to make about whether to assume, reject, or, in some cases, assume and then assign your lease. See BC 365(f). Because you represent the estate (it's your business at stake!), the Code allows you to make a decision whether to assume or reject a lease based on your business judgment.

Before you make this choice, however, you should determine whether your lease constitutes a true lease or a disguised security agreement (see Chapter 17). If you conclude that your lease does indeed constitute a true lease, you then have the right to assume or reject an unexpired lease with Bankruptcy Court approval. See BC 365(a). However, if your lease constitutes a disguised security agreement, you take a different approach as discussed in the following section called "Consequences of entering disguised security agreements."

If your lease constitutes a true lease, then you focus on whether your lease constitutes an *unexpired lease*. You can think of an unexpired lease as one that still has life in it, legally speaking, or as a lease that has some time remaining before it expires. You don't have time remaining on your lease if it expires on its own terms, or your lessor terminates the lease before you file your petition in bankruptcy. Your lessor generally terminates your lease by getting a court order and/or sending you a notice telling you, for example, that your lease has been terminated by reason of your default due to nonpayment of rent. An unexpired lease is part of your bankruptcy estate, but a terminated or expired lease is not. If a lease is not in effect, you have no leasehold interest or right to use or possess the leased property. In short, you can't assume or reject a lease that doesn't exist.

It is critical to understand that only the debtor in possession or his trustee can assume, reject, or assume and then assign the lease. See BC 365. The non-debtor party (usually the lessor) remains bound by the terms of the lease. Once you conclude that your lease constitutes an unexpired lease, then you, as the debtor/lessee, or the trustee can assume or reject the lease.

If the Bankruptcy Court, at your request, treats your lease as a security agreement (in which you granted a security interest to your lessor), then you can't even consider assuming or rejecting a lease because no true lease exists. Consequently, you (or your trustee) can

✔ **Avoid the lien and perfection of the lien.** You (or your trustee) can try to avoid (or set aside) the lien of your lessor if your lessor did not properly perfect her security interest in the leased property (which becomes collateral for a loan). See BC 544.

✔ **Use the property/collateral subject to a security interest, but pay less for it.** You can use the property, but you must provide the lessor/lender adequate protection of its security interest. See BC 361. You don't have to cure defaults or provide adequate assurance of future performance like you do with respect to leases. *Adequate protection* is the lender's version of adequate assurance for a lessor. Adequate protections takes the forms, takes the form, for example, of an equity cushion in the value of the property (that is, collateral value exceeding the debt), cash payments to the lessor, administrative claims against the estate with super-priority over other creditors (see BC 503), and replacement liens on other property (that is, liens with a similar value on different property, not on the original leased property/collateral of the lessor/lender). See BC 362 and 363.

After confirmation of your plan of reorganization, you may, as part of the plan, continue to use the property subject to your lease and pay only the value of the collateral. If the lessor's cost (the principal amount) of your lease (which is a loan) exceeds the value of the leased property (which is the collateral), you may only have to pay the collateral value without obligation to pay the deficiency under the principal amount. Even if the property value exceeds the debt, you may still pay less interest or have different loan terms than you did before your bankruptcy. See BC 1129(b)(2).

Assuming your lease

If the lease constitutes a true lease, as debtor/lessee, you can assume a lease and thereby continue your use of the leased property. See BC 365. Unless a lease is assumed in the Bankruptcy Court, your lease is automatically deemed rejected (as discussed in the next section). To assume your lease:

✔ You must cure all defaults (such as paying all prepetition rent) or provide adequate assurance to your lessor that you will promptly cure defaults. See BC 365(b)(1).

✔ You must provide adequate assurance of future performance to your lessor. You can provide adequate assurance if you:

• Have sufficient unencumbered assets to pledge to a lessor

• Post a bond or letter of credit to cover that value

• Have sufficient assets to pay all amounts due under the lease

> ✔ You must compensate your lessor for all money losses that the lessor suffered or provide adequate assurance to your lessor that you will compensate the lessor for all losses caused by your default.

Once your estate assumes a lease, your lessor's claim for rent constitutes an expense of administration, which gives your lessor priority in the distribution of your assets over unsecured creditors if you breach the assumed lease. See BC 365(g)(2) and 503(b)(1).

Rejecting your lease

If the lease constitutes a true lease, as debtor/lessee, you can also *reject* a lease. When you reject your lease, you officially terminate all your lease obligations with the help of a Bankruptcy Court order, regardless of how long the lease term lasts or what it says. The power to reject your lease comes from a trustee's power to abandon assets that, in his business judgment, place an unacceptable burden on your bankruptcy estate. You can't walk away from your lease without consequences, however. Your lessor has rights at that point (after the automatic stay is lifted/ended) to:

> ✔ Repossess the leased property (which your lessor can do with a state court order).
>
> ✔ File an administrative claim to pay for the use of the property for the period *after* you filed your petition in bankruptcy (that is, the post-petition period), and before you returned the property to the lessor.
>
> ✔ File a proof of claim for the prepetition damages under your lease.

Assigning your lease

Either you, as debtor/lessee, or your trustee, can assign an unexpired lease to a third party on two conditions. See BC365(f).

> ✔ You must assume the lease (meeting the requirements for assumptions described in the preceding assumption section) and then assign a lessee to an assignee.
>
> ✔ The *assignee,* the party who takes over for you, must provide adequate assurance that she can perform under the lease in the future.

The Five Ps of Bankruptcy: A Lessor's Perspective

When I began to think about how to describe some essential information to you, as the lessor, about a lessor's views of bankruptcy of his lessees, I thought of five key words, which coincidentally all started with the letter *P*. In this section, the five Ps are

- ✔ **Prepare** (getting ready for your lessee's possible bankruptcy)

- ✔ **Payment** (pursuing payments before and during bankruptcy)

- ✔ **Perfection** (perfecting your security interests in case you enter into a disguised security agreement/secured loan instead of a true lease)

- ✔ **Preferences** (knowing whether you may have to give back money or other value to the lessee that you received before bankruptcy in preference to other creditors)

- ✔ **Proof of Claims** (filing a claim to collect unpaid rent and other obligations arising before the bankruptcy filing of your lessee)

Prepare for bankruptcy early

You know the signs of your lessee's financial trouble. They include nonpayment of rent, irregular payments to trade creditors, nondelivery of financial reports, deficient equipment maintenance, and failure to maintain insurance.

A bankruptcy filing can cause disruption to scheduled rent payments, challenge to the validity of your lease as a true lease, consume valuable management time and cash flow, and result in significant deterioration in value of your leased property, to name a few problems. At the first sign of financial trouble, gather appropriate personnel and establish a game plan to protect your leased property and other financial interests.

You can take several actions before a bankruptcy filing:

- ✔ **Conduct a lease and credit review.** Call your internal lawyers and/or external bankruptcy/leasing counsel and ask them to review your leases to ensure that these documents have been properly organized and signed correctly and also represent the deal that you believe is in effect.

- ✔ **Make sure that you have made correct precautionary filings under the UCC.** Do this even if you believe that your lease constitutes a true lease. If you know that your lease is a loan in lease clothing, make sure that you have perfected your security interest properly and have possession or control of the original lease. See Chapter 17 on perfecting your security interest in chattel paper.

- ✔ **Initiate efforts by your credit staff to obtain the most recent financial information about your lessee from the lessee and other resources.** That way, you can evaluate the potential for defaults and financial distress. Set up appropriate loss reserves. Increase your on-site inspections of the leased property and of the books and records of the lessee. Communicate regularly with the lessee's chief financial officer and other appropriate senior executives. Review credit applications to find a basis to put the lease in default and to exercise immediate remedies. For example, misstatements in credit applications may trigger a default because the statements constitute a breach of the lessee's representations and warranties in the lease.

✔ **Improve your legal and financial position.** Even though the lessee may challenge you later, you should consider taking the following actions:

- File additional UCC financing statements or amendments to correct any deficiencies in your existing filings. Revised Article 9 changes some collateral classifications that may affect your transactions as well as required filing rules for financing statements. See Chapter 17. Watch out for the transition rules under Revised Article 9, which affect whether your remain perfected in collateral for transactions completed *before* and after the effective date of Revised Article 9 (July 1, 2001 for most states).

- Make corrections to your documents so that your lease documents accurately reflect your intended deal.

- Request that your lessee hire turnaround professionals to nurse the lessee's business back to health or even alter his management team to effectively handle his problems.

- Enter into *forbearance agreements*, if necessary. Such agreements help the lessee when the lessee has defaulted or may default in her obligations by giving the lessee time to comply with her obligations and financial relief such as rent deferrals and restructuring. In exchange for this forbearance, you can ask for additional collateral to support the lease obligations. You can also ask for a letter of credit (good luck on this one for a lessee in distress!), and personal guarantees (if you don't already have them) of the owners or senior officers. You can also ask for various representations, acknowledgments and waivers from the lessee (for example, that your lease is a true lease, the amount necessary to cure any and all defaults under the lease and the lessee has no equity in the leased property). The waivers may limit a lessee's challenges to your interests if the lessee has equal (or similar) business sophistication (to you), good legal representation, and receives value from you for the waivers. For example, you can ask for waivers of the automatic stay (should the lessee commence a bankruptcy); any jury trial (which helps avoid a sympathy vote of a jury for the lessee); and defenses and claims against you.

Although a Bankruptcy Court may not enforce waivers, the waivers may help you direct the behavior of the lessee before a bankruptcy while you attempt to minimize your credit and legal risks. Representations can help disclose credit problems and other possible basis for defaults that allow you to exercise remedies before a bankruptcy stay stops you.

✔ **Terminate your lease and attach the leased property.** If a filing in bankruptcy seems likely, and you can establish strong basis for exercising remedies, such as nonpayment of rent or cancellation of insurance coverage, then consider terminating your lease by notice to, or state court action against, your lessee. If you terminate your lease before bankruptcy, your lessee can neither assume nor reject the lease because the lease no longer exists. You can and should thereafter try to repossess the equipment before a filing occurs using powers of the appropriate courts, through attachment or sequestration actions.

Payment: Pursue it early and often

You should remain diligent before bankruptcy that the lessee pays your rent on time. However, once the lessee files his petition and the automatic stay comes into effect, your rights to payment may change dramatically. If the Bankruptcy Court treats your lease as a disguised security agreement, you can experience reduced and delayed payments. If your lease constitutes a true lease, the debtor/lessee must perform all of his obligations, including paying rent, starting 60 days after the lessee files his petition in bankruptcy. See BC 365(d)(10). The payments must continue until the lessee assumes or rejects the lease, which may occur at any time before the confirmation of the plan of reorganization or the deadline set by the Bankruptcy Court. See BC 365(d)(2). During the first 59 days, you can (and should) seek payment of your rent. You must demonstrate that the actual use or benefit of the leased property was a necessary expense to preserve the bankruptcy estate. See BC 363(b).

Your efforts early and often in participating in the bankruptcy proceeding may lead to higher payments on your lease. For example, watch for lenders who try to use available cash collateral to pay their loans to the exclusion of your rent payments. See BC 363 and 364(d). Don't get behind in collecting that rent, if possible; otherwise, you may have to accept only a pro rata share of available cash flow of the lessee with other creditors (and that pro rata payment may be insufficient to fully pay the rent). Diligence, even at some expense, pays! Further, leasing property to a lessee that is critical to the lessee's operations may help get you out of the ditch before other lessors (which lease less important assets to the debtor/lessee).

Perfection and preferences

A debtor in possession under the Code has all the avoiding powers of a trustee in bankruptcy. See BC 1107(a) and 1108. The *avoiding powers* give a debtor/lessee the right to challenge any transfer made to you (or others) that may constitute an unperfected security interest, preferential transfer, or *fraudulent conveyance* (a transfer in fraud of creditors of the lessee). This section focuses on the perfection and preferences.

Bankruptcy really tests the legal strength of your interests. One such test occurs when the debtor/lessee uses her strong-arm powers. These powers vest in the debtor/lessee (or a trustee) the powers of the hypothetical lien creditor. See BC 544. The *hypothetical lien creditor* gives the debtor/lessee (or a trustee) the right to step into the shoes of a (make-believe) creditor of the debtor/lessee and challenge any lien that any creditor did not properly perfect before the bankruptcy. For example, if no financing statement had been filed with respect to your lease, and the Bankruptcy Court construes your lease as a disguised security agreement, the debtor/lessee can argue that the Bankruptcy Court should avoid your security interest. A true lease doesn't face much exposure because generally the debtor/lessee may only have leasehold rights to use and possess the property (for unexpired leases), and the lessor alone owns the leased property.

Under the Code, all creditors have equal positions relative to the debtor/lessee. No one creditor can gain a preferential position over any other creditor within 90 days (and within one year for insiders) before a bankruptcy filing. *Insiders* for corporate debtors/lessees include its officers, directors, general partners, and persons who have control over the debtor/lessee. See BC 101(31). If the lessee/debtor makes any such transfer on account of debt that existed before the bankruptcy filing, the debtor/lessee (or his trustee) has rights to recover any payment or avoid any security interest. The idea is to put the creditor back in the same relative (equal) position without favor or preference over others. See BC 547. Any such transfer or payment in violation of this rule may represent a preference that the Code permits the debtor/lessee to recover.

Three key reasons exist for the right to challenge preferences in bankruptcy. First, a distressed lessee should not be able to play favorites among her creditors who each have bargained for their positions and accepted risks according to their original deals with the lessee. Second, because no one gets a preference after a bankruptcy filing, no creditor has an incentive to race to exercise it rights and thereby to dismember the lessee. Third, the preference rules help create an orderly process in Bankruptcy Court (as hard as that may be to believe when you experience the process!) for the rehabilitation of the debtor/lessee and/or the fair distribution of her assets.

The Code describes a *preference* as follows in Section 547(b) of the Code:

> **A transfer** (usually a payment or grant of security interest) **to or for the benefit of a creditor** (even if not directly a recipient, a creditor benefits) **of property of the debtor** (property of the bankruptcy estate in which the debtor has some equity interest) **for or on account of an antecedent debt** (a transfer to pay debt that existed before the transfer and bankruptcy occurred and is not new debt incurred at the time of the transfer) **made while the debtor was insolvent** (when the sum of the lessee's debts exceeded the fair value of it assets) **made within 90 days before a debtor/lessee files a petition in bankruptcy** (the period that you look back from the date that the bankruptcy case was filed is 90 days, and any

transfer in that 90-day period, or one year for insiders, may be challenged as a preference) **that enables the creditor to receive more than it would have received in a liquidation of the lessee's assets in a Chapter 7 case** (a lessor can't receive a greater percentage of its claims than it would have in a liquidation of the lessee's assets taking into account exemptions and priority of administrative claims).

The debtor/lessee (or trustee) must prove every element of a preference to reclaim payments to you as a preference. See BC 547(b). In addition, your normal lease payments arguably should not be treated as preferences for two reasons. First, one exception (called an *affirmative defense*) to the preference rules says that if a debtor/lessee makes payments in the ordinary course of business, then those payments are not preferences. The *ordinary course of business* refers to a debtor/lessee incurring the obligation and making the payment or transfer in a normal business or financial manner. The payment can not be caused by unusual credit or other problems, and must be made on normal business terms (both for it and the creditor/lessor who receives the transfer from the lessee). See BC 547(c)(2). Second, rent paid on a regularly scheduled basis, paid in advance, and when due does not relate to antecedent debt; it is arguably a current obligation, paid as the obligation arises.

Two other affirmative defenses exist. First, preference claims expire two years after the filing of a petition under Chapter 11 (that is, the period of the *statute of limitations*). Second, and more important, if you or any creditor gives new value for property transferred to you, the exchange is current value for current property is not a preference because it does not relate to debt existing prepetition.

Preference litigation often occurs in bankruptcy cases. It tends to be extremely technical based on the requirements of the preference law, affirmative defenses that may exist, and the facts of each case. Don't take this issue on without the help of knowledgeable bankruptcy counsel.

Proof of claims: Forms for payment

A *proof of claim* is the official form required in the bankruptcy case by which you assert your claim or right to payment for your prepetition losses or damages against a lessee's bankruptcy estate for unpaid rent and other breaches of the lease. If the lessee lists your claim on his official bankruptcy schedules filed with the Bankruptcy Court and does not list your debt as in dispute, contingent, or uncertain as to its amount, then you do not need to file a proof of claim. Otherwise, you can obtain a prescribed form of Proof of Claim and complete it and send it in to the Bankruptcy Court within the required time period based on local Bankruptcy Court rules of procedure. Once your Proof of Claim is filed, it is deemed allowed unless someone objects to it. Otherwise, you should receive your pro rata portion of any funds distributed to similarly situated creditors with claims similar to yours.

Bankruptcy Involving Aircraft, Vessels, and Railroads

When you talk to lessors, conditional sale vendors, and secured lenders involved in leasing aircraft, vessels, or railroad rolling stock, they routinely confirm that their documents include protective language under Sections 1110 and 1168 of the Code. They have good reason for concern because these provision say that the debtor/lessee must, within 60 days after filing her petition in bankruptcy, cure all defaults that occurred before she filed the petition. The financing parties may extend the 60-day period.

These provisions also require that lessees perform all obligations when due under the lease documents (such as paying rent and maintaining the leased property). These promises do not prevent lessees from assuming or rejecting the lease later, but if the lessee does not provide this protection to the lessor, the lessor, unlike other creditors, can repossess his aircraft, vessels, or railroad equipment.

Without these provisions, the automatic stay would apply as it does in every other case, and the financing parties would face issues such as reduced payments, valuation of the collateral, and adequate protection. With these provisions, if a debtor/lessee fails to perform within the 60 days, then creditors/lessors may exercise the self-help remedy of retaking possession of the leased property.

Requirements for aircraft and vessels under Section 1110

Section 1110 has several essential requirements for a creditor/lessor to use his protections:

- ✔ Section 1110 applies only to bankruptcy petitions filed under Chapter 11. See BC 103(f).

- ✔ The sole remedy under Section 1110 is the self-help remedy of repossessing the aircraft (leased property). See BC 1110(a).

- ✔ The lease must include an agreement that it will be treated as a true lease for Federal income tax purposes. See Chapter 13; BC 1110(c).

- ✔ The leased property must consist of an aircraft, aircraft engine, propeller, appliance, or spare part (see 49 U.S.C. Section 40102), or documented vessels. See 46 U.S.C. Section 30101(1); BC 1110(a). Chapter 12 covers documenting a vessel.

- A lessor of aircraft must enter into the lease with a debtor/lessee that is a citizen of the United States. See 49 U.S.C. 40102; BC 1110(a)(2); BC 1110(a)(2). See Chapter 11 on citizenship requirements.

- The debtor/lessee must, in the case of aircraft, hold an air carrier operating certificate issued by the Secretary of Transportation for aircraft capable of carrying 10 or more individuals or 6,000 pounds or more of cargo.

- The debtor/lessee must, in the case of vessels, hold a certificate of public convenience and necessity or other permit issued by an appropriate federal agency.

In other words, Section 1110 provides that the lessee can keep the leased property if she cures initial defaults within 60 days of filing her petition under Chapter 11 (or within 30 days for any subsequent default). If the lessee fails to comply with all of the lease terms, lessors can exercise the self-help remedy of repossessing the leased property. Section 1110 therefore enables transportation businesses to continue operating and lessors to continue receiving rent during a reorganization of a debtor/lessee under Chapter 11 of the Code if lessee cure defaults and stays current in her meeting her obligations thereafter. Note that Section 1110 also applies to conditional sale vendors and secured lenders.

If you lease equipment subject to Section 1110, the lessee should represent in writing in his lease that he meets each of the citizenship, true lease, equipment type, usage, and certification requirements described in this section. Also, you should include detailed repossession rights so that a lessor can fully and effectively use self-help to recover the leased property in a default.

Requirements for rail equipment under Section 1168

If a lessee of railroad equipment turns out to be a poor credit risk and goes into bankruptcy, a lessor, a secured party, or a conditional vendor may use Section 1168 of the Code (a parallel provision to Section 1110 of the Bankruptcy Code for aircraft) to gain relief similar to Section 1110. Section 1168 allows the lessor secured party or conditional vendor in certain cases to recover possession of the rolling stock equipment or accessories used on such equipment (new and rebuilt), including superstructures and racks, within 60 days after a bankruptcy filing. The lessee may continue to use the equipment if she cures past defaults (for example, pays up past due rent) and promises to perform all obligations including the timely payment of rent within 60 days after the bankruptcy filing. See BC 1161 through 1168. The true lease requirement exists under Section 1168, but the citizenship, certification, and equipment usage requirements do not.

Part V

Products and Programs Worldwide

The 5th Wave   By Rich Tennant

Before we go in, let me ask you—do you like to bowl?

FOR SALE

In this part . . .

You can enter into outbound or inbound cross-border leases as a lessee or a lessor. You can even do leases wholly within a country outside the United States. In this part, you find information on the international world of leasing, as well as how you do business with federal, state, and local government entities in the United States. You also discover the world of vendor leasing, venture leasing, and e-leasing.

Chapter 19

Doing Business with Federal, State, and Local Government Entities

*E*very year, the federal government leases billions of dollars of equipment and other personal property under its own arcane system. Unfortunately, many banks and financial institutions that "buy" these federal leases don't always understand the unusual risks of these transactions or pay the appropriate prices for them.

In a whole different sphere, state and local governments also lease equipment and other personal property every day. However, the type of lessees, the lease structures, the credit risks, and the tax treatment, among other factors, set these transactions apart from commercial leasing and federal leasing. This chapter briefly describes leasing to federal, state, and local government entities and provides tips that you won't find in the rulebooks.

Leasing to the Federal Government

Leasing to the federal government involves more regulations and twists and turns than you can image, but for all its risks, leasing of this kind can provide a reasonable investment — for those who learn how to play the game.

Get to know the rules and the risks unique to federal leasing. Don't assume that the rules or the risks are the same as in commercial leasing. They aren't. In some cases, commercial rules won't apply at all. Realize that you will be bound by the federal rules, even when they aren't spelled out. (Many rules are just incorporated into your lease.) Find a competent federal government leasing lawyer who can help you navigate through the

- ✔ Federal Acquisition Regulation (FAR), which governs the entire lease/buy process work

- ✔ Assignment of Claims Act and the Anti-Assignment Act, which permit the assignment of federal lease revenue to a financial institutions while prohibiting the assignment of any other contract rights

Knowing how it works

Operating under the banner of the United States of America, a vast group of *contracting agencies*, as federal lessees, help Uncle Sam lease any property that it needs to run the government, ranging from computers to aircraft and copy machines to tractor-trailers. Federal lessees, called *federal agencies* in this chapter, include, for example, the U.S. military, the Treasury Department, the National Institutes of Health, and the FBI.

Federal agencies develop and implement leasing strategies. They lease (as opposed to buy) equipment, not because a particular lease is a good deal for the lessor, but strictly because the lease benefits the federal government. Federal leasing shifts onto the private sector lessor (known as the *government contractor*) almost all the economic risk that a federal agency ordinarily would take if the agency were to purchase the equipment.

Leasing enables federal agencies to commit to use and pay for leased property only for the shortest possible period — typically on a renewable year-to-year basis. The term of the typical federal lease doesn't obligate the federal agency to pay you, as the government contractor or its assignee, enough monthly payments to cover the cost of the leased property or to pay you an acceptable return on your investment. For you to recover your investment, the federal agency must generally renew the lease several times. And you can't count on these renewals. After a short time (say, after one or two years), the federal agency can replace your equipment and end your lease payments. It can just walk away from your deal and use another source to lease newer equipment.

You should enter into these deals knowing that this power of a federal agency to walk away puts you, as the government contractor or the buyer of the lease stream from the federal lease (assignee), at unusual economic risk, much more than under a customary commercial lease. This risk may require you, for example, to refurbish and remarket the leased property or to structure your lease to recover your investment a quickly as possible under prevailing market conditions.

Acting as the lessee

Who are the government officials who wield the power of the federal agency? Two individuals, working together, call the shots. The *Program Manager* and the *Contracting Officer* decide on and enter into leases for the federal agency. These two government officials first establish the need to lease the type of leased property for the federal agency and then negotiate and authorize the terms and conditions of the lease.

In essence, the Program Manager decides whether a lease best fulfills a federal agency's needs, and, if so, how much federal money goes toward the lease. The Contracting Officer, in effect, acts as the Program Manager's business agent to carry out the complicated federal contracting process that brings about a federal lease that will bind both the federal agency and the government contractor. The Program Manager also plays a critical role in determining whether to renew or extend the lease. If the Program Manager is convinced at the end of a lease term that the leased property continues to meet the needs of the federal agency and that the lease rate represents a good value, then the Program Manager directs the Contracting Officer to renew or extend your lease.

Under federal procurement law, only the Contracting Officer has the legal authority to award, modify, renew, or extend your federal lease. This rule is written in stone. The Program Manager doesn't have this authority, and nothing that the Program Manager does or says to modify, renew, or extend a federal lease is binding on the federal agency unless the Contracting Officer agrees and then issues the formal federal lease award, modification, renewal, or extension in writing.

Acting as the lessor

Only a *government contractor* (effectively, acting as the lessor) can enter into leases with federal agencies (which become its lessee). Similar to the private sector, a government contractor supplies the leased property to the federal agency. A federal agency has a contractual obligation *only* to the government contractor. It recognizes and deals *only* with the government contractor. For example, if the federal agency elects to renew the lease, upgrade or replace the leased property, or make claims for additional payment, it works only through and with the government contractor. The government contractor enjoys the direct relationship with the federal agency that, in legalese, puts it in *privity of contract* with the federal agency.

In the private sector, sometimes a purchaser of the stream of lease payments becomes the lessor, but that's not the case in the federal leasing world. A bank or other financial institution that buys the right to receive federal agency payments (that is, the lease receivable) under an assignment of payments from the government contractor doesn't qualify as a government contractor. In other words, the assignee doesn't step into the shoes of a lessor/government contractor. The federal agency doesn't listen to the assignee, and the government contractor remains in control of the leasing relationship with the federal agency, even if you, as the assignee, tell the federal agency that you own the lease.

For example, say that federal agency ABC wants to lease 500 computers. Federal agency ABC enters into a one-year lease, with four one-year options with XYZ. XYZ then sells and assigns to you, a financial institution or bank, all of XYZ's right in the lease receivable and the equipment for a discounted price, typically on a nonrecourse basis. Federal agency ABC recognizes *only* XYZ as the government contractor. Under the Anti-Assignment Act and the Assignment of Claims Act, any right that the federal agency exercises, or any right that you want to exercise, must go through XYZ, as the government contractor, regardless of any assignment to you and the fact that it's your money at risk. For example, federal agency ABC only deals with the government contractor should it want to renew or extend the lease.

If you buy the right to receive payments under federal leases from government contractors or their brokers, choose your government contractors carefully. Your payment stream remains at risk of being terminated if your chosen government contractor defaults on any of its obligations (for example, maintenance) under a federal lease. Select a government contractor that can and you expect will fully perform its obligations to the federal agency under the lease and under any separate maintenance contract. Base your decision on the demonstrated history of past performance, credibility, integrity, and financial strength/creditworthiness. Confirm that the federal agency legally awarded the federal lease to your government contractor under federal procurement laws to protect yourself as the buyer of a lease stream and to test the binding nature of the government lease. Avoid any government contractor that insists that you buy the lease from it on a nonrecourse basis but doesn't demonstrate financially how the government contractor can help you solve any nonpayment, nonrenewal, or other problem with the federal agency. For example, as a buyer of a federal lease, you may pay full price to the government contractor for a five-year lease receivable, which the government agency can end after one year. You may have no recourse against the government contractor for the four-year shortfall. Be aware of this risk and others described in the next section, and, before you buy, figure out how you can recover your investment with the help of the government contractor.

In addition, you should, as the potential government contractor or purchaser of the lease receivable, ask the following questions before you enter into a lease or assignment agreement:

- ✔ Why is the federal agency entering into this lease?
- ✔ What does the Program Manager look for in your deal?
- ✔ What is the federal agency's need for the leased property now and in the future?

Each Program Manager begins to address these questions by no later than March of the current year. At that point, the Program Manager begins planning for the period covered by the next government fiscal year (that is, from October 1 of the current year through September 30 of the following year).

Whether you're the government contractor or a bank or other financial institution with an interest in the federal lease, you should develop a good working relationship with the Contracting Officer and the Program Manager. Their decisions can and will affect your respective interests. You should also know enough about the government agency and its needs to justify your risks of a lease to the federal agency. In other words, the answers to the preceding questions should convince each of you that the lease investment you make with the particular federal agency is attractive and represents an acceptable risk for you.

Handling the risks

During a lease term, each federal agency can exercise additional powers that present some serious risks for you, as a government contractor or a buyer of the lease, including the following:

- ✔ **Termination for convenience.** A federal agency can, whenever it wants, decide that your leased property no longer provides the best value. It can make that decision for various reasons, such as the property's age or technological obsolescence. Alternatively, the federal agency may not need the particular property during the current lease term. (That is, it can decide that, at any time before lease expiration, it does not need your stuff.) In official speak, a federal agency can determine that your transaction "is not in the government's interest." The federal agency can terminate your lease (and cash flows) for the "convenience of the government" without blame or fault on your part. At that point, you have to find a new lessee or buyer for the leased property.

  You can limit this risk at the time of entering into the federal lease, if the federal agency is willing to include in your federal lease a termination value schedule that protects your economics (of both the lessor and any assignee/buyer). In other words, the termination value should pay both of you your respective yields as of the termination date, taking into account the most likely fair market value of the leased property (which will be returned to the government contractor) at the time of the termination for convenience.

  If the federal lease doesn't contain this termination value schedule, a financial institution or bank, as assignee, who takes an assignment of payments due under the federal lease, should ensure that its assignment document includes an equivalent termination value schedule that makes the government contractor liable to the assignee. In any event, the government contractor (but not the assignee) may have a right under the federal lease to pursue a termination for convenience claim and settlement against the federal agency. Any assignee of payments under a federal lease should ensure that the assignment documents obligate the government contractor to prepare and present a proper termination for convenience claim to the federal agency. At the same time, the assignee should reserve the right to settle the claim.

✔ **Nonrenewal.** The federal agency can decide not to renew a lease for many reasons, including budget cuts, the failure of the government contractor to perform its obligations or the desire to get better quality property from a new contractor.

If your government contractor fails in its duties, the federal agency can decide not to renew your lease simply to avoid the litigation risk regarding such nonperformance. Assess the likelihood that your federal lease will be renewed at least six months before the renewal date. Ask the federal agency to give you a 90-day notice of intent not to renew (which is customarily under federal procurement regulations). Use your relationship with the Program Manager and the Contracting Officer to scope out any possible nonrenewal and try to solve any problems they perceive to exist before they make the decision not to extend or renew your federal lease.

✔ **Nonappropriation.** If the U.S. Congress doesn't appropriate funds that cover payments under your federal lease, then your lease ends.

✔ **Default by a government contractor.** If your government contractor fails to perform its obligations to the federal agency, the federal agency can terminate the lease for default. This termination may create liability for you, as the assignee, or for your government contractor. Uncle Sam can charge you for its *reprocurement cost,* which is the difference between the rents under your federal lease and the rent payable by the federal agency for a replacement lease. This is a double-whammy: no more lease and damages to boot!

Leasing to State and Local Governments

This section discusses tax-exempt leases for state and local governmental units. It does not cover leases to other tax-exempt entities, such as private universities, museums, research centers, and hospitals, under Section 501(c)(3) of the Internal Revenue Code of 1986, as amended (Code), which involves governmental sponsors.

If you, as a lessee or a lessor, get the urge to say that state and local government leasing works just the same as leasing to the federal government, stop! You stand to make some huge mistakes. The governments do *not* operate alike or enter leasing transactions in any similar manner.

Leasing opportunities for government lessees

As a government entity and tax-exempt lessee, you have significant opportunities to use leasing to make nearly all of your essential acquisitions at competitive rates. Leasing can provide you with the flexibility to match the lease financing with your other capital resources and your budgetary allocations, acquire assets for the period that you need them, and retain ownership of the leased property (or even donate it when you don't need it any more). Perhaps best of all, you can often avoid *constitutional debt limitations* (governmental debt restrictions as contrasted with GAAP reporting of debt) and the cumbersome debt approval processes.

Leasing can even provide you with a financial tool that beats bond financing. You can match the term of your lease with the useful life of the leased property, plan your leases with more flexible timing than with bonds, and secure low rates without the fees that you pay for bonds. Generally speaking, you can use most leases to spread out the cost of the property over the budget years for which you intend to use the property.

Section 103 of the Code generally enables states and their political subdivisions to enter into tax-exempt leases. Political subdivisions of a state include, for example, its cities, public universities, counties, and even its fire, park, utility, school, and water districts. Each of these units can lease real property (prisons, anyone?) and personal property, including intangible assets such as certain software licenses.

As a lessee-government entity, you can test whether you qualify for tax-exempt financing by looking at your charter to see whether you have one or more of the following sovereign powers:

- ✔ The power to levy and collect taxes
- ✔ The power to police a specified area
- ✔ The power of *eminent domain* (that is, take property for governmental use)

If you are not sure, retain counsel specializing in reviewing governmental bonds and other governmental borrowing.

Lessors include vendors, banks, independent leasing companies, and other institutional investors who want tax-exempt income from leasing as a part of their portfolios.

A *tax-exempt lease* refers to a lease consisting of a principal and interest component in which the interest component is exempt from federal income taxation. In some cases of municipal leases, the interest is free from state income taxation, too. A tax-exempt lease looks and acts like a lease-purchase transaction, or a conditional sale for federal income tax purposes — you buy your property now and pay for it over time. For accounting purposes your tax-exempt lease constitutes a capital lease obligation (see Chapter 15) that you record as a liability on your balance sheet (if that matters to you).

For a lessor to claim the exemption from income taxation, you, as a lessee, must file appropriate information forms with the IRS, but most lessors assume responsibility for the filing of the forms to ensure that the filing occurs in a timely manner. Ask your tax guys or lessor about the Form 8038G and other similar forms.

Lease structure and nonappropriation

You usually structure your lease as a lease purchase agreement (nontax-oriented lease), with a variety of names or similar structures used in the market such as a conditional sale, installment sales agreement, or installment payment contract. You pay your lease payments periodically (often monthly, semiannually or annually) in the amount needed to amortize the entire lessor's cost of the leased property. Generally, a lease expires at the end of your fiscal year but automatically renews for the next fiscal year unless you, as the lessee, do not appropriate funds to make your lease payments under your lease for the next fiscal year. A nonappropriation can occur as a result of the exercise of rights under a nonappropriation clause or an annual appropriation clause.

A nonappropriation doesn't constitute a default. It represents a contractual right to condition the payment of lease payments on the appropriation of funds by the governmental unit. In other words, funding for your lease is subject to an annual budgetary process. Consequently, your lessor can generally only repossess the leased property and collect appropriated but unpaid lease payments should a nonappropriation occur. If you treat the lease payments as an annual obligation, you normally don't run afoul of rules setting limitation on your debt. You need special approvals to incur debt, which is a longer term obligation than paying lease payments for an annual period.

As a lessee, use this nonappropriation right at the risk of your financial health The bond and debt markets now view such use as shirking your responsibilities, which probably will result in a downgrading of your credit rating and a corresponding increase in your interest rates on your subsequent leases and/or bond issues.

Your lease may contain a *nonsubstitution clause,* or your lessor may ask for one. This clause says that if you, as the lessee, do exercise the nonappropriation right, you cannot replace the leased property with similar property for a certain period of time (for example, 18 months thereafter).

If your lessor asks for the nonsubstitution clause, just tell your lessor to forget it! The trend in the courts seems to indicate that these clauses undermine the nonappropriation right, which your lessor must respect. If the trend continues, your lessor probably can't (and the courts won't) enforce the clause.

Amortization schedules

Your lease must separately state (generally, in an amortization schedule) the principal and interest components of your "lease" payment for income tax purposes so that your lessor can readily identify and claim tax-exempt interest. With exceptions, as the lessee, you typically hold the title to the "leased" property during the term. You grant your lessor a security interest in the property as collateral for payment and other obligations under the lease. On payment of the final lease payment, the lessor releases the security interest and you own the property free and clear of the liens and the lease. You do have obligations to insure and maintain the property, but most government lessees self-insure for property loss. Because you hold title, you can usually avoid property tax (if any); otherwise, if your lessor holds title, you may end up paying those taxes through your lease payments.

Lessors risks and strategies

As a lessor in tax-exempt leases, you face some risks that you can and should address:

✔ **Nonappropriation.** You don't have to be a sitting duck for nonappropriation risk. Include a covenant in your lease that your lessee must give you at least a 30-day notice of any potential nonappropriation and require your lessee to take other lawful steps to continue funding for your lease.

You may not be able to enforce this agreement because some argue it may create unconstitutional debt (undermining the power of government), but it may give you some warning of a nonappropriation. Remind lessees that the nonappropriation clause (sometimes called the *funding-out clause*) should not be used lightly. Governmental entities that, as noted in the preceding section, have used these clauses as a convenience or to acquire more updated equipment can do serious damage to their credit in the financial marketplace. To protect yourself, as lessor, against a loss of funding, you should consider including language in your lease that allows only the governing body (as opposed to a government employee) to make such a decision on funding.

✔ **Default and other nonperformance risks.** To minimize the effect of these risks:

- Lease essential purpose property, critical governmental operations such as social services, or tax collection (assets tied to revenue production or cost/energy savings).

- Improve underwriting of your leases. Check closely for the lessee's credit capability; sources to make lease payments; cash reserves/liquidity; budget flexibility to make lease payments; vulnerability to significant reductions in its resources; revenue concentrations; and diversity of revenue base from taxes and other sources. Government leases have been viewed as safe investments, but history reveals that your diligence can avoid big goofs.

- Offer short lease terms with higher *front-loaded payments* (you collect a larger proportion of principal early in the term) so that you have less investment to recover if you have to take back the leased property (and remarket it) after a nonappropriation or default.

- Negotiate strong documents that include representations and warranties that the lessee has full power to enter into and perform your specific type of lease transaction; have full authorization through correct approval processes to perform its duties; and have not, in entering into the lease, violated any law or regulation, such as bidding, usury or debt limitations, and no voter approval is required to execute, deliver, and perform the lease (like debt/bond issues may require).

Require a legal opinion from either the lessee's counsel or outside bond counsel who has special expertise in the issuance of bonds and government leases that the lease is valid, binding, and enforceable against the lessee as written. Such opinions have become an important and accepted practice in most tax-exempt transactions.

✔ **Protect against loss of tax-exempt treatment.** Obtain special representations, warranties, and covenants for IRS purposes that:

- The lessee is properly organized as a governmental body and will *gross up* the interest rate if the government body does not qualify as a tax-exempt entity. In other words, if the entity is not tax-exempt, the lessee will pay an amount of interest that gives you, as the lessor, an equivalent yield after you pay taxes on the interest.

- The property being acquired is "essential" for the operation of government and that it is not being acquired for private use (see Section 141 of the Code).

- The lessee is not borrowing "tax-exempt" money for the purpose of investing it at a higher rate of interest (see Section 148 of the Code).

- The lessee will keep/file all appropriate documents (such as Code Form 8038-G).

Chapter 20

Leasing Around the Globe

· ·

In This Chapter

▶ Categorizing international transactions as inbound or outbound from your country

▶ Considering the special advantages and risks of cross-border and international leasing

▶ Evaluating the tax, legal, and accounting issues in international leasing transactions

▶ Describing products and structures used in cross-border leasing

· ·

*T*his chapter discusses how you can participate in international leasing transactions — both within foreign countries and across borders of countries. This chapter generally views these transactions from a U.S. perspective. However, for readers who lease in other countries, you can, for most of this chapter, put yourself in place of the U.S. party and apply the general concepts in relationship to your foreign markets.

The Basics of International Leasing

Fundamentally, you can enter into international leasing transactions that look very similar to the type of leases discussed throughout this book. The international elements simply add sophistication and complexity for the sake of moving capital around the world in the most advantageous pricing structures. Most of this chapter discusses *cross-border leases*, which generally refer to leases by a lessor located in one country to a lessee located in another country.

Taking a perspective from the United States, you can describe cross-border activity as inbound or outbound transactions. An *outbound* lease refers a lease by a U.S. lessor to a lessee located in another country. For example, as a U.S. lessor, you can lease an aircraft to a French lessee. An *inbound* lease refers to a lease from a foreign person to a lessee located in the United States. For example, as a Japanese lessor, you can lease a printing press to a U.S. lessee.

You can lease almost any personal property in international transactions, just like in the domestic markets of the United States. The leaders in cross-border transactions, at least the big-ticket deals, include railroad rolling stock, aircraft, power plants and related assets, manufacturing and technology equipment, containers, and vessels. The international marketplace for leasing remains dynamic and ever changing. The countries that often lead the pack in cross-border and international leasing transactions other than the United States include Canada, France, Germany (at least before current regulation), Ireland, Japan, Sweden, and the United Kingdom. These transactions offer a range of deals from relatively straightforward single-investor aircraft leases to sophisticated large-ticket leveraged leases of vessels to Japanese operating leases of aircraft and vessels.

As a lessee, cross-border leasing boils down, in most cases, to finding the lowest cost financing that you can arrange (assuming that you have the creditworthiness to entice international lessors to enter into a lease with you). The other benefits of leasing play a lesser role. So what else is new? Money talks around the world.

The economic benefit of cross-border transactions worldwide is universally defined as the net present value (NPV) of the tax benefit realized by the foreign lessor. The lessor then shares the benefit with the lessee. The average NPV ranges from 4 to 6 percent but can reach 12 percent or so for the most complex transactions.

As a lessor, you may or may not, institutionally, have the desire or willingness to lease property outside of your own country. If you respond negatively, you have lots of company (at least with a lessor in the U.S. market). However, international lessors find that many opportunities exist outside their countries to obtain attractive tax and economic benefits in less efficient markets to increase profits and build their portfolio of leases. Like the United States, as international leasing markets begin to mature, competition for deals increases, and you may experience downward pressure on your margins. However, innovative structures can add profit to the bottom line and create economically attractive transactions that produce higher after-tax benefits for lessors and lessees.

Risk Factors to Consider

Lessors often shy away from international markets for fear of the unknown risks and rules of the game, or known risks that seem difficult to manage within their own business objectives, models, and experience. While a prudent approach makes sense, as a lessor, you can identify and manage most risks of leasing in international markets, including the risks discussed in this section. As a lessee, you can help limit these risks in such a way as to interest lessors from other countries in providing financing to you in your country.

 You may feel a bit overwhelmed by the risks and complexity of cross-border or other international aspects of leasing. Keep in mind, however, that as a lessee or lessor (or lender), you can gain from opportunities in international markets to grow your respective businesses. You can find advisors and use other resources of all types to help you through the challenges. You not only can surmount these challenges, but you may also find the journey quite rewarding and interesting!

Country risk

Also called *political risk*, the term *country risk* refers to everything that can go wrong in a country affecting its political stability and business predictability. For example, these risks include war, civil strife, *nationalization* (the act of taking ownership or control of property by a government), political violence, or *expropriation* (seizure of property by government without adequate compensation), riots, or other governmental orders. You can experience licensing and tax requirements that make it difficult to deliver or repossess lease property, or other limitations that may result in a loss of your investment. You can lessen these risks. As a lessor or lessee, you can purchase

- ✔ **Private political risk insurance.** An insurer such as American International Underwriters (AIG) may pay an owner-lessor if the insurer determines that the occurrence was caused by a government action or resulted from a commercial risk. See `aiu.aig.com/aiu/wr000001.htm#wr000001` (called "Worldrisk" coverage at AIG).

- ✔ **Governmental insurance.** You can obtain governmental insurance from the Export-Import Bank of the United States (or similar agencies), which covers long-term lease transactions, such as leases of new commercial jet aircraft, offshore drilling rigs, or other leased property of significant value. The Ex-Im Bank's Insurance Program covers medium-term lease transactions of capital equipment. See `www.exim.gov/leg.html`. For more information on other well-known international lease insurers, see `www.miga.org/` or `www.opic.gov/Insurance/home.htm`.

Regardless of available insurance, as a lessor or a lessee, you can reduce your risk by leasing in a country that has been politically and economically stable for an extended period of time. The country should have no projected changes (as if anyone really knows!) of significance during the term of your lease. If you use insurance, confirm that your insurer has registered and can issue insurance coverage and/or perform its functions in the countries in which you need it.

As a lessor, you can use resources such as extensive publications of the United States Department of State to make judgments about country risk. For example, you can update your business information generally about a country by reviewing the Country Commercial Guides (CCGs) prepared annually by U.S. embassies with the assistance of several U.S. government agencies. These reports review in detail most countries' commercial environments, using economic, political and market analysis. See `www.state.gov/e/eb/rpt/index.cfm?id=270`. Also review a Lloyd's of London description of country risks and status at `www.lloyds.com/un/en/countrybriefings`.

If you don't have an office in the country, and even if you do, you can probably make an even more informed decision by hiring good local professionals (such as lawyers, accountants, and appraisers) who understand the local market and its customs, risks, laws, and political climate. Alternatively, you can co-invest in a transaction by joining a local leasing company with a deep knowledge and significant investments in the market. You know how this works: If you both stand to lose money when a big problem situation occurs, you can have greater certainty that your co-investor will focus on a solution.

Currency concerns

Although most countries of the world have confidence in the U.S. greenback, all currencies fluctuate in value relative to other currencies. As a lessor or lessee, select a currency of a country that should remain stable. You look for a country with a prudent fiscal and monetary policy, and independent and nondiscriminatory regulatory system — a big phrase for a country with a sound economy that plays fair. From a U.S. perspective, most lessors either require or prefer that their lessees make payments in U.S. dollars regardless of where a lessee uses the leased property. For example, as a lessee in Canada, your lessor may require you to pay it in U.S. dollars for all amount due under your lease. Even if the relative values of currency remain stable, not all countries allow automatic rights of conversion of currency, especially the ones that need your type of currency in their economy, such as China.

Ask about any currency controls or regulations that may limit the amount of any particular currency in which lessees can make payments and the right to convert the local currency into the currency of your choice. If fees, restrictions, or conversion problems exist, as the lessor, require your lessee to bear the economic risk to make adjustments in your rent to compensate you so that you don't receive less than a full rent payment when due as a result of these problems. Otherwise, if you receive payment in different currencies (for all or part of any rent or other payment), you can

- ✔ Establish mechanisms in your documents to adjust payments (upward or downward) so that you receive the U.S. dollar equivalent rent and other sums due under the lease.

- ✔ Purchase *currency hedges* or *swaps* (financial instruments that adjust and compensate for changes in value of currency, for a fee, of course) at the lessee's cost to pay for the differences in value of the currency that you must use. Watch for accounting rules related to using hedges or swaps of foreign currency. The financial tools do not always work in predictable ways.

- ✔ Obtain insurance for inconvertibility of the currency into your chosen currency. (For example, you can't convert a currency into U.S. dollars and take that cash back to the United States.) You can insure this risk through organizations like OPIC (the Overseas Private Investment Corporation).

If a default occurs, as a lessor, you may end up with payments in the local currency because the court or liquidator in that country orders payment in that currency. That local currency, like all others, can fluctuate in value. Plan for this contingency if feasible with hedges or other protections, such as accelerating lease payments, to minimize your risk.

Language differences

Cultural and language differences can play more than a subtle role in international transactions. Between a lessor and a lessee, your primary business languages may differ. If so, you should agree on a controlling language for all your documents and business transactions to gain the best meaning of the language used in your deal. Generally, the English language prevails, but not always.

Reliability of legal structure

Related to country risk, as lessor and lessee, you both should satisfy yourselves that you can exercise and enforce your rights against the other. Legal systems and rules differ dramatically and can affect the success of your deal.

You should select a competent foreign/local lawyers to help you in all cross-border/international transactions at a known (preferably internationally known) law firm. You should also understand the approach of the legal system regarding leasing as a business person so that you can explain the risks to your approval committees and/or board. As a lawyer, you should routinely get copies of the significant laws on which you receive advice if they have been translated into your language. If not, you should consider finding a translator to help you if the laws significantly affect your deal. Finally, you both should, at least in large-ticket transactions, seek legal opinions of foreign counsel to confirm the validity and enforceability of your transaction documents and structure.

Creditworthiness of the lessee

For lessors, in evaluating the creditworthiness of your lessee, especially in a big-ticket, cross-border deal, you look for credit rating of companies by Standard & Poor's or Moody's Investor Services. The *Financial Times* also publishes a list at www.info.ft.com/crinternational.shtml of ratings of more than 30,000 individual entities covering sovereigns, corporations, and financial institutions in a single volume.

In smaller international deals, as the lessor, you can take the most prudent approach and consider the lessee's credit as if you cannot find or regain access to your leased property. You may, in these deals, find that lessees don't want to provide financial statements to you, or that they prepare their financial information under a system other than GAAP (or its equivalent). You may have to evaluate the more limited amount of information available to you and determine from it alone whether you can approve the financing. Alternatively, you can structure your deal so that you have additional credit support, such as a letter of credit, personal guarantees, or additional collateral. For example, you can, as lessor, collect rent from a lessee affiliate, formed in your own country, which can guaranty the lease and arrange payment to you from an acceptable bank in your own country.

Finally, inquire locally about any credit application or other governmental approvals required in the lessee's country for your lease, regardless of size, and determine whether any usury risks affect (that is, limit) your lease rates or compensation.

Access to leased property and residual realization

I hear lessors express legitimate concern that they don't want to do international deals for fear that they can't find or secure the return of the leased property due to pragmatic and legal concerns: The property sits far away and is subject to laws that they don't fully understand.

As a lessor, you should inspect your leased property periodically to assure that it still exists, and that the lessee has maintained it as required by the lease. You should also plan on how to get your leased property back if the lessee does not buy it at the end of the lease, or worse, defaults. Before the lease starts, as a lessor, determine whether any local restrictions exist on the sale, lease, or other disposition (for example, conditional sale or exchange) of the leased property.

Ask your local advisors for help. Stay in touch with your lessee. Hire local inspectors to locate and inspect your leased property. Before your lease starts, put legal agreements in place to access your leased property at all times (such as landlord or owner waivers and access agreements). Also, determine from your local counsel how you can remove or dispose of the leased property under local laws at the end of the lease. Watch out for tax liability, transfer costs, mortgage or lien fees, and other registration fees that may limit your upside or inhibit repossession. Identify these costs and negotiate with your lessee as to which of you has to pay the various costs at lease expiration. Many countries respect your right to repossess equipment under various lien principles. Look for help from international conventions, such as the Geneva Convention discussed in Chapter 11.

Lessor Alternatives for Intolerable Risks

If, as a lessor, you determine that the economic impact or degree of perceived risk is too negative for you, you can still complete the transaction in several ways:

- ✔ Refer the transaction to another lessor in the country and take a fee.

- ✔ Find a local vendor with an appropriate exemption from tax or regulation to complete the deal and let the vendor act as your "front" person under an agency arrangement where the vendor acts for you.

- ✔ Create a joint venture with a local lessor and provide the funds for all or a part of the deal, with cooperation on billing, collecting, and managing the lessee.

Your counsel can help you prepare the necessary agreements and still do your deal.

Tax Issues in International Leasing

Tax issues often dominate the discussion of international leasing transactions. In many cases, tax benefits drive the economics of these deals. Consider each of the following taxes in your planning, as a lessee or a lessor.

The pickling of a lease transaction

As cross-border lease transactions became more prevalent in the 1980s, U.S. Representative J.J. Pickle sponsored legislation that prevented U.S. taxpayers from taking accelerated depreciation and other tax benefits on property leased to any non-U.S. taxpayer called *tax-exempt use property*. *Tax-exempt use property* refers to property used by a tax-exempt entity, namely the foreign lessee in this case. This arrangement became known as a *Pickle lease*. For a brief definition of, and rationale for not supporting a Pickle lease structure in its guaranty programs, see www.exim.gov/manuals/policyhb/pickle.html.

Uncle Sam did not want a non-U.S. taxpayer (a foreign lessee) to benefit from the lessor's U.S. accelerated depreciation deductions and other tax incentives and used the Pickle rules to end this loss of U.S. tax revenue. However, in time, clever tax lawyers and accountants devised ways such as the so-called *replacement lease* or *accelerator* (or *turbo*) structures to get the accelerated depreciation back into cross-border deals.

The *replacement lease* structure provides for a shortened initial lease term coupled with a longer (immediately following) replacement lease term, which preserves the benefits of the longer term transaction for debt, equity and lessee players in a leveraged lease. By keeping the initial lease term short, the lessor takes faster depreciation during the initial lease term.

In 1996, Uncle Sam tried again to limit Pickle leases and promulgated the so-called *Pickle Regulations*, which slammed the door on these tax structures and required lessors to depreciate tax-exempt use property under the slow poke alternative depreciation system (ADS) discussed in Chapter 13. Under the Pickle Regulations, Uncle Sam required lessors to add the term of the replacement lease to the immediately preceding term of the initial lease. A longer aggregate lease term slowed down the depreciation benefits so much as to make the replacement lease structure uneconomical and noncompetitive.

ADS provides that, as a lessor/owner, you can only depreciate tax-exempt use property on a straight-line (level) basis over the longer of the asset's class life or 125 percent of the lease term. See §168(i)(3) of the Internal Revenue Code of 1986, as amended (the "Code" in this chapter). To apply this rule, say that a lease term extends 16 years for an aircraft. A lessor can only take straight-line depreciation over 20 years (which equals 125 percent of 16 years) in a Pickle lease. The slower depreciation fails to even come close to the economic benefits of a leveraged lease under MACRS for lessors and lessees. As a result, in every lease to a foreign lessee (alias, a Pickle lease), tax lawyers try to get around the Pickle Regulations.

Withholding taxes

Some countries impose withholding taxes, which redirect part of a lease payment to the local government to pay a lessor's domestic income taxes. As a result, the lessee could, in theory, make a lesser payment to the lessor than required by the lease. Lessors do not accept such reductions and want to receive rent in full when due. Lessees should plan to pay these taxes so that lessors receive full rents, or at least develop an approach to minimize the economic effect on the lessor. Certain structuring of leases may also help avoid such taxes, such as using offsetting tax credits in the U.S. against income taxes payable by the lessor. For this kind of planning, you need to consult both local and foreign tax planners.

Cross-border transfer taxes and fees

Although unavoidable in many transactions, lessors can sometimes structure leases to minimize or avoid transfer, stamp, and other taxes in cross-border transactions.

As a lessor, you probably can avoid some of these taxes, with certainty, only if you have a business operation in the country of the lessee. If you do, then you may not have some cross-border taxes (only because you don't necessarily have a cross-border element of your transaction regardless of where your chief executive office is located).

To *repatriate* your earnings, or bring money home from another country, you may have a more complex question to discuss with your tax planners if you decide to return funds earned in one country to another country. When you, as lessor, import and/or export leased property, check on taxes, duties, licenses, or other restrictions with your tax accountants and tax lawyers. Similarly, you should consult your tax and accounting professionals if you plan to keep the earnings and payments in the same country as that requires more planning.

As a lessee, you can expect your lessor to ask you to pay all these amounts so that the lessor receives its intended yield and cash flow. Because of possible taxation, as a lessee, you indemnify the lessor not only as you normally do in a U.S. lease, but also for any of these special taxes, fees, and related costs that you incur in international deals.

Tax treaties and international conventions

Tax treaties are bilateral agreements between two countries that try to avoid the double taxation of income arising in one country in the hands of a resident of the other country. Such treaties often reduce withholding taxes. Look at the effect of any tax treaty for the jurisdiction in which you lease property for income tax impact of local law so that, as a lessor, your price your deal correctly, and, as a lessee, you receive the value of the tax benefits available to your lessor. For further information and an illustration of such treaties, see `www.oecd.org//daf/fa/treaties/treaty.htm` (the OECD Model Income Tax Conventions) and `www.treas.gov/taxpolicy/t0txmod1.htm` (U.S. Model Income Tax Convention). See Chapter 11 for a discussion of international conventions affecting aircraft.

If you pick any area of pricing to understand the best in international leasing, pick taxes. Taxes can make or break your pricing, whether you are a lessor or lessee. To get the lowest rent, study all applicable international and local taxes and ask international tax accountants (especially in Europe) or tax lawyers to help you structure the most tax effective lease, both in respect of taking and receiving tax benefits as well as paying taxes related to your lease.

Change of tax law and accounting rules

Tax laws in the United States and elsewhere in the world change. As a lessor, you often bear this risk unless you can get your lessee to indemnify you for a structure problem rather than the more normal acts and omissions indemnity. Good luck on that one!

Accounting treatment for leases (see Chapter 15) can directly impact the value and desirability of leasing in a corporate lessee's strategy. For a discussion of Europe's accounting rules, see www.leaseurope.org. Stay tuned for changes in international accounting that adopts an asset/liability approach as FASB has indicated that it may consider to replace the current benefits/risks approach in lease accounting.

As lessees and lessors, you both should examine the applicable accounting rules in your respective countries to confirm that you can account for your lease in a way that benefits or at least satisfies your financial planning and balance sheet objectives.

Legal Issues in International Leasing Transactions

As a lessor, you should choose a law, such as New York law, that helps you resolve commercial disputes under well-developed legal principles and court structure. (Yes, I know; you can debate all about New York law and court structure, such as it is!).

As a lessee, you may have different ideas. You may want the laws of your country to apply (if other than the United States). In jurisdictions such as the United Kingdom, Canada, and Brazil, the choice of law there may work. If a country is more unstable or unpredictable, such as Colombia or China, select a law outside of that jurisdiction such as New York, UK, or Swiss law. In any event, confirm under local law that the courts in the chosen jurisdiction can (and will) enforce your choice of law.

As a lessor or a lessee, select a *forum* (a court system and location) in your agreements that regularly and fairly handles commercial disputes. For lessors and lessees, your first choice of forum may understandably differ from each other. If any choice involves an unstable country, select a third neutral but well-developed country with courts that handle commercial matters to settle your disputes. Because any foreign litigation costs a bunch to pursue (but lawyers will love you for it!), consider *alternative dispute resolution (ADR)*, a noncourt settlement process that should cost you less and speed up the process of reaching a final decision in your matter.

For example, as lessee or lessor, you can demand arbitration or mediation. Well-established arbitration rules and procedures exist with various international bodies to settle disputes, and you can negotiate and customize those rules and procedures. Consider the following entities for help on international ADR:

Your agreements in lease documentation can help you mitigate or manage various risks. You should therefore ask local counsel as well as your transactional counsel to draft lease documents that include strong indemnities and protections for the special liabilities and obligations under the foreign laws, such as license fees, withholding taxes, insurance, and other costs beyond rent payable to the lessor.

Unfortunately, not all countries have well-developed judicial systems or legal structures for the enforcement of rights and remedies under leases. Local restrictions may limit the availability of courts to enforce leases. You're more likely to find that another country has no similar registration system like the Personal Property Security Act in Canada (*PPSA*) or the UCC in the United States to perfect your respective interests, as lessor and lessee, in leased property.

You need to determine the type of lien or title filing system, if any, that exists in the country/location in which the lessee uses the leased property. By doing so, you can assure that you perfect your rights, as lessee or lessor, in the lease transaction and the equipment. Note that a local law can control perfecting your interests in certain parts of property, while a national or international law or treaty may require additional or different filings. For example, in the United States, most aircraft transactions involve filings at the FAA and under the UCC. International treaties, such as Unidroit, the Chicago Convention, and the Geneva Convention (see Chapter 11), can also affect rights in aircraft. If no comparable system exists, ask about using the rules and regulation of a developed system and incorporate those rights in your agreements to the extent that they help you achieve your transaction goals. As a lessor, you should perform due diligence to determine whether anyone else has (or may later secure) conflicting rights in your leased property. If so, to the extent that you can identify the other party, ask the other party, like a bank or landlord, to waive its rights that may affect the leased property.

In addition, as a lessor, you can enter into leases with governmental or other sovereign entities. You may not know in all cases that your lessee enjoys *sovereign immunity*. Sovereign immunity refers to a special right afforded to governmental entities or specially designated groups that stops or limits your judicial or other remedies under your lease. These entities or groups receive special protections by law, as a matter of public policy in their own country, to insulate them from a barrage of lawsuits and claims that could undermine their existence or purpose. As a lessor, you could face these kinds of barriers to enforcing your lease.

To offset this risk, you should obtain representations from your lessee that he does not have sovereign immunity or an affirmative covenant that your lessee is bound by commercial law. If in doubt, you should obtain a waiver of that immunity or as much of it as you can with the advice of counsel. You may find this subject creates a lively negotiation. Evaluate your credit risks closely should your lessee keep all or part of these special rights and obtain extra collateral protection to assure your lease payments.

Cross-Border Structures and Products

In this section, I introduce you to a few tax-oriented, cross-border products that can decrease the cost of leasing for lessees and enhance the yields of lessors.

Because of the sophistication of these products and the rapid changes that occur legislatively around the world, you can fully expect these structures and products to change. You can also expect the leasing industry to adapt to new laws and continue or expand leasing transactions as a result of the changes. Many other products exist that only the tax gurus really understand. Ask them and be prepared for a very long answer!

Service contract

A *service contract* structure effectively does an end run around the Pickle Regulations. You use a service contract in the place of the replacement lease. If structured correctly, the service contract generates depreciation benefits for a lessor similar to the old replacement lease for the benefit of lessees located in foreign countries (that is, in the lingo, the outbound cross-border lessees).

The service contract must meet criteria that fundamentally distinguish it from a lease. In a service contract, the lessor (called the service provider) controls and operates the property for the benefit of the lessee (called the service recipient). In a lease, the lessee controls and operates the leased property under a net lease in which he possesses, maintains, and operates the leased property at his expense and risk. A service recipient (lessee) pays services fees (alias, rent) to the service provider (alias, the lessor).

You can, as a lessor or lessee, use the service contract structure with the most confidence, due to favorable presumptions in the tax law, on selected energy assets. These assets consist of:

- A "qualified solid waste disposal facility" for residents of "governmental units" (a facility that disposes of solid waste collected from the general public)

- A "cogeneration facility" (a power plant that uses the same energy to produce sequential useful electrical and thermal energy)

- An "alternative energy facility" (a power plant using fuel other than oil, natural gas, or nuclear fuel)

- A "water treatment works facility" (a processing plant meeting certain environmental standards)

QTE

A *QTE transaction* refers to a lease to a foreign lessee by a U.S. lessor covering *qualified technological equipment (QTE)*. QTE includes computers or related peripherals, aircraft simulators, high-technology telephone stations and switching equipment, air traffic control equipment, automated mail sorting equipment, telecommunications equipment, and high-technology medical equipment. The lessee can be either a foreign governmental entity or private foreign corporation.

Don't fall out of your chair. This class of specific assets is exempt from the Pickle Regulations! As a lessor, you can recover the cost of QTE on a straight-line basis over five years. This product generally attracts industrial finance companies, banks, insurance companies, and utilities that act as a passive, equity investor and probably want tax benefits that shelter their income unrelated to the QTE transaction (and an acceptable return on their investment as a passive investor).

Due to the age of the definition of QTE in the Code and its regulations, as a lessor, you may have some uncertainty about what equipment qualifies for the exemption. Ask your tax counsel for current tax rulings to help.

Double dips

A *double dip* lease takes advantage of inconsistent tax laws in the two countries involved in a cross-border lease and entitles both a lessor and a lessee to claim tax benefits for the same property in the same transaction in their own country. Such a deal! Because two taxpayers (lessor and lessee) receive tax benefits, you get two benefits for the price of one lease deal or a "double dip" of the tax benefits consisting primarily (if not entirely) of depreciation write-offs. The effect creates a lower effective cost of financing for the lessee and an improved after-tax return, in some deals, for the lessor. Double dip leases can arise in outbound or inbound lease transactions. See Chapter 13 regarding true lease criteria in the United States.

In the inbound transaction, a foreign lessor enters into a lease with a U.S. lessee. The foreign lessor claims the tax title and tax benefit attributable to the leased property under its law because the foreign law treats the lessor (which resides or is incorporated in the foreign country) as the legal/tax owner. At the same time, U.S. law treats the U.S. lessee as borrower or conditional sale buyer of the leased property entitled to tax benefits under U.S. law as tax owner in the United States. Presto! You have a double dip lease.

In the outbound transaction, a foreign lessee enters a true tax lease with a U.S. lessor. In a twist on the inbound lease, in this transaction the foreign jurisdiction may treat the lease as a transfer of ownership to the foreign lessee (under its foreign law). At the same time, U.S. tax law may treat the U.S. lessor as the tax owner of the leased property entitled to depreciation benefits in the United States. Consequently, the U.S. taxpayer/lessor and the foreign lessee may each receive tax benefits of ownership under the law in their respective jurisdictions, creating an outbound double dip lease.

Although U.S. tax law evaluates transactions based on substance over form, other countries may accept the opposite — form over substance, labels that alone establish that the deal constitutes a lease regardless of its substance. As a U.S. lessor, these labels may enable you to do a double dip. For a shot at these deals, you can check out combining U.S. law with, among other laws, the tax laws in Denmark, France, Japan, and Germany. These laws change frequently, so keep checking.

ETI structure

Most nations tax only the income of corporations within their borders. However, Uncle Sam taxes American corporations on their worldwide income. On the other hand, if you, as a U.S. corporation, sell your products through a branch in Switzerland, Uncle Sam taxes the income on that sale. However, if a Swiss corporation sells its products through a branch in the U.S., Switzerland does not tax the income generated by the Swiss corporation in the U.S. Consequently, U.S. taxpayers shoulder a heavier tax burden that may put them at a competitive disadvantage. To even the playing field, Congress has enacted various exceptions to the general rule to provide tax breaks.

An *ETI structure* replaced the Foreign Sale Corporation (FSC) laws. It says that if you have income earned outside of the United States attributable to *qualifying foreign trade income,* you can exclude a portion of that income from your gross income. If you lower your gross income, Uncle Sam has less income on which to impose income taxes. For leasing, as a lessor, you can exclude 30 percent of your foreign sale and leasing income earned outside of the United States.

The lessors that use this product consist of the same players who use the QTE structure. As a lessee, you can use this product if lessors accept your credit-worthiness and you want to use qualifying equipment abroad for a period of 15 to 20 years. FSCs received substantial use from domestic and foreign airlines. ETIs, as the successor, probably draws from the same pool of lessees. However, as a lessor or a lessee, you can use ETIs on any equipment that has less than 50 percent imported/foreign parts/content with useful lives, ideally in excess of 35 years, to extend the deferral associated with leasing that equipment. See Chapter 7 on lessor pricing concerning the value of tax deferral.

Chapter 21

Tapping Diverse Markets: Vendor, Venture, and e-Leasing

In This Chapter

▶ Expanding markets and sales with vendor leasing

▶ Venturing into the high-risk leasing arena with early stage companies

▶ Trying the electronic world of leasing on the Web

*L*easing offers opportunities for almost every business. This chapter briefly describes vendor leasing, venture leasing, and e-leasing, which all involve leasing in the creation and sale of different kinds of products andservices. For vendor and venture programs, leasing provides a means to an end — a way to increase sales for vendors and to enable entrepreneurs to create new products and services in the unique environment of early-stage/venture capital -backed companies. For now, e-leasing, an emerging new business may just be an end in itself: a new channel for any business to lease property. Check out this chapter and judge for yourself how these programs can help you.

Vendor Leasing Programs

This section primarily speaks to vendors. However, if you are a lessor or lender, you can gain an understanding of how you can expect vendor programs to work for you, too.

If, as a vendor, you sell equipment, products, or services and need a way to increase your sales, a vendor leasing program may work for you.

A *vendor leasing program* refers to an organized way for vendors to increase sales by arranging or providing financing for their customers to acquire their products and/or services. The customer uses the financing to pay the purchase price to the vendor and then repays the financing over time in the form of a lease or installment payment obligation. You can create a vendor program for virtually any item of equipment and/or software.

As a vendor, you can provide the financing yourself directly to your customer. You can also form a captive finance company in the business of providing financing to your customers. However, like many vendors, you may resist forming a captive because independent lessors already have the infrastructures and business models to meet your needs and the needs of your customer in a cost-effective manner. Consequently, you can, as an alternative, arrange for outside leasing and/or other financial services companies to provide financing to your customers through vendor programs structured for the benefit of your business.

The benefits and risks

When you enter into a vendor program, as the vendor, you can benefit when you:

- ✔ Increase your sales volume with no or reduced discounts in your sale prices.

- ✔ Maintain the perception that you provide full service, a veritable one-stop shop for your customer, by offering products, services, and financing.

- ✔ Focus on selling instead of financing your inventory by involving independent lessors and lenders.

- ✔ Control your markets including your secondary or used equipment market.

- ✔ Reduce your borrowing costs to carry your customer's leases or installment purchases by substituting the funding of independent lessors and lenders.

- ✔ Decrease your inventory by increasing sales using this financing.

As a lessor, you can benefit from vendor programs when you:

- ✔ Establish a relationship with a vendor whose creditworthiness and business model works for you and meets your approval standards.

- ✔ Produce a flow of profitable transactions (you hope!) that builds your deal volume.

- ✔ Diversify your credit risk by funding multiple lessees identified by your vendors rather than (or in addition to) the vendor itself.

- ✔ Gain opportunities for potential residual upside from the property that you lease.

Trust me when I tell you that if you don't realize these benefits, you find out quickly the risks of vendor financing. As a lessor, your key risk, however, comes from failing to select a vendor with acceptable products, organizational infrastructure, and creditworthiness.

Establishing the right vendor programs

As a vendor you try to shape your vendor program to fit your needs to sell your particular products and services. You can lay out the terms of your relationship with the lessor (and lenders) in a *vendor program agreement* (or similar name).

As a vendor, you don't have to enter into program agreements with lessors or lenders. You can just identify transactions and ask the lessors or lenders to bid terms that work for you and your customer at the time.

However, vendor program agreements help establish order and clarity on such issues as:

- The kind of program structure that, as a vendor, you need (for example, exclusive or non-exclusive programs with one or more lessors)

- The procedures for lessors to win the business of your customer, including credit standards, bidding for customers, and processing time for their transactions, and to interact with or compete for your customer

- The kinds of property (or service) the lease can cover, such as equipment, software, and maintenance

- The business and legal terms and form of lease documentation (the form of which may be attached to the agreement)

- The economics of each transaction, such as lease rates that your customer pays to the lessor or sharing residual value of leased property with your lessor

- The responsibility for remarketing the leased property

- How the billing and collecting of rents work

  Vendors sometimes remain in the lease transactions with the customer to bill and collect rents for the lessor and to control the customer relationship, rather than let the lessor interact directly with the customer. Lessors agree to this approach for creditworthy vendors, but this right remains a key issue of negotiation of vendor programs because lessors (or lenders) want to have access to the lessee and the leased property in any problem/default situation. Even in a default scenario, lessors (and lenders) often allow vendors to solve the problem during limited time periods such as 90 days after a default occurs

- How you, as the vendor, resolve legal disputes with your lessors or lenders

As a vendor, you may find that your lessors typically want to have complete freedom to set their rental or spreads or increase them for any particular deal or program, regardless of the economics that you stipulate in your program agreement. You can ask that all increases be made only on a fixed margin over an index, such as the prime lending rate or comparable term Treasury Notes. These limitations help avoid excessive rate increases by the lessor. Alternatively, you can limit how often a lessor changes its rates (for example, only on a quarterly or semi-annual basis).

Types of vendor programs

As vendors, you can create the following types of typical vendor programs:

- **Direct programs.** In direct programs you act as the supplier of products, and a lessor leases the products to your customer directly. Upon entering the lease, the lessor pays you the purchase price of the leased property, and you complete your sale. A *vendor program agreement* establishes the ground rules for your relationship with the lessor based on the types of issues set out in the preceding section. Lenders use a similar approach for making loans to your customers.

- **Private label programs.** You can establish a private label program. A *private label program* refers to an arrangement in which your customer finances her purchases through you (or at least the customer thinks that you provide the financing). In reality, you act only as the supplier, and the lessor provides the money under a program agreement sometimes called a *vendor sale and assignment agreement* (or similar name). You can typically structure private label programs of two basic types:

  - **Notification program.** A *notification program* refers to an arrangement in which you (and/or your lessor) notify your customer that the lessor has provided the financing that you initially put in place with the customer. In legal terms, you enter into a lease with the customer for your product. On that day or any time thereafter (during the lease term), you assign the entire lease (including title to the product) or just the rent payments to a lessor. From that point on, your customer pays rent for the benefit of the lessor. If you only assign the rents, you effectively split the lease into two pieces: You keep the residual value, and your lessor gets the rent payments. For example, say that you convince your customer to acquire a tractor that you manufacture by leasing it for 60 payments of $1,000 per month. You complete the lease on a form pre-approved by your lessor, which your customer signs. Then, five months later, you assign the tractor lease to your lessor (the tractor and 55 remaining payments). You tell your lessee at the time about the lessor taking over the lease. In the notice, your lessor may ask your lessee/customer to confirm, among other things, that the equipment works, the lessee has 55 rent payments left at $1,000 per month, and that the lessee has not prepaid the rent or defaulted under the lease.

- **Non-notification program.** If you don't tell your customer about your financing arrangements, you can call your program a *non-notification program*. The lessor pays you the purchase price for the lease (a discounted value of the rents and residual value) or for the rents only. You book the sale and assign the entire lease or the rent payments to a lessor. The customer may continue to pay you. Alternatively, the customer may make payments to a location that you designate (which may be lessor's lockbox or bank). In each case, the customer/lessee has no knowledge that you assigned the lease or the just the payments to a lessor. However, if a vendor or a lessee/customer defaults (fails to meet her obligations), most lessors insist that that they can take over billing and collecting and can *lift the veil* (disclose its existence and rights to enforce the lease directly against the lessee). You can resolve the tension between your controls and your lessor's need to take over the deal when problems arise by prescribing appropriate procedures in your vendor program agreement.

Many variations exist in these vendor programs. For a lessor, an *assumed name program* can work like "tractors-are-us," where an independent lessor acts like a captive finance company with a name that sounds like yours. (A vendor can own a real captive finance company, too.) Lessors can offer the back office and financing capability that you lack, and your customer won't know that it's not you on the other end of its deal.

Lenders, too, participate in vendor programs. They can purchase an installment purchase agreement or make loans to you against rent or installment purchase payments that your customer agrees to pay you.

You can finance all kinds of equipment and services (including software) if a reliable cash flow from rents or similar streams of cash exists. The fundamental objective remains the same: You sell products and services, and the lessor or lender helps you and your customer by providing the financing.

Venture Leasing Programs

Venture leasing refers to leasing various types of personal property to emerging growth companies in which professional venture capitalists have made equity investments.

You can identify an *emerging growth company* as a start-up or early stage company generally involved in the development of unique products and services under the direction of entrepreneurs, scientists, big company defectors, and/or other very creative, hard-working people who want to do what others have not accomplished. The company generally uses up cash resources rather than making a profit in its early years of existence. The pace at which it burns cash is sometimes called the *burn rate.* Some companies earn income from joint development or similar arrangements. Most, however, manage on fixed amount of cash and control the burn rate. They need non-equity capital, and venture leasing can provide it.

Venture capitalists (*VCs*) fund these companies. As professional investors in early-stage or other high-potential growth companies, they usually sit on the board of directors and either maintain control or exert substantial influence over the business affairs of the company. VCs tend to have vision of the company's future growth and an appetite for high-risk investments. They also expect commensurate returns on investment, which can range from the 30 percent of the capital investment up to the stars — or so they hope. They enter their transactions with an *exit strategy,* which means a way to unload their investment within a three- to seven-year time frame. Two of the most common exit strategies in which the venture capitalists sell their stock are to:

- ✔ Complete an initial public offering (IPO) of stock of the company

- ✔ Sell the venture-backed company to a larger company, which may even include an existing joint venture partner

For a list of VCs, and more about investing by VCs, see `www.pwcmoneytree.com/fundsaz.asp?az=yes&year=2001&qtr=1` (the Web site of PriceWaterhouseCoopers and Venture One on venture capital investing).

Fundamental characteristics

Venture leasing players (including banks) respect and value the involvement of experienced venture capitalists, whose expertise and cash help motivate a venture lessor to provide lease financing. Venture leasing transactions not only include leasing products, but also secured loans. For purposes of this chapter, just consider all the deals as leases. A friend of mine described venture leasing (being a venture lessor) as follows: "Venture leasing is more about venture than about equipment leasing."

Look for three essential characteristics in most venture leasing transactions:

- ✔ **Professional venture capitalists have invested at least one round (and usually more than one round) of financing in the lessee company.** A *round of financing* (or similar terminology) refers to a transaction in which VCs invest cash for equity. Specifically, a VC often receives preferred stock, such as a Series A Preferred Stock, representing its investment. An early stage company may call its subsequent rounds of stock sales Series B Preferred Stock, then a Series C Preferred Stock, and so on. Preferred stock carries certain liquidation, payment, and other rights that other common stock does not. The VCs reserve Common Stock for founders, key employees, and an option pool.

✔ **The lessor in a venture leasing transaction almost always obtains equity from the lessee as part of making its lease investment, usually in the form of preferred or common stock warrants.** A *warrant* represents the contractual right to purchase an equity security of the issuing venture backed company within a certain time (such as ten years) and at a particular price (such as $2.50 per share) called the *strike price*. The company benefits by receiving non-equity capital at very low dilution. *Dilution* refers to spreading out the existing value of a company among its equity holders when it issues additional stock or other equity. In other words, although the warrants, if converted into stock, dilute the value of a company's equity, the cash invested in the leased property does not. If a company uses equity capital to purchase the same leased property, the investment results in higher dilution. You can bet that VCs want to limit dilution. For lessors, the equity upside (sometimes called the *equity kicker*) is crucial to a lessor's total return and reason for investing in an emerging growth company. Consequently, the lessor wants to minimize dilution. Also, the lease dollars invested by the lessor give the young company several more months of cash to further develop its business before raising additional capital.

✔ **The lessee has a quality management team and a business plan.** While equipment values and a lessee's credit rating traditionally play an important role in leasing of more mature companies, venture leasing companies often focus more (but not exclusively) on the quality of the VCs, management, and business plan for the lessee company.

Industries funded by venture leasing

As venture leasing has grown over the last decade, so have the industries that receive lease financing. They include biopharmaceuticals, manufacturing, consumer, retail, electronics, medical device, healthcare, semiconductor, information systems, software, Internet, and technology companies. In each of these industries, the equipment financed ranges from office furniture to telecommunications equipment, testing equipment to computers, and industrial equipment to specialized manufacturing equipment fabricated by the lessee to build its new product. However, venture lessors tend to focus on areas of their expertise and the industries in which top-tier venture capitalists make their investments — often technology in the broadest sense — rather than a specific industry. For more on definitions and industry classifications in which VCs invest for equity, see www.pwcmoneytree.com/definitions.asp (the Web site of PriceWaterhouseCoopers and Venture One).

Structure and business terms

Venture lessors tend to do master leases or some single-delivery leases with a lessor's cost ranging from under $100,000 to $5,000,000. See the form of the

Master Lease Agreement in the Appendix. Rent is usually higher than more mature companies with one or two months of advance rent paid up front. Some venture lessors prefer deals that start at $500,000 to lessen the impact of transaction and administration costs and to increase the equity upside potential in the warrants or stock. Leases often include a fixed buyout or fair market value options. In some deals, lessors require the lessee to exercise the "option" to assure the lessor of her own exit strategy with respect to the leased property. Bank lessors may want more fees, financial covenants, and higher equipment value in exchange for lower lease or lending rates and fewer warrants.

Because venture leases can involve a high degree of risk, lessors generally limit their lease terms to 24 to 36 months. Some venture lessors may, on occasion, extend a term out to 48 months or more, for later round (better capitalized) companies. One of the important factors to banks and some independent lessors seems to be the collateral value of the leased property on a liquidation or resale by the lessor. For deals involving leased property without collateral/resale value, such as software, tenant improvements, and demonstration equipment, venture lessors often stick to a term of 24 to 30 months. For leased property with some collateral value, such as testing or production equipment, venture lessors may extend the term to 36 months or more.

However, equipment value is not the really the name of the game. The equity upside in these deals, unlike traditional deals focused on strong financials and valuable leased property, such as production equipment or aircraft, lies in the warrants or other *equity kickers* issued by the lessee. Consequently, venture lessors may enter deals with little collateral value in the leased property (for example, less than 15 percent of lessor's cost).

Most lessors want their lessees to have substantial cash on hand to burn during the early part of the lease term, and some indication that the VCs can and will support the company for the term of the lease. The lessee should be able to demonstrate that the cash on hand will last until the next milestone that results in additional cash investments. In effect, a venture lessor want to see enough cash to survive the lease term.

Warrant coverage or value

Coverage refers to a negotiated number of warrants issued to a lessor. You can express coverage, for example, as a percentage of the investment made by the lessor. Coverage often ranges between 5 percent and 10 percent on a lessor's cost of leased property. The calculation of coverage can vary, depending on the lessor and VCs. Some venture lessors, for example, focus on the valuation of the lessee company. For the earlier stage/round companies, these lessors want a lower valuation so that they can get a bigger *upside* (future stock price relative to the strike price of the warrant/equity) on selling their warrants or other equity stake.

When I started negotiating venture leases, the lessor could negotiate his rights under the warrant. Very quickly, however, VCs put an end to that approach. VCs typically require venture lessors to conform to (or take less equity rights than) the VCs regarding the capital stock of the company. For example, a VC may have rights to force a lessee to register his stock for an IPO, but a venture lessor probably does not. One of the most important features that a venture lessor wants is an acceptable *multiple* to sell his warrants (for example, three times his strike price per share of stock) on an acquisition or IPO. If he doesn't get that bang, he generally wants to retain his warrant (or other equity stake) until the optimal time to sell to capture the upside. After an IPO, the investment bankers may insist that the company remove the warrant from the company's balance sheet and corporate books. As a result, the warrant either terminates or, if a venture lessor keeps it, it probably converts to preferred or common stock. As a lessor, you should be aware at the outset of your deal of this issue and negotiate, if possible, that your warrant survives any IPO. By keeping your warrant, you can maintain your upside potential intact as well as your original investment return model and analysis.

E-Leasing: The Internet and Leasing

When I visited Mexico with my younger daughter last year, we signed up to go horseback riding. When we arrived at the ranch, we participated in a game with the donkeys. The leader, with a guttural laugh, explained the rules this way: "Here are the rules in Mexico — no rules."

The leader's phrase suggests an apt view of e-leasing. The diversity of the leasing marketplace and the emergence of new technology make *e-leasing* (engaging in all aspects of leasing on the Internet) like Mexico. It has no rules, or at least very few of them in full use, prescribing how e-leasing business can and will be done.

As reality sets in, however, the leasing industry has not exactly been moving at light speed to embrace the use of the Internet to lease personal property. In fact, many lessors fear that the use of the World Wide Web may "commoditize" the leasing business, "cannibalize" existing customers, and detract from the value of relationships in the leasing business.

Perhaps, to some extent, these deflating effects can and do occur. However, the Web should not hurt most lessees or lessors. Instead, the Web can provide a way for the small-ticket and middle-ticket markets to expand the meeting and greeting of lessees and lessors, online, and to do some deals there. For the broader market, the Web has increased (and may continue to increase) the speed and efficiency of transactions, heighten customer expectations, enhance communications, and encourage the exchange and analysis of information among lessors, lessees, and lenders.

So, for you, what does all of this activity really mean?

Web portals to leasing

After many of the dot-coms turned into dot-bombs, I am not clear whether e-leasing fits in the "new economy" or the old one. The Web has expanded the access to information about sources of financing, the speed of exchanging drafts of transaction documents, and the volume of credit applications for processing loans and leases. However, the completion of deals online through various Web *portals* still seems to be in its infancy.

A *portal* refers to an entrance or a gateway to something specific. An Internet service provider (*ISP*) opens a portal for you to access the Web. A portal in the leasing business refers to a pathway to the various types of entities that provide you with sources of money and leasing/lending expertise (for example, regarding structuring and analyzing lease and loan transactions). You can think of these portals as a meeting place to exchange information and do deals.

As a lessor, your use of the Web probably gives you little competitive advantage because most lessors have seized upon the use of the Web to convey a message about themselves and their products and services. Your business model, strategy, execution, and customer relationships, rather than a Web presence, should still win the day. Yet the Web represents a growing tool in leasing (and lending), and today almost every leasing company uses conventional and technological means to purvey their products and services, making each of them a so-called "click and mortar business."

Some of the largest and many of the smallest players in leasing, individually and in joint ventures, have established Web portals that provide a range of services and types of financing and purchasing opportunities. Behind the screen sit real people with a variety of experience who say that they can add value to help you, as a lessee, efficiently find sources of capital and even help you close a deal with an identified source of capital. Those who operate the portals, in short, provide a service driven, or at least assisted, by Web technology.

As a lessee, you can use a leasing Web portal to:

- Identify competing capital resources
- Make application to, and gain transaction approvals from, lessors and lenders (in minutes or hours) online who can provide money for your deal
- Create custom payment schedules
- Close your lease or loan

You can also combine the power of the Web to find money with the value-added service of the experts (yes, real people) at a Web portal. You can, for example, ask the Web portal experts to do the following:

✔ Analyze your company and lease transaction that you submitted to it online

✔ Prepare and post a report online accessible to the Web portal's client base of lessors and lenders or personally contact the lenders and lessors, and present your transaction

✔ Prescreen potential lessors or lenders who show an interest in your deal

✔ Assist you in making contact with the most appropriate source of capital

✔ Participate in obtaining approvals for your transaction with the selected capital source

✔ Help you prepare documents, online or offline, and close the transaction

For these services, you may pay fees, including processing or posting fees and various success fees, which may range from ½ percent up to more than 2 percent of the lessor's cost or principal amount of loans.

As a lessor (or lender), you can access a variety of services and opportunities online that save you time and cost (or so the pitch goes) to develop lessee/borrower relationships. For example, you can

✔ Create your own Web portal to process applications for, and provide financing to, lessees and other borrowers (such as vendors)

✔ Sign up with independent Web portal services to provide financing for lessees and borrowers

✔ Store documents in *electronic vaults,* which refer to safe and secure locations (servers) controlled by a Web portal for the permanent storage of documents in electronic form

You can, at least in theory, engage in purely electronic closings of leases. The legal and technical structure exist (or so it seems at least in an early form) to do so. For example, under emerging state and federal law, you can now use electronic signatures and contracts to close real deals, and no state can deny that your deal is effective solely because you documented, signed, and closed it electronically.

Three significant laws back up the idea that courts must enforce your deals closed using any kind of electronic media:

✔ Revised Article 9 of the UCC. See Chapter 17 regarding electronic chattel paper.

✔ The Uniform Electronic Transactions Act (UETA). See Chapter 10. UETA assures that electronic transactions cannot be denied legal effect or enforceability solely because you use an electronic record in the formation (closing) of your deal (that is, you signed and/or stored contracts in electronic media). Other state laws control the substance of your deal.

✔ Title I of the Federal Electronic Signatures in Global and National Commerce Act (ENSIGN). ENSIGN became effective October 1, 2000. Similar to UETA, it says that states that do not adopt UETA cannot deny the legal effect, validity or enforceability to a signature or contract solely because it is in electronic form. ENSIGN complements and does not preempt (that is, replace) UETA.

Web sites that illustrate e-leasing

Here are Web sites that provide leasing services and products:

Sites for *turnkey leasing programs* (that is, a complete marketplace package that creates and initiates a complete financing program for vendors, lessors, and lenders) include

✔ www.efinance.com (eFinance Corporation site, contains a fraud detection feature)

✔ www.emarketcapital.com (eMarket Capital, Inc. site, offers an online lease program for vendors, including site design and training)

✔ www.eoriginal.com/industry_solutions/leasing.html (eOriginal, Inc. site, offers paperless transaction, including electronic storage of documents upon completion of transaction)

Portals for lessees to obtain financing include

✔ www.financetrust.net/online_finance.cfm (Finance Trust.net site, enables both entities and individuals to apply for financing)

✔ www.leaseloan.com (LeaseLoan.com, Inc. site, contains a leasing university for lessees to become educated on the leasing process)

✔ www.livecapital.com/leasing.html (LiveCapital site, provides information on business financing and an easy step-by-step method to apply for financing)

✔ www.tfc.textron.com (Textron Financial Corporation site, a major lessor that says that it can provide lessees financing in as little as 24 hours)

Part VI
The Parts of Ten

The 5th Wave — By Rich Tennant

"See if this is covered in our lease agreement."

In this part . . .

Before the end of the book, I step back from some of the business of structuring and closing leases and look at ten bigger issues of lessors and ten other issues of lessees that, in your respective positions, you should consider in deciding how to succeed in leasing, now and in the future.

Chapter 22

Ten Points for Successful Leasing by Lessees

*W*hen you approach opportunities in leasing today, you can be certain that at least parts of the business and its products will not be the same tomorrow. Leasing has grown based in part on what you and millions of other lessees need and want. The process to get what you want doesn't rest only in your hands or in the hands of your lessors. Rather, the economy, change of laws, accounting discussions, and an increasingly global business climate all affect you and your opportunities.

This chapter offers ten points to help you get the most out of leasing and to understand some of the real market pressures that you face. Most points can withstand the test of time, but others may change. If you start from here, you not only can build the foundation for these changes, but also can use the changes to your advantage over time.

Try Leasing; You'll Like It!

Leasing has become a widely used but often misunderstood financial tool. Although 80 percent of the businesses in the United States use leasing for some or all their capital asset financing, many people shy away from it for various reasons. For example, you may not really grasp how leasing works or how it can benefit you. You may want to own your property at the end of the day. You may not want someone else telling you how to run your business or maintain your property. You may even think that leasing represents a somewhat underhanded or dishonest approach to financing.

For those of you who have tried leasing, most of you, I imagine, achieved your objectives. For those of you who lease in the future, you can expect lessors to create a positive impression of the lessor and leasing. Why is that so? Lessors know that you, and your business, mean nearly everything to their success. They recognize that you must have a good experience in leasing.

While leasing doesn't work for every deal or every business, it provides a source of financing from savvy players who think differently than your bankers. Leasing guys and gals think and act differently. They know that, if you properly maintain your leased property, you both can enjoy the benefits of residual upside. You can capture some of that benefit through various purchase options (see Chapter 8) and in reduced rents. Lessors also know that if structured properly, they have some unique protection in your bankruptcy (should that unfortunate event occur).

In Chapter 4, I describe how you pick the right lessor. When you need financing next, review that chapter. Contact lessors. Let them compete for your business and demonstrate their creativity, innovation, and pricing capabilities to help you lease property and build your business by doing so. Try leasing and try it again. The better you understand it, the better terms you can get. It can help your business and provide money for growth that's potentially more cost-effective and more available that other types of financing.

Expect Tougher Credit Standards

In a slowing economy, many people face a tougher challenge to find financing. Lessors now more often make the so-called *flight to quality*, which means that they want only reliable, strong, proven, and creditworthy lessees, without too much risk. If you qualify as one of the quality guys, then you may experience some benefits that others won't. On the other hand, if you fall under the quality line that lessors draw, you need to plan on a significant effort to find the financing that you need. If you do find financing, you may also discover that it's more expensive than you expect. Fortunately, because lessors need and want to complete deals, that cost may not always be higher. Further, because lessors often understand the value and residual value of leased property, they may take too much credit risk on your deal that other financial institutions may not.

Lessors don't always want to turn you down, but they, too, face funding challenges — their lenders don't want the lessors to take your credit risk. Guess who rules? The lenders and other entities that finance your lessor ultimately set the standards for your deal with the lessor. A lessor can't provide you funding if the lessor herself lacks funding. That's the reality — especially in a slowing economy.

If you find that you're funding challenged — and perhaps in any case — try the Web portals discussed in Chapter 21 as a source of capital where other more conventional means prove unsatisfactory. Keep existing financing relationships in tact and create business plans that take into account a potential limit on available capital.

Evaluate Financing Alternatives

You need to decide first what alternatives you may have for financing your property. Here's a little rhyme for you: Unless you have very strong credit, and even if you do, plan to shop for the right financing for you. A rhyme that has reasons, this you can see, but the challenge for you is to find some money!

All my bad limericks aside, consider the following decision points:

- ✔ **Pricing.** Your choice of financing (if you have choices at all) often boils down to the lowest price. Review your least cost alternatives first. See Chapter 6 on how you analyze pricing. Take a peek into the lessor-pricing world in Chapter 7 to see how lessors decide on pricing for you. Consider the lease versus buy discussion in Chapter 6.

- ✔ **Other features.** Decide what additional features merit your consideration that may change your approach and/or lead you to the selection of the best financing. For example, if you have an existing relationship with a bank, you may feel more comfortable asking your account officer for direction to his leasing people or products. Alternatively, a leasing company may offer faster speed of closing and more predictable closing costs. Vendor programs available to you from the people who sell products (such as hardware and software or machinery or even aircraft) may also offer competitive pricing and speed to close, too. See Chapter 21. Whether you choose to lease, look closely at the various costs, and what the financing types can do for you, to meet your objective on your schedule.

- ✔ **Test of speed and quality.** Before you make a final decision, decide whether you believe in the lessor or lender's viability, reliability, and capability to meet your expectations. For example, ask how quickly a lessor or lender can provide a final credit approval for a deal on terms acceptable to you. Determine whether, in any case, the quality and general service approach of the lender or lessor meet your needs. Remember, as you decide, that when you close a lease or loan, you also begin a new long-term relationship that can affect your future.

✔ **Transaction costs.** Don't forget to ask about the transaction costs that you have to pay to close a deal. Lessors and lenders usually put that cost on you if they can (at least attorneys and appraisal fees from their outside specialists). Transaction costs can increase the cost of one deal over another enough to sway your decision. Leasing companies may bury some of that cost in your rent pricing, and lessen the immediate burden. Be sure to ask about what costs you pay and when you pay them.

Retain Experienced Lease Advisors

Would you hire an electrician to fix your water pipes just because he owns a pipe wrench that he seldom, if ever, uses? Of course, you don't do that. You find the electrician who does the kind of work that you need. Similarly, you should hire advisors, such as packagers, investment bankers, lawyers, accountants, appraisers, and engineers, who understand your needs and the business that you want to do. I have too often worked with well-meaning and bright professionals who don't do the stuff I talk about in this book, and it shows. Find experienced help!

Fortunately for you, the leasing business offers a wide array of lease advisors. Although quality varies, you can find help. First if, and only if, they can offer objective input, ask your current accountants, lawyers, and business associates. Look in the relevant chapters of this book for tips and Web sites to help you. In addition, look at Internet resources by subject matter. To find lessors, brokers, lawyers, accountants, and investment bankers who specialize in leasing and can assist you, visit the Web site www.elaonline.com/memberDir/(the Equipment Leasing Association directory of members). Then inquire.

Many lessees believe that they understand how to lease property, and many do, especially in small-ticket transactions. However, as soon as any pricing and structure considerations become important, you often can benefit from hiring specialists to advise you. By doing so, your real costs may drop more than enough to pay for these services; and even if you increase your cost somewhat, the improved terms of your deal may protect your business and assets in ways that may prove valuable to you in the long term.

Develop a Good Relationship with Your Lessor

Lessors now realize more than ever that a good relationship with you really counts. However, developing a good relationship is not a one-way street. You, too, should work hard to create a good relationship with your lessor. At the beginning, get to know the people who make up the lessor's team. Ask them important questions about the relationship and your obligations, in good times and bad. For example, as a minute sampling, ask your lessor (or prospective lessor):

> ✔ Who is your competition, and why are you better for me?
>
> ✔ If I have questions after I close, whom can I call?
>
> ✔ How do I know whether I am meeting your standards when it comes to maintaining the leased property?
>
> ✔ If I should encounter financial problems, tell me what really happens? Do you try to work it out, or do you jump on me when (and if) I first stumble?

Tell the lessor that your questions relate to how leasing really works for the lessor, and that you are not negotiating the lease terms or asking the lessor to waive his rights. In short, get to know your lessor because if you do perform, your lessor, within his credit and business constraints, probably wants to help you with your leasing needs again. And if you run into financial trouble, your relationship may enable you to get that extra time or break that you need to get out of the ditch.

Seek Requests for Proposals

At the inception of a lease transaction, you can exchange ideas with a lessor in five minutes or in months of lengthy meetings. You can, as one approach, for large-ticket leases and some complex middle-market leases, use a broker, investment banker, or lease advisor to send out *requests for proposals*, or *RFPs*, to lessors. The RFPs elicit interest in financing and can often produce the best pricing and terms for you.

You may wonder how much a transaction costs in legal and other transaction fees if you negotiate a proposal with the help of your outside lawyers and then negotiate definitive lease documents, too. The actual cost depends, of course, on the complexity of the transaction and whom you use as advisors. Counsel in large cities, such as Chicago, Dallas, New York, San Francisco, or Los Angeles, can, with the right experience, cost $250 to $550 per hour. Advisors usually get paid from ½ percent to 4 percent of the lessor's cost depending on the type of deal.

That cost may serve you well, however. Structuring leases properly may not only identify funding sources and drive down pricing, but also help you gain control over the leased property through lease options and negotiated terms regarding the maintenance and return of leased property.

Allow Time for the Proposal Process

You may have a good idea how long it takes to complete a lease transaction. Small-ticket transactions can take hours or days after an approval. However, you may want or need to do a large-ticket deal or one of any size with some "hair on it" — the vernacular for a difficult transaction with unusual structures, credit issues, or other risks.

As I suggest to lessors in Chapter 23, the drafting and negotiating stages can take more time than you expect. Just because a transaction keeps your singular focus or takes a high priority in your business, don't expect everyone else to feel the same way. The lessor may have ten deals like yours to do, or the lessor may have to go through extraordinary internal approvals to get your deal done. You can, of course, help others understand the urgency of your need, but the point should be clear: Anticipate that your deal takes longer than predicted. Don't count on completing your deal before your lessor can respond in the ordinary course of its business. If you want to close a deal urgently, let your lessor know early and often and make sure that your advisors meet or beat any deadline that you set. Most lessors can keep the pace if you give them the "heads up."

Sign Proposals with All Major Business Points

Regardless of the size of your deal, except for some small-ticket transactions, you can generally sign some kind of a proposal letter describing the terms of your lease. These proposals vary significantly in detail from a page or two to dozens of pages. Here's the key for you: Include all significant terms in your proposal. Critical areas for errors or omissions include your economics (such as when your lessor fixes the rental rate), options (including early buyout options and fixed price purchase options), conditions to close and fund, and return requirements for the leased property.

You can make a list of many of these terms by reviewing the Schedule in the Appendix. You should cover each business issue relevant to your deal. By doing so, you avoid giving your lessor leeway to impose her ideas on you when you negotiate your lease documents. You should gain a common understanding first.

Negotiate Your Documentation

In middle-ticket and large-ticket leases, negotiation is the name of the game. Lessors usually draft documents based on forms that give them the advantage. Lessors expect you to negotiate, although most don't care if you do. Like any negotiation, pick your battles. Read Chapter 8, which provides negotiating points worth pursuing and others that you can just pass by because lessors generally won't budge. In most cases, if you identify issues important to your business, negotiate them. Lessors generally try to accommodate you unless you have just about taken your last gasp financially, and the lessor knows that he has the advantage in a risky deal. Even in that case, many lessors negotiate, so don't hesitate to fully negotiate significant points.

Try Different Types of Leases

Leasing can solve your financing needs in many ways. You just have to figure out what kind of leasing works for you. Even though some leasing products may appear complicated or confusing, they generally all consist of a patchwork of basic concepts discussed in this book. Lessors have mixed and matched the various concepts to compete for your business. So, don't be afraid to try something new or different.

Like hand in glove, leases can be made for you. Insist on it. For example, you can enter into TRAC leases (see Chapter 12) to finance vehicles. As a lessee, TRAC leases provide you benefits including the following:

- ✔ You make lower payments than with an equivalent loan because the lessor takes into account the tax benefits and passes most of the tax benefits to you through lower payments.

- ✔ You can establish fixed-price purchase and renewal rates at the start of the lease.

- ✔ You can, if you have good credit, encourage your lessors to take into account substantial residual values. In effect, your rent payments go down as the lessor's residual value assumption goes up.

Use cross-border leases to finance property for your operations located in another country (see Chapter 20) and vendor leases if you want to purchase and finance products and services today (see Chapter 21).

Don't forget a synthetic lease, which is a hybrid transaction that takes advantage of inconsistencies in the accounting and federal income tax rules. In a synthetic, you not only keep your lease off of your balance sheet loan (under the FAS 13), but you also claim the tax benefits as the tax owner of leased property under Rev. Proc. 75-21 and related federal tax precedent. See Chapter 15.

With the force of competition and your knowledge of leasing, you can arrange optimal leases for your business. In the final analysis, one type of lease may not suffice.

Chapter 23

Ten Points for Successful Leasing by Lessors

· ·

In This Chapter

▶ Developing your relationships

▶ Branding your business

▶ And more tips you need to know for successful leasing

· ·

*R*egardless of how long you have acted as a lessor, or even if you want to join the ranks as one, you probably realize (or soon will) that the leasing business continues to change and evolve. As the economy slows and technology advances, you can benefit from looking at some of the bigger concepts and pitfalls in leasing to improve your chances of success in the business. This chapter offers you ten tips to help you succeed in leasing. The ideas here reflect current trends and some conventional wisdom that I have developed from practicing this stuff for a long time.

Develop Your Relationships

When I first started in the leasing business, some lessors seemed to want to close, close, and close more and more deals, to build volume, often without apparent concern for the importance of their new relationship with the lessee. Times change, and the idea that you can simply build volume at the expense of your relationships has, in my view passed — and that's good. My point in this section is simple: Relationships count!

The development and nurturing of relationships should remain a paramount objective. You can profit in the broadest sense when you demonstrate the sustained desire and effort to provide quality service to your lessees and add exceptional value for your vendors, partners, and other suppliers. Treat each of these relationships as assets. Maintain and care for them. Add value to these relationships by helping meet needs better than the next lessor or lender. Act on these few basics:

✔ **Deliver for your lessee.** Respond to the concerns of your lessee quickly and negotiate with fairness, competence, and integrity. Deliver on your promises today and over the long term. Demonstrate deep knowledge of your products. Balance your approach by taking into account the characteristics of your customer, such as his creditworthiness, size, and management. Don't ignore your lessee after you close and book the deal. "Walk the talk" of attentive customer service for your lessee. Large or small, show respect for your lessee because, in the end, he feeds you!

✔ **Create and build relationships with your partner-investors and find the right people to help you.** Help your partners and investors achieve their objectives within the constraints of their business models and strategies. Invest their money, build their portfolios, manage their assets worldwide, and provide advisory services that distinguish you from the pack of other lessors. For example, use your full capabilities to provide equipment and risk management, as well as financial structuring, and state and federal tax planning services. If, on the other hand, you need these kinds of services, find experts or other advisors who can help you until you can manage on your own (if you choose to do so).

✔ **Know the businesses of your vendors.** In vendor financing, understand your customer's business as well (or better) than she does so that you can anticipate her needs and objectives and meet them before your competition takes the business from you. The same understanding, coupled with persistent efforts, can help you win the business of vendors.

Build a Brand

Branding has become the name of the game for many businesses, not just in leasing. *Branding* seems to defy simple definitions. It generally refers to creating a lasting and consistent identity for your business. For example, when you think of IBM, Coca-Cola, McDonald's, CIT, or Mercedes, do you develop an image in your mind of these businesses and what they do or sell? A brand can create confidence based on the values that you promote. A brand can separate you and your products from the pack. You can create a look, feel and approach that sets you apart like the *For Dummies* people who bring you this book have done.

Although branding costs money, look closely at building your brand. You can do it through advertising, direct mail, e-mail, advertising, direct marketing, and, most importantly, your everyday actions in business. Know your products and services and convey to your customers the qualities that define you. For example, do you want the markets to know you as a boutique cross-border firm, an efficient small-ticket vendor lessor, a sophisticated residual value player, or a model captive of an equipment manufacturer? Consider building a brand for your business, and if you do, keep it simple, clear, and positive. Focus your brand on what you do best because in this complex business, you cannot satisfy everyone's need everywhere all the time.

Improve Your Business Infrastructure

Business infrastructure refers, in my view, to the organization of people and systems that make your business go and grow. If, in the relentless drive to build volume, you fail to build your infrastructure, you only inhibit your own chances for sustained growth and success. I encourage you to evaluate whether you always:

- ✔ **Nurture and manage your human resources.** This concept is far from novel — treat your employees well, train them, value them, and help them evolve into your next leaders and the leaders in the leasing industry. The leasing business has struggled with finding and keeping competent employees and leaders. Recognize the value in your people and reward them for helping you grow and solve problems.

- ✔ **Retain experienced advisors as needed.** No one knows everything about every thing, in leasing or any other subject. Many lessors have developed large and sophisticated organizations with a bevy of experts in tax, insurance, equipment, pricing, contracts, legal, accounting, and structuring issues. However, even the big guys, and certainly the smaller guys, sometimes need help from the outside — especially when they find their staff stretched or overburdened by the demands of the business.

  You may find that outside help not only provides better quality service, but also costs less. Throughout this book, I urge you to hire experts in various areas. As you look through the chapters, watch for my tips because you can gain ideas where experts that you hire can make the difference between winning a deal or losing it. For example, you can hire:

  - Sophisticated lessor advisors who may provide you with structuring capability that you don't have and enable you to beat out a competing lessor with a similar, or even lower, cost of funds or higher tax rate

  - An equipment expert may provide you remarketing capability that you lack, appraisals that you need to approve a transaction, and reliable residual value assumptions to support your pricing efforts

  In making these staffing decisions, balance the economics of using outside help and the real value of developing internal talent, in each case with the goal of running your business most effectively, knowledgeably, and competitively.

- ✔ **Invest in technology.** The cost to acquire technology and use it may be high for you. The failure to do so may be deadly. As technology and the Internet create some transparency in leasing, you need good technology to compete. *Transparency* refers to the idea that everyone knows what every lessor is doing — unveiling at alarming speed lessor secrets and innovation. Technology can increase the speed and decrease the cost of doing business. Technology can also improve your internal operations and information management systems. With the backbone of your operation humming, you can focus on relationships, volume, and new products. Without technology, you may experience the frustrating reality of your competitors stealing your deals. It's a choice.

Manage Through Each Business Cycle

Changes in the economy around the world perplex the best and the brightest. The recent economy shows marked weakness in many different markets after about a decade of sustained growth. Leasing, like other businesses, faces challenges in a slowing economy, including less capital investment, diminishing funding resources, and significant credit concerns about lessees and lessors alike. To help you manage your business well in every business cycle, try a few suggestions:

- **Take time out.** Like a gravitational pull, your business routine pulls on you every day. However, you should stop and invest the time to study how the current economy affects you and how you can benefit from the changes that it brings into your markets.

- **Build where you add the most value.** Study the markets and identify the business segments in which you can add the most value, even if not at the lowest cost. Identify your niche and find ways to beat your competitors. Focus on your strengths. Evaluate deals realistically, and take prudent risks defined by your business model, structure, strategies, and markets.

- **Don't pass by deals because of unfamiliarity.** For example, don't forsake foreign markets because they are foreign to you. Don't avoid new products or structures, even distressed credits, just because you have not done it recently or ever. Learn new skills that help you manage with confidence. Hire people who understand your issues. With uncertainty, whether about a lessee or the economy, comes opportunity. Work hard to manage the risks, but accept them as part of the ever-changing business cycles.

Add Securitizations to Your Strategies

As you well know, leasing companies continue to consolidate with the result that capital formation has not only become a challenge, but also a critical problem, for many lessors. The strong lessors continue to have funding for the right deals, but not always the best funding structures to make the best deal. Smaller lessors more frequently can't secure funding that they need just to do their basic business. You need to diversify your funding strategies regardless of your size. This section describes securitizations and how you can use them to fund your business. Securitizations can level the playing field among companies seeking liquidity by allowing investors to receive a large part of the cash flow from a pool of leasing transactions owned by a lessor.

A *securitization* refers to a process in which you, as the lessor and the sponsor, convert pools of your cash generating leases (and other financial assets) into securities. A *security* (in this context) refers to any certificate, note, bond or similar evidence of an interest in the pool of leases created and managed by the lessor/sponsor. Also called *asset-backed securitizations,* leases and leased property serve as collateral to the investors for the payment of the return in their investments.

Functionally, as sponsor, you select leases that, as a group or a pool, produce reliable cash flow. You typically transfer the leases and the property covered by the leases (for example, an aircraft, or a printing press) to a *special purpose entity* (a corporation, partnership, business trust, grantor trust, or other legal entity) whose only purpose to exist is to hold the pool of leases.

A *trust* is a legal entity created by banks or trust companies that hold assets, such as the leases and the leased property covered by the leases. The trustee of the trust holds legal title to these assets for the benefit of others who own and direct the affairs of the trust, called *beneficial owners* or *trustors.* A beneficial owner can in general freely sell or transfer its interest in the trust, called a *beneficial interest.* As a sponsor, you can be the beneficial owner of the trust or the owner of the stock or other securities of the special purpose entity.

A special purpose entity, sometimes called a *bankruptcy remote entity,* maintains a separate existence from the lessor/sponsor, on a financial and legal basis. If the lessor files bankruptcy, the special purpose entity should not be consolidated with, or become a part of, the bankruptcy estate of the lessor. As a result, purchasers of the securities treat the special purpose entity as having a higher decree of creditworthiness than the lessor has in many cases, which should result in a lower cost financing of the pool of leases for the sponsor.

The special purpose entity then issues to the investors (and the investors buy) the securities in the form of debt or equity interests (such as passthrough bonds, commercial paper, or notes). The investors may include financial institutions, banks, and even leasing companies. You can complete securitizations as public sales or private offerings. In either case, you comply with state and federal securities laws. The issued securities represent an undivided share of the leased property and lease receivables (the pool of leases) owned by the special purpose entity. The terms on which the special purpose entity issues the securities depends on the cash flows and quality of the underlying lease receivables (the credit of the lessees).

Securitizations differ from most other funding of a sponsor because they do not generally depend on the sponsor's credit. The issuer/special purpose entity pays the sums due on the securities primarily, if not exclusively, from the cash flow generated by the leases in the pools instead of the credit of the sponsor. In other words, in the perfect world, as the sponsor of the securitization financing, you shouldn't be required to put your personal credit at risk. The pool of leases (or other financial assets) should alone provide the payment and security. The credit rating of the securities depends only on the quality and the cash flows of the lease receivables and not on your credit. As a result, the securities may be more easily transferred and sold than the leases within the pools.

Alas, the world is not perfect, and you may have to support the securitization to attract investors, perhaps only in part for first losses in the pool, depending on the quality of the leases in the pool and the state of the market.

Alternatively, you can often further reduce your cost of the financing if you arrange for other *independent credit enhancements,* which refers to an additional dependable source of payment, such as letters of credit, credit insurance, reserve accounts or pools, and extra tangible collateral.

As the lessor/sponsor, you should, in completing a securitization, realize several benefits:

- ✔ Book a gain on the sale of the leased property and related leases (which may constitute an acceleration of gain represented by receiving the present value of these lease receivables rather than wait to collect rent over the various lease terms)

- ✔ Raise capital at lower rates while earning fees for servicing the transactions

- ✔ Improve your financial ratios because the leases are removed from your balance sheet, and you can record all or a part of your gain on sale as new equity

- ✔ Gain access to an otherwise limited financial market to acquire capital to expand your portfolio of lease investments

Your investors gain also in the following ways:

- ✔ They receive securities that represent a well-collateralized investment.

- ✔ They value the use of a *bankruptcy-remote structure* (a trust or special purpose entity that stands apart from credit risks of the lessor).

- ✔ They get an investment that offers relatively predictable and stable interest payments with little risk of prepayment.

Increase Earnings with Syndications

If you need to accelerate earnings, increase cash flow, improve fee income, and reduce credit exposure to certain customers, you can do so with syndications. *Syndications* refer to a sale of all or any part of a single lease transaction or group of transactions to raise capital, generate fees, recognize asset sale income, or reduce credit exposure to a particular lessee. You can syndicate leases in several ways:

✔ **You can sell all or any part of your interest in the lease and leased property.** You can sell the lease and all of its related documents together with the leased property, or sell all or a portion of your beneficial interest if you formed a trust that owns the leased property.

In either case, this transaction may be characterized as a true sale. A *true sale* refers to a transaction in which you sell, assign, and transfer all of your interest and obligations to another person or entity, and treat the transaction as a sale and not a financing (a secured loan) for legal, accounting, and tax purposes.

✔ **You can sell a participation in the lease.** A *participation* refers to a transfer of a share of your rights and interests in a lease transaction to other persons or entities who have no direct legal relationship with the lessee. The participants stand behind you whether the lessee knows that you have sold a participation in the lease to others. You stay in the deal as the lead participant, which means that you exercise all rights and interests that you have with your lessee on behalf of all participants and yourself. You act as the face person who maintains the exclusive relationship with your lessee in most circumstances.

True leases create tax benefits, and sharing actual ownership interests may create partnerships. Forming partnerships create other tax issues. See Chapter 13. You can more effectively handle these deals by assigning interests to your buyers like the sale described in the preceding section. You can expect the participants to vote on important actions, such as changing rents or declaring the lessee to be in default. Each participant shares rent payments in proportion to his percentage of participation in the entire deal.

✔ **You can discount or leverage the stream of rent payments.** You can borrow money using your lease and leased property as the collateral, sometimes called a *back-leveraged lease*. A *back-leveraged lease* exists when your investor lends money to you after you have already closed and funded your lease. A *front-leveraging* looks more like a leveraged lease in that your investor lends you money at the same time as you close the lease. You essentially borrow money secured by the rent stream in either case.

Add Support for Your Credit Risk

Whether the economy cruises along or it falters, you probably start the approval process of every deal with an evaluation of the prospective lessee's credit. Chapter 3 discusses credit issues as a risk of leasing. Credit experts may view these issues as the foundation of deciding whether you, as the lessor, can expect to be paid by your lessee as required by your lease. If they sign off with a negative point of view, kiss your deal goodbye!

It is certainly understandable that, as the economy tries mightily to sustain its growth (or avoid recession), it's easy to clam up and not offer financing to anyone who seems even remotely marginal on credit. Before you make that decision, you may want to try the following:

- ✔ **Evaluate structures that support the credit of the lessee.** Consider using third-party support, such as letters of credit, additional collateral, guaranties, credit insurance, and deposit and reserve accounts, to assure you that your lessee can make her payments.

- ✔ **Shorten the term of your leases.** By keeping your leases short and increasing early payments, you can minimize your risk (subject to tax restraints for true leases).

- ✔ **Lease mission critical property.** If your lessee leases property that he must have to operate his business, and the lessee's credit has reasonable strength, you can usually count on getting paid in the absence of huge business/credit problems.

In short, don't let changing economies stop you from doing business. Structure your leases to protect your downside and monitor the lessee's business on a periodic basis as needed. Working with lessees in a slow economy fairly but prudently can help you forge a long and mutually beneficial relationship.

Allow Time for the Proposal Process

Drafting and negotiating proposals and/or commitments can take several weeks to several months depending on the nature of the leased property and the complexity of the lease structure. Start your efforts with more than sufficient time before your lessee intends to place the property in service, to preserve tax benefits and financing options. Add to the negotiating schedule the time you need to identify the best advisors and lessors to handle your business. Even small-ticket transactions take time, but small-ticket transactions on form documents can move faster and cheaper than other deals.

Avoid Common Errors in Your Proposals

In the proposal, try to clearly set out all major terms of your deal. Certain terms can spoil your fun if not clearly stated in the proposal. Three examples help make this point:

✔ **Locking lease rates.** Some lessors forget to maintain flexibility to set their rates based on the prevailing interest rates or cost of funds at the time of paying the lessor's cost. Avoid locking rates if you can, especially in volatile interest rate environments, if you don't plan to close within a few days; otherwise, say in your proposal that you set rates two days or so before funding. You can set rates based on a recognized index such as LIBOR, the prime rate, or Treasury Notes. See `www.federalreserve.gov/releases/H15/data.htm` as a place to find and set rates daily.

✔ **Paying for transaction expenses.** Clearly establish responsibility for transaction costs. Try to avoid fixing or capping these costs when your lessee's negotiating style can force you to endure delays and complications — unless you like signing blank checks, of course, that reduce your yield and cash flow.

✔ **Deciding whether to commit yourself to the deal.** If you intend to be bound by your proposal, say so explicitly in writing in your proposal or commitment. In every other case, you should be equally clear that you do not intend to be bound and offer the terms only as nonbinding proposal. See Chapter 4.

Selecting Lease Versus Loan Structures

As part of your business model, you know, generally, whether you have the tax appetite to do a tax-oriented lease, a lease without tax benefits, or a secured loan. Work through the true lease Guidelines discussed in Chapter 13 and use all of your pricing programs to get the lease structure right. The challenge is to avoid mixing them up and ending up with a loan that you want to be a lease. For that reason, you need to gather your legal, pricing, and business types and decide on which type of deal you intend to do. This decision helps you avoid challenges from your lessee in or out of its bankruptcy.

Stay Tuned to Change

As leasing continues to evolve, you face a myriad of economic, regulatory, tax, and other changes around the globe that impact your business. You should, at least, stay tuned to the significant changes before and after they occur. While this book helps you understand some basic (and not so basic) concepts in leasing and secured lending, you can and should build on what you read here. To give you some initial direction, review the following short list of changes that affect you now and in the future:

- ✔ **Accounting.** The FASB and its counterparts around the world plan to analyze whether to replace the benefits/risk model with an asset/liability model of accounting for leases, which could put many leases back on a lessee's balance sheet. See Chapter 15.

- ✔ **Bankruptcy.** Congress has been working on changes in the bankruptcy law. As discussed in Chapter 18, bankruptcy law clearly affects you, especially in a slowing economy.

- ✔ **Federal Income Tax.** The Internal Revenue Code of 1986, as amended (the Code to many of you), is a powerful tool for economic and policy changes, and Congress has made huge amendments recently to return tax money to the economy. Watch for changes in depreciation schedules, including tax rules affecting cross-border transactions, and other tax changes as they occur. Remember to update your leasing programs as soon as any change in the Code occurs and get the right training to implement the changes in your pricing. See Chapters 7, 13, and 20.

- ✔ **Revised Article 9.** Revised Article 9 of the Uniform Commercial Code is here, as of July 1, 2001, for most states (and January 1, 2002, for a few others). It affects almost every leasing and secured loan transaction you do. You may not have to be a guru on this law, but if you know its fundamentals, you can do a better job of structuring your deals. See Chapter 17.

- ✔ **State Tax.** As this book goes to the production guys, the states continue to work on the Streamlined Sales Tax Project discussed in Chapter 15. Because sales taxes, in the aggregate, can exceed your yield as a percentage of lessor's cost in any given transaction, you should probably follow or get involved in this ongoing effort to simplify (and probably increase) sales taxes nationwide.

- ✔ **Technology.** Although technology has its ups and downs in the economy, it produces changes of all kinds ranging from laws governing electronic signatures at the state and federal level to Web-based equipment transactions. This area is here to stay and will remain dynamic if not profitable. Read Chapters 10 and 21 for more.

Happy leasing!

Appendix

This appendix presents a form of Master Lease Agreement (*Lease*) updated to reflect Revised Article 9 (see Chapter 17). The Lease works best for middle-ticket deals with corporate lessees. A form of Schedule appears at the end of this Lease. Square brackets [ ] indicate business terms that typically vary depending on the type of transaction.

This form may contain provisions that may not be right for you. Do not use the Lease (or any part of it) without seeking advice from your counsel. See Chapters 1, 8, 10, 11, and 12 to better understand the Lease.

Master Lease Agreement

MASTER LEASE AGREEMENT, dated as of _____, 200__ (as amended, supplemented or modified from time to time, this "Lease"), between ABC Company, a _____ corporation, with a mailing address at _____ ("Lessee"), and XYZ Leasing Corp., a Delaware corporation, with a mailing address at _____ ("Lessor").

The parties agree to a lease Property under this Lease as follows:

AGREEMENT:

1. DEFINITIONS: Unless otherwise defined in this Lease, capitalized terms shall have the following meanings:

"Basic Rent" means the periodic rent set forth in the applicable Schedule other than Interim Rent, payable by Lessee during the initial Term.

"Delivery Date" means, with respect to any Schedule, the date set forth on such Schedule as the "Delivery Date."

"executed" means to sign or otherwise authenticate a document or record within the meaning of Article 9 of the UCC, in effect as _____.

"Fair Market Value" or "Fair Rental Value," as the case may be, means an amount equal to the value which would obtain in an arm's-length transaction between an informed and willing buyer-user or lessee-user (other than a used equipment dealer), as appropriate, and an informed and willing seller or lessor under no compulsion to sell or lease. Such values shall be based on the assumptions that the Units: (i) are being sold "in place and in use;" (ii) are free and clear of all liens and encumbrances; and (iii) are in the condition required upon the return of the Units under Section 19 of this Lease. In such determination, costs of removal from the location of current use shall not be a deduction from such value(s).

"<u>Lease Documents</u>" means this Lease and all Schedules together with all documents, records, instruments, and agreements related thereto.

"<u>Lessor's Cost</u>" means, with respect to a Unit, Lessor's total cost to purchase such Unit as set forth in the applicable Schedule.

"<u>Property</u>" means all equipment (including all related software, whether embedded therein or otherwise), fixtures, and other personal property, tangible or intangible, subject to any Schedule, together with all replacement parts, additions, substitutions, and accessions to such equipment, fixtures and other personal property, and insurance proceeds, agreements, records, security deposits, and general intangibles related thereto.

"<u>Rent Commencement Date</u>" means the date on which the Lessee first pays Rent as set forth in the applicable Schedule, which shall be the first day of the calendar [month] immediately following the Delivery Date set forth in such Schedule.

"<u>Rent</u>" means all payments of rent during the Term, including Interim Rent, Basic Rent, and any renewal rent.

"<u>Schedule</u>" or "<u>Schedule No.___</u>" means a schedule to lease Property substantially in the form of <u>Exhibit A</u> hereto.

"<u>Term</u>" means the period that Property is subject this Lease, including any renewal or extension of this Lease.

"<u>UCC</u>" means the UCC in effect in the state set forth in <u>Section 22(e)</u> hereof.

"<u>Unit</u>" means each item of Property.

2. LEASE: Lessor agrees to lease to Lessee, and Lessee agrees to lease from Lessor, the Property described in each Schedule on the terms and subject to the conditions specified herein and therein. Lessee may, until not later than _____, 200__ (the "<u>Commitment Expiration Date</u>"), submit to Lessor a written request, in form and substance satisfactory to Lessor, to lease certain property to Lessee under this Lease. Lessor may, in its sole discretion, commit in writing to fund (each a "<u>Commitment</u>") all or any portion of such request under this Lease. Lessor's obligation (if any) to fund shall expire and terminate [30] days after the Commitment Expiration Date.

3. TERM OF LEASE: THIS LEASE SHALL BE EFFECTIVE UPON EXECUTION AND DELIVERY HEREOF by Lessee and Lessor. The Term for Property covered by a Schedule shall commence on the applicable Delivery Date and end on the "<u>Lease Expiration Date</u>" set forth in such Schedule. Lessee may extend this Lease beyond the existing Term in accordance with its renewal options set forth in <u>Section 16(a)(iii)</u> of this Lease.

4. RENT: (a) Lessee agrees to pay all Rent when due as provided herein and in the applicable Schedule. Lessor may charge Lessee interest at a rate of 1.5% per month, or, if less, the then highest lawful rate, on any past due amount, including late Rent payments.

(b) Lessee shall pay an interim rent ("<u>Interim Rent</u>") in an amount equal to the product of (i) the total annual Basic Rent for the first year of the initial Term under the applicable Schedule divided by [360], and (ii) the actual number of days from and including such Delivery Date to but excluding such Rent Commencement Date. The Interim Rent for each Schedule shall be due and payable, in advance, on the Delivery Date set forth in such Schedule.

(c) Basic Rent payments shall be due and payable, in advance, commencing on such Rent Commencement Date and thereafter on the same day of each succeeding [month] during the Term, as specified in the applicable Schedule.

(d) Lessor shall make reasonable efforts to send Lessee invoices for Rent, but the failure to do so or the incorrectness of any invoice shall not relieve Lessee of its obligation to pay any amount due under this Lease.

5. NET LEASE; UNCONDITIONAL OBLIGATIONS: This Lease is a net lease, and Lessee acknowledges and agrees that Lessee's obligations hereunder and under every Schedule, including, without limitation, its obligations to pay all Rent, shall be absolute and unconditional under any and all circumstances. Rents shall be paid without notice or demand and without any abatement, reduction, diminution, setoff, withholding, defense, counterclaim, or recoupment whatsoever whether they are due or alleged to be due to, and regardless of any past, present or future claims which Lessee may have against Lessor, the Property or any part thereof, or against any other person for any reason whatsoever even giving effect to any present or future law. This Lease may be terminated only as expressly provided in herein.

6. LESSEE'S REPRESENTATIONS, WARRANTIES AND COVENANTS: Lessee warrants and represents the following as of the date hereof and as of each Delivery Date: (a) Lessee is a [corporation] duly organized, validly existing and in good standing under the laws of _____, and is duly qualified and authorized to do business in the state where the Property will be located. (b) The information set forth under lessee's signature line and in the first paragraph of this Lease is true and complete, and Lessee will furnish Lessor with at least 10 days prior written notice of any change in such information. (c) Lessee's name on the signature page of this Lease is its exact legal name. (d) Lessee has the full [corporate] power, authority and legal right, and has obtained all necessary approvals and consents, and given all notices, to execute and deliver the Lease Documents to which it is a party and to perform the terms thereof, including each Schedule. (e) There is no action, proceeding or claim pending or, insofar as Lessee knows, threatened against Lessee or any of its subsidiaries before any court or administrative agency, which might have a material adverse effect on the business, condition or operations of Lessee or such subsidiary. (f) This Lease has been, and each Schedule and the other Lease Document to which Lessee is a party will be, duly executed and delivered by Lessee and constitute or will constitute the valid, binding and enforceable obligations of Lessee in accordance with their terms. (g) Lessee is in compliance with all applicable laws, rules and regulations affecting, in any material respect, the Lessee, the Units, this Lease or any other Lease Document.

7. DISCLAIMER OF WARRANTIES: Lessee acknowledges that it has made the selection of each Unit based upon its own judgment. The manufacturer or supplier of such Unit is not, and will not be, an agent of Lessor under any circumstances. Lessor will in no event be deemed an agent of any manufacturer or supplier. LESSOR MAKES NO EXPRESS OR IMPLIED WARRANTIES, INCLUDING, WITHOUT LIMITATION, THOSE OF DESCRIPTION, INFRINGEMENT, MERCHANTABILITY OR FITNESS FOR A PARTICULAR USE OR PURPOSE WITH RESPECT TO THE PROPERTY, AND HEREBY DISCLAIMS THE SAME. Lessor shall have no liability for any damages, whether direct or consequential, incurred by Lessee as a result of any defect or malfunction of a Unit. Lessee agrees to look solely to the manufacturer or supplier of any defective or malfunctioning Unit for the repair or replacement of such Unit and to continue to make all Rent with respect to such Unit in spite of such defect or malfunction. Lessor hereby assigns to Lessee, for and during the Term, any warranty, guaranty or indemnity of the manufacturer or supplier issued or transferred to Lessor with respect to any Unit.

8. GENERAL INDEMNIFICATION: Lessee agrees to indemnify, reimburse, and hold Lessor (including, without limitation, its employees, officers, directors, agents, representatives, attorneys, and partners) and each of their respective successors and assigns, harmless from and against all liabilities, losses, damages, actions, suits, demands, infringements, claims of any kind and nature (including, without limitation, claims relating to environmental discharge, cleanup, or compliance), and all costs and expenses whatsoever to the extent they may be incurred or suffered by such indemnified party in connection therewith (including, without limitation, reasonable attorneys' fees and expenses), fines, penalties (and other charges of applicable governmental authorities), licensing fees relating to any Unit, damage to or loss of use of Property (including, without limitation, consequential or special damages to third parties or damages to Lessee's property), or bodily injury to or death of any person (including, without limitation, employees, officers, directors, agents, representatives, attorneys and partners of Lessee), directly or indirectly relating to or arising out of the acquisition, use, lease or sublease, ownership, operation, possession, control, storage, or condition of any Unit (regardless of whether such Unit is at the time in the possession of Lessee), the falsity of any nontax representation or warranty of Lessee or Lessee's failure to comply with the terms of any Lease Document during the Term.

9. GENERAL TAX INDEMNIFICATION AND PAYMENT: Lessee agrees to pay if and when due, and indemnify and hold Lessor harmless from and against, in addition to other amounts due hereunder and under each Schedule, all fees and assessments, and all sales, use, property, privilege, transfer, stamp, value added, excise and other taxes and charges (including all interest and penalties) (collectively "Taxes"), now or hereafter imposed by any governmental body or agency upon any of the Property or upon the purchase, ownership, possession, leasing, operation, use, rentals or other payments, or disposition hereunder whether payable by Lessor or Lessee (exclusive of taxes on or measured by Lessor's net income). Lessee agrees to prepare and file promptly with the appropriate offices any and all tax and similar returns required to be filed with respect thereto, or, if requested by Lessor, to notify Lessor of such requirements and furnish Lessor with all information required by Lessor so that it may effect such filing, at Lessee's expense. Any Taxes paid by, or imposed on, Lessor on behalf of Lessee shall become immediately due and payable on Lessor's demand.

10. INCOME TAX INDEMNIFICATION: Lessor, as owner, shall be entitled to any and all of the most accelerated depreciation deductions with respect to the Property as provided under the Internal Revenue Code of 1986, as amended from time to time, and any and all other such state, local or federal tax benefits as may now or hereafter be available to an owner of such Property (collectively, "Tax Benefits"). If as a result of (i) the inaccuracy or breach of any of Lessee's representations, warranties and covenants in any Lease Document, or (ii) the acts or failure to act of Lessee or any person claiming an interest in the Property through the Lessee (other than a casualty or other event described in Section 14 hereof with respect to which Stipulated Loss Value shall have been paid by Lessee), Lessor or any of its assigns shall lose, or shall not, in its reasonable opinion, have the right to claim, or there shall be disallowed, deferred or recaptured, any portion of the Tax Benefits with respect to a Unit (a "Loss of Tax Benefits"), or there shall be included in Lessor's gross income any amounts other than Rent in respect of the purchase price of any Unit (an "Inclusion"), then, on and after the next succeeding Rent payment date after written notice to Lessee by Lessor, Lessee agrees to pay Lessor an amount in cash that will cause Lessor's after-tax yield and cash flow in respect of the Property to equal that which Lessor would have realized if Lessor had not incurred such a Loss of Tax Benefits or had such an Inclusion. If any claim or contest regarding any tax indemnity covered by this Section 10 shall arise, such claim or contest shall be addressed or conducted, at Lessee's expense, in the manner reasonably specified by Lessor.

11. USE; MAINTENANCE; QUIET ENJOYMENT: (a) Lessee, at its expense, agrees to make all necessary site preparations and cause the Property to be operated in accordance with any applicable manufacturer's manuals or instructions. So long as no Event of Default has occurred and is continuing, Lessee shall have the right to quietly possess and use the Property as provided herein without interference by Lessor.

(b) Lessee, at its expense, shall maintain the Property in good condition, reasonable wear and tear excepted, and will comply with all laws, ordinances and regulations to which the use and operation of the Property may be or become subject. Such obligation shall extend to repair and replacement of any partial loss or damage to the Property, regardless of the cause. If the manufacturer mandates maintenance, Lessee shall also obtain and keep in effect at all times during the Term maintenance service contracts with suppliers approved by Lessor, such approval not to be unreasonably withheld. All parts furnished in connection with such maintenance or repair shall immediately become part of the Property. All such contracts, maintenance, repair, and replacement services shall be paid for and performed by Lessee when due with the result that no lien will attach to the Property. Only qualified personnel of Lessee shall operate the Property. The Property shall be used only for the purposes for which it was designed.

(c) Lessee agrees not to make or permit any material changes or alterations to be made to the Property without Lessor's prior written approval, such approval not to be unreasonably withheld. All accessories, replacements, parts and substitutions to the Property shall become the property of Lessor, be included in the definition of Property and be subject to this Lease.

12. TITLE AND LOCATION: Lessor and Lessee hereby confirm their intent that: (a) the Property shall remain personal property; (b) such Property shall be readily removable from, and not primarily leased hereunder for the operation of, the real property, if applicable, on which it is situated; and (c) title to the Property shall remain vested solely in Lessor. At any time during the Term, and at Lessor's request, Lessee agrees to place in a conspicuous location on each Unit (or any lot of Property as determined by Lessor) a tag, to be provided by Lessor, which reads substantially as follows: "Property leased by XYZ LEASING CORP." as Owner/Lessor." Lessee may not remove the Property from its place of installation without Lessor's prior written consent, which consent shall not be unreasonably withheld. Lessor shall have the right to inspect the Property during regular business hours, with reasonable notice, and in compliance with Lessee's reasonable security procedures.

13. INSURANCE: Lessee shall obtain and maintain for the Term, at its own expense, insurance on and relating to the Property in such amounts, with such deductibles and issued by such insurers as Lessor shall reasonably request or approve. Such insurance shall include: (i) "all risk" insurance against loss or damage to the Property, (ii) commercial general liability insurance (including contractual liability, products liability and pollution coverages), and (iii) such other insurance against such other risks of loss and with such terms, as shall in each case be reasonably satisfactory to, or reasonably required by, Lessor. *(See Chapter 9 for a longer form insurance provision that can replace this section.)*

14. LOSS; DAMAGE; DESTRUCTION AND SEIZURE: (a) Lessee agrees to bear the risk of the Units being lost, stolen, destroyed, damaged, or seized by governmental authority for any reason whatsoever at any time until the latest to occur of (i) the expiration or termination of the Term or (ii) any storage period thereafter or (iii) the return of the subject Unit to Lessor (if authorized hereunder), and shall proceed diligently and cooperate fully to recover any and all damages, insurance proceeds or condemnation awards.

(b) Except as described in <u>Section 14(c)</u> hereof, if during the Term or the storage period thereafter, any Unit shall be lost, stolen, destroyed, irreparably damaged or seized by governmental authority for a period equal to at least the remainder of the Term, Lessor shall receive from the proceeds of insurance obtained pursuant to <u>Section 13</u> hereof, from any award paid by the seizing governmental authority and, to the extent not received from the proceeds of such insurance or award, or both, from Lessee, on or before the third Rent payment date next succeeding such loss, theft, destruction, damage or governmental seizure: (i) all accrued and unpaid rent in respect of such Unit including rent due on all Rent payment dates following the date of such loss or seizure; (ii) the Stipulated Loss Value of such Unit, determined as of the first such Rent payment date next following such loss or seizure; (iii) all other sums, if any, that shall have become due and payable hereunder; and (iv) interest on the foregoing at the lower of the rate equal to 1.5% per month or the then highest lawful rate from the due dates(s) of such payment(s) to the date of payment.

On receipt by Lessor of the amount specified herein above with respect to each such Unit so lost, stolen, destroyed, damaged or seized, (i) this Lease shall be deemed terminated as to such Unit and Rent in respect of such Unit shall be deemed abated, as of the Rent payment date next succeeding such loss, theft, destruction, damage or seizure; and (ii) so long as no default or Event of Default has occurred and is continuing hereunder, Lessor shall on demand, transfer title to such Unit, "AS IS, WHERE IS, WITH ALL FAULTS AND WITHOUT RECOURSE, REPRESENTATION OR WARRANTY," to Lessee, or, if appropriate in Lessor's sole judgment, which judgment shall be exercised in a reasonable manner, and on prior notice to Lessee, to Lessee's insurance carrier. Any proceeds of insurance payable to Lessor pursuant to this <u>Section 14</u> and <u>Section 13</u> hereof received by Lessee shall be paid to Lessor promptly upon their receipt by Lessee. If any proceeds of insurance or awards received from governmental authorities are in excess of the amount owed under this <u>Section 14(b)</u>, Lessor shall promptly remit to Lessee the amount in excess of the amount owed to Lessor.

(c) So long as no Event of Default shall have occurred and be continuing, any proceeds of insurance obtained pursuant to <u>Section 13</u> hereof received with respect to any Unit the repair of which is practical shall, at the election of Lessee, be applied either to the repair of such Unit or, upon Lessor's receipt of evidence of the repair of the Unit reasonably satisfactory to Lessor, to the reimbursement of Lessee for the cost of such repair.

(d) Lessee shall promptly, but in any event within [30] days thereafter, notify Lessor in writing in reasonable detail of any loss, theft, destruction, damage or seizure described in this <u>Section 14</u>.

(e) The Stipulated Loss Value payable by Lessee under this Lease shall be that percentage of Lessor's Cost of the affected Unit(s) set forth in the table annexed to the applicable Schedule opposite the Rent payment date next following the event giving rise to Lessee's obligation to pay the Stipulated Loss Value. Stipulated Loss Values and Rent shall not be prorated.

15. CONDITIONS TO LEASE AND FUNDING: Lessor may, in its sole discretion, terminate any Commitment herein at any time if the following conditions shall not be met to the satisfaction of Lessor.

(a) On the date of this Lease, Lessee and Lessor shall have executed and delivered this Lease and the following other Lease Documents in form and substance satisfactory to Lessor: (i) an unconditional guaranty of Lessee's obligations under the Lease Documents from ABC Guaranty Co., Lessee's parent company ("<u>Guarantor</u>"), in favor of Lessor (the "<u>Guaranty</u>"); (ii) copies, certified by the Secretary or Assistant Secretary of Lessee, of Lessee's and Guarantor's charter documents and resolutions authorizing the transactions contemplated hereby; (iii) a good standing certificate, including franchise tax status, and proof of the organizational number (if any) with respect to Lessee and Guarantor from Lessee's and Guarantor's respective states of organization; (iv) all necessary consents of shareholders and other third parties with respect to the subject matter of the Lease Documents; and (v) a legal opinion of Lessee's and Guarantor's legal counsel.

(b) On each Delivery Date, Lessor and Lessee shall have executed and delivered in form and substance satisfactory to Lessor: (i) a Schedule (with Guarantor's written approval and acceptance thereon) covering the Units being delivered and accepted by Lessee under this Lease on such date; (ii) appraisals or valuations and, on Lessor's request, inspections of the Units to be delivered and accepted on such Delivery Date; (iii) landlord waivers and/or mortgagee waivers relating to the real property on which the Units will be located, (iv) bills of sale, purchase orders, invoices, and certificates of acceptance with respect to the Units covered by such Schedule; (v) an assignment of each purchase order, invoice, or agreement, as appropriate, with respect to the Units, with the consent of the supplier/manufacturer; (vi) insurance coverage with respect to the Units covered by such Schedule in compliance with this Lease; (vii) precautionary financing statements under the UCC requested by and in favor of Lessor with respect to such Units including, among others, words therein to the effect that any act by Lessee prohibited by <u>Section 18(b)</u> hereof shall violate the rights of Lessor under this Lease; and (vii) all other Lease Documents as Lessor may reasonably request.

(c) On the date of this Lease and on each Delivery Date, no Event of Default shall exist, and Lessor and Lessee shall also have met the requirements of the next to the last two sentences in <u>Section 22(f)</u> hereof with respect to this Lease and each Schedule.

16. OPTIONS OF LESSEE: (a) Provided that this Lease has not been terminated and that no Event of Default or event which, with notice or lapse of time or both, would become an Event of Default shall have occurred and be continuing, Lessee may elect one of the following options with respect to each Schedule:

(i) <u>Lessee's Option to Early Terminate this Lease</u>: On the [third] anniversary of the Rent Commencement Date of Schedule No. 1, Lessee may elect to terminate all, but not less than all, of the Schedules to this Lease. Lessee may arrange for the Units to be sold to an unrelated third person on or before the termination date. If the purchase price is less than the greater of the Stipulated Loss Value or the Fair Market Value thereof as of the termination date of this Lease plus any applicable sales or other transfer tax, Lessee shall pay Lessor the difference in cash on such termination date. If Lessee fails to arrange for such sale to the satisfaction of Lessor, this Lease shall continue in full force and effect, and this option shall thereupon expire and terminate.

(ii) <u>Lessee's Early Buy-Out Option</u>: On the [third] anniversary of the Rent Commencement Date of each Schedule, Lessee may, elect to purchase all, but not less than all, of the Units under such Schedule for a purchase price equal to the Fair Market Value thereof plus any applicable sales or other transfer tax.

(iii) <u>Lessee's Option to Renew</u>: At the expiration date of the initial Term of each Schedule, Lessee may elect to renew this Lease with respect to all, but not less than all, the Units under such Schedules for not less than [twelve (12)] months nor more than [twenty-four (24)] months for a rent equal to the Fair Rental Value of such Units for such additional period, which rent shall be paid [monthly] in advance.

(iv) <u>Lessee's Option to Purchase at End of Term</u>: At the expiration date of the initial Term of each Schedule, Lessee may elect to purchase all, but not less than all, of the Units under such Schedule for a purchase price equal to the Fair Market Value thereof as of the end of the initial Term of such Schedule plus any applicable sales or other transfer tax.

(b) If none of the foregoing options is duly exercised by Lessee at the expiration of the Term of a Schedule, Lessee shall return the Units subject to such Schedule to Lessor in the condition required by this Lease. Any of the foregoing options shall be exercised by written notice delivered to Lessor not less than [120] days prior to the relevant option date. The purchase of the Units by Lessee pursuant to its option in <u>Sections 16 (a)(ii) or (iv)</u> hereof shall be "AS IS, WHERE IS", "WITH ALL FAULTS" without recourse to or any warranty by Lessor, other than a warranty that the Units are free and clear of liens and encumbrances created by Lessor.

(c) For purposes of this section, if Lessor and Lessee have not agreed upon a determination of the Fair Market Value or Fair Rental Value of any

Unit, as the case may be, within [30] days after one of the parties has requested such determination, that determination shall be made by a certified independent appraiser approved by both Lessor and Lessee, such approvals not to be unreasonably withheld. The appraiser shall be furnished with a letter of instruction concerning the preparation of the appraisal, together with a copy of this Lease and the applicable Schedule and, to the extent available, related purchase orders, agreements, and invoices. The appraiser shall be instructed to make such determination within [30] days following appointment. The determination made by the appraiser shall be final and binding on both Lessor and Lessee. The Lessee and Lessor shall each pay half of the fees and expenses of any appraisal.

17. LESSOR'S RIGHTS OF FIRST REFUSAL: (a) Lessor shall have the right of first refusal to provide additional financing for Lessee's upgrades or improvements to any Unit prior to Lessee seeking such financing from any other person.

(b) If Lessee intends to seek financing described in Section 17(a) hereof, Lessee may seek bona fide, arms-length bids for such financing. Lessee shall provide to Lessor copies of such bids and related information distributed to other potential bidders. Lessor shall have least [20] days after receipt of such bids and information to elect to provide such financing on substantially the same terms as such bid or decline to provide such financing. If Lessor elects to provide any such financing, Lessor shall have [60] days after receipt of such bids and information from Lessee to close and fund such financing. Lessee and Lessor shall act diligently and in good faith under this Section 17. If Lessor fails to close and fund such financing within such [60]-day period, Lessee may thereafter close and fund the other financing evidenced by such bids free of the Lessor's rights under this Section for a period ending [90] days after Lessor's receipt of such bids. After such [90]-day period expires, however, Lessee shall comply with the provisions of this Section again with respect to bids provided to Lessor in accordance with this Section 17 hereof.

18. SUBLEASE, ASSIGNMENT: (a) Lessee acknowledges and agrees that Lessor may, subject to the terms of this Lease, sell, assign, grant a security interest in, or otherwise transfer all or any part of its rights, title and interest in the Lease Documents and the Property without notice to or the consent of the Lessee. Upon Lessor's written notice, Lessee shall, if requested, pay directly to such assignee without abatement, reduction, diminution, set off, withholding, defense, counterclaim, or recoupment (collectively, "defense") in respect of any such amount that becomes due hereunder. Lessee waives and agrees it will not assert against such defense against assignee. Such assignee shall have and be entitled to exercise any and all rights and remedies of Lessor hereunder, and all references herein to Lessor shall include Lessor's assignee. Lessee acknowledges that such a sale, assignment, grant or transfer would neither materially change Lessee's duties nor materially increase the burdens or risks imposed on the Lessee under this Lease.

(b) LESSEE MAY NOT, WITHOUT LESSOR'S PRIOR WRITTEN CONSENT, (i) SUBLEASE, TRANSFER, DISPOSE OF, OR ASSIGN ITS RIGHTS IN RESPECT OF ANY UNIT OR DELEGATE ITS OBLIGATIONS UNDER THIS LEASE or (ii) ASSIGN, GRANT A SECURITY INTEREST IN, OR OTHERWISE TRANSFER ALL OR ANY PART OF ITS RIGHTS, TITLE AND INTEREST IN AND TO THIS LEASE OR THE PROPERTY.

19. RETURN: At the expiration or earlier termination of this Lease, Lessee, at its own risk and expense, agrees to cause the Property to be delivered promptly to Lessor free of all hazardous materials under applicable environmental laws, rules and regulations and in the same condition as when delivered hereunder, ordinary wear and tear excepted, and in compliance with Section 11 hereof. Lessee agrees to redeliver such Property to such point in the United States as Lessor may designate and in such a manner as is consistent with the manufacturer's recommendations, if any, for transportation and packaging of such Property. All charges to cover equipment transportation, removal, storage until returned, packing, and handling and all other costs associated with a return of the Property to the location designated by Lessor shall be paid by Lessee. Lessee shall, at its sole expense, properly store the Property at the location of its last use for up to 180 days on Lessor's request.

20. EVENTS OF DEFAULT: An "Event of Default" shall occur if (a) Lessee (i) fails to make any Rent payment or other payment required hereunder when due and such failure continues for a period of 3 days; or (ii) excluding Section 13, fails to perform or observe any other covenant, condition or agreement hereunder or breaches any provision contained herein or in any other Lease Document to which it is a party, and such failure or breach continues for a period of [30] days after written notice by Lessor; or (iii) makes any representation or warranty herein or in any document furnished in connection herewith, which shall have been materially false or inaccurate when made; or (iv) fails to maintain insurance under Section 13 of this Lease; or (v) shall admit in writing that it is unable to pay its debts as they become due, become insolvent or bankrupt or make an assignment for the benefit of its creditors or consent to the appointment of a trustee or receiver, or insolvency proceedings shall be instituted by or against Lessee; or (b) Guarantor shall be in breach or violation of its Guaranty.

21. REMEDIES: Upon the occurrence of any Event of Default and at any time thereafter, Lessor may, in its discretion, do any one or more of the following, all of which Lessor and Lessee expressly agree are commercially reasonable under the UCC and any other applicable law: (i) terminate this Lease; (ii) claim: (A) all unpaid Rent and sums due and payable under this Lease (other than amounts payable under clause (B) hereof, if any) plus (B) an amount equal to the greater of the then applicable Stipulated Loss Value (which value Lessee acknowledges is liquidated damages and not a penalty, and has a reasonable discount rate implicit therein) or the then applicable Fair Market Value of the Property as determined by Lessor; (iii) require that Lessee return all Property to Lessor in accordance with <u>Section 19</u> hereof; (iv) enter upon the premises where such Property is located without breaching the peace, and take immediate possession of and remove the same, all without liability to Lessor or its agents for such entry; (v) sell any or all of the Property at public or private sale, without prior notice to Lessee or Guarantor, or advertisement, or otherwise dispose of, hold, use, operate, lease to others or keep idle such Property, all free and clear of any rights of Lessee or Guarantor and without any duty to account or give other notice to Lessee or Guarantor for such action or inaction or for any proceeds with respect thereto subject in any event to the requirements of applicable law) to applicable law; (vi) retain all or any part of the Property in satisfaction of any deficiency of Lessee should this Lease be determined constitute a security agreement; (vii) charge all costs, fees, and expenses of Lessor (including fees and expenses of Lessor's counsel) arising from or related to any or every Event of Default; and (viii) exercise any other right or remedy which may be available under the UCC or other applicable law. Lessee acknowledges that Lessor shall not make and may disclaim any and all warranties, express or implied, of quiet enjoyment, title, and the like, arising from its exercise of remedies under this <u>Section 21</u>. All sales or other disposition of Property under this <u>Section 21</u> shall be made "as is where is" with "all faults."

22. MISCELLANEOUS: (a) This Lease shall constitute a "finance lease" under Article 2A of the UCC. Lessee waives any and all rights and remedies conferred upon Lessee by UCC Sections 2A-508 through 2A-522, including, without limitation, Lessee's rights to (i) cancel or repudiate this Lease, (ii) reject or revoke acceptance of any Unit, (iii) recover damages from Lessor for breach of warranty or for any other reason, (iv) claim a security interest in any rejected Property in Lessee's possession or control, (v) deduct from Rent all or any part of any claimed damages resulting from Lessor's default under this Lease, (vi) accept partial delivery of the Property, (vii) "cover" by making any purchase or lease of other property in substitution for Property to be leased from Lessor, (viii) recover from the Lessor any general, special, incidental, or consequential damages, for any reason whatsoever, and (ix) seek specific performance, replevin, or the like for any of the Property.

(b) The Units shall be leased for commercial purposes only, and not for consumer, personal, home, or family purposes, The Units shall not constitute "consumer goods" and this Lease shall not be deemed to be a "consumer lease" under the UCC.

(c) Without limiting <u>Section 22(a)</u> hereof, this Lease describes the terms of, and is intended by the parties hereto to be, a true lease; provided, however, that the parties acknowledge that the terms and conditions of this Lease may, alternatively, constitute a security agreement. If any Schedule constitutes a security agreement (all provisions of this Lease being incorporated therein), the Lessee (i) represents, with respect to such Schedule, that it has rights in, or the power to transfer rights in, the Property subject thereto; (ii) hereby grants a security interest to Lessor in all of Lessee's right, title and interest in such Property (including Units described in such

Schedule) and the proceeds thereof, whether now or hereafter existing, to secure all of Lessee's obligations under the Lease Documents.

(d) It is not the intent of the parties to create rent or other payment obligations of Lessee, which will be considered usurious under applicable law. However, if any such payment shall be found to be usurious by a court of competent jurisdiction, then Rent or such other amounts shall automatically be reduced to the then highest rate or amounts and the usurious portion of the Rent or such other amounts shall be applied to the Lessee's remaining obligations under this Lease in a manner reasonably determined by Lessor.

(e) ALL MATTERS INVOLVING THE CONSTRUCTION, VALIDITY, PERFORMANCE AND ENFORCEMENT OF THIS LEASE WILL BE GOVERNED BY THE LAWS OF THE STATE OF [_____] WITHOUT GIVING EFFECT TO PRINCIPLES OF CONFLICTS OF LAW.

(f) This Lease and each Schedule may be executed by the parties hereto in separate counterparts, each of which when so executed and delivered shall be an original, but all such counterparts shall together constitute one and same instrument; provided, however, that to the extent, if any, that this Lease and any Schedule constitutes chattel paper (as such term is defined in the UCC), no security interest in this Lease or such a Schedule may be created through the transfer, control (for electronic chattel paper) or possession of any counterpart of this Lease or the Schedule, as the case may be, other than the executed original counterpart of each of those documents. Each counterpart of this Lease and such Schedules shall be marked as "Lessor's Original" or words to a similar effect. All other counterparts shall be marked as a "duplicate" or words to a similar effect to the satisfaction of Lessor. Each Schedule shall be deemed to incorporate all of the terms of this Lease and to constitute a separate lease for all purposes.

(g) NONE OF THE PROVISIONS OF THIS LEASE MAY BE AMENDED, MODIFIED OR WAIVED EXCEPT IN A WRITING SIGNED BY LESSOR AND LESSEE.

(h) Whether any Unit is funded or accepted under this Lease, Lessee shall pay all fees and expenses of Lessor (including the fees and expenses of its counsel), on Lessor's demand, with regard to this Lease or any document relating hereto or any amendment of any thereof. Lessor may in its sole discretion include such fees and expenses as part of the Lessor's Cost.

(i) Lessee shall execute and deliver such further documents, instruments, agreements, and other records (as defined in Article 9 of the UCC) relating to the Property, and take such other actions as the Lessor may request, to carry out the intent and purposes of this Lease and the Schedules. Lessee authorizes Lessor to file Lease Documents without being executed by, or further act of Lessee, as Lessor may require, to the fullest extent permitted by law.

IN WITNESS WHEREOF, Lessee and Lessor have executed and delivered this Lease as of the date first written above.

LESSOR: XYZ LEASING CORP.

By: _____

Name/Title: _____

LESSEE: ABC COMPANY

By: _____

Name/Title: _____

Organizational No.: _____

Tax Identification No.: _____

Exhibit A

Schedule No. _____ to Master Lease Agreement

Schedule No. _____ dated as of _____, 200__ (this "Schedule") to Master Lease Agreement, dated as of _____, 200__ (the "Lease") between ABC Company, a _____ corporation, as "Lessee," and XYZ Leasing Corp., as "Lessor." Capitalized terms used but not defined herein have the meaning given to them in the Lease. The parties agree to the lease of the Property covered hereby pursuant to the Lease as follows:

1. Delivery Date: _____, 200__

2. Rent Commencement Date: _____, 200__ (Basic Rent)

3. Basic Rent Payment Date: _____ (day of each [month])

4. Basic Rent Payment: $_____ per [month] of _____Basic Rent Payments.

5. Lease Expiration Date: _____, 200__ (of this Schedule)

6. Interim Rent Payment: $_____ (due on the date of this Schedule)

7. The Stipulated Loss Values: As set forth on Annex A attached hereto [Not Attached] The "Property" subject to this Schedule: as listed in Annex B attached hereto, including the "Lessor's Cost" and location of each Unit [Not Attached].

8. The Lessor's Cost for this Schedule: not exceed a total amount of $_____.

Lessee represents and warrants that no Event of Default, or any event which, with the lapse of time or notice, or both, would constitute an Event of Default, has occurred and is continuing on the date of this Schedule. This Schedule incorporates all of the terms and conditions of the Lease as if such provisions were set forth at length herein. This Schedule shall constitute a separate lease for all purposes.

LESSOR: XYZ LEASING CORP.

By:_____

Name/Title:_____

LESSEE: ABC COMPANY

By:_____

Name /Title:_____

Organizational No.:_____

Tax Identification No.:_____

APPROVED AND ACCEPTED AS OF THE DATE HEREOF:

GUARANTOR: ABC GUARANTY CO.

By:_____

Name /Title:_____

Index

● *T* ●

YOUR ONLINE RESOURCE

WWW.DUMMIES.COM

Discover Dummies Online!

The Dummies Web Site is your fun and friendly online resource for the latest information about *For Dummies* books and your favorite topics. The Web site is the place to communicate with us, exchange ideas with other *For Dummies* readers, chat with authors, and have fun!

Ten Fun and Useful Things You Can Do at www.dummies.com

1. Win free *For Dummies* books and more!
2. Register your book and be entered in a prize drawing.
3. Meet your favorite authors through the Hungry Minds Author Chat Series.
4. Exchange helpful information with other *For Dummies* readers.
5. Discover other great *For Dummies* books you must have!
6. Purchase Dummieswear exclusively from our Web site.
7. Buy *For Dummies* books online.
8. Talk to us. Make comments, ask questions, get answers!
9. Download free software.
10. Find additional useful resources from authors.

Link directly to these ten fun and useful things at
www.dummies.com/10useful

SURF THE NET

WWW.DUMMIES.COM

For other titles from Hungry Minds,
go to **www.hungryminds.com**

Not on the Web yet? It's easy to get started with *Dummies 101: The Internet For Windows 98* or *The Internet For Dummies* at local retailers everywhere.

Find other *For Dummies* books on these topics:
Business • Career • Databases • Food & Beverage • Games • Gardening
Graphics • Hardware • Health & Fitness • Internet and the World Wide Web
Networking • Office Suites • Operating Systems • Personal Finance • Pets
Programming • Recreation • Sports • Spreadsheets • Teacher Resources
Test Prep • Word Processing

Hungry Minds™

FOR DUMMIES
BOOK REGISTRATION

Register
This Book
and Win!

We want to hear from you!

Visit **dummies.com** to register this book and tell us how you liked it!

- ✔ Get entered in our monthly prize giveaway.

- ✔ Give us feedback about this book — tell us what you like best, what you like least, or maybe what you'd like to ask the author and us to change!

- ✔ Let us know any other *For Dummies* topics that interest you.

Your feedback helps us determine what books to publish, tells us what coverage to add as we revise our books, and lets us know whether we're meeting your needs as a *For Dummies* reader. You're our most valuable resource, and what you have to say is important to us!

Not on the Web yet? It's easy to get started with *Dummies 101: The Internet For Windows 98* or *The Internet For Dummies* at local retailers everywhere.

Or let us know what you think by sending us a letter at the following address:

For Dummies Book Registration
Dummies Press
10475 Crosspoint Blvd.
Indianapolis, IN 46256

™
...FOR
DUMMIES

BESTSELLING
BOOK SERIES